FABLES: WITCHES

FABLES CREATED BY BILL WILLINGHAM

Bill Willingham
Writer

Mark Buckingham
Steve Leialoha
David Lapham
Jim Fern
Andrew Pepoy
Craig Hamilton
Daniel Green
Artists

Lee Loughridge
Colorist

Todd Klein
Letterer

Joao Ruas
Cover Art and Original Series Covers

KAREN BERGER
Senior VP – Executive Editor

SHELLY BOND
Editor – Original Series

ANGELA RUFINO
Associate Editor – Original Series

BOB HARRAS
Group Editor – Collected Editions

SCOTT NYBAKKEN
Editor

ROBBIN BROSTERMAN
Design Director – Books

DC COMICS

DIANE NELSON
President

DAN DIDIO AND **JIM LEE**
Co-Publishers

GEOFF JOHNS
Chief Creative Officer

PATRICK CALDON
EVP – Finance and Administration

JOHN ROOD
EVP – Sales, Marketing and
Business Development

AMY GENKINS
SVP – Business and Legal Affairs

STEVE ROTTERDAM
SVP – Sales and Marketing

JOHN CUNNINGHAM
VP – Marketing

TERRI CUNNINGHAM
VP – Managing Editor

ALISON GILL
VP – Manufacturing

DAVID HYDE
VP – Publicity

SUE POHJA
VP – Book Trade Sales

ALYSSE SOLL
VP – Advertising and Custom Publishing

BOB WAYNE
VP – Sales

MARK CHIARELLO
Art Director

*This collection of baseball and other
forms of witchcraft is dedicated to
Stacey Brook, a fan of both.*
— Bill Willingham

*For Elena, Roberto, Ricardo and Luis.
For good friendship and constant support.*
— Mark Buckingham

Logo design by Brainchild Studios/NYC

FABLES: WITCHES

Published by DC Comics. Cover and compilation
Copyright © 2010 Bill Willingham and
DC Comics. All Rights Reserved.

Originally published in single magazine form
as FABLES 86-93. Copyright © 2009, 2010
Bill Willingham and DC Comics.
All Rights Reserved. All characters, their
distinctive likenesses and related elements
featured in this publication are trademarks of
Bill Willingham. VERTIGO is a trademark of
DC Comics. The stories, characters and incidents
featured in this publication are entirely fictional.
DC Comics does not read or accept unsolicited
submissions of ideas, stories or artwork.

DC Comics, 1700 Broadway, New York, NY 10019
A Warner Bros. Entertainment Company.
Printed in the USA. First Printing.
ISBN: 978-1-4012-2880-4

SUSTAINABLE
FORESTRY
INITIATIVE
Certified Fiber Sourcing
www.sfiprogram.org
Fiber used in this product line meets the
sourcing requirements of the SFI program.
www.sfiprogram.org PWC-SFICOC-260

Table of Contents

Who's Who in Fabletown 4

Boxing Days 7
Pencils by Jim Fern • Inks by Craig Hamilton

Witches
Pencils by Mark Buckingham
Chapter One: Bufkin 31
Inks by Andrew Pepoy
Chapter Two: Totenkinder 53
Inks by Steve Leialoha (pages 53-57, 62-74) and Andrew Pepoy (pages 58-61)
Chapter Three: Baba Yaga 75
Inks by Steve Leialoha (pages 75-76, 78-88, 91-93, 96) and Andrew Pepoy (pages 77, 89-90, 94-95)
Chapter Four: Ozma 97
Inks by Steve Leialoha (pages 97-106, 112-118) and Andrew Pepoy (pages 107-111)
Chapter Five: Geppetto 119
Inks by Steve Leialoha (pages 119-122, 126-127, 129, 133-138) and Daniel Green (pages 123-125, 128, 130-132, 139-140)

Out to the Ball Game 141
Art by David Lapham

Cover Gallery by Joao Ruas 185

WHO'S WHO IN FABLETOWN

FRAU TOTENKINDER

The Black Forest Witch and current leader of Fabletown's cabal of spellcasters.

OZMA

An ambitious rival of Frau Totenkinder's whos[e] innocent appearance be[lies] her power.

BIGBY

The Big Bad Wolf of house-blowing fame, now a respected husband and father.

SNOW WHITE

The former deputy mayor of Fabletown and wife of Bigby.

KING COLE

Fabletown's mayor-in-exile.

GEPPETTO

Once Fabletown's most terrible adversary, in def[eat] he has become a widely hated fellow citizen.

FLYCATCHER

The former Frog Prince and janitor, now ruling the Kingdom of Haven in the liberated Homelands.

RED RIDING HOOD

Flycatcher's court hostess and all-around right-hand girl.

BABA YAGA

A formidable sorceress hungry for vengeance after being freed from captivity in Fabletown's business office.

BUFKIN

A flying monkey residing in the business office.

BEAUTY

The current deputy mayor and wife of Beast.

BEAST

Beauty's husband and the sheriff of Fabletown.

PINOCCHIO

Geppetto's first-carved son, transformed centuries ago into a real boy by the Blue Fairy.

THE BARLEYCORN BRIDES

Exceptionally wee girls born from enchanted seeds.

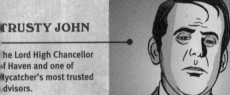

TRUSTY JOHN

The Lord High Chancellor of Haven and one of Flycatcher's most trusted advisors.

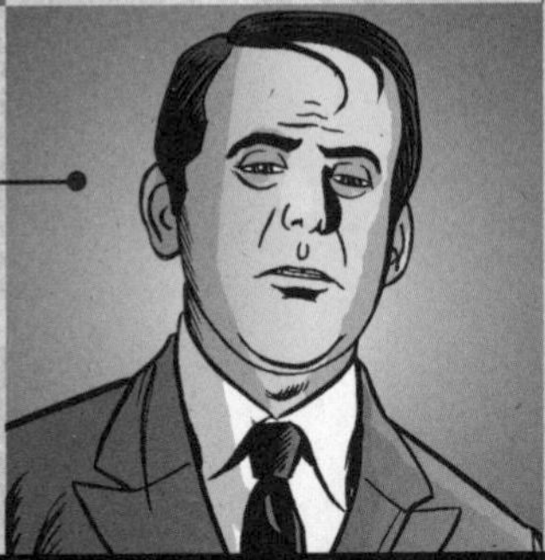

WEYLAND SMITH

Haven's royal Builder of the Kingdom.

THE STORY SO FAR

The battle to save Fabledom (and possibly all of reality) from Kevin Thorne, the literal embodiment of storytelling, is over. Thorne and all of the other Literals have been banished to a new unwritten universe, leaving the denizens of this one to fend for themselves from now on. But the Dark Man still lurks in the ruins of old Fabletown, and his threat is not likely

FABLES: WITCHES

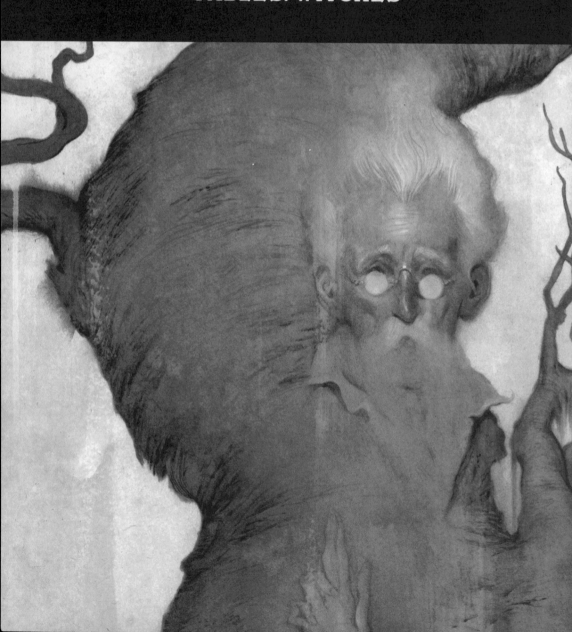

WHO AM I?
I'M THE THING BARELY SEEN IN THE SHADOWS. THE DARK ONE JUST OUT OF THE CORNER OF YOUR EYE.
I'M THE CREATURE LURKING UNDER YOUR CHILD'S BED AND HIDING IN HIS CLOSET.
BULLFINCH STREET
EVEN WHEN THEY HAD ME BOXED UP AND TUCKED SAFELY AWAY, MY SHADOW TOUCHED EVERY WORLD, EVERY MAN'S SOUL.

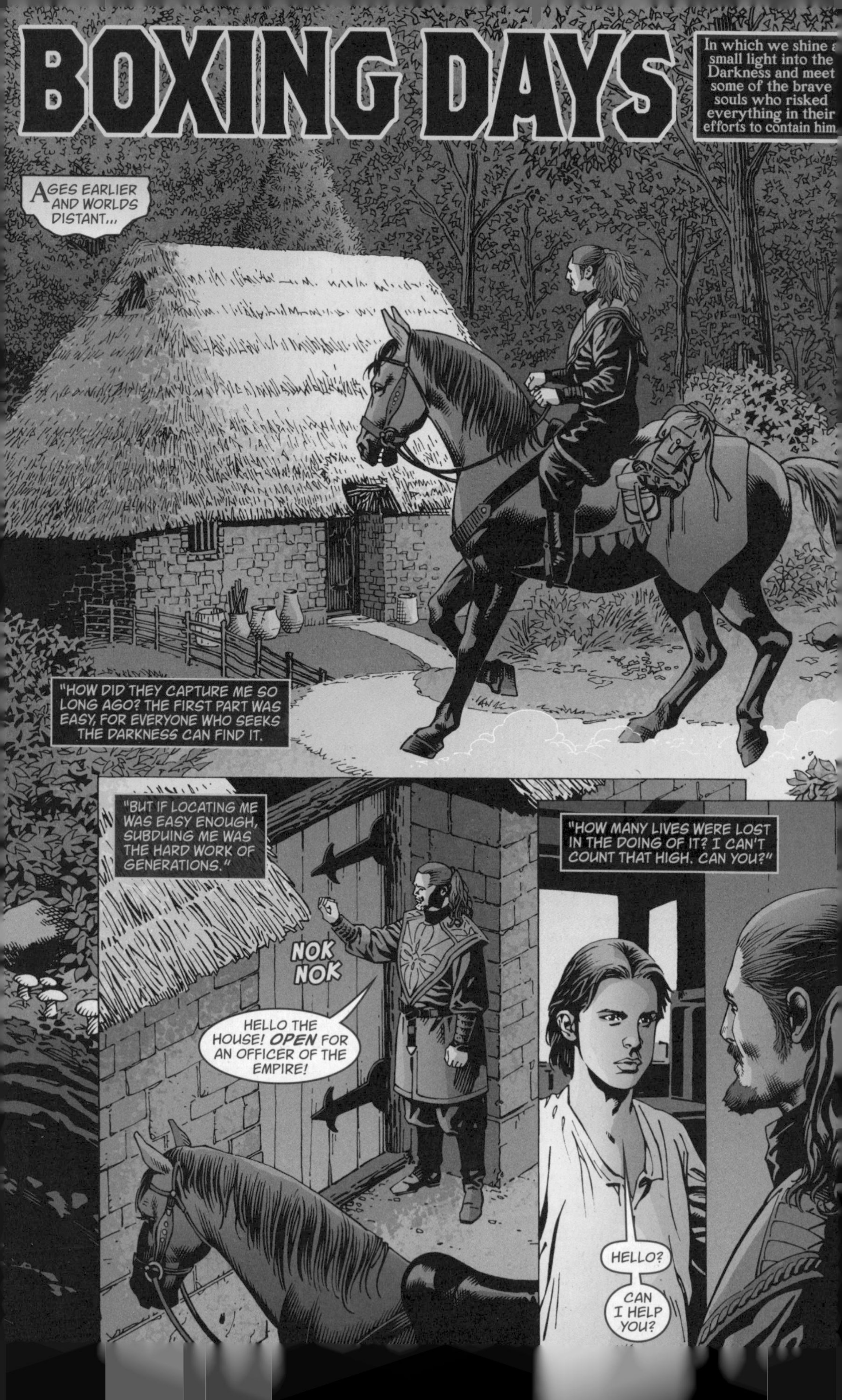

BOXING DAYS
In which we shine a small light into the Darkness and meet some of the brave souls who risked everything in their efforts to contain him.
AGES EARLIER AND WORLDS DISTANT...
"HOW DID THEY CAPTURE ME SO LONG AGO? THE FIRST PART WAS EASY, FOR EVERYONE WHO SEEKS THE DARKNESS CAN FIND IT.
"BUT IF LOCATING ME WAS EASY ENOUGH, SUBDUING ME WAS THE HARD WORK OF GENERATIONS."
NOK NOK
HELLO THE HOUSE! OPEN FOR AN OFFICER OF THE EMPIRE!
"HOW MANY LIVES WERE LOST IN THE DOING OF IT? I CAN'T COUNT THAT HIGH. CAN YOU?"
HELLO?
CAN I HELP YOU?

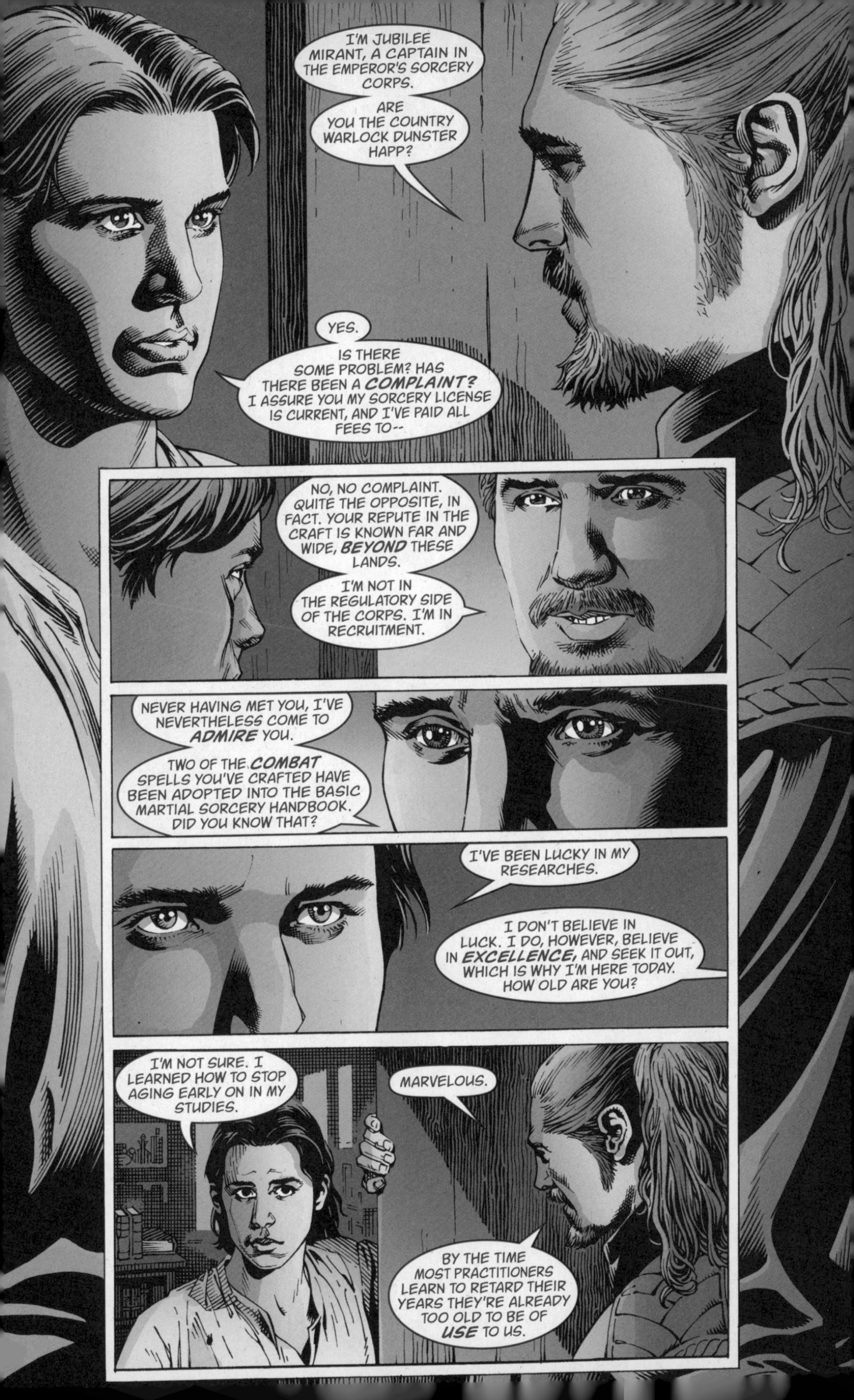
I'M JUBILEE MIRANT, A CAPTAIN IN THE EMPEROR'S SORCERY CORPS.
ARE YOU THE COUNTRY WARLOCK DUNSTER HAPP?
YES.
IS THERE SOME PROBLEM? HAS THERE BEEN A COMPLAINT? I ASSURE YOU MY SORCERY LICENSE IS CURRENT, AND I'VE PAID ALL FEES TO--
NO, NO COMPLAINT. QUITE THE OPPOSITE, IN FACT. YOUR REPUTE IN THE CRAFT IS KNOWN FAR AND WIDE, BEYOND THESE LANDS.
I'M NOT IN THE REGULATORY SIDE OF THE CORPS. I'M IN RECRUITMENT.
NEVER HAVING MET YOU, I'VE NEVERTHELESS COME TO ADMIRE YOU.
TWO OF THE COMBAT SPELLS YOU'VE CRAFTED HAVE BEEN ADOPTED INTO THE BASIC MARTIAL SORCERY HANDBOOK. DID YOU KNOW THAT?
I'VE BEEN LUCKY IN MY RESEARCHES.
I DON'T BELIEVE IN LUCK. I DO, HOWEVER, BELIEVE IN EXCELLENCE, AND SEEK IT OUT, WHICH IS WHY I'M HERE TODAY. HOW OLD ARE YOU?
I'M NOT SURE. I LEARNED HOW TO STOP AGING EARLY ON IN MY STUDIES.
MARVELOUS.
BY THE TIME MOST PRACTITIONERS LEARN TO RETARD THEIR YEARS THEY'RE ALREADY TOO OLD TO BE OF USE TO US.

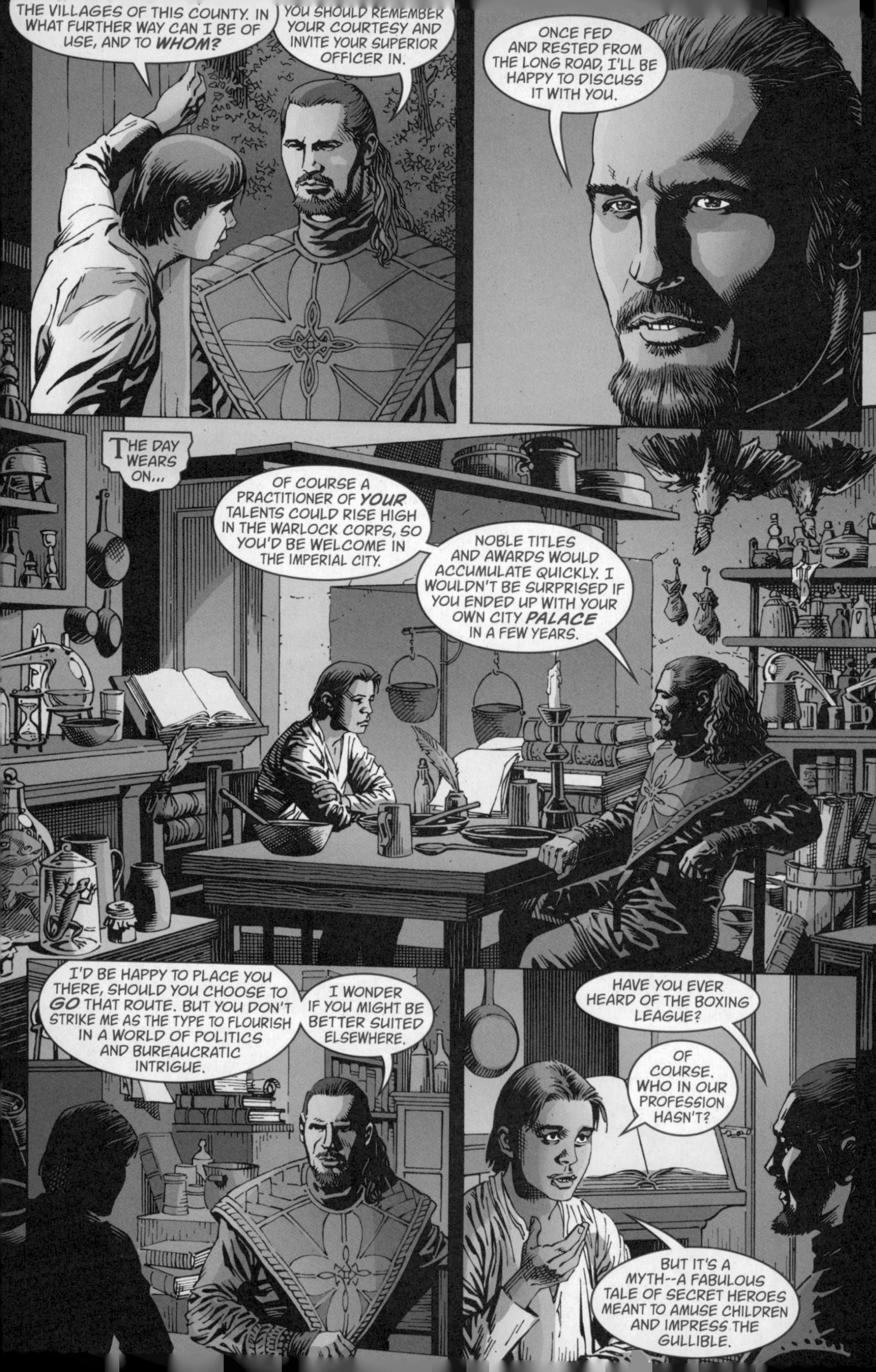
THE VILLAGES OF THIS COUNTY. IN WHAT FURTHER WAY CAN I BE OF USE, AND TO WHOM?
YOU SHOULD REMEMBER YOUR COURTESY AND INVITE YOUR SUPERIOR OFFICER IN.
ONCE FED AND RESTED FROM THE LONG ROAD, I'LL BE HAPPY TO DISCUSS IT WITH YOU.
THE DAY WEARS ON...
OF COURSE A PRACTITIONER OF YOUR TALENTS COULD RISE HIGH IN THE WARLOCK CORPS, SO YOU'D BE WELCOME IN THE IMPERIAL CITY.
NOBLE TITLES AND AWARDS WOULD ACCUMULATE QUICKLY. I WOULDN'T BE SURPRISED IF YOU ENDED UP WITH YOUR OWN CITY PALACE IN A FEW YEARS.
I'D BE HAPPY TO PLACE YOU THERE, SHOULD YOU CHOOSE TO GO THAT ROUTE. BUT YOU DON'T STRIKE ME AS THE TYPE TO FLOURISH IN A WORLD OF POLITICS AND BUREAUCRATIC INTRIGUE.
I WONDER IF YOU MIGHT BE BETTER SUITED ELSEWHERE.
HAVE YOU EVER HEARD OF THE BOXING LEAGUE?
OF COURSE. WHO IN OUR PROFESSION HASN'T?
BUT IT'S A MYTH--A FABULOUS TALE OF SECRET HEROES MEANT TO AMUSE CHILDREN AND IMPRESS THE GULLIBLE.

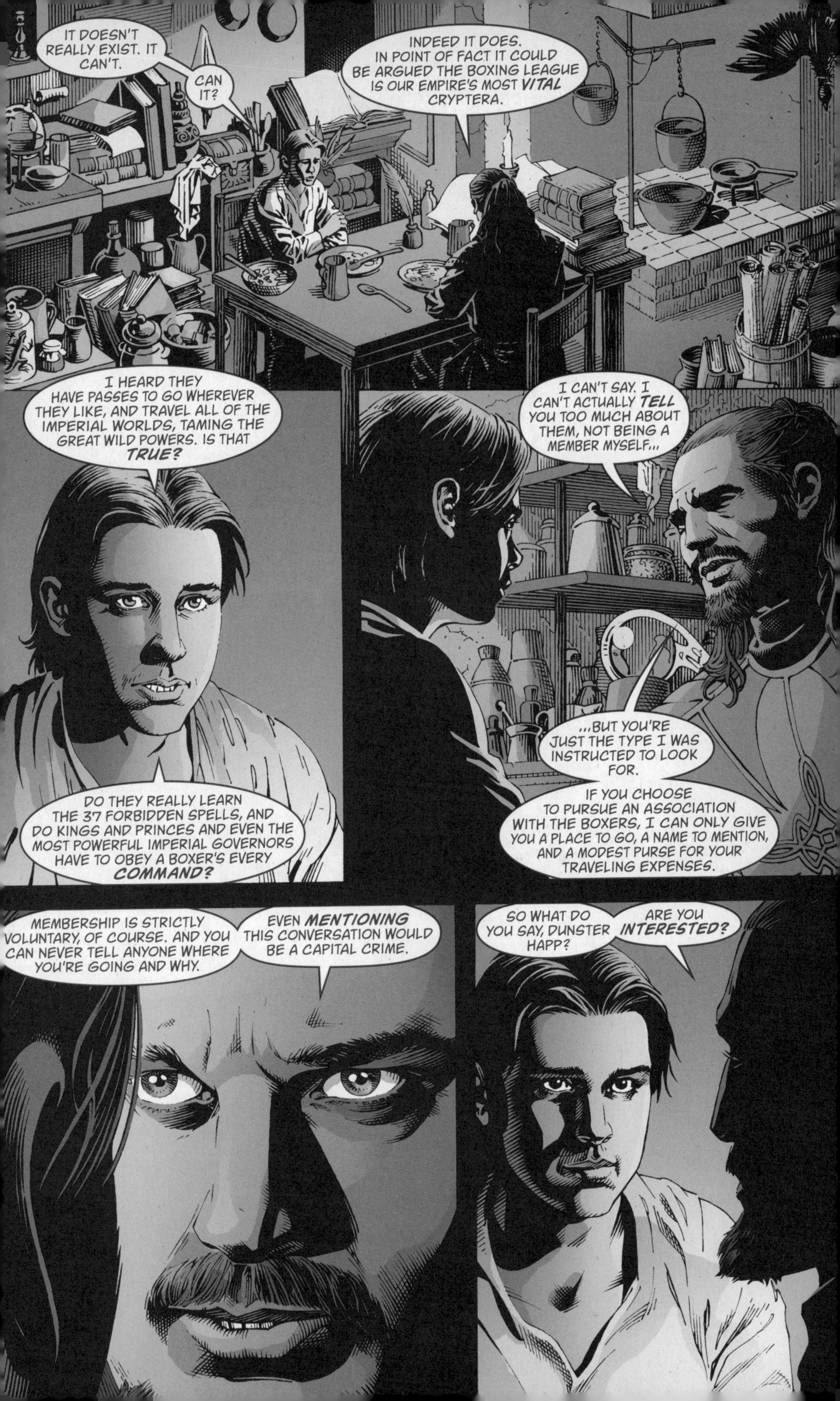
IT DOESN'T REALLY EXIST. IT CAN'T.
CAN IT?
INDEED IT DOES. IN POINT OF FACT IT COULD BE ARGUED THE BOXING LEAGUE IS OUR EMPIRE'S MOST VITAL CRYPTERA.
I HEARD THEY HAVE PASSES TO GO WHEREVER THEY LIKE, AND TRAVEL ALL OF THE IMPERIAL WORLDS, TAMING THE GREAT WILD POWERS. IS THAT TRUE?
DO THEY REALLY LEARN THE 37 FORBIDDEN SPELLS, AND DO KINGS AND PRINCES AND EVEN THE MOST POWERFUL IMPERIAL GOVERNORS HAVE TO OBEY A BOXER'S EVERY COMMAND?
I CAN'T SAY. I CAN'T ACTUALLY TELL YOU TOO MUCH ABOUT THEM, NOT BEING A MEMBER MYSELF...
...BUT YOU'RE JUST THE TYPE I WAS INSTRUCTED TO LOOK FOR.
IF YOU CHOOSE TO PURSUE AN ASSOCIATION WITH THE BOXERS, I CAN ONLY GIVE YOU A PLACE TO GO, A NAME TO MENTION, AND A MODEST PURSE FOR YOUR TRAVELING EXPENSES.
MEMBERSHIP IS STRICTLY VOLUNTARY, OF COURSE. AND YOU CAN NEVER TELL ANYONE WHERE YOU'RE GOING AND WHY.
EVEN MENTIONING THIS CONVERSATION WOULD BE A CAPITAL CRIME.
SO WHAT DO YOU SAY, DUNSTER HAPP?
ARE YOU INTERESTED?

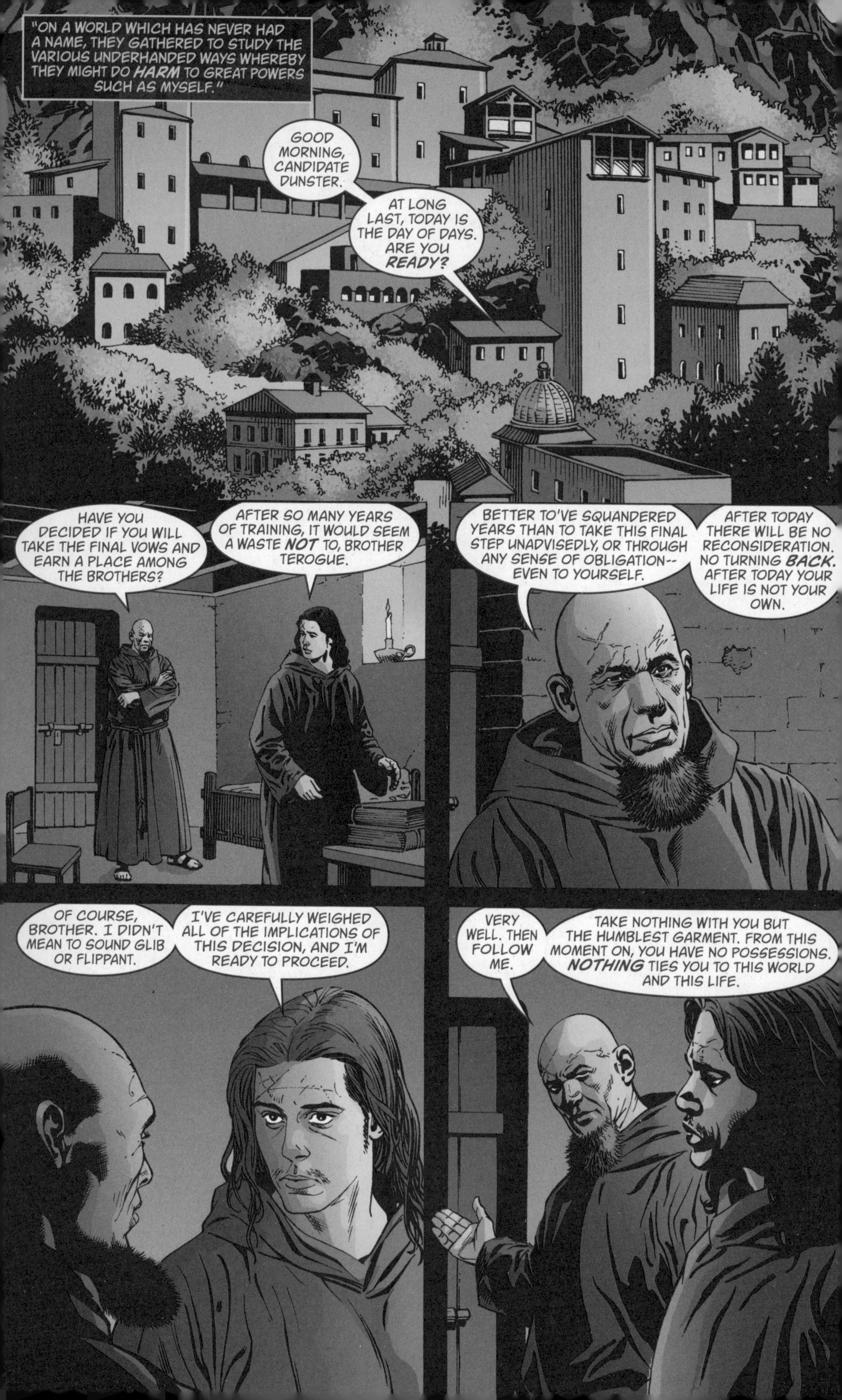
"ON A WORLD WHICH HAS NEVER HAD A NAME, THEY GATHERED TO STUDY THE VARIOUS UNDERHANDED WAYS WHEREBY THEY MIGHT DO HARM TO GREAT POWERS SUCH AS MYSELF."
GOOD MORNING, CANDIDATE DUNSTER.
AT LONG LAST, TODAY IS THE DAY OF DAYS. ARE YOU READY?
HAVE YOU DECIDED IF YOU WILL TAKE THE FINAL VOWS AND EARN A PLACE AMONG THE BROTHERS?
AFTER SO MANY YEARS OF TRAINING, IT WOULD SEEM A WASTE NOT TO, BROTHER TEROGUE.
BETTER TO'VE SQUANDERED YEARS THAN TO TAKE THIS FINAL STEP UNADVISEDLY, OR THROUGH ANY SENSE OF OBLIGATION-- EVEN TO YOURSELF.
AFTER TODAY THERE WILL BE NO RECONSIDERATION. NO TURNING BACK. AFTER TODAY YOUR LIFE IS NOT YOUR OWN.
OF COURSE, BROTHER. I DIDN'T MEAN TO SOUND GLIB OR FLIPPANT.
I'VE CAREFULLY WEIGHED ALL OF THE IMPLICATIONS OF THIS DECISION, AND I'M READY TO PROCEED.
VERY WELL. THEN FOLLOW ME.
TAKE NOTHING WITH YOU BUT THE HUMBLEST GARMENT. FROM THIS MOMENT ON, YOU HAVE NO POSSESSIONS. NOTHING TIES YOU TO THIS WORLD AND THIS LIFE.

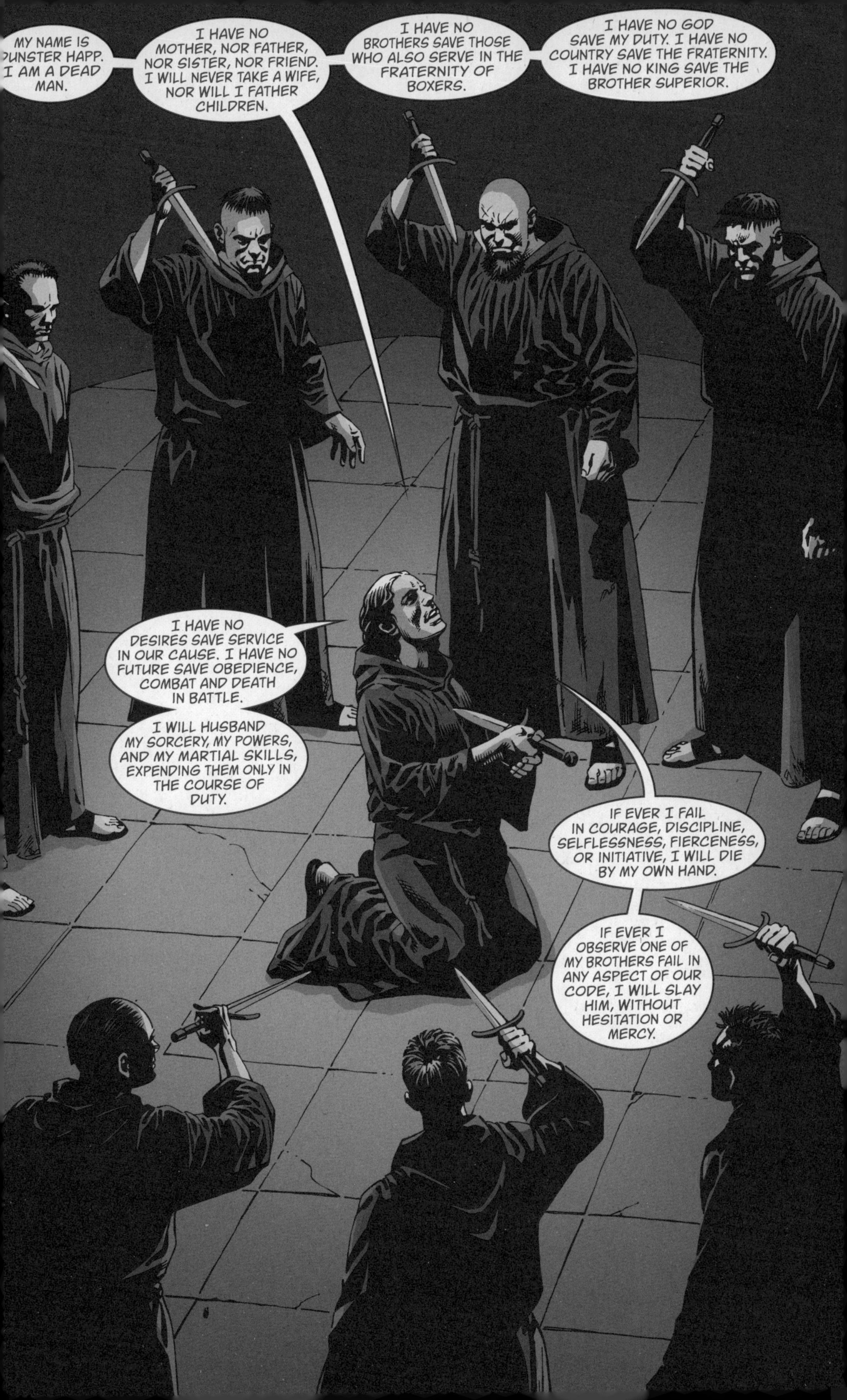
MY NAME IS DUNSTER HAPP. I AM A DEAD MAN.
I HAVE NO MOTHER, NOR FATHER, NOR SISTER, NOR FRIEND. I WILL NEVER TAKE A WIFE, NOR WILL I FATHER CHILDREN.
I HAVE NO BROTHERS SAVE THOSE WHO ALSO SERVE IN THE FRATERNITY OF BOXERS.
I HAVE NO GOD SAVE MY DUTY. I HAVE NO COUNTRY SAVE THE FRATERNITY. I HAVE NO KING SAVE THE BROTHER SUPERIOR.
I HAVE NO DESIRES SAVE SERVICE IN OUR CAUSE. I HAVE NO FUTURE SAVE OBEDIENCE, COMBAT AND DEATH IN BATTLE.
I WILL HUSBAND MY SORCERY, MY POWERS, AND MY MARTIAL SKILLS, EXPENDING THEM ONLY IN THE COURSE OF DUTY.
IF EVER I FAIL IN COURAGE, DISCIPLINE, SELFLESSNESS, FIERCENESS, OR INITIATIVE, I WILL DIE BY MY OWN HAND.
IF EVER I OBSERVE ONE OF MY BROTHERS FAIL IN ANY ASPECT OF OUR CODE, I WILL SLAY HIM, WITHOUT HESITATION OR MERCY.

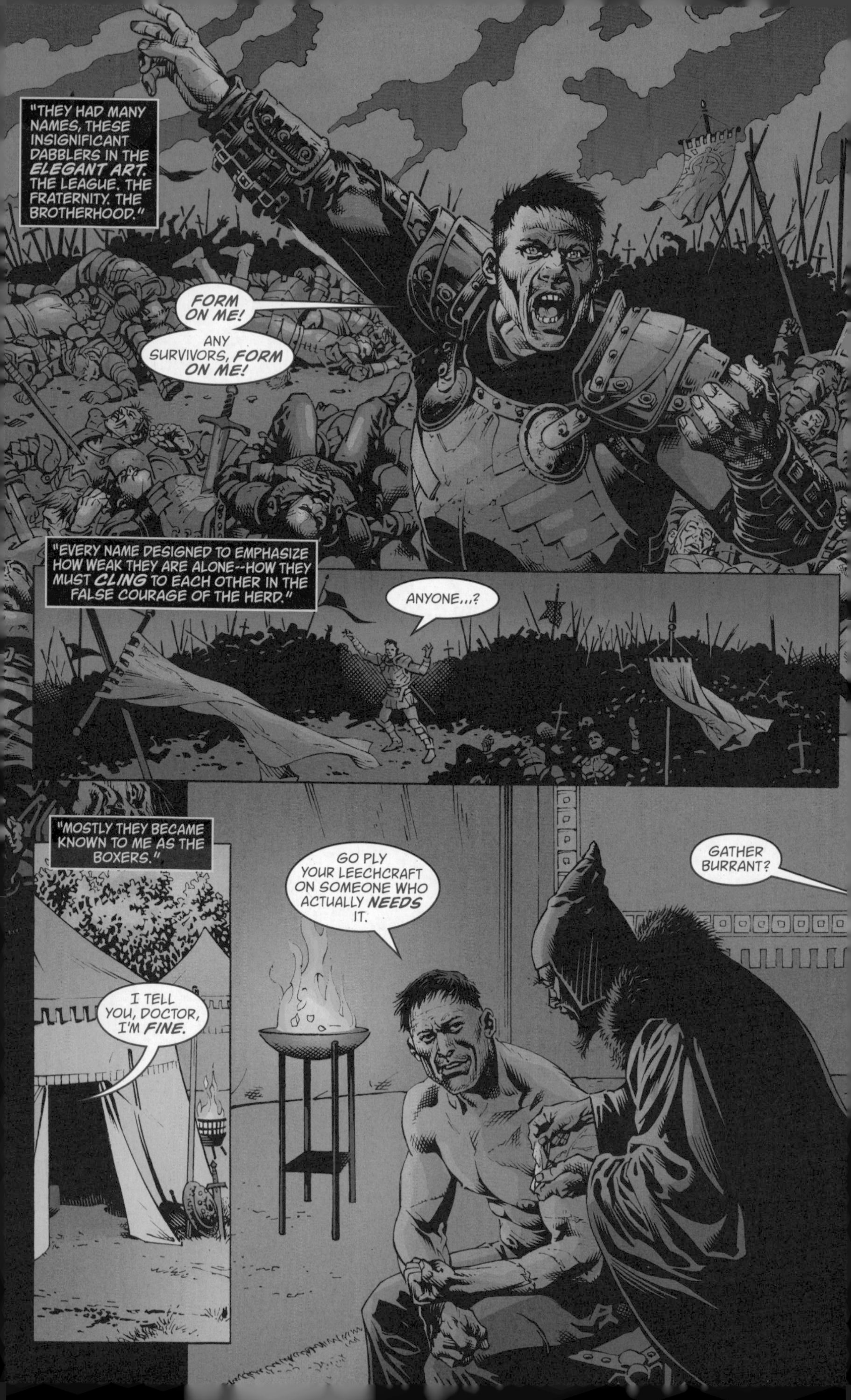
"THEY HAD MANY NAMES, THESE INSIGNIFICANT DABBLERS IN THE ELEGANT ART. THE LEAGUE. THE FRATERNITY. THE BROTHERHOOD."
FORM ON ME!
ANY SURVIVORS, FORM ON ME!
"EVERY NAME DESIGNED TO EMPHASIZE HOW WEAK THEY ARE ALONE--HOW THEY MUST CLING TO EACH OTHER IN THE FALSE COURAGE OF THE HERD."
ANYONE...?
"MOSTLY THEY BECAME KNOWN TO ME AS THE BOXERS."
GATHER BURRANT?
I TELL YOU, DOCTOR, I'M FINE.
GO PLY YOUR LEECHCRAFT ON SOMEONE WHO ACTUALLY NEEDS IT.

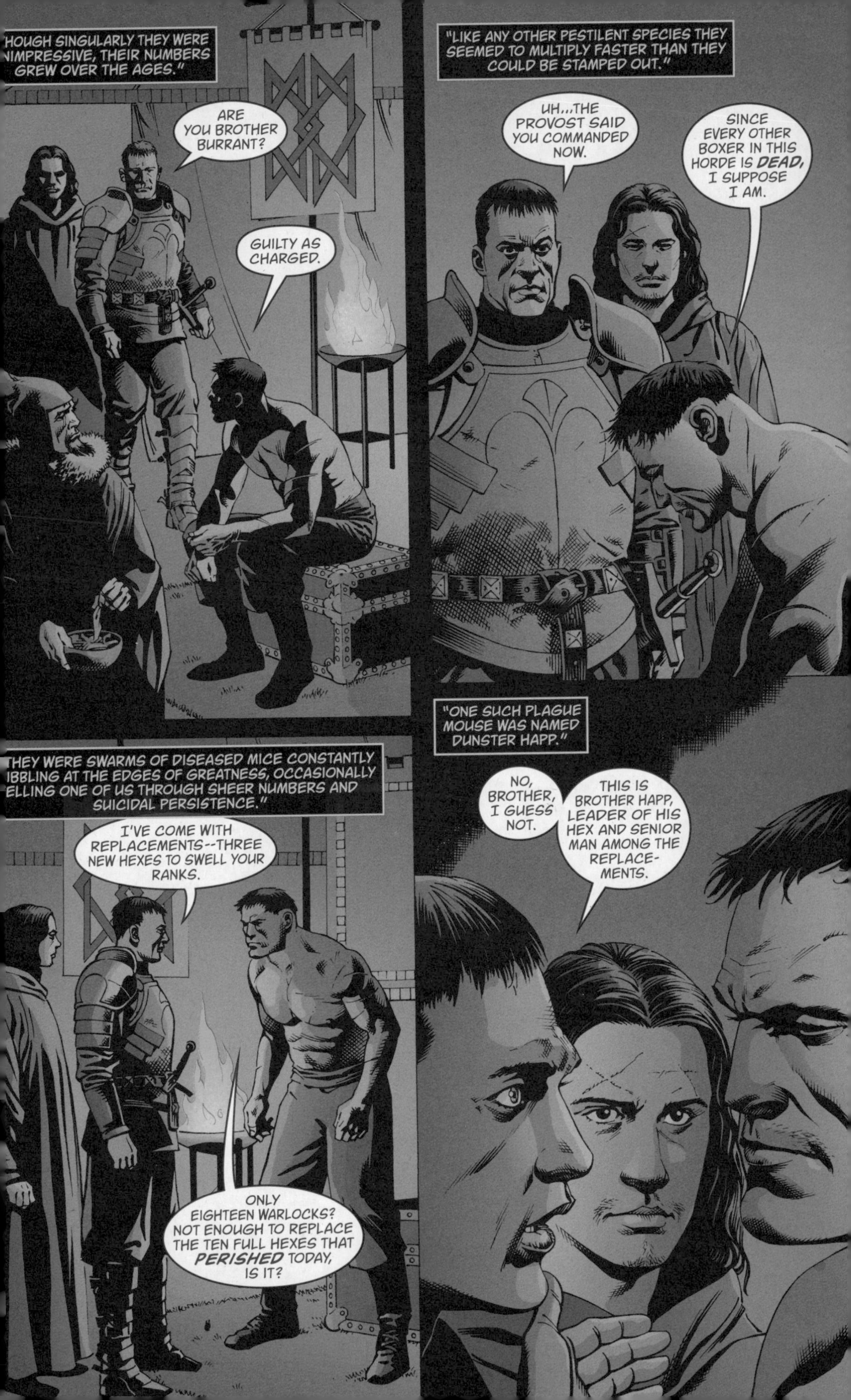
HOUGH SINGULARLY THEY WERE NIMPRESSIVE, THEIR NUMBERS GREW OVER THE AGES."
ARE YOU BROTHER BURRANT?
GUILTY AS CHARGED.
"LIKE ANY OTHER PESTILENT SPECIES THEY SEEMED TO MULTIPLY FASTER THAN THEY COULD BE STAMPED OUT."
UH...THE PROVOST SAID YOU COMMANDED NOW.
SINCE EVERY OTHER BOXER IN THIS HORDE IS DEAD, I SUPPOSE I AM.
THEY WERE SWARMS OF DISEASED MICE CONSTANTLY IBBLING AT THE EDGES OF GREATNESS, OCCASIONALLY ELLING ONE OF US THROUGH SHEER NUMBERS AND SUICIDAL PERSISTENCE."
I'VE COME WITH REPLACEMENTS--THREE NEW HEXES TO SWELL YOUR RANKS.
ONLY EIGHTEEN WARLOCKS? NOT ENOUGH TO REPLACE THE TEN FULL HEXES THAT PERISHED TODAY, IS IT?
"ONE SUCH PLAGUE MOUSE WAS NAMED DUNSTER HAPP."
NO, BROTHER, I GUESS NOT.
THIS IS BROTHER HAPP, LEADER OF HIS HEX AND SENIOR MAN AMONG THE REPLACE-MENTS.

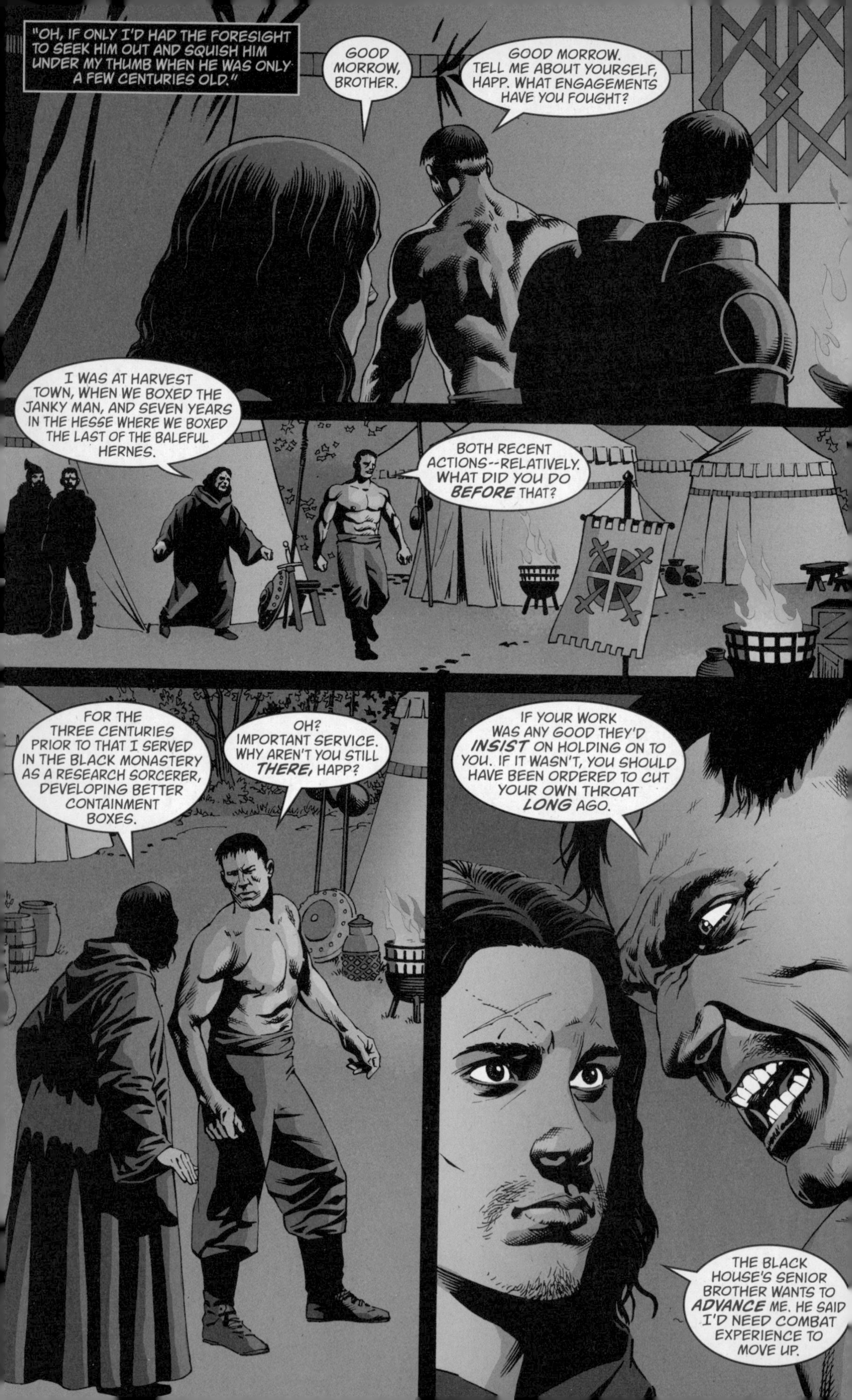
"OH, IF ONLY I'D HAD THE FORESIGHT TO SEEK HIM OUT AND SQUISH HIM UNDER MY THUMB WHEN HE WAS ONLY A FEW CENTURIES OLD."
GOOD MORROW, BROTHER.
GOOD MORROW. TELL ME ABOUT YOURSELF, HAPP. WHAT ENGAGEMENTS HAVE YOU FOUGHT?
I WAS AT HARVEST TOWN, WHEN WE BOXED THE JANKY MAN, AND SEVEN YEARS IN THE HESSE WHERE WE BOXED THE LAST OF THE BALEFUL HERNES.
BOTH RECENT ACTIONS--RELATIVELY. WHAT DID YOU DO *BEFORE* THAT?
FOR THE THREE CENTURIES PRIOR TO THAT I SERVED IN THE BLACK MONASTERY AS A RESEARCH SORCERER, DEVELOPING BETTER CONTAINMENT BOXES.
OH? IMPORTANT SERVICE. WHY AREN'T YOU STILL *THERE,* HAPP?
IF YOUR WORK WAS ANY GOOD THEY'D *INSIST* ON HOLDING ON TO YOU. IF IT WASN'T, YOU SHOULD HAVE BEEN ORDERED TO CUT YOUR OWN THROAT *LONG* AGO.
THE BLACK HOUSE'S SENIOR BROTHER WANTS TO *ADVANCE* ME. HE SAID I'D NEED COMBAT EXPERIENCE TO MOVE UP.

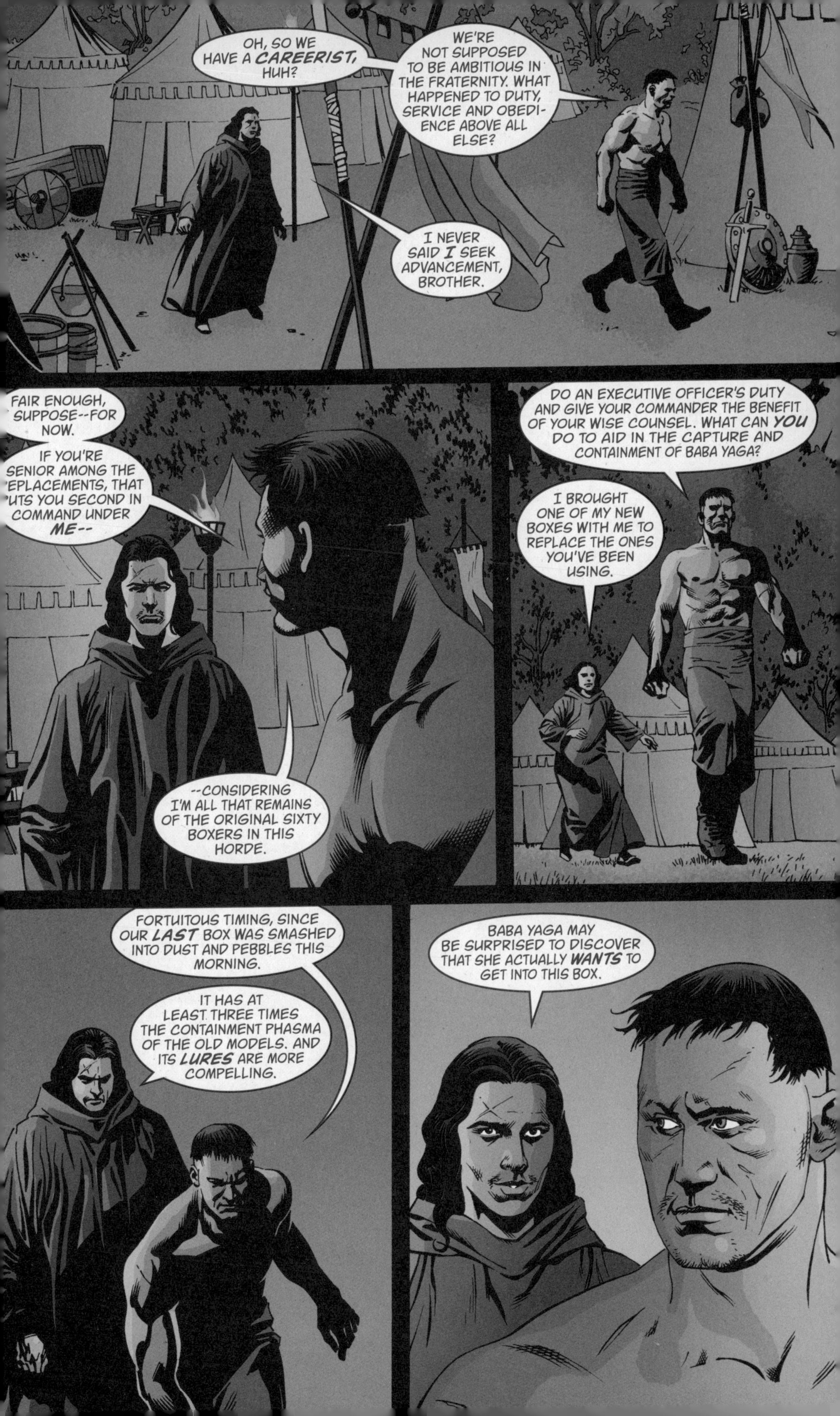
OH, SO WE HAVE A CAREERIST, HUH?
WE'RE NOT SUPPOSED TO BE AMBITIOUS IN THE FRATERNITY. WHAT HAPPENED TO DUTY, SERVICE AND OBEDIENCE ABOVE ALL ELSE?
I NEVER SAID I SEEK ADVANCEMENT, BROTHER.
FAIR ENOUGH, SUPPOSE--FOR NOW.
IF YOU'RE SENIOR AMONG THE EPLACEMENTS, THAT UTS YOU SECOND IN COMMAND UNDER ME--
--CONSIDERING I'M ALL THAT REMAINS OF THE ORIGINAL SIXTY BOXERS IN THIS HORDE.
DO AN EXECUTIVE OFFICER'S DUTY AND GIVE YOUR COMMANDER THE BENEFIT OF YOUR WISE COUNSEL. WHAT CAN YOU DO TO AID IN THE CAPTURE AND CONTAINMENT OF BABA YAGA?
I BROUGHT ONE OF MY NEW BOXES WITH ME TO REPLACE THE ONES YOU'VE BEEN USING.
FORTUITOUS TIMING, SINCE OUR LAST BOX WAS SMASHED INTO DUST AND PEBBLES THIS MORNING.
IT HAS AT LEAST THREE TIMES THE CONTAINMENT PHASMA OF THE OLD MODELS. AND ITS LURES ARE MORE COMPELLING.
BABA YAGA MAY BE SURPRISED TO DISCOVER THAT SHE ACTUALLY WANTS TO GET INTO THIS BOX.

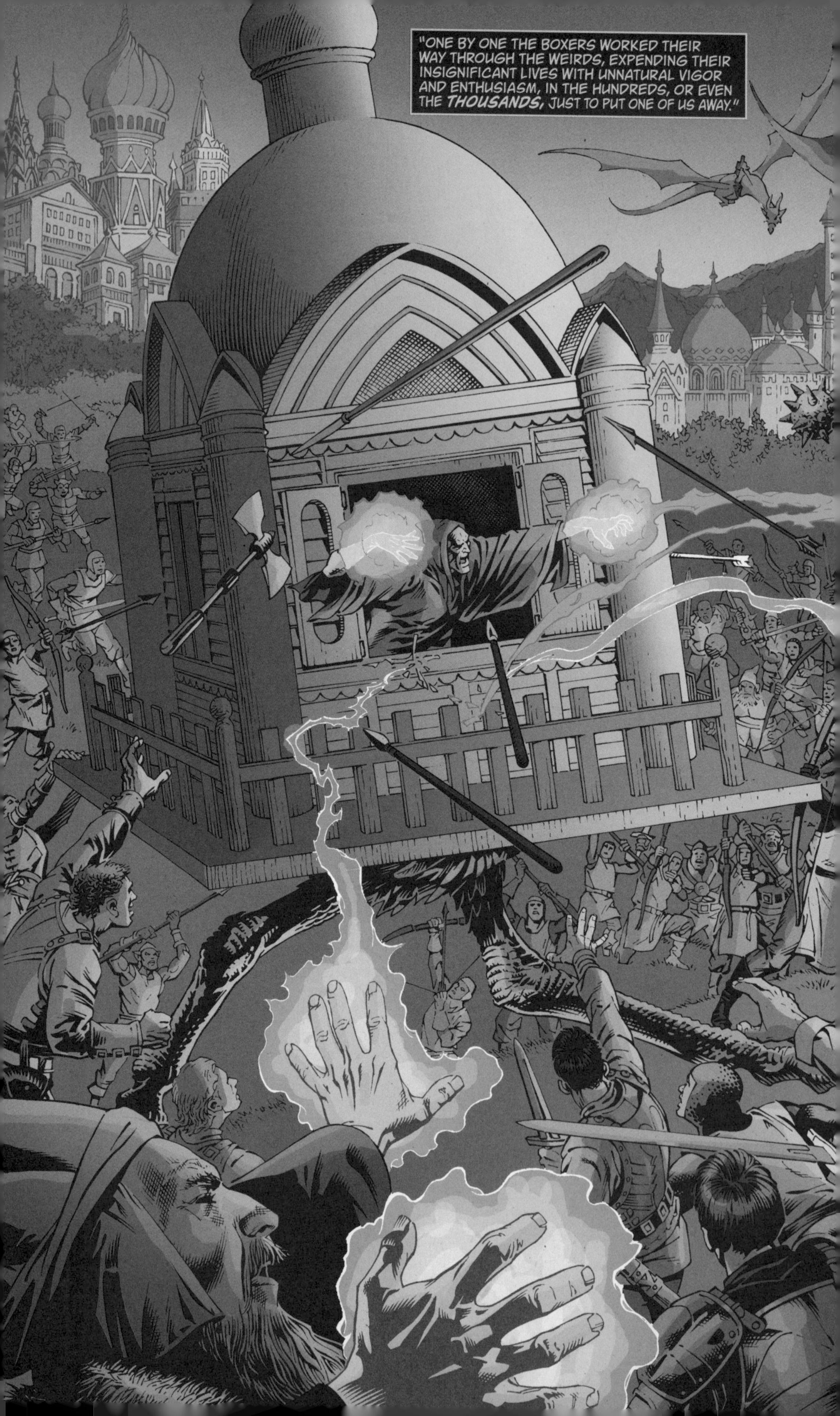
"ONE BY ONE THE BOXERS WORKED THEIR WAY THROUGH THE WEIRDS, EXPENDING THEIR INSIGNIFICANT LIVES WITH UNNATURAL VIGOR AND ENTHUSIASM, IN THE HUNDREDS, OR EVEN THE *THOUSANDS,* JUST TO PUT ONE OF US AWAY."

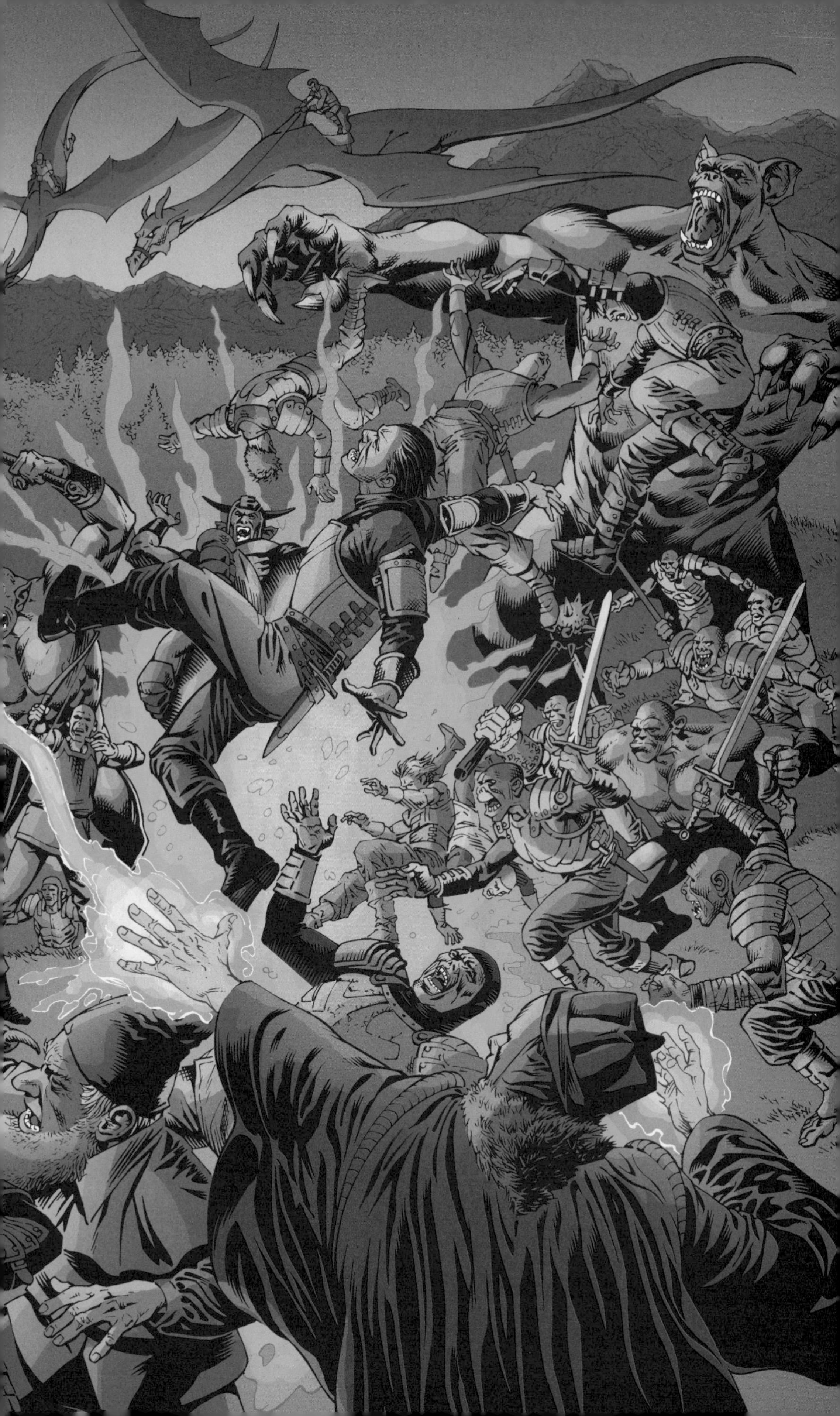

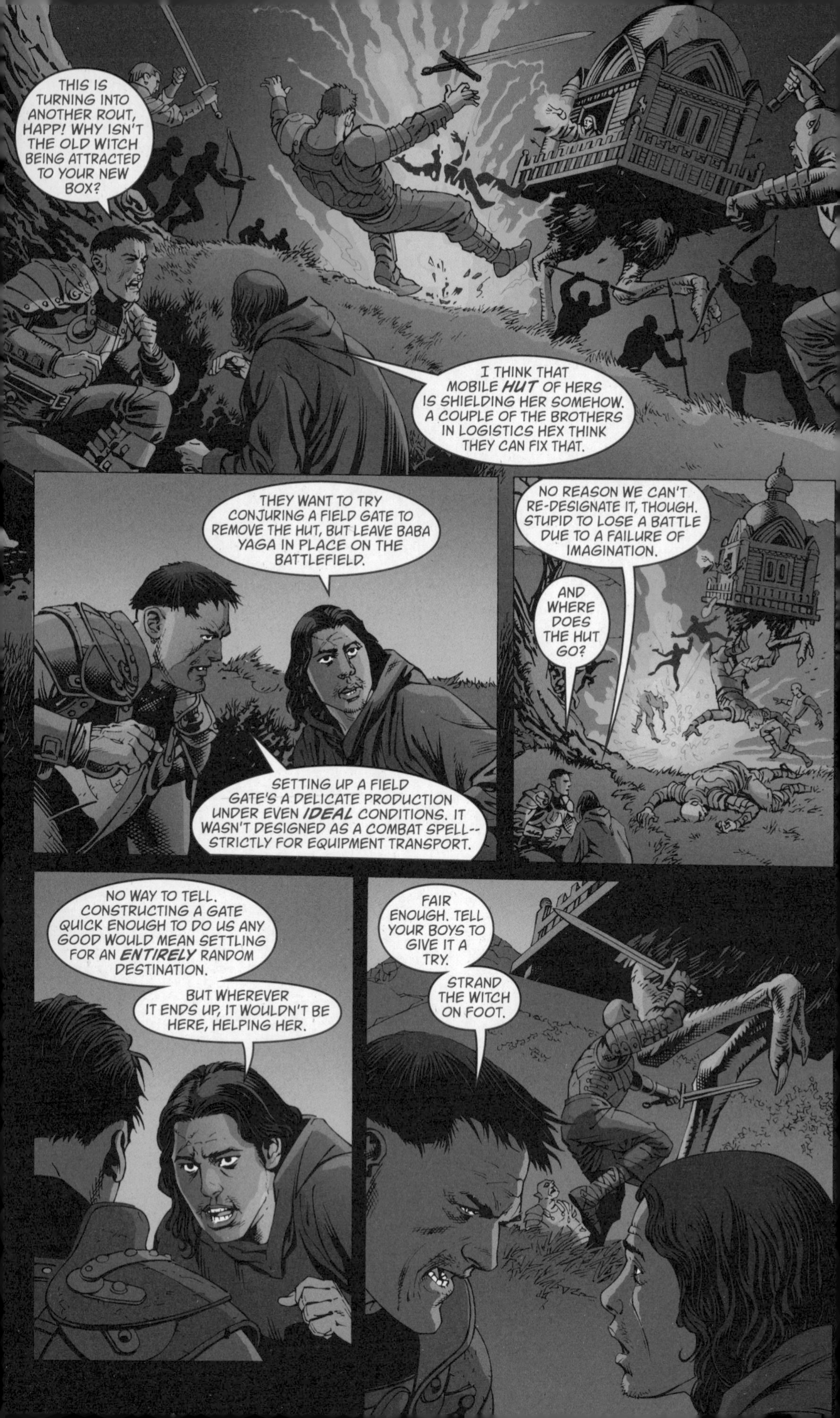

THIS IS TURNING INTO ANOTHER ROUT, HAPP! WHY ISN'T THE OLD WITCH BEING ATTRACTED TO YOUR NEW BOX?
I THINK THAT MOBILE HUT OF HERS IS SHIELDING HER SOMEHOW. A COUPLE OF THE BROTHERS IN LOGISTICS HEX THINK THEY CAN FIX THAT.
THEY WANT TO TRY CONJURING A FIELD GATE TO REMOVE THE HUT, BUT LEAVE BABA YAGA IN PLACE ON THE BATTLEFIELD.
SETTING UP A FIELD GATE'S A DELICATE PRODUCTION UNDER EVEN IDEAL CONDITIONS. IT WASN'T DESIGNED AS A COMBAT SPELL-- STRICTLY FOR EQUIPMENT TRANSPORT.
NO REASON WE CAN'T RE-DESIGNATE IT, THOUGH. STUPID TO LOSE A BATTLE DUE TO A FAILURE OF IMAGINATION.
AND WHERE DOES THE HUT GO?
NO WAY TO TELL. CONSTRUCTING A GATE QUICK ENOUGH TO DO US ANY GOOD WOULD MEAN SETTLING FOR AN ENTIRELY RANDOM DESTINATION.
BUT WHEREVER IT ENDS UP, IT WOULDN'T BE HERE, HELPING HER.
FAIR ENOUGH. TELL YOUR BOYS TO GIVE IT A TRY.
STRAND THE WITCH ON FOOT.

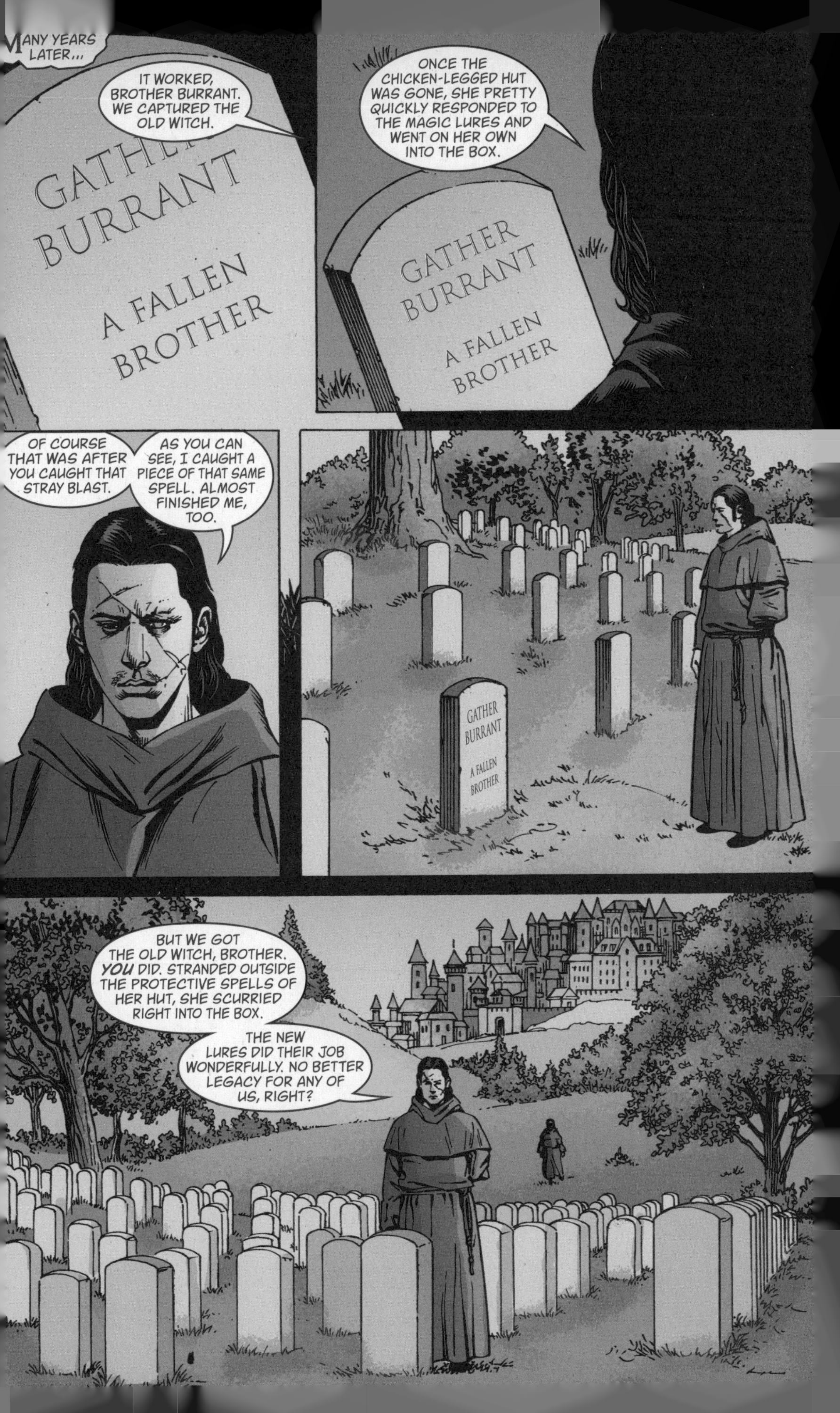
MANY YEARS LATER...
IT WORKED, BROTHER BURRANT. WE CAPTURED THE OLD WITCH.
GATHER BURRANT
A FALLEN BROTHER
ONCE THE CHICKEN-LEGGED HUT WAS GONE, SHE PRETTY QUICKLY RESPONDED TO THE MAGIC LURES AND WENT ON HER OWN INTO THE BOX.
GATHER BURRANT
A FALLEN BROTHER
OF COURSE THAT WAS AFTER YOU CAUGHT THAT STRAY BLAST.
AS YOU CAN SEE, I CAUGHT A PIECE OF THAT SAME SPELL. ALMOST FINISHED ME, TOO.
GATHER BURRANT
A FALLEN BROTHER
BUT WE GOT THE OLD WITCH, BROTHER. YOU DID. STRANDED OUTSIDE THE PROTECTIVE SPELLS OF HER HUT, SHE SCURRIED RIGHT INTO THE BOX.
THE NEW LURES DID THEIR JOB WONDERFULLY. NO BETTER LEGACY FOR ANY OF US, RIGHT?

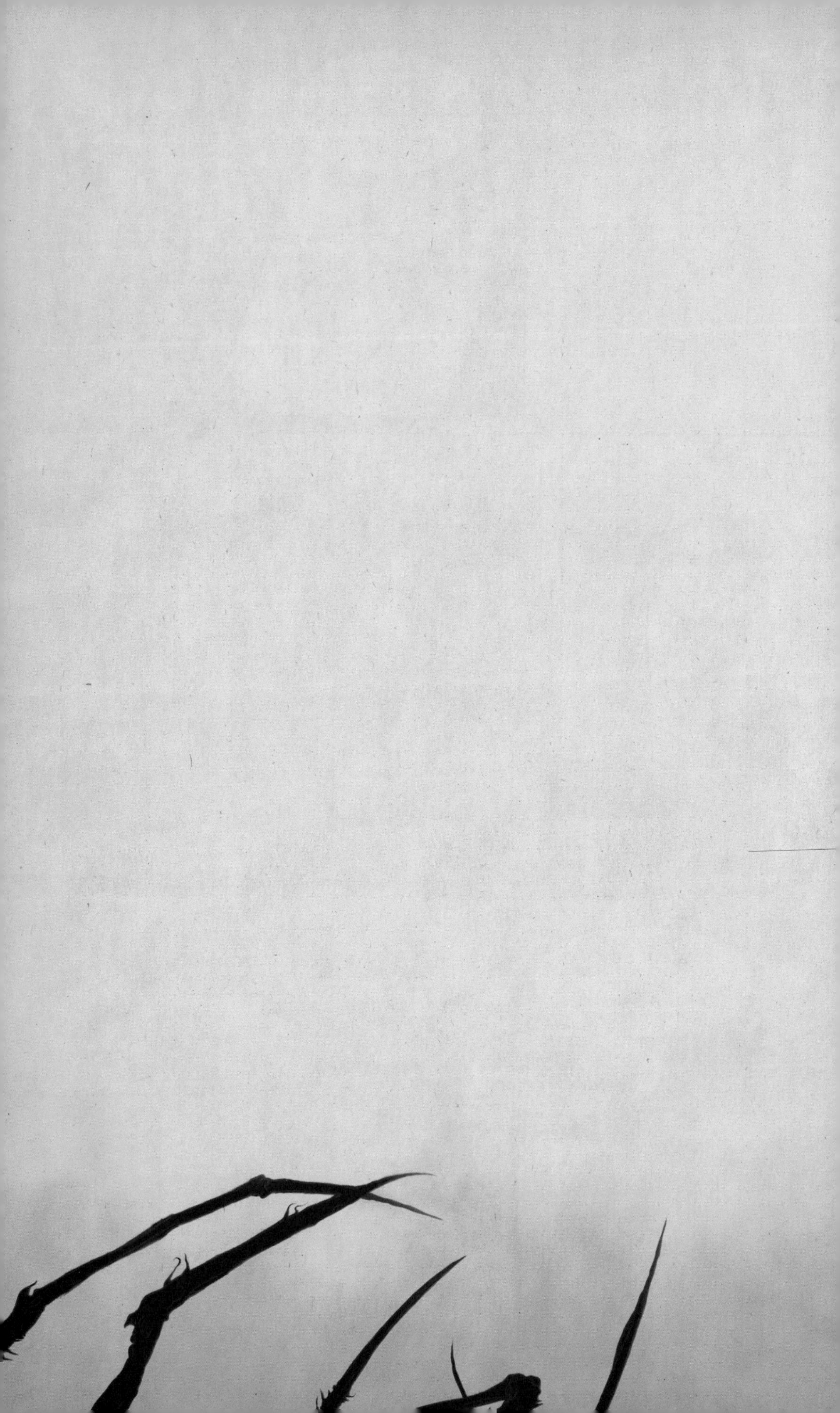

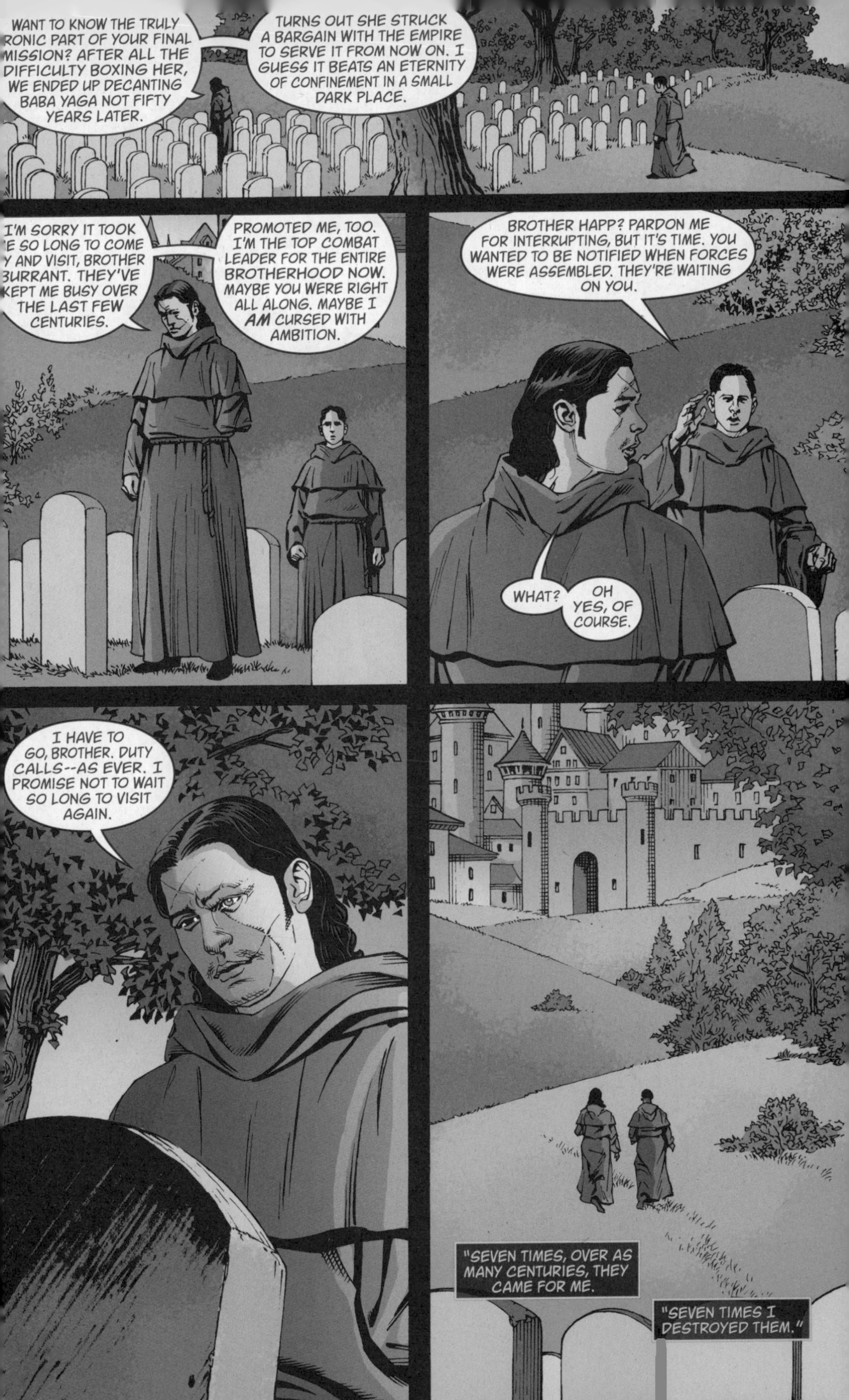
WANT TO KNOW THE TRULY RONIC PART OF YOUR FINAL MISSION? AFTER ALL THE DIFFICULTY BOXING HER, WE ENDED UP DECANTING BABA YAGA NOT FIFTY YEARS LATER.
TURNS OUT SHE STRUCK A BARGAIN WITH THE EMPIRE TO SERVE IT FROM NOW ON. I GUESS IT BEATS AN ETERNITY OF CONFINEMENT IN A SMALL DARK PLACE.
I'M SORRY IT TOOK E SO LONG TO COME Y AND VISIT, BROTHER BURRANT. THEY'VE KEPT ME BUSY OVER THE LAST FEW CENTURIES.
PROMOTED ME, TOO. I'M THE TOP COMBAT LEADER FOR THE ENTIRE BROTHERHOOD NOW. MAYBE YOU WERE RIGHT ALL ALONG. MAYBE I AM CURSED WITH AMBITION.
BROTHER HAPP? PARDON ME FOR INTERRUPTING, BUT IT'S TIME. YOU WANTED TO BE NOTIFIED WHEN FORCES WERE ASSEMBLED. THEY'RE WAITING ON YOU.
WHAT?
OH YES, OF COURSE.
I HAVE TO GO, BROTHER. DUTY CALLS--AS EVER. I PROMISE NOT TO WAIT SO LONG TO VISIT AGAIN.
"SEVEN TIMES, OVER AS MANY CENTURIES, THEY CAME FOR ME.
"SEVEN TIMES I DESTROYED THEM."

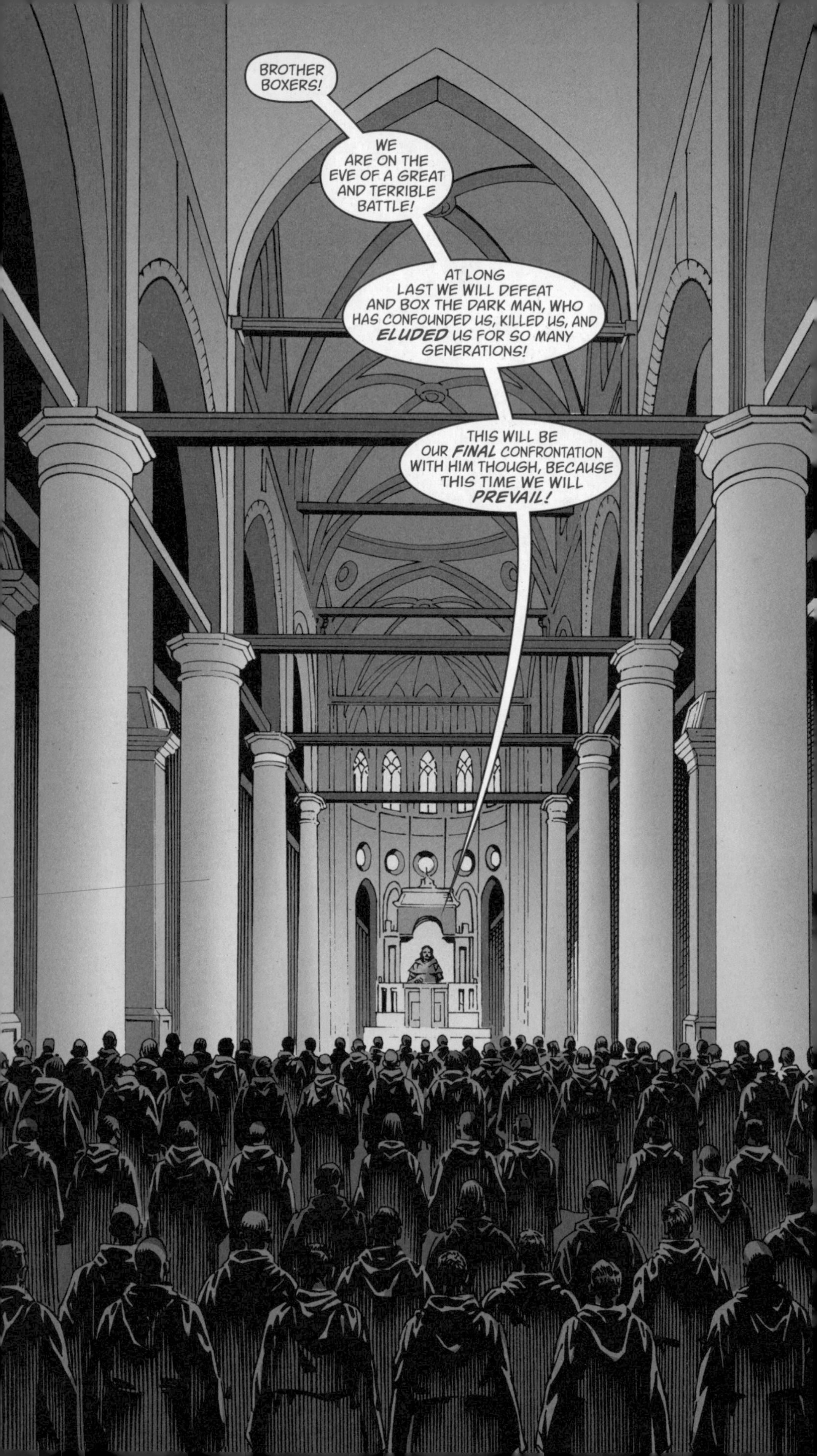
BROTHER BOXERS!
WE ARE ON THE EVE OF A GREAT AND TERRIBLE BATTLE!
AT LONG LAST WE WILL DEFEAT AND BOX THE DARK MAN, WHO HAS CONFOUNDED US, KILLED US, AND ELUDED US FOR SO MANY GENERATIONS!
THIS WILL BE OUR FINAL CONFRONTATION WITH HIM THOUGH, BECAUSE THIS TIME WE WILL PREVAIL!

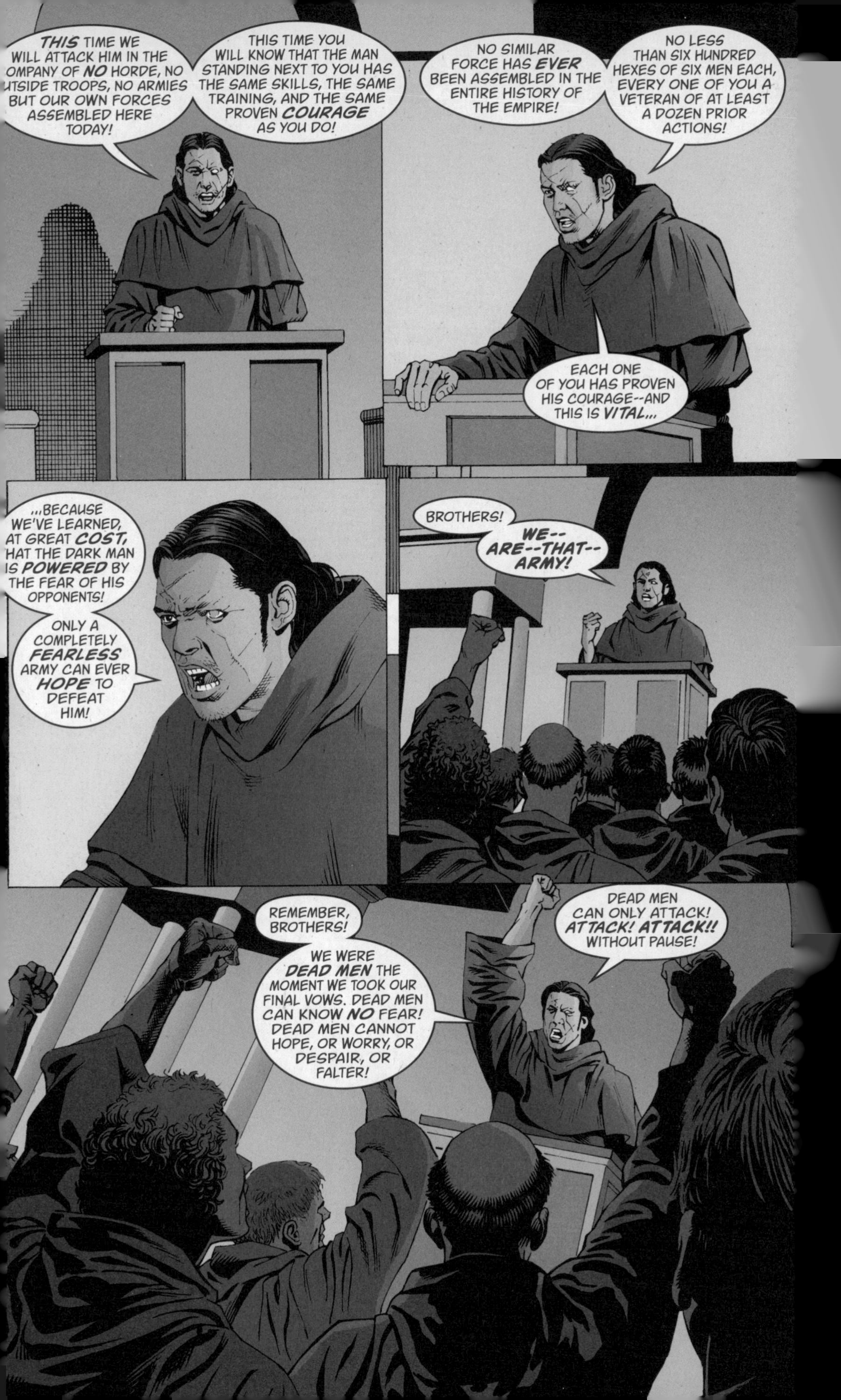
THIS TIME WE WILL ATTACK HIM IN THE OMPANY OF NO HORDE, NO UTSIDE TROOPS, NO ARMIES BUT OUR OWN FORCES ASSEMBLED HERE TODAY!
THIS TIME YOU WILL KNOW THAT THE MAN STANDING NEXT TO YOU HAS THE SAME SKILLS, THE SAME TRAINING, AND THE SAME PROVEN COURAGE AS YOU DO!
NO SIMILAR FORCE HAS EVER BEEN ASSEMBLED IN THE ENTIRE HISTORY OF THE EMPIRE!
NO LESS THAN SIX HUNDRED HEXES OF SIX MEN EACH, EVERY ONE OF YOU A VETERAN OF AT LEAST A DOZEN PRIOR ACTIONS!
EACH ONE OF YOU HAS PROVEN HIS COURAGE--AND THIS IS VITAL...
...BECAUSE WE'VE LEARNED, AT GREAT COST, HAT THE DARK MAN IS POWERED BY THE FEAR OF HIS OPPONENTS!
ONLY A COMPLETELY FEARLESS ARMY CAN EVER HOPE TO DEFEAT HIM!
BROTHERS!
WE--ARE--THAT--ARMY!
REMEMBER, BROTHERS!
WE WERE DEAD MEN THE MOMENT WE TOOK OUR FINAL VOWS. DEAD MEN CAN KNOW NO FEAR! DEAD MEN CANNOT HOPE, OR WORRY, OR DESPAIR, OR FALTER!
DEAD MEN CAN ONLY ATTACK! ATTACK! ATTACK!! WITHOUT PAUSE!

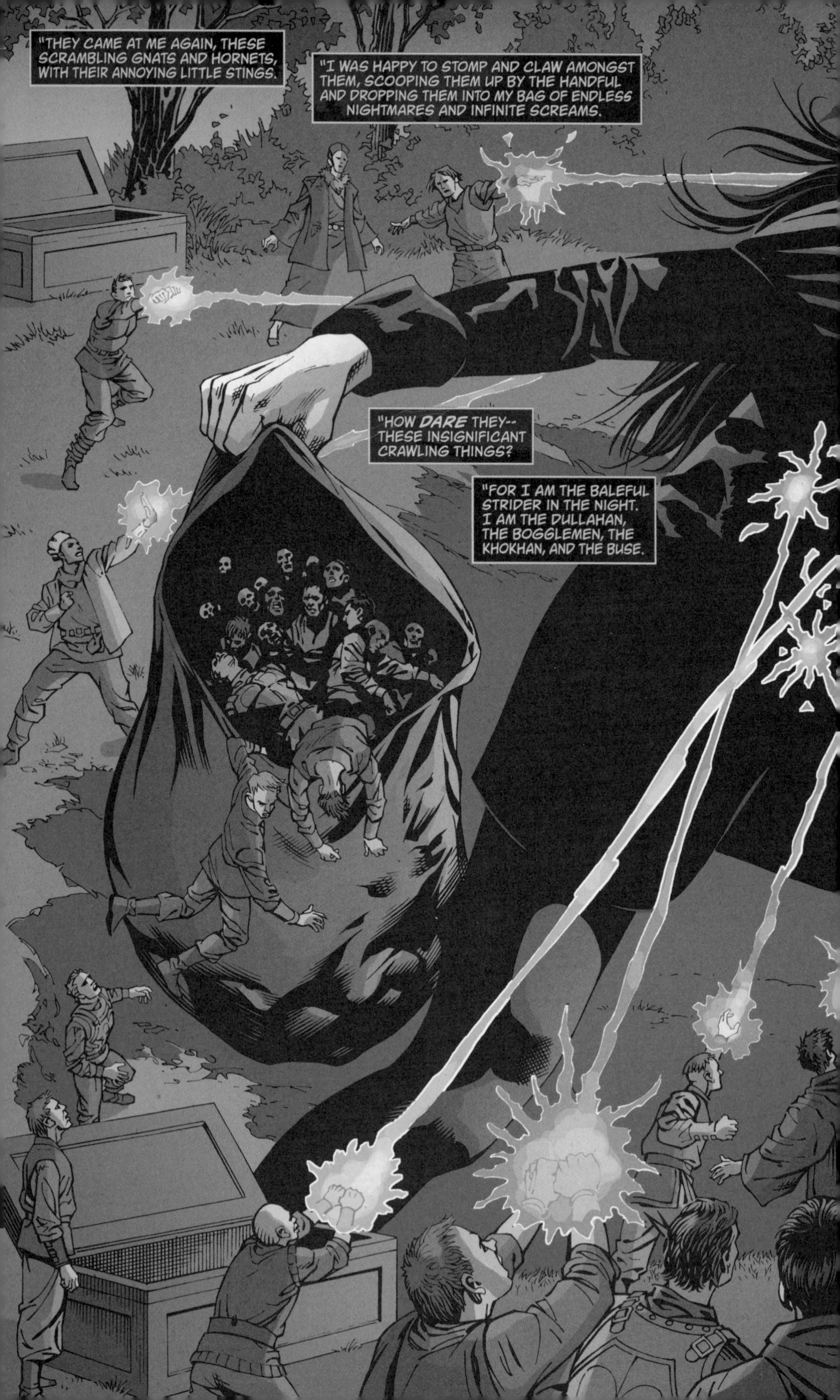
"THEY CAME AT ME AGAIN, THESE SCRAMBLING GNATS AND HORNETS, WITH THEIR ANNOYING LITTLE STINGS.
"I WAS HAPPY TO STOMP AND CLAW AMONGST THEM, SCOOPING THEM UP BY THE HANDFUL AND DROPPING THEM INTO MY BAG OF ENDLESS NIGHTMARES AND INFINITE SCREAMS.
"HOW *DARE* THEY-- THESE INSIGNIFICANT CRAWLING THINGS?
"FOR I AM THE BALEFUL STRIDER IN THE NIGHT. I AM THE DULLAHAN, THE BOGGLEMEN, THE KHOKHAN, AND THE BUSE.

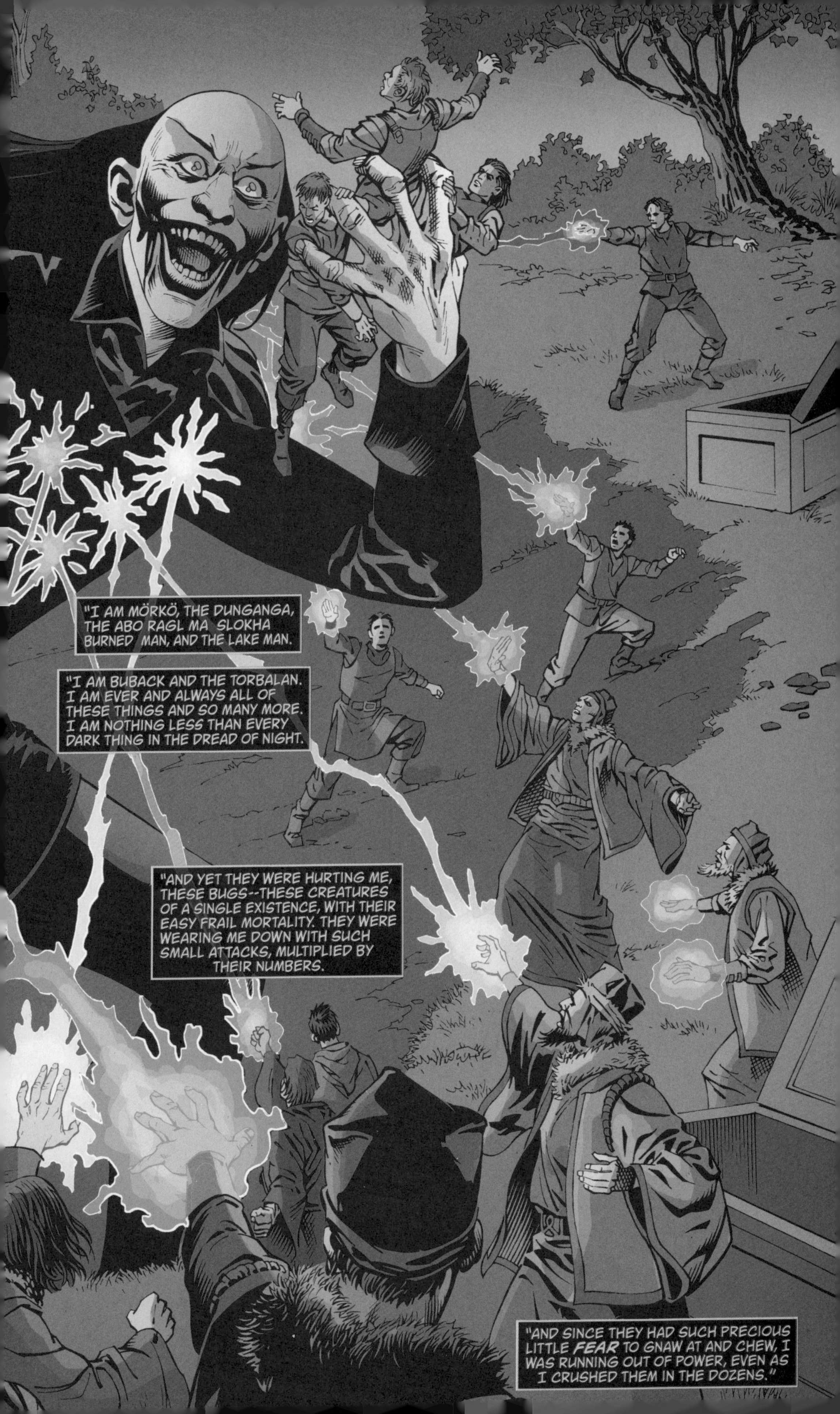
"I AM MÖRKÖ, THE DUNGANGA, THE ABO RAGL MA SLOKHA BURNED MAN, AND THE LAKE MAN.
"I AM BUBACK AND THE TORBALAN. I AM EVER AND ALWAYS ALL OF THESE THINGS AND SO MANY MORE. I AM NOTHING LESS THAN EVERY DARK THING IN THE DREAD OF NIGHT.
"AND YET THEY WERE HURTING ME, THESE BUGS--THESE CREATURES OF A SINGLE EXISTENCE, WITH THEIR EASY FRAIL MORTALITY. THEY WERE WEARING ME DOWN WITH SUCH SMALL ATTACKS, MULTIPLIED BY THEIR NUMBERS.
"AND SINCE THEY HAD SUCH PRECIOUS LITTLE FEAR TO GNAW AT AND CHEW, I WAS RUNNING OUT OF POWER, EVEN AS I CRUSHED THEM IN THE DOZENS."

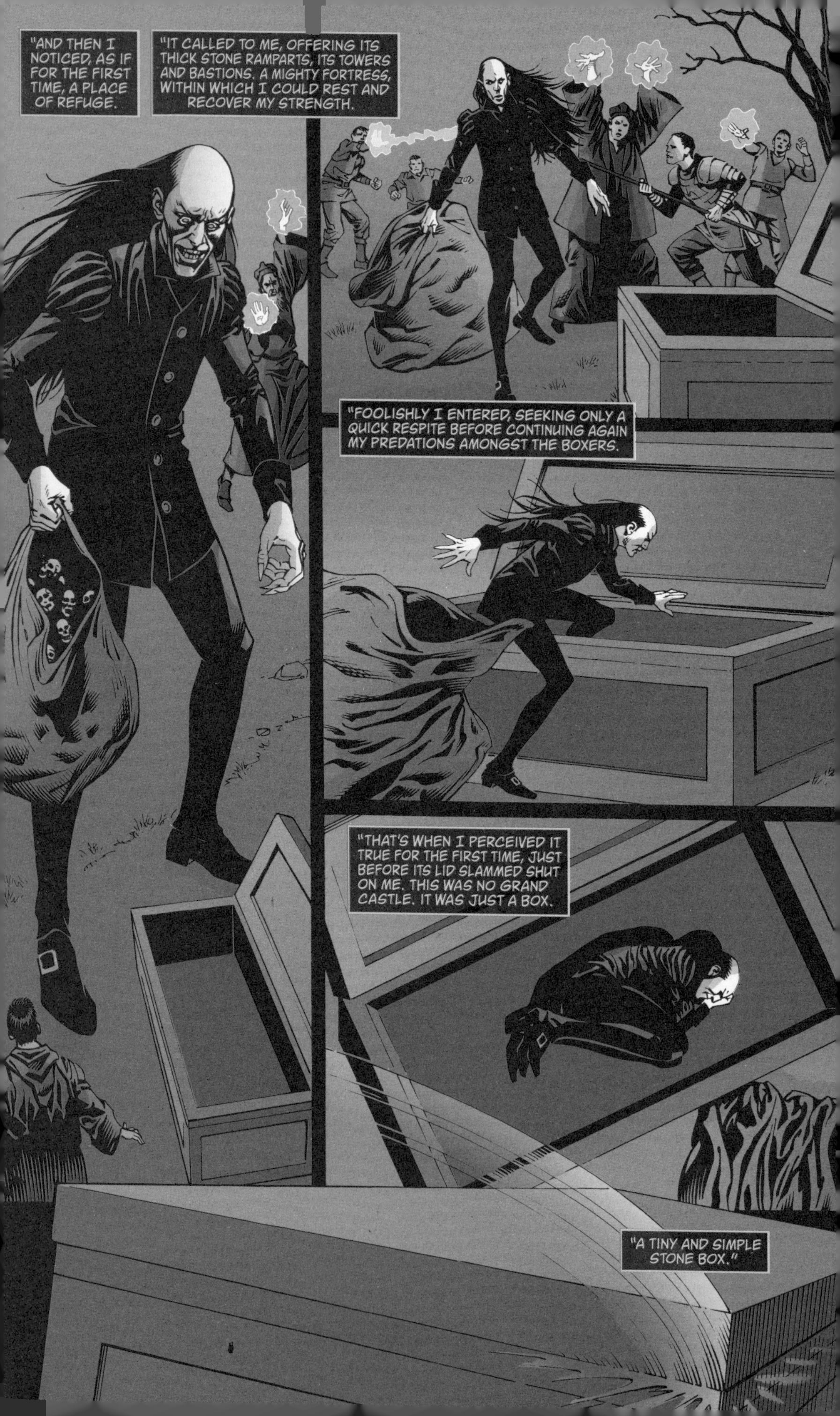
"AND THEN I NOTICED, AS IF FOR THE FIRST TIME, A PLACE OF REFUGE.
"IT CALLED TO ME, OFFERING ITS THICK STONE RAMPARTS, ITS TOWERS AND BASTIONS. A MIGHTY FORTRESS, WITHIN WHICH I COULD REST AND RECOVER MY STRENGTH.
"FOOLISHLY I ENTERED, SEEKING ONLY A QUICK RESPITE BEFORE CONTINUING AGAIN MY PREDATIONS AMONGST THE BOXERS.
"THAT'S WHEN I PERCEIVED IT TRUE FOR THE FIRST TIME, JUST BEFORE ITS LID SLAMMED SHUT ON ME. THIS WAS NO GRAND CASTLE. IT WAS JUST A BOX.
"A TINY AND SIMPLE STONE BOX."

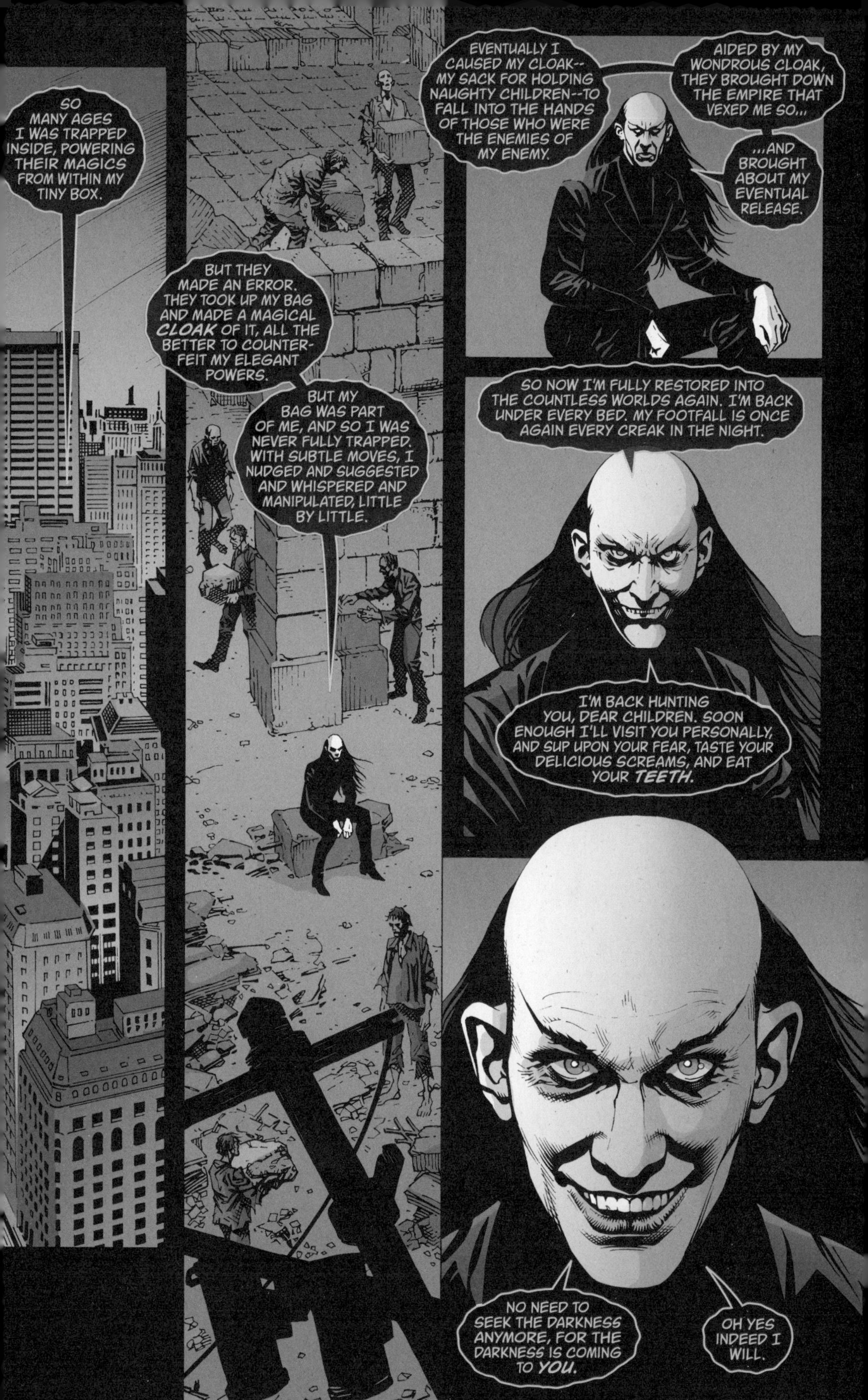
SO MANY AGES I WAS TRAPPED INSIDE, POWERING THEIR MAGICS FROM WITHIN MY TINY BOX.
BUT THEY MADE AN ERROR. THEY TOOK UP MY BAG AND MADE A MAGICAL CLOAK OF IT, ALL THE BETTER TO COUNTER-FEIT MY ELEGANT POWERS.
BUT MY BAG WAS PART OF ME, AND SO I WAS NEVER FULLY TRAPPED. WITH SUBTLE MOVES, I NUDGED AND SUGGESTED AND WHISPERED AND MANIPULATED, LITTLE BY LITTLE.
EVENTUALLY I CAUSED MY CLOAK-- MY SACK FOR HOLDING NAUGHTY CHILDREN--TO FALL INTO THE HANDS OF THOSE WHO WERE THE ENEMIES OF MY ENEMY.
AIDED BY MY WONDROUS CLOAK, THEY BROUGHT DOWN THE EMPIRE THAT VEXED ME SO...
...AND BROUGHT ABOUT MY EVENTUAL RELEASE.
SO NOW I'M FULLY RESTORED INTO THE COUNTLESS WORLDS AGAIN. I'M BACK UNDER EVERY BED. MY FOOTFALL IS ONCE AGAIN EVERY CREAK IN THE NIGHT.
I'M BACK HUNTING YOU, DEAR CHILDREN. SOON ENOUGH I'LL VISIT YOU PERSONALLY, AND SUP UPON YOUR FEAR, TASTE YOUR DELICIOUS SCREAMS, AND EAT YOUR TEETH.
NO NEED TO SEEK THE DARKNESS ANYMORE, FOR THE DARKNESS IS COMING TO YOU.
OH YES INDEED I WILL.

Next: Baba Yaga

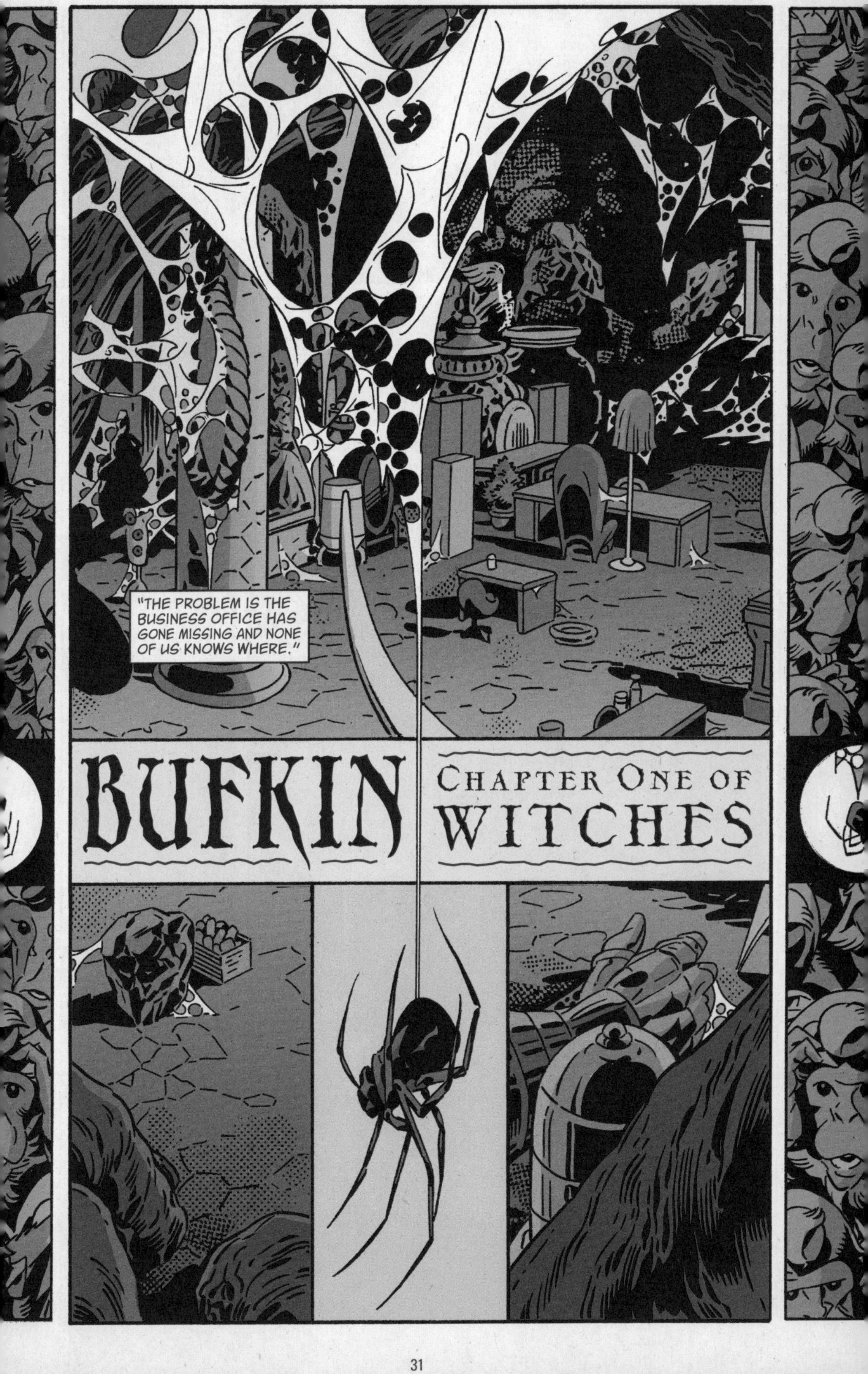

"THE PROBLEM IS THE BUSINESS OFFICE HAS GONE MISSING AND NONE OF US KNOWS WHERE."
BUFKIN
CHAPTER ONE OF
WITCHES

THE FARM.
EXCEPT THAT YOU DO. YOU PLACED IT, ARDELIA. YOU MUST KNOW WHERE IT IS.
OR ARE YOU BULAH TODAY? OR BIRDIE? OR CHERISH?
CAN YOU TRY REALLY HARD TO RECALL WHERE YOU PUT THE BUSINESS OFFICE OH SO LONG AGO?
I THINK THE PUDDING IS READY FOR THE BREAD NOW.
FORGET IT, FRAU TOTENKINDER. SHE'S NEVER GOING TO REMEMBER HOW SHE CONSTRUCTED THE BUSINESS OFFICE SPELLS OR WHERE IT ACTUALLY IS.
THE POWERFUL FAIRY WITCH OF YEARS AGO IS GONE. HER MIND WENT WHEN SHE WAS REMOVED FROM LEADERSHIP.

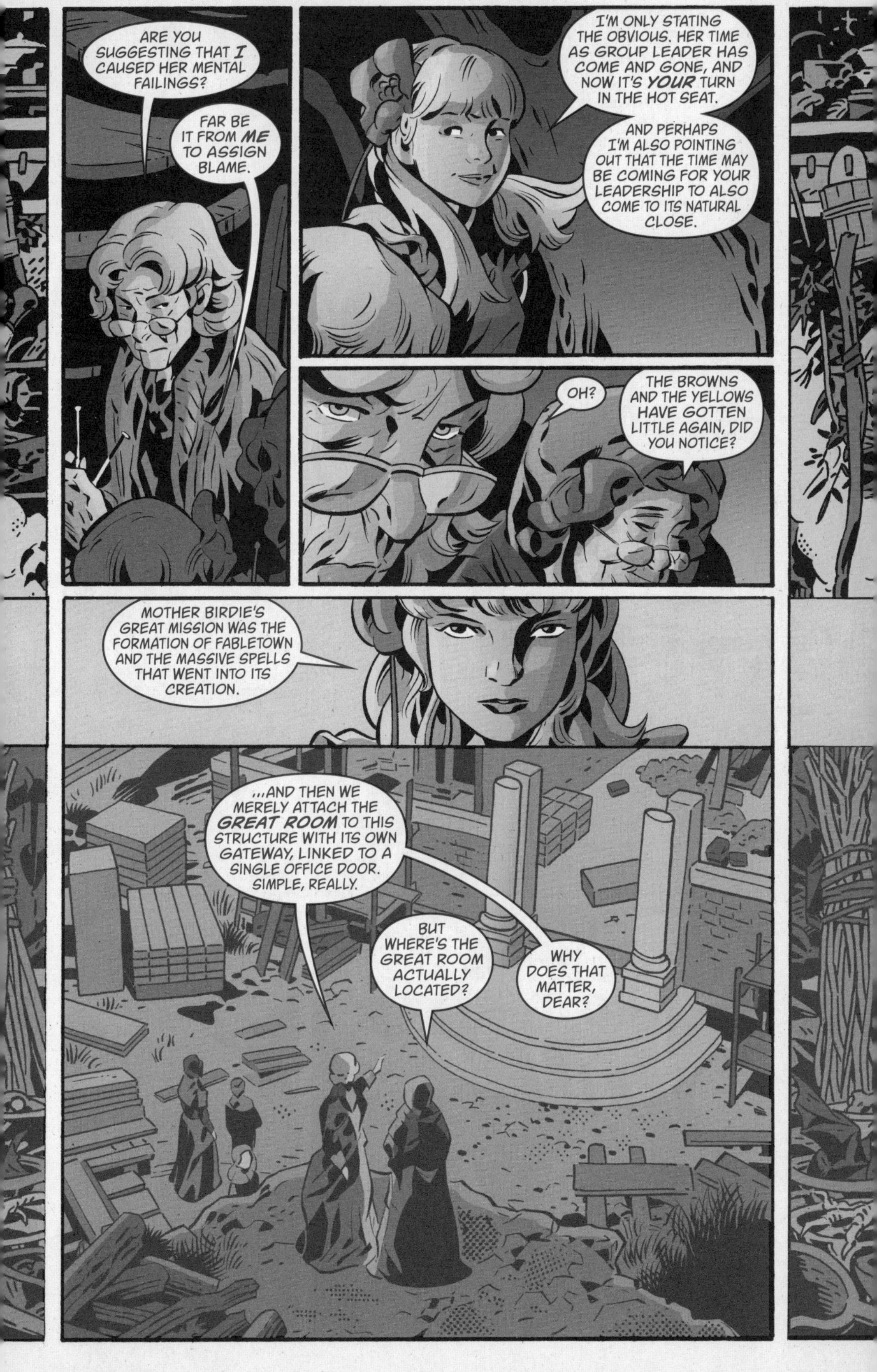
ARE YOU SUGGESTING THAT I CAUSED HER MENTAL FAILINGS?
FAR BE IT FROM ME TO ASSIGN BLAME.
I'M ONLY STATING THE OBVIOUS. HER TIME AS GROUP LEADER HAS COME AND GONE, AND NOW IT'S YOUR TURN IN THE HOT SEAT.
AND PERHAPS I'M ALSO POINTING OUT THAT THE TIME MAY BE COMING FOR YOUR LEADERSHIP TO ALSO COME TO ITS NATURAL CLOSE.
OH?
THE BROWNS AND THE YELLOWS HAVE GOTTEN LITTLE AGAIN, DID YOU NOTICE?
MOTHER BIRDIE'S GREAT MISSION WAS THE FORMATION OF FABLETOWN AND THE MASSIVE SPELLS THAT WENT INTO ITS CREATION.
...AND THEN WE MERELY ATTACH THE GREAT ROOM TO THIS STRUCTURE WITH ITS OWN GATEWAY, LINKED TO A SINGLE OFFICE DOOR. SIMPLE, REALLY.
BUT WHERE'S THE GREAT ROOM ACTUALLY LOCATED?
WHY DOES THAT MATTER, DEAR?

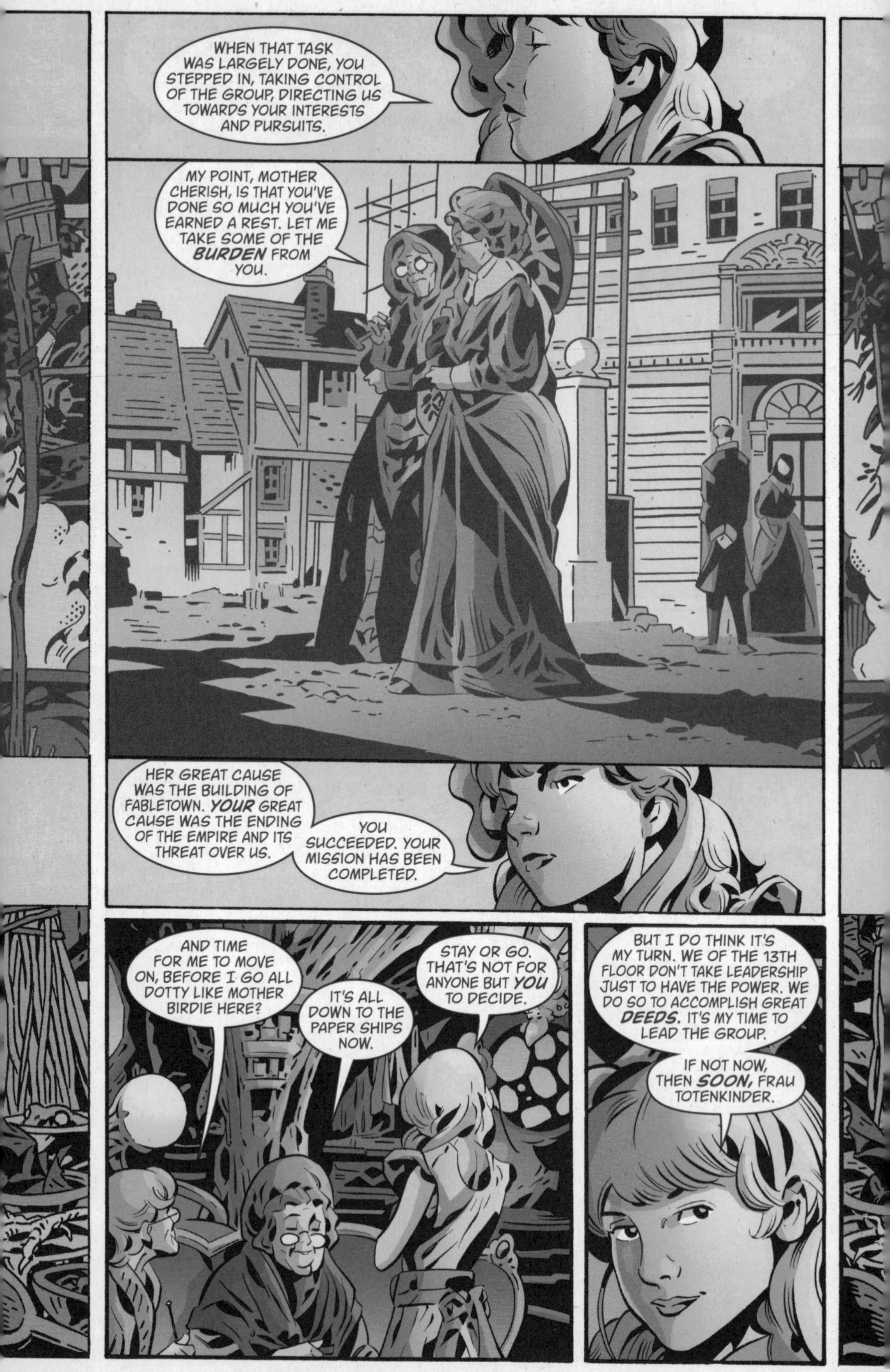
WHEN THAT TASK WAS LARGELY DONE, YOU STEPPED IN, TAKING CONTROL OF THE GROUP, DIRECTING US TOWARDS YOUR INTERESTS AND PURSUITS.
MY POINT, MOTHER CHERISH, IS THAT YOU'VE DONE SO MUCH YOU'VE EARNED A REST. LET ME TAKE SOME OF THE *BURDEN* FROM YOU.
HER GREAT CAUSE WAS THE BUILDING OF FABLETOWN. *YOUR* GREAT CAUSE WAS THE ENDING OF THE EMPIRE AND ITS THREAT OVER US.
YOU SUCCEEDED. YOUR MISSION HAS BEEN COMPLETED.
AND TIME FOR ME TO MOVE ON, BEFORE I GO ALL DOTTY LIKE MOTHER BIRDIE HERE?
IT'S ALL DOWN TO THE PAPER SHIPS NOW.
STAY OR GO. THAT'S NOT FOR ANYONE BUT *YOU* TO DECIDE.
BUT I DO THINK IT'S MY TURN. WE OF THE 13TH FLOOR DON'T TAKE LEADERSHIP JUST TO HAVE THE POWER. WE DO SO TO ACCOMPLISH GREAT *DEEDS*. IT'S MY TIME TO LEAD THE GROUP.
IF NOT NOW, THEN *SOON*, FRAU TOTENKINDER.

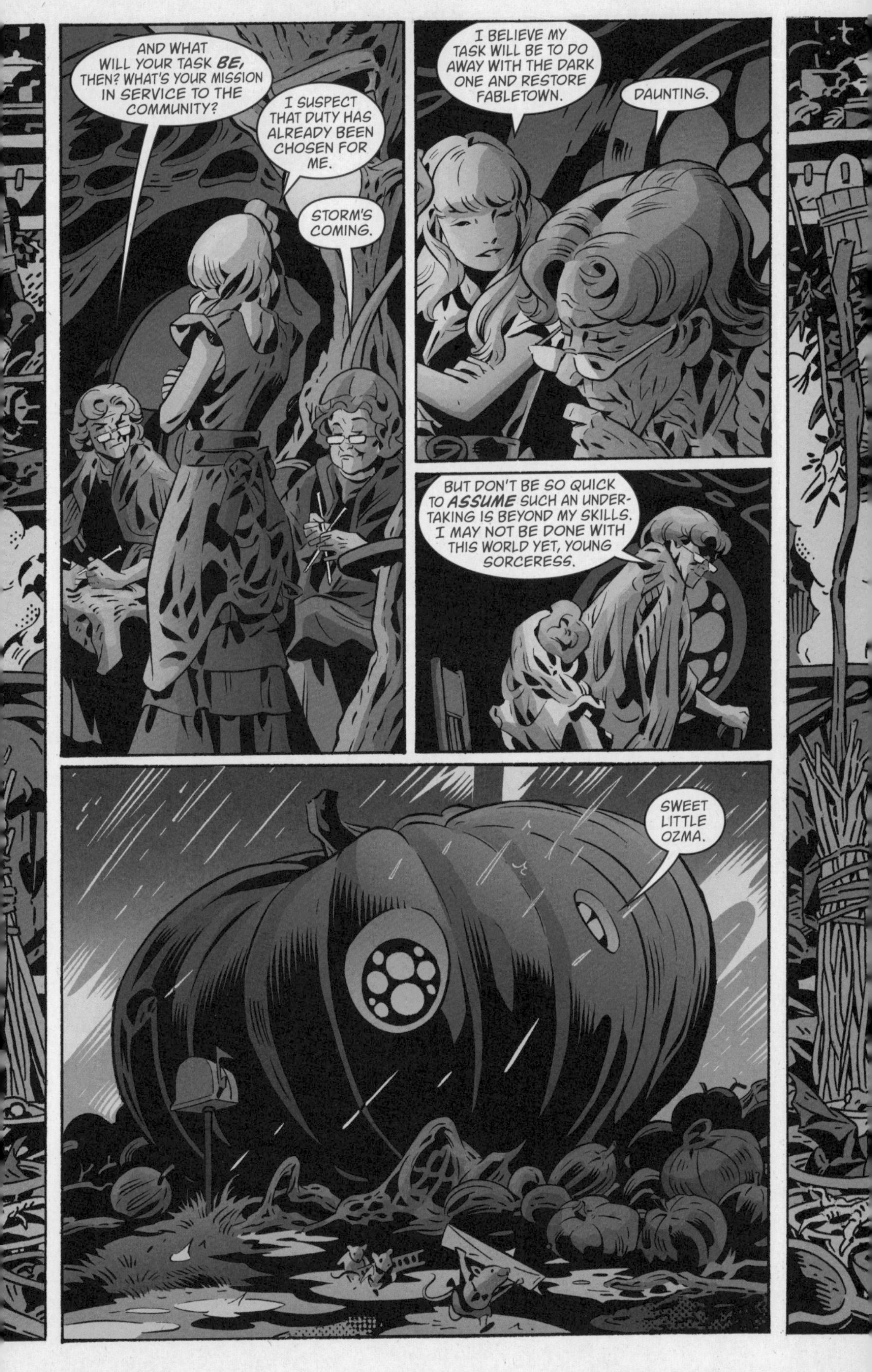

AND WHAT WILL YOUR TASK BE, THEN? WHAT'S YOUR MISSION IN SERVICE TO THE COMMUNITY?
I SUSPECT THAT DUTY HAS ALREADY BEEN CHOSEN FOR ME.
STORM'S COMING.
I BELIEVE MY TASK WILL BE TO DO AWAY WITH THE DARK ONE AND RESTORE FABLETOWN.
DAUNTING.
BUT DON'T BE SO QUICK TO ASSUME SUCH AN UNDERTAKING IS BEYOND MY SKILLS. I MAY NOT BE DONE WITH THIS WORLD YET, YOUNG SORCERESS.
SWEET LITTLE OZMA.

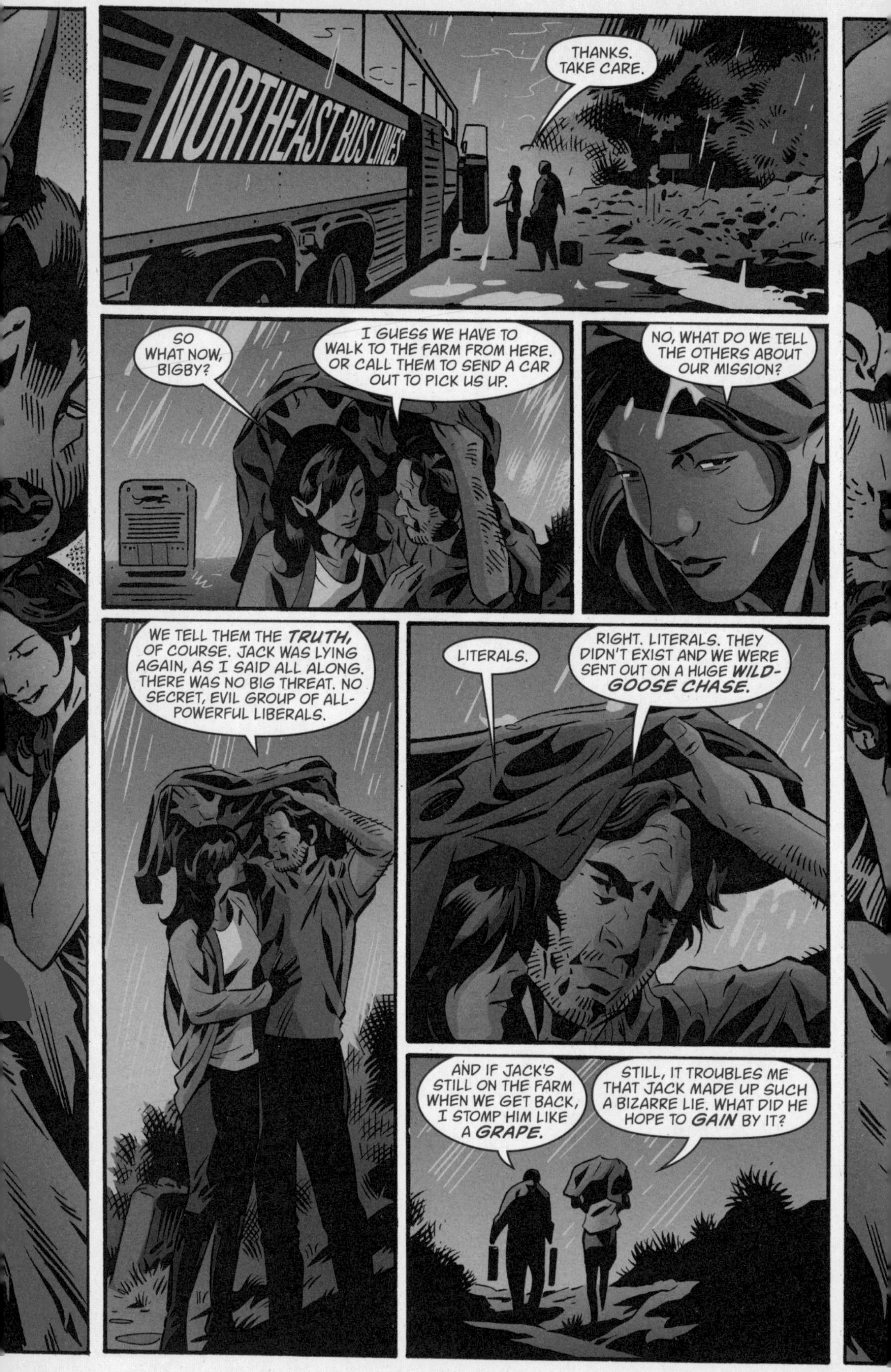
NORTHEAST BUS LINES
THANKS. TAKE CARE.
SO WHAT NOW, BIGBY?
I GUESS WE HAVE TO WALK TO THE FARM FROM HERE. OR CALL THEM TO SEND A CAR OUT TO PICK US UP.
NO, WHAT DO WE TELL THE OTHERS ABOUT OUR MISSION?
WE TELL THEM THE TRUTH, OF COURSE. JACK WAS LYING AGAIN, AS I SAID ALL ALONG. THERE WAS NO BIG THREAT. NO SECRET, EVIL GROUP OF ALL-POWERFUL LIBERALS.
LITERALS.
RIGHT. LITERALS. THEY DIDN'T EXIST AND WE WERE SENT OUT ON A HUGE WILD-GOOSE CHASE.
AND IF JACK'S STILL ON THE FARM WHEN WE GET BACK, I STOMP HIM LIKE A GRAPE.
STILL, IT TROUBLES ME THAT JACK MADE UP SUCH A BIZARRE LIE. WHAT DID HE HOPE TO GAIN BY IT?

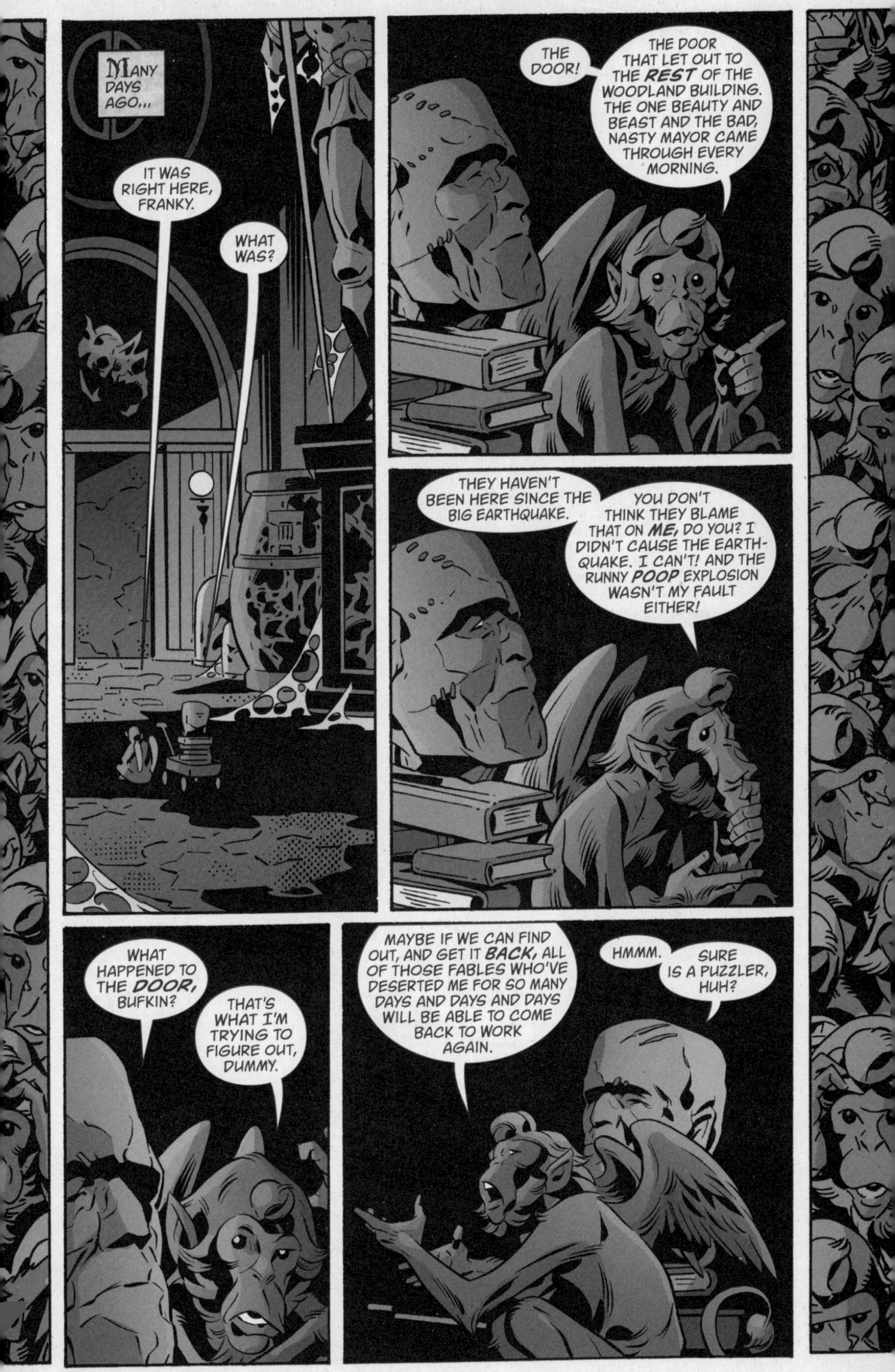
MANY DAYS AGO...
IT WAS RIGHT HERE, FRANKY.
WHAT WAS?
THE DOOR!
THE DOOR THAT LET OUT TO THE REST OF THE WOODLAND BUILDING. THE ONE BEAUTY AND BEAST AND THE BAD, NASTY MAYOR CAME THROUGH EVERY MORNING.
THEY HAVEN'T BEEN HERE SINCE THE BIG EARTHQUAKE.
YOU DON'T THINK THEY BLAME THAT ON ME, DO YOU? I DIDN'T CAUSE THE EARTH-QUAKE. I CAN'T! AND THE RUNNY POOP EXPLOSION WASN'T MY FAULT EITHER!
WHAT HAPPENED TO THE DOOR, BUFKIN?
THAT'S WHAT I'M TRYING TO FIGURE OUT, DUMMY.
MAYBE IF WE CAN FIND OUT, AND GET IT BACK, ALL OF THOSE FABLES WHO'VE DESERTED ME FOR SO MANY DAYS AND DAYS AND DAYS WILL BE ABLE TO COME BACK TO WORK AGAIN.
HMMM.
SURE IS A PUZZLER, HUH?

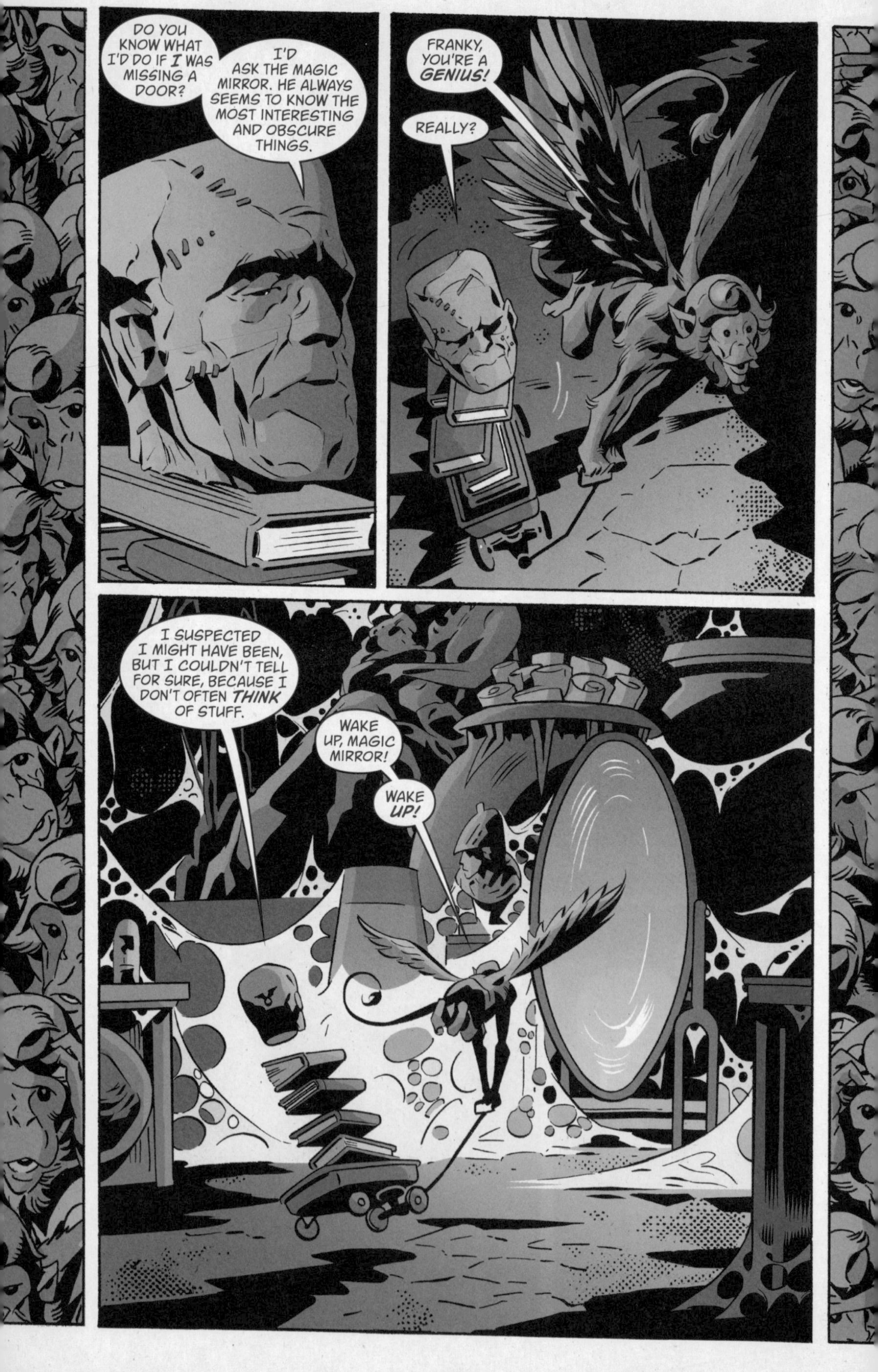
DO YOU KNOW WHAT I'D DO IF I WAS MISSING A DOOR?
I'D ASK THE MAGIC MIRROR. HE ALWAYS SEEMS TO KNOW THE MOST INTERESTING AND OBSCURE THINGS.
FRANKY, YOU'RE A GENIUS!
REALLY?
I SUSPECTED I MIGHT HAVE BEEN, BUT I COULDN'T TELL FOR SURE, BECAUSE I DON'T OFTEN THINK OF STUFF.
WAKE UP, MAGIC MIRROR!
WAKE UP!

YOU HAVE TO RHYME.

OH, YEAH.

FORGOT.

MIRROR, MIRROR ON THE FLOOR!

HELP ME FIND THE MISSING DOOR!

NNNG-- HNNN--UH-- -SNORT- --UHM...

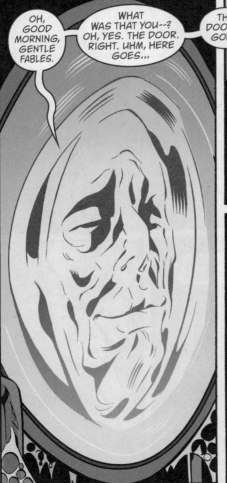

OH, GOOD MORNING, GENTLE FABLES.

WHAT WAS THAT YOU--? OH, YES. THE DOOR. RIGHT. UHM, HERE GOES...

THE DOOR IS GONE.

IT'S DIED AWAY.

ONLY A NEW SPELL CAN BRING IT BACK SOMEDAY.

CAN I BE OF ANY FURTHER ASSIS- TANCE?

THAT'S IT?

THAT'S ALL YOU'VE GOT?

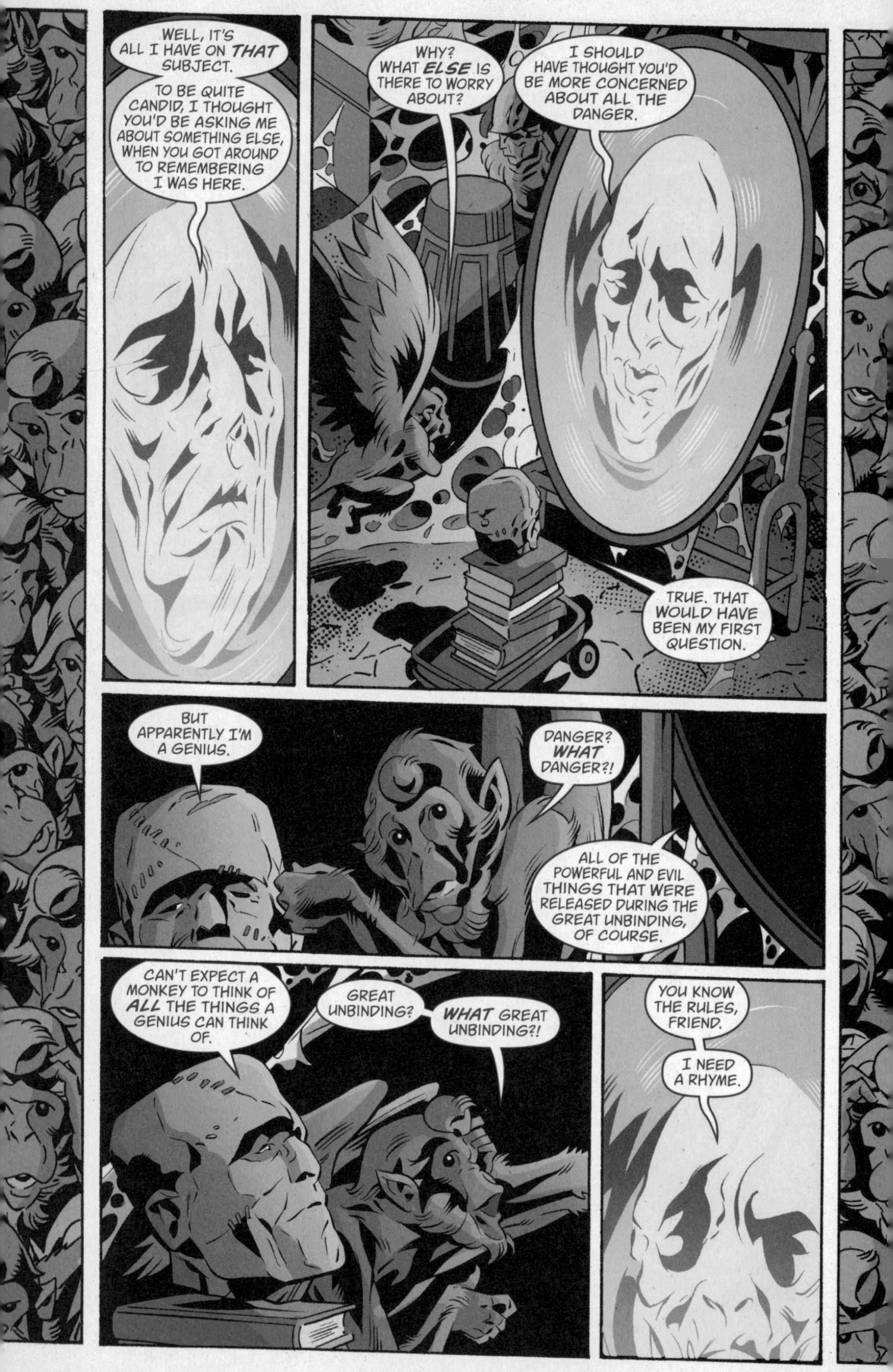
WELL, IT'S ALL I HAVE ON THAT SUBJECT.
TO BE QUITE CANDID, I THOUGHT YOU'D BE ASKING ME ABOUT SOMETHING ELSE, WHEN YOU GOT AROUND TO REMEMBERING I WAS HERE.
WHY? WHAT ELSE IS THERE TO WORRY ABOUT?
I SHOULD HAVE THOUGHT YOU'D BE MORE CONCERNED ABOUT ALL THE DANGER.
TRUE. THAT WOULD HAVE BEEN MY FIRST QUESTION.
BUT APPARENTLY I'M A GENIUS.
DANGER? WHAT DANGER?!
ALL OF THE POWERFUL AND EVIL THINGS THAT WERE RELEASED DURING THE GREAT UNBINDING, OF COURSE.
CAN'T EXPECT A MONKEY TO THINK OF ALL THE THINGS A GENIUS CAN THINK OF.
GREAT UNBINDING?
WHAT GREAT UNBINDING?!
YOU KNOW THE RULES, FRIEND.
I NEED A RHYME.

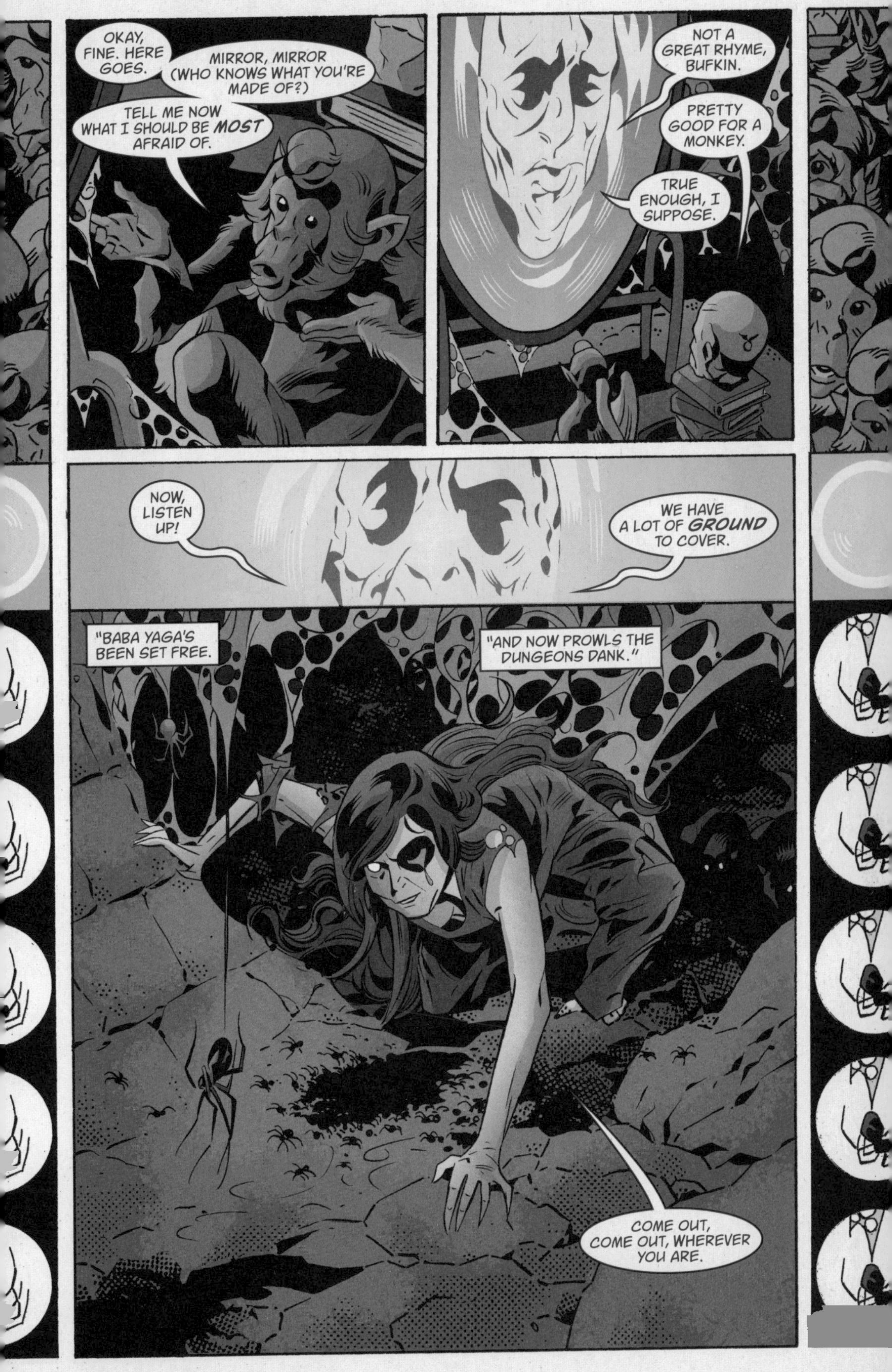
OKAY, FINE. HERE GOES.
MIRROR, MIRROR (WHO KNOWS WHAT YOU'RE MADE OF?)
TELL ME NOW WHAT I SHOULD BE MOST AFRAID OF.
NOT A GREAT RHYME, BUFKIN.
PRETTY GOOD FOR A MONKEY.
TRUE ENOUGH, I SUPPOSE.
NOW, LISTEN UP!
WE HAVE A LOT OF GROUND TO COVER.
"BABA YAGA'S BEEN SET FREE.
"AND NOW PROWLS THE DUNGEONS DANK."
COME OUT, COME OUT, WHEREVER YOU ARE.

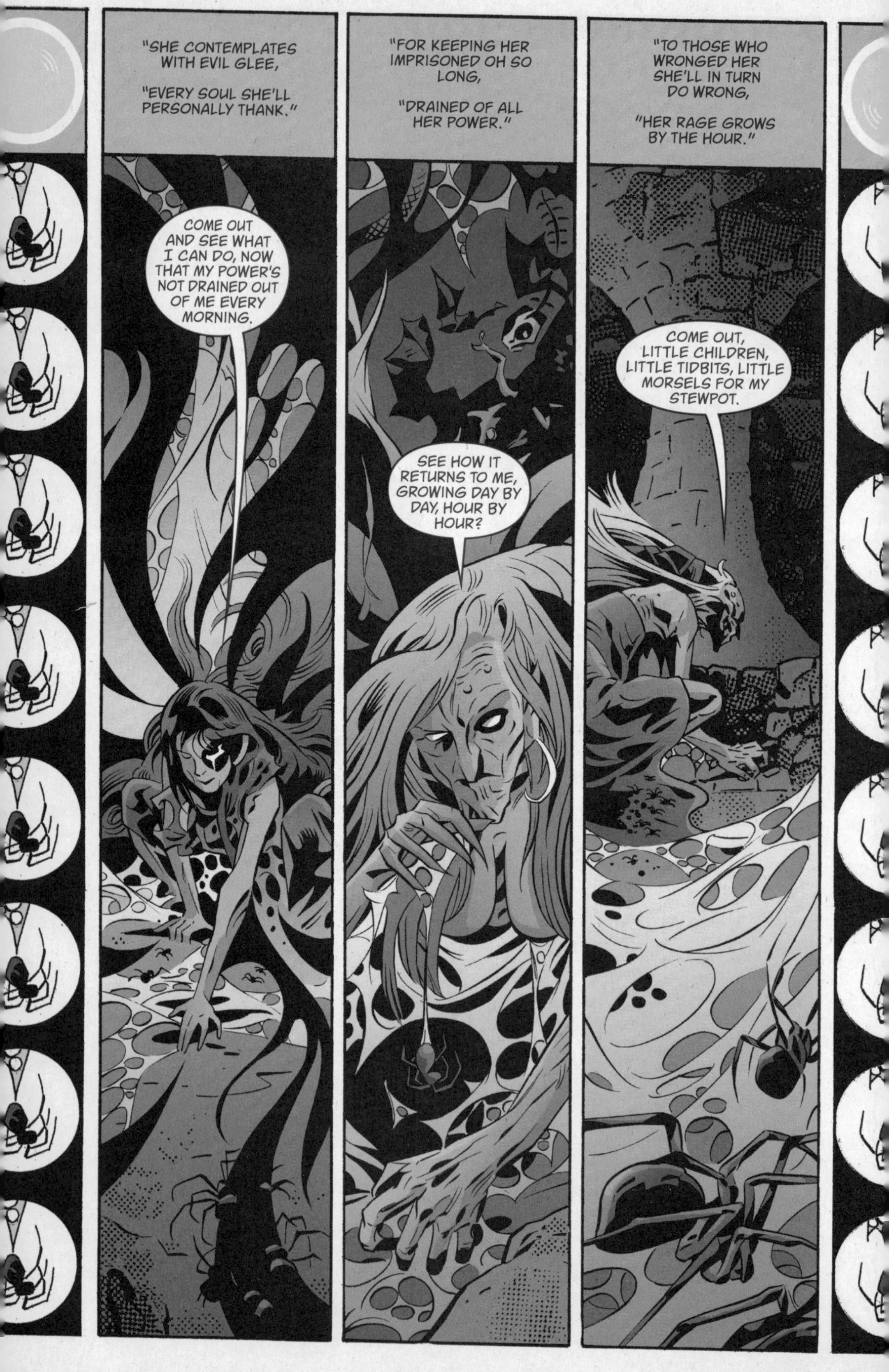
"SHE CONTEMPLATES WITH EVIL GLEE,
"EVERY SOUL SHE'LL PERSONALLY THANK."
COME OUT AND SEE WHAT I CAN DO, NOW THAT MY POWER'S NOT DRAINED OUT OF ME EVERY MORNING.
"FOR KEEPING HER IMPRISONED OH SO LONG,
"DRAINED OF ALL HER POWER."
SEE HOW IT RETURNS TO ME, GROWING DAY BY DAY, HOUR BY HOUR?
"TO THOSE WHO WRONGED HER SHE'LL IN TURN DO WRONG,
"HER RAGE GROWS BY THE HOUR."
COME OUT, LITTLE CHILDREN, LITTLE TIDBITS, LITTLE MORSELS FOR MY STEWPOT.

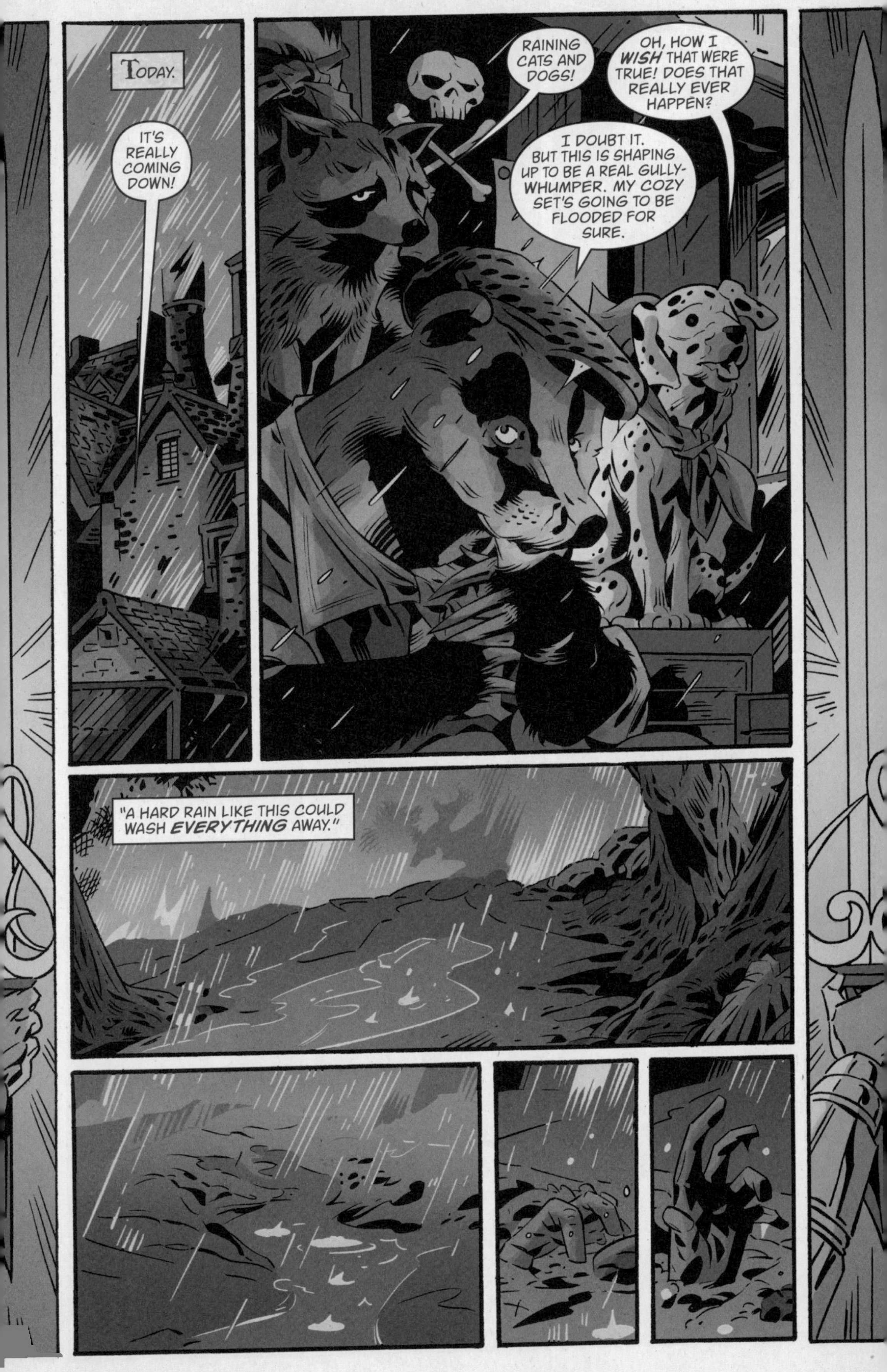
TODAY.
IT'S REALLY COMING DOWN!
RAINING CATS AND DOGS!
OH, HOW I WISH THAT WERE TRUE! DOES THAT REALLY EVER HAPPEN?
I DOUBT IT. BUT THIS IS SHAPING UP TO BE A REAL GULLY-WHUMPER. MY COZY SET'S GOING TO BE FLOODED FOR SURE.
"A HARD RAIN LIKE THIS COULD WASH EVERYTHING AWAY."

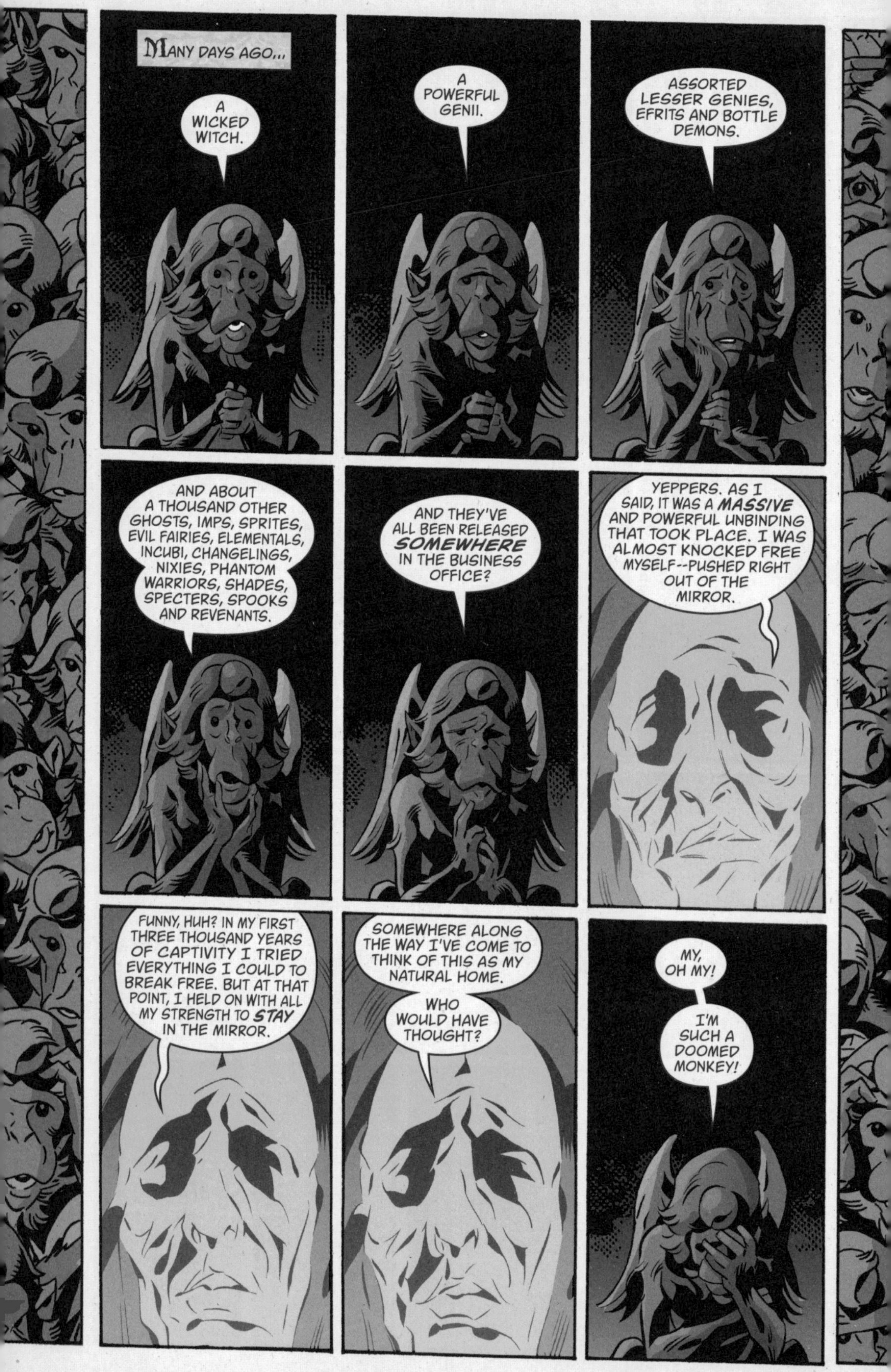
MANY DAYS AGO...
A WICKED WITCH.
A POWERFUL GENII.
ASSORTED LESSER GENIES, EFRITS AND BOTTLE DEMONS.
AND ABOUT A THOUSAND OTHER GHOSTS, IMPS, SPRITES, EVIL FAIRIES, ELEMENTALS, INCUBI, CHANGELINGS, NIXIES, PHANTOM WARRIORS, SHADES, SPECTERS, SPOOKS AND REVENANTS.
AND THEY'VE ALL BEEN RELEASED SOMEWHERE IN THE BUSINESS OFFICE?
YEPPERS. AS I SAID, IT WAS A MASSIVE AND POWERFUL UNBINDING THAT TOOK PLACE. I WAS ALMOST KNOCKED FREE MYSELF--PUSHED RIGHT OUT OF THE MIRROR.
FUNNY, HUH? IN MY FIRST THREE THOUSAND YEARS OF CAPTIVITY I TRIED EVERYTHING I COULD TO BREAK FREE. BUT AT THAT POINT, I HELD ON WITH ALL MY STRENGTH TO STAY IN THE MIRROR.
SOMEWHERE ALONG THE WAY I'VE COME TO THINK OF THIS AS MY NATURAL HOME.
WHO WOULD HAVE THOUGHT?
MY, OH MY!
I'M SUCH A DOOMED MONKEY!

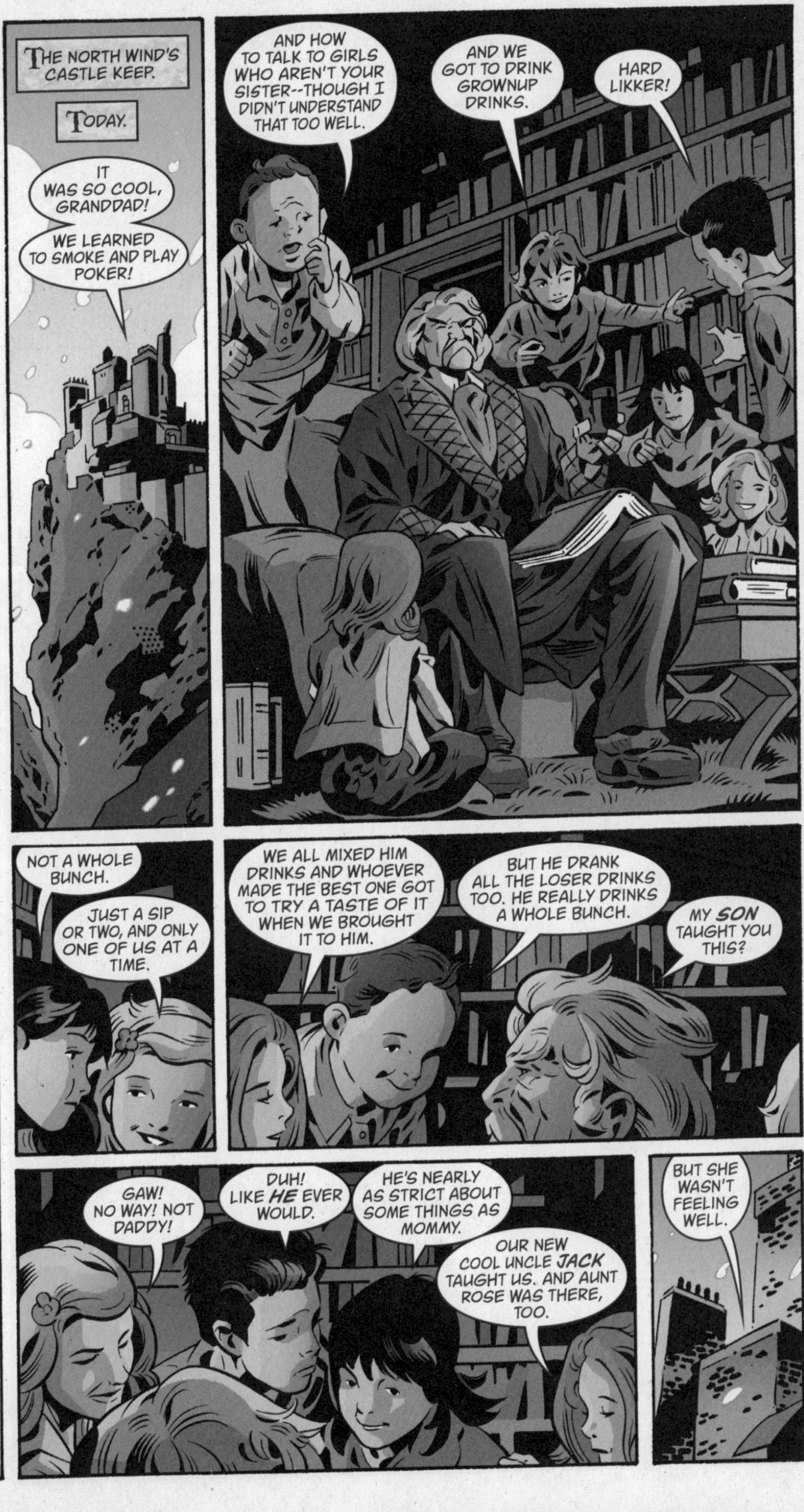
THE NORTH WIND'S CASTLE KEEP.
TODAY.
IT WAS SO COOL, GRANDDAD!
WE LEARNED TO SMOKE AND PLAY POKER!
AND HOW TO TALK TO GIRLS WHO AREN'T YOUR SISTER--THOUGH I DIDN'T UNDERSTAND THAT TOO WELL.
AND WE GOT TO DRINK GROWNUP DRINKS.
HARD LIKKER!
NOT A WHOLE BUNCH.
JUST A SIP OR TWO, AND ONLY ONE OF US AT A TIME.
WE ALL MIXED HIM DRINKS AND WHOEVER MADE THE BEST ONE GOT TO TRY A TASTE OF IT WHEN WE BROUGHT IT TO HIM.
BUT HE DRANK ALL THE LOSER DRINKS TOO. HE REALLY DRINKS A WHOLE BUNCH.
MY SON TAUGHT YOU THIS?
GAW! NO WAY! NOT DADDY!
DUH! LIKE HE EVER WOULD.
HE'S NEARLY AS STRICT ABOUT SOME THINGS AS MOMMY.
OUR NEW COOL UNCLE JACK TAUGHT US. AND AUNT ROSE WAS THERE, TOO.
BUT SHE WASN'T FEELING WELL.

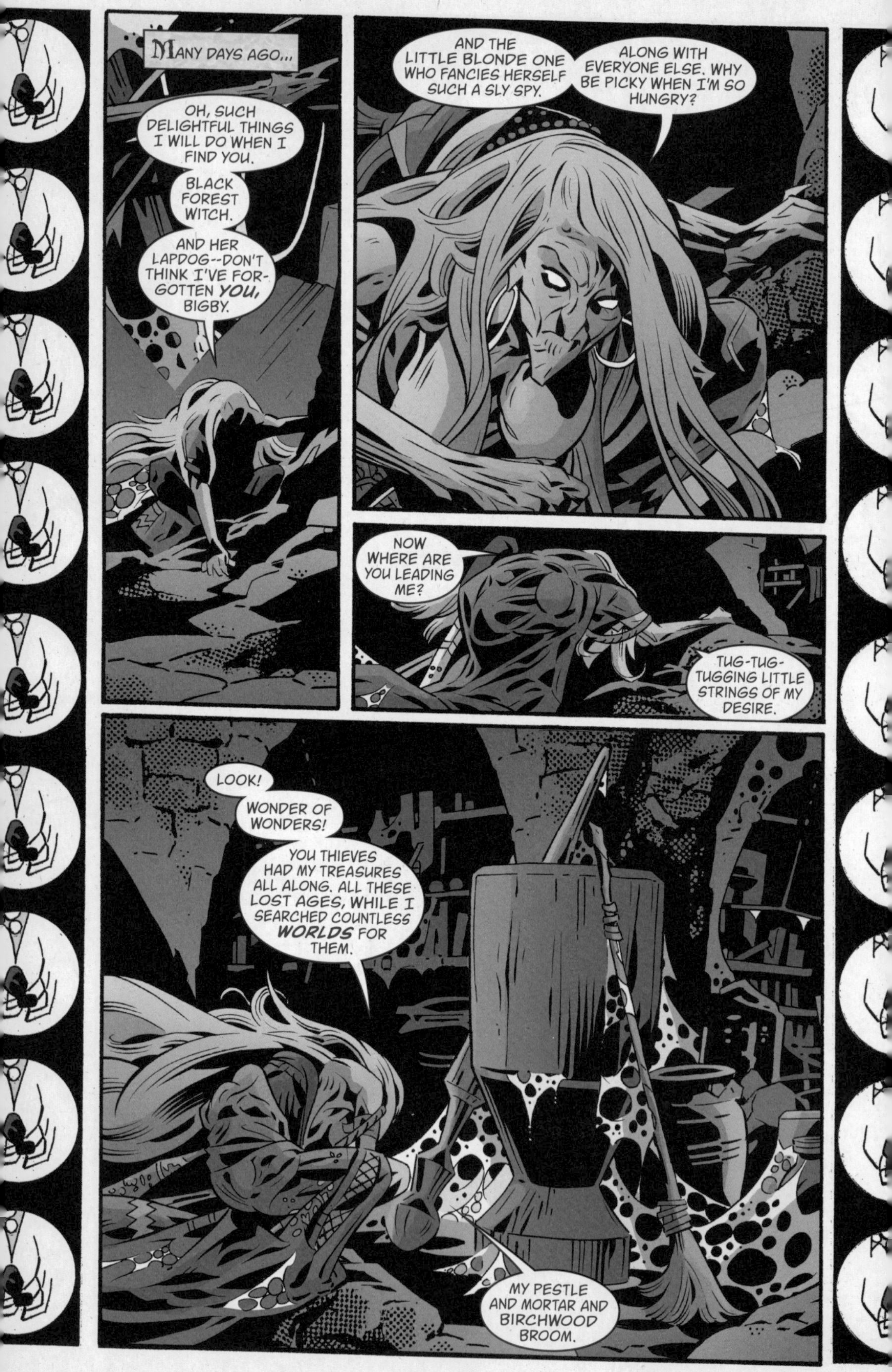
MANY DAYS AGO...
OH, SUCH DELIGHTFUL THINGS I WILL DO WHEN I FIND YOU.
BLACK FOREST WITCH.
AND HER LAPDOG--DON'T THINK I'VE FORGOTTEN YOU, BIGBY.
AND THE LITTLE BLONDE ONE WHO FANCIES HERSELF SUCH A SLY SPY.
ALONG WITH EVERYONE ELSE. WHY BE PICKY WHEN I'M SO HUNGRY?
NOW WHERE ARE YOU LEADING ME?
TUG-TUG-TUGGING LITTLE STRINGS OF MY DESIRE.
LOOK!
WONDER OF WONDERS!
YOU THIEVES HAD MY TREASURES ALL ALONG. ALL THESE LOST AGES, WHILE I SEARCHED COUNTLESS WORLDS FOR THEM.
MY PESTLE AND MORTAR AND BIRCHWOOD BROOM.

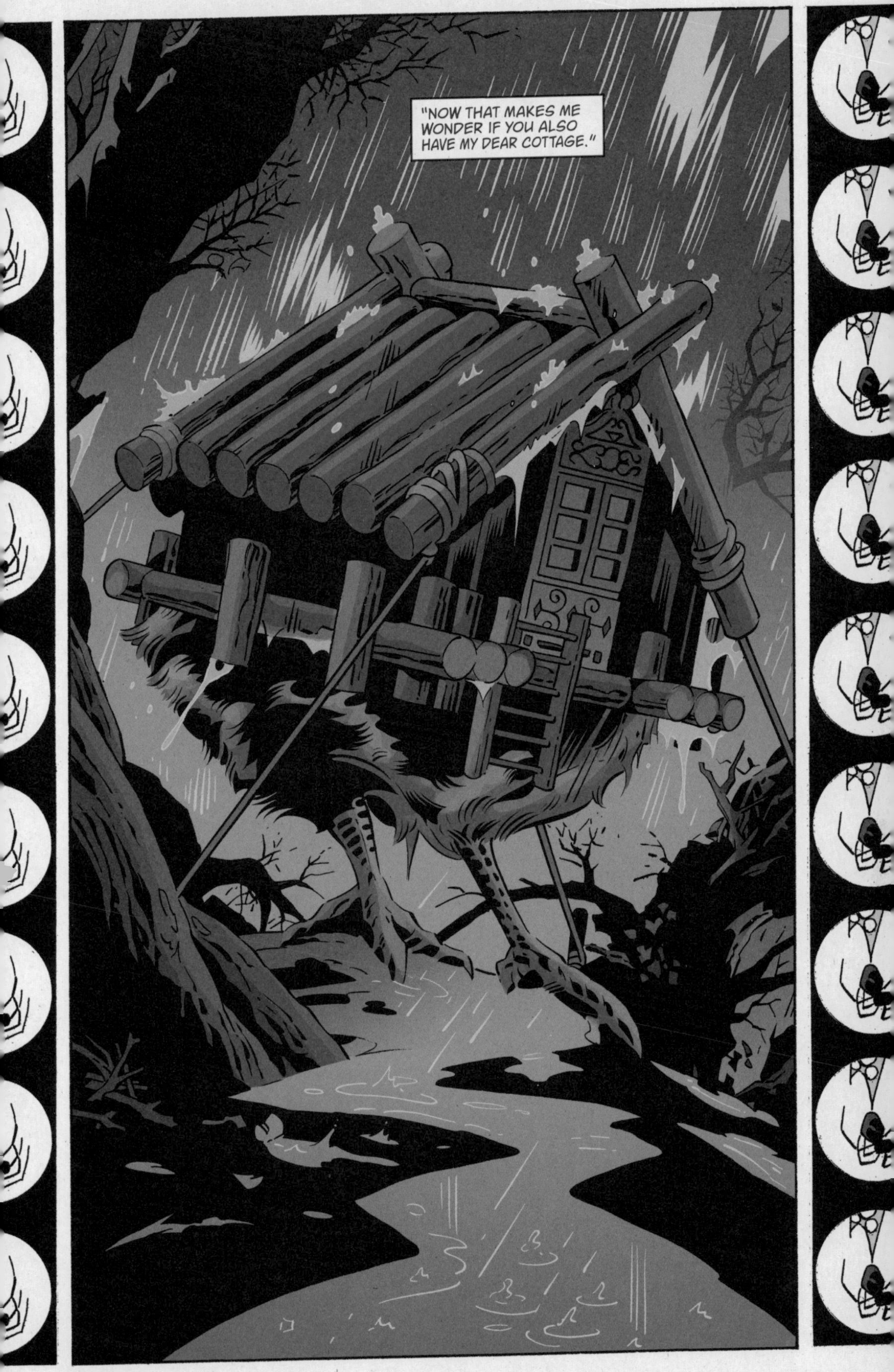
"NOW THAT MAKES ME WONDER IF YOU ALSO HAVE MY DEAR COTTAGE."

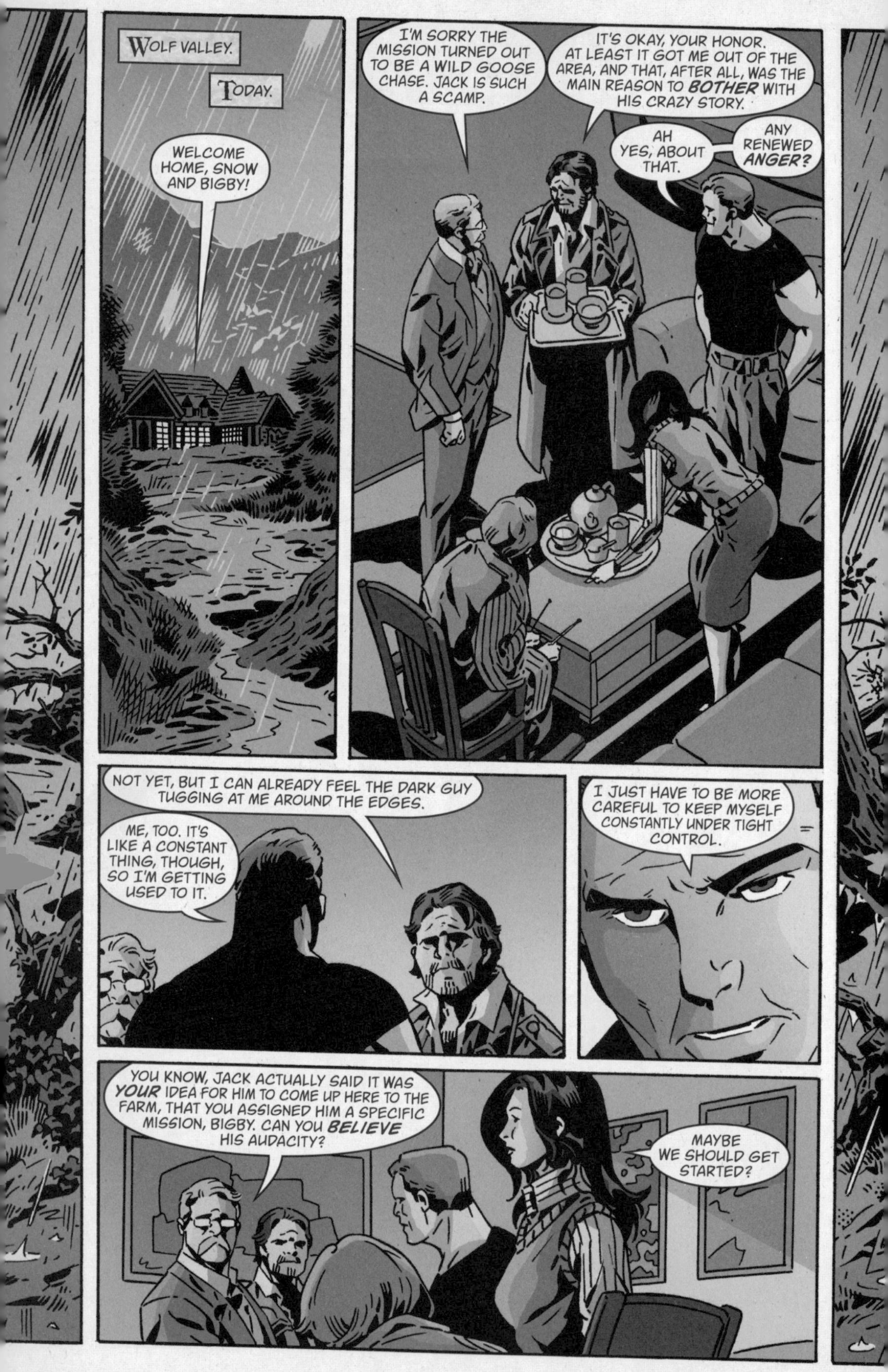
WOLF VALLEY.
TODAY.
WELCOME HOME, SNOW AND BIGBY!
I'M SORRY THE MISSION TURNED OUT TO BE A WILD GOOSE CHASE. JACK IS SUCH A SCAMP.
IT'S OKAY, YOUR HONOR. AT LEAST IT GOT ME OUT OF THE AREA, AND THAT, AFTER ALL, WAS THE MAIN REASON TO BOTHER WITH HIS CRAZY STORY.
AH YES, ABOUT THAT.
ANY RENEWED ANGER?
NOT YET, BUT I CAN ALREADY FEEL THE DARK GUY TUGGING AT ME AROUND THE EDGES.
ME, TOO. IT'S LIKE A CONSTANT THING, THOUGH, SO I'M GETTING USED TO IT.
I JUST HAVE TO BE MORE CAREFUL TO KEEP MYSELF CONSTANTLY UNDER TIGHT CONTROL.
YOU KNOW, JACK ACTUALLY SAID IT WAS YOUR IDEA FOR HIM TO COME UP HERE TO THE FARM, THAT YOU ASSIGNED HIM A SPECIFIC MISSION, BIGBY. CAN YOU BELIEVE HIS AUDACITY?
MAYBE WE SHOULD GET STARTED?

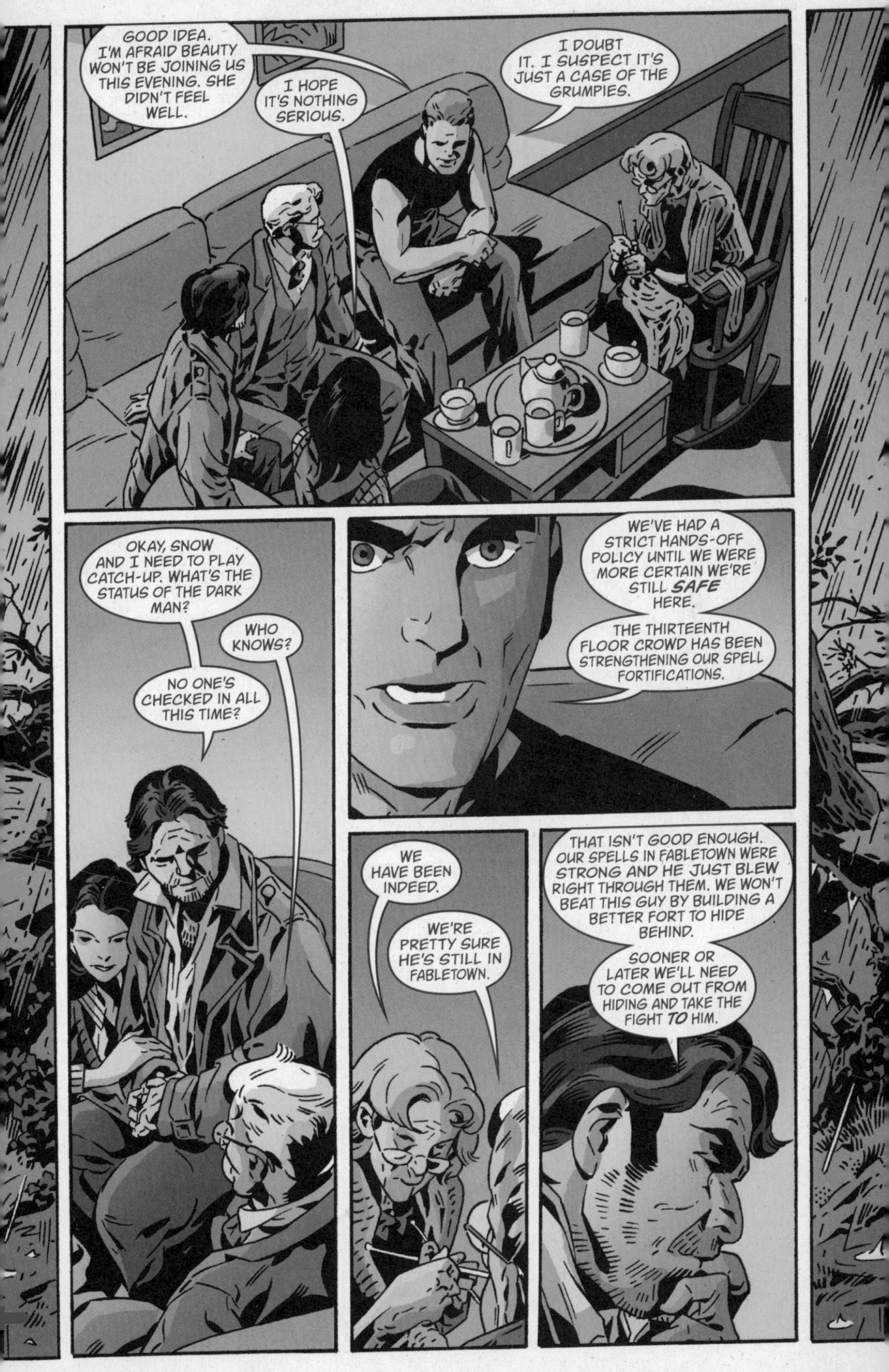
GOOD IDEA. I'M AFRAID BEAUTY WON'T BE JOINING US THIS EVENING. SHE DIDN'T FEEL WELL.
I HOPE IT'S NOTHING SERIOUS.
I DOUBT IT. I SUSPECT IT'S JUST A CASE OF THE GRUMPIES.
OKAY, SNOW AND I NEED TO PLAY CATCH-UP. WHAT'S THE STATUS OF THE DARK MAN?
WHO KNOWS?
NO ONE'S CHECKED IN ALL THIS TIME?
WE'VE HAD A STRICT HANDS-OFF POLICY UNTIL WE WERE MORE CERTAIN WE'RE STILL SAFE HERE.
THE THIRTEENTH FLOOR CROWD HAS BEEN STRENGTHENING OUR SPELL FORTIFICATIONS.
WE HAVE BEEN INDEED.
WE'RE PRETTY SURE HE'S STILL IN FABLETOWN.
THAT ISN'T GOOD ENOUGH. OUR SPELLS IN FABLETOWN WERE STRONG AND HE JUST BLEW RIGHT THROUGH THEM. WE WON'T BEAT THIS GUY BY BUILDING A BETTER FORT TO HIDE BEHIND.
SOONER OR LATER WE'LL NEED TO COME OUT FROM HIDING AND TAKE THE FIGHT TO HIM.

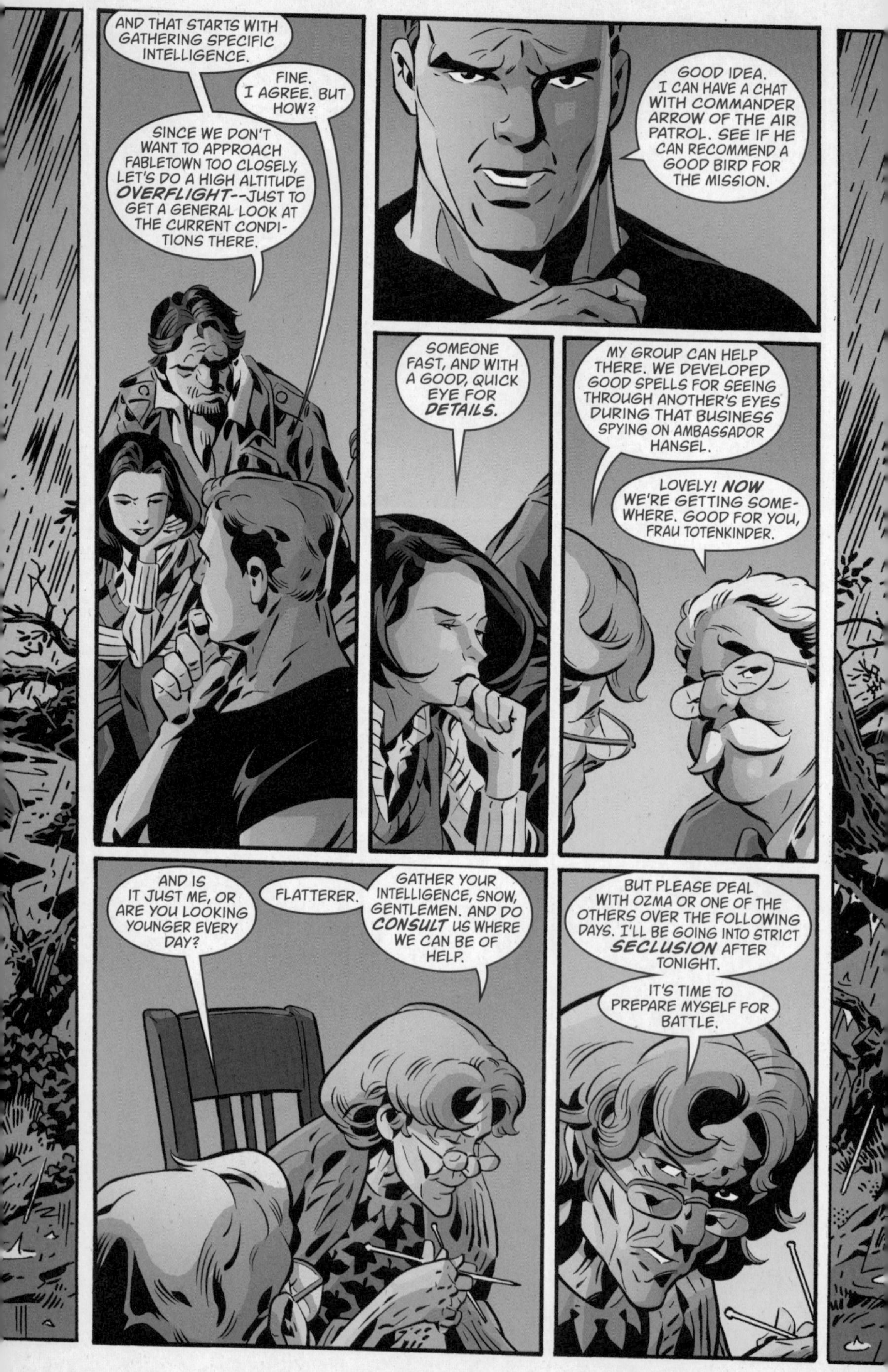
AND THAT STARTS WITH GATHERING SPECIFIC INTELLIGENCE.
FINE. I AGREE. BUT HOW?
SINCE WE DON'T WANT TO APPROACH FABLETOWN TOO CLOSELY, LET'S DO A HIGH ALTITUDE OVERFLIGHT--JUST TO GET A GENERAL LOOK AT THE CURRENT CONDITIONS THERE.
GOOD IDEA. I CAN HAVE A CHAT WITH COMMANDER ARROW OF THE AIR PATROL. SEE IF HE CAN RECOMMEND A GOOD BIRD FOR THE MISSION.
SOMEONE FAST, AND WITH A GOOD, QUICK EYE FOR DETAILS.
MY GROUP CAN HELP THERE. WE DEVELOPED GOOD SPELLS FOR SEEING THROUGH ANOTHER'S EYES DURING THAT BUSINESS SPYING ON AMBASSADOR HANSEL.
LOVELY! NOW WE'RE GETTING SOMEWHERE. GOOD FOR YOU, FRAU TOTENKINDER.
AND IS IT JUST ME, OR ARE YOU LOOKING YOUNGER EVERY DAY?
FLATTERER.
GATHER YOUR INTELLIGENCE, SNOW, GENTLEMEN. AND DO CONSULT US WHERE WE CAN BE OF HELP.
BUT PLEASE DEAL WITH OZMA OR ONE OF THE OTHERS OVER THE FOLLOWING DAYS. I'LL BE GOING INTO STRICT SECLUSION AFTER TONIGHT.
IT'S TIME TO PREPARE MYSELF FOR BATTLE.

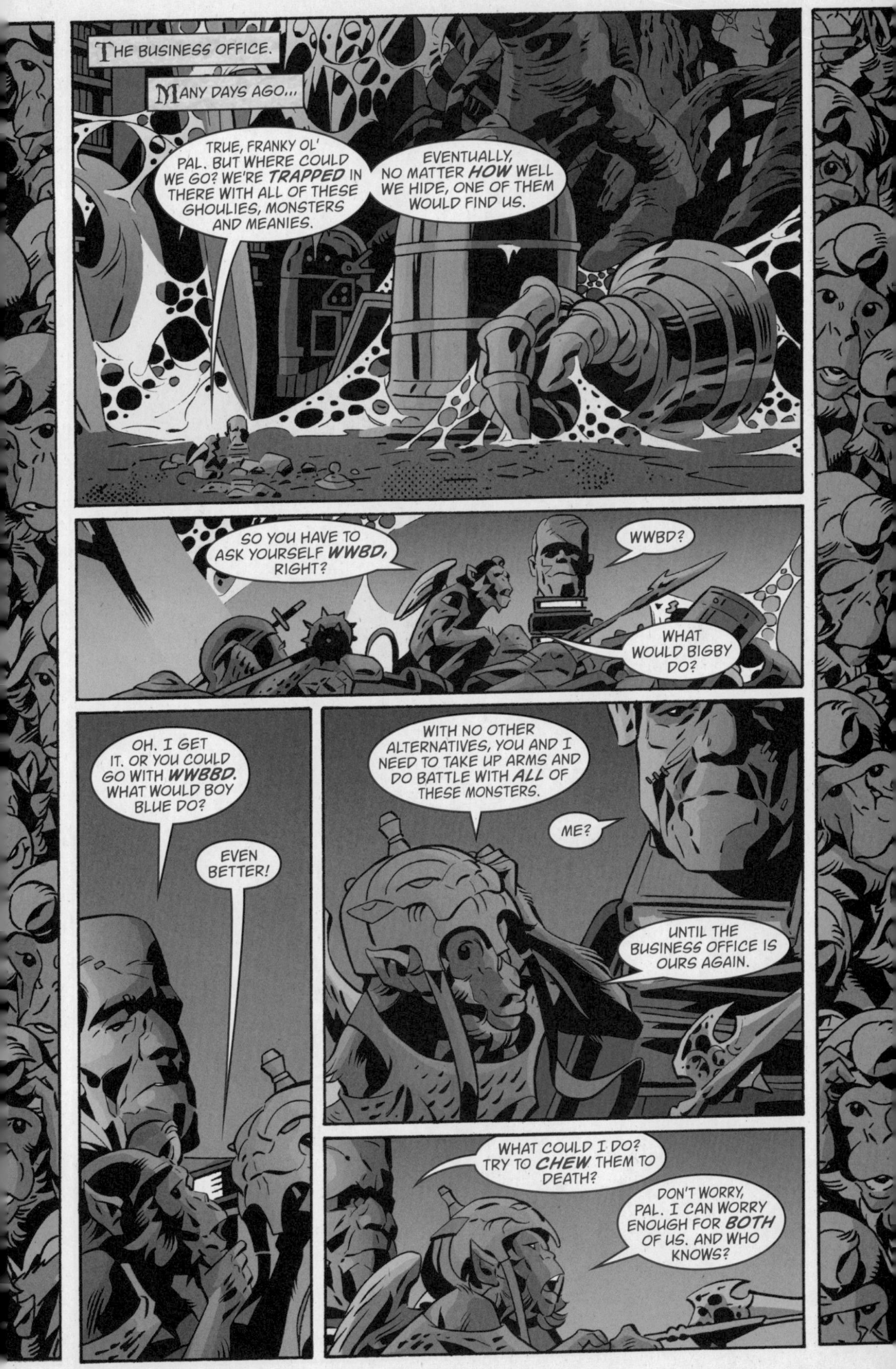
THE BUSINESS OFFICE.
MANY DAYS AGO...
TRUE, FRANKY OL' PAL. BUT WHERE COULD WE GO? WE'RE TRAPPED IN THERE WITH ALL OF THESE GHOULIES, MONSTERS AND MEANIES.
EVENTUALLY, NO MATTER HOW WELL WE HIDE, ONE OF THEM WOULD FIND US.
SO YOU HAVE TO ASK YOURSELF WWBD, RIGHT?
WWBD?
WHAT WOULD BIGBY DO?
OH. I GET IT. OR YOU COULD GO WITH WWBBD. WHAT WOULD BOY BLUE DO?
EVEN BETTER!
WITH NO OTHER ALTERNATIVES, YOU AND I NEED TO TAKE UP ARMS AND DO BATTLE WITH ALL OF THESE MONSTERS.
ME?
UNTIL THE BUSINESS OFFICE IS OURS AGAIN.
WHAT COULD I DO? TRY TO CHEW THEM TO DEATH?
DON'T WORRY, PAL. I CAN WORRY ENOUGH FOR BOTH OF US. AND WHO KNOWS?

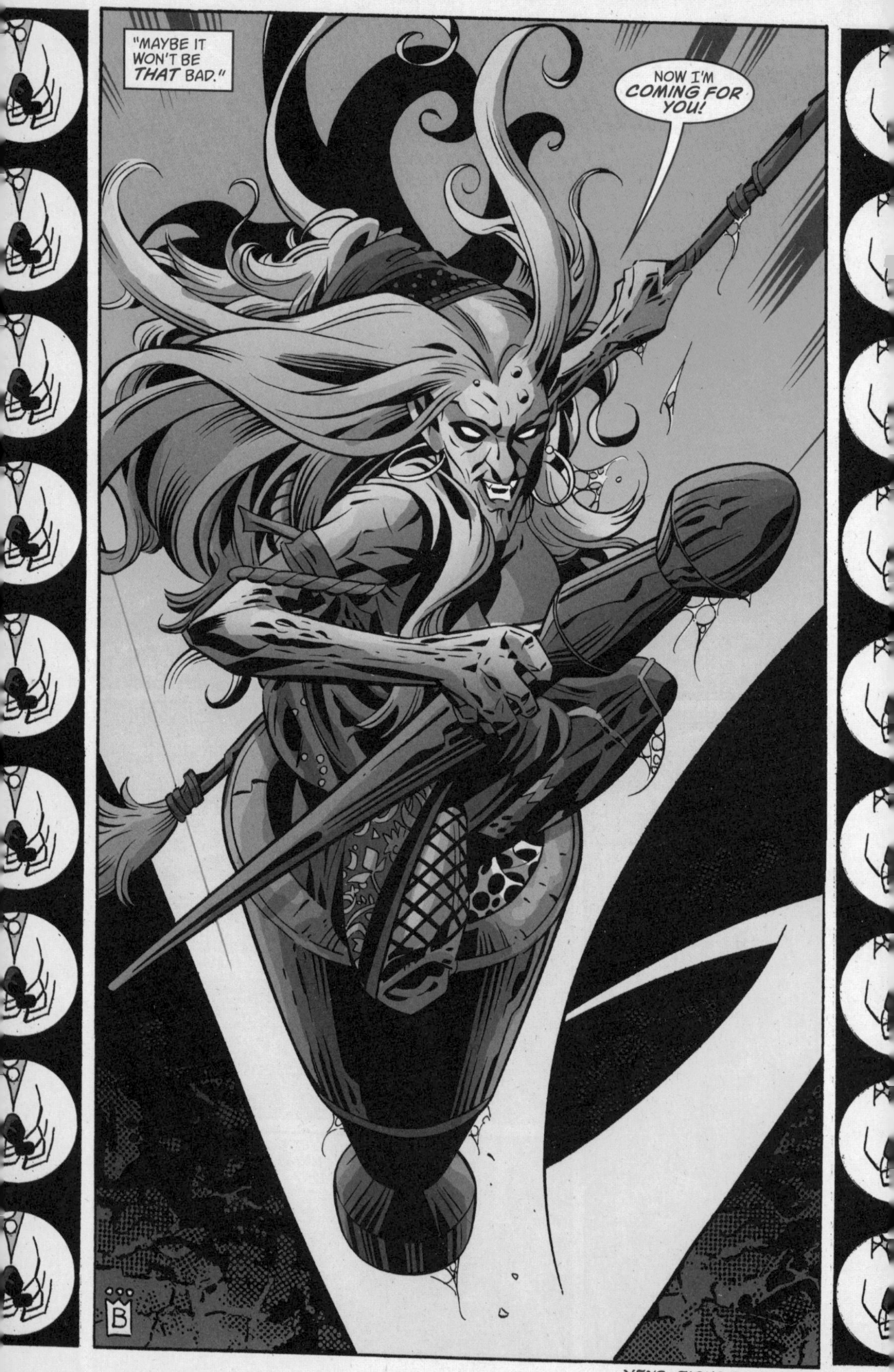
"MAYBE IT WON'T BE *THAT* BAD."
NOW I'M COMING FOR YOU!

NEXT: *FIGHT OR FLIGHT!*

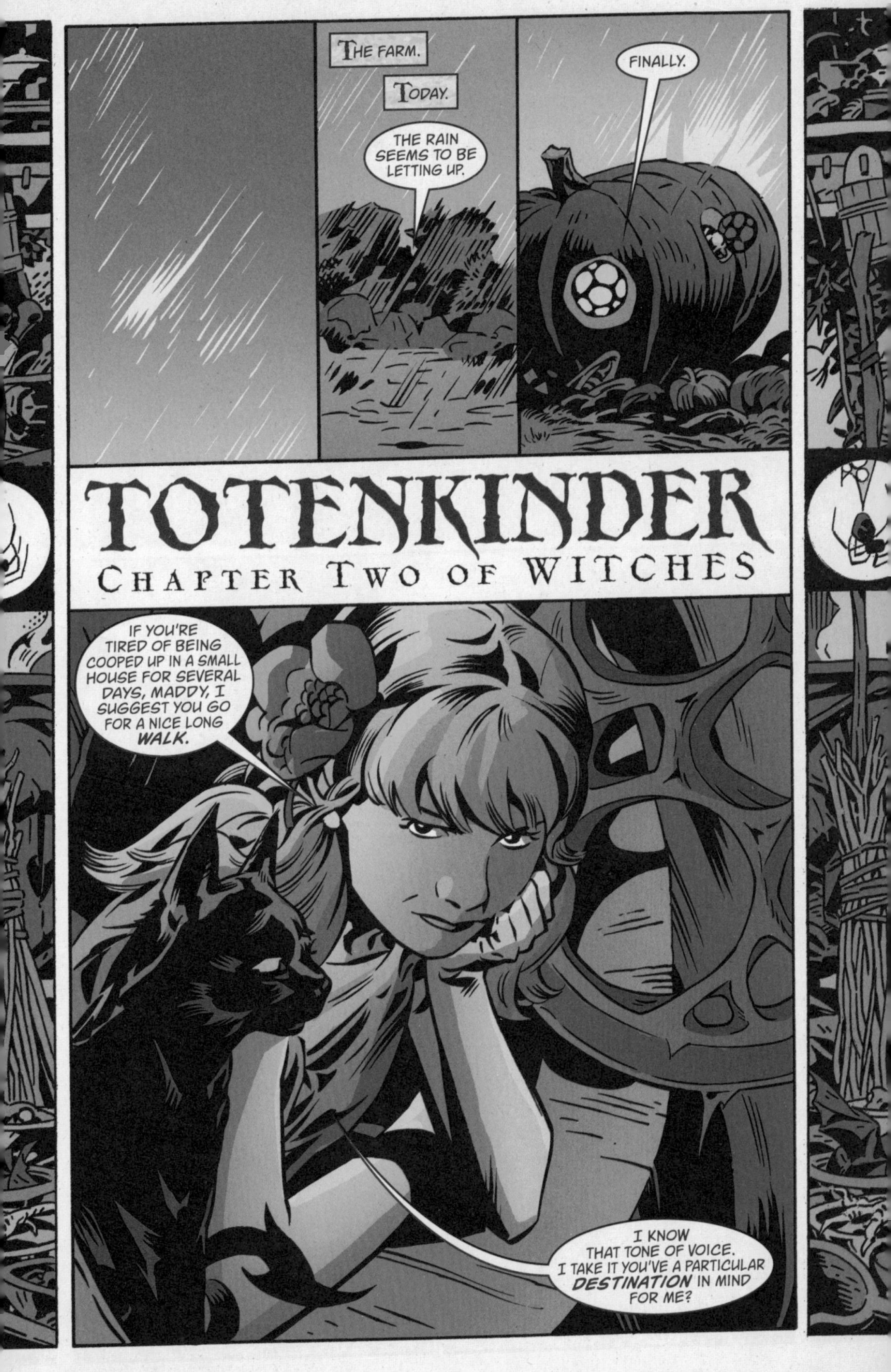
THE FARM.
TODAY.
THE RAIN SEEMS TO BE LETTING UP.
FINALLY.
TOTENKINDER
CHAPTER TWO OF WITCHES
IF YOU'RE TIRED OF BEING COOPED UP IN A SMALL HOUSE FOR SEVERAL DAYS, MADDY, I SUGGEST YOU GO FOR A NICE LONG WALK.
I KNOW THAT TONE OF VOICE. I TAKE IT YOU'VE A PARTICULAR DESTINATION IN MIND FOR ME?

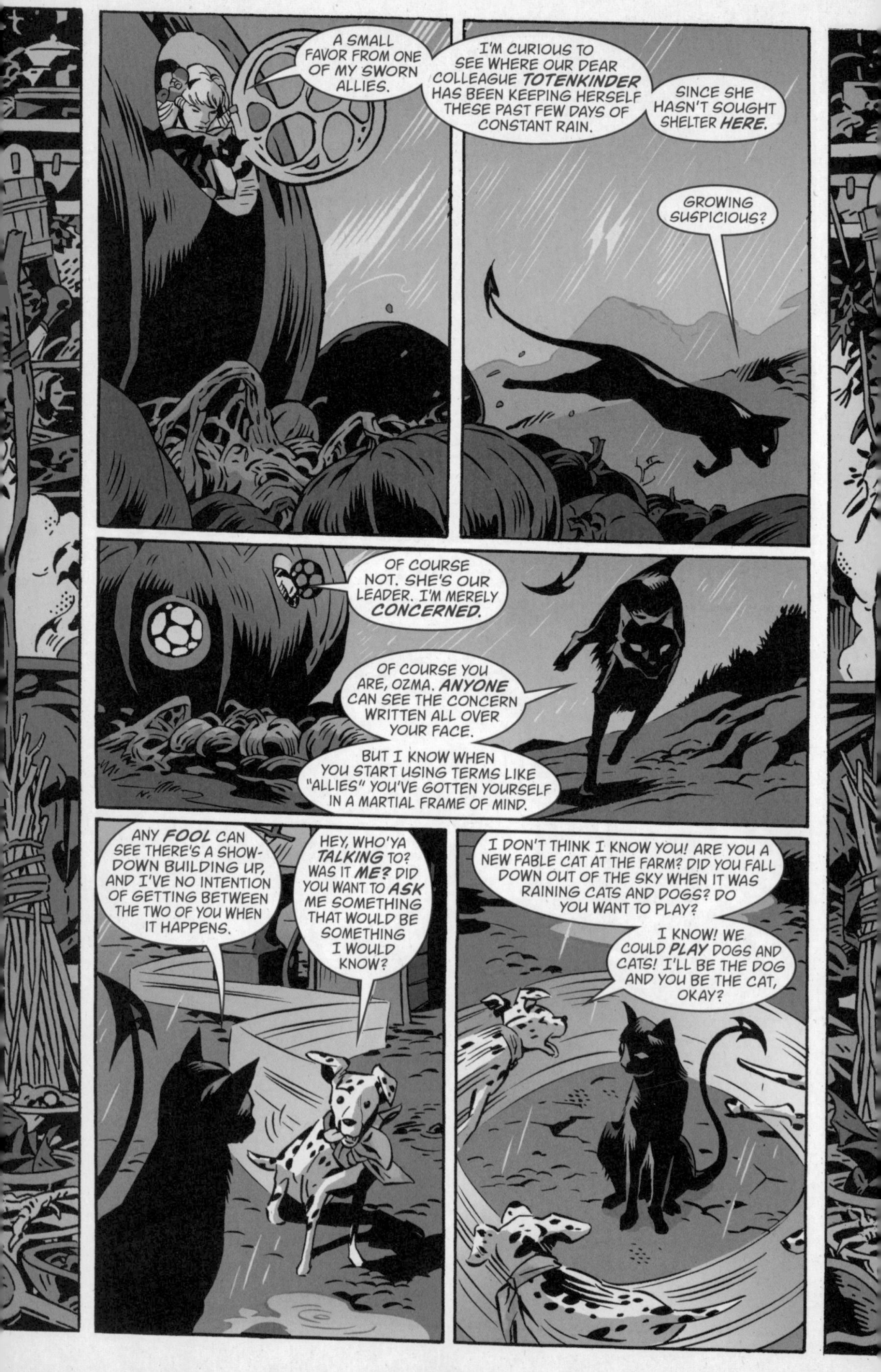
A SMALL FAVOR FROM ONE OF MY SWORN ALLIES.
I'M CURIOUS TO SEE WHERE OUR DEAR COLLEAGUE TOTENKINDER HAS BEEN KEEPING HERSELF THESE PAST FEW DAYS OF CONSTANT RAIN.
SINCE SHE HASN'T SOUGHT SHELTER HERE.
GROWING SUSPICIOUS?
OF COURSE NOT. SHE'S OUR LEADER. I'M MERELY CONCERNED.
OF COURSE YOU ARE, OZMA. ANYONE CAN SEE THE CONCERN WRITTEN ALL OVER YOUR FACE.
BUT I KNOW WHEN YOU START USING TERMS LIKE "ALLIES" YOU'VE GOTTEN YOURSELF IN A MARTIAL FRAME OF MIND.
ANY FOOL CAN SEE THERE'S A SHOW-DOWN BUILDING UP, AND I'VE NO INTENTION OF GETTING BETWEEN THE TWO OF YOU WHEN IT HAPPENS.
HEY, WHO'YA TALKING TO? WAS IT ME? DID YOU WANT TO ASK ME SOMETHING THAT WOULD BE SOMETHING I WOULD KNOW?
I DON'T THINK I KNOW YOU! ARE YOU A NEW FABLE CAT AT THE FARM? DID YOU FALL DOWN OUT OF THE SKY WHEN IT WAS RAINING CATS AND DOGS? DO YOU WANT TO PLAY?
I KNOW! WE COULD PLAY DOGS AND CATS! I'LL BE THE DOG AND YOU BE THE CAT, OKAY?

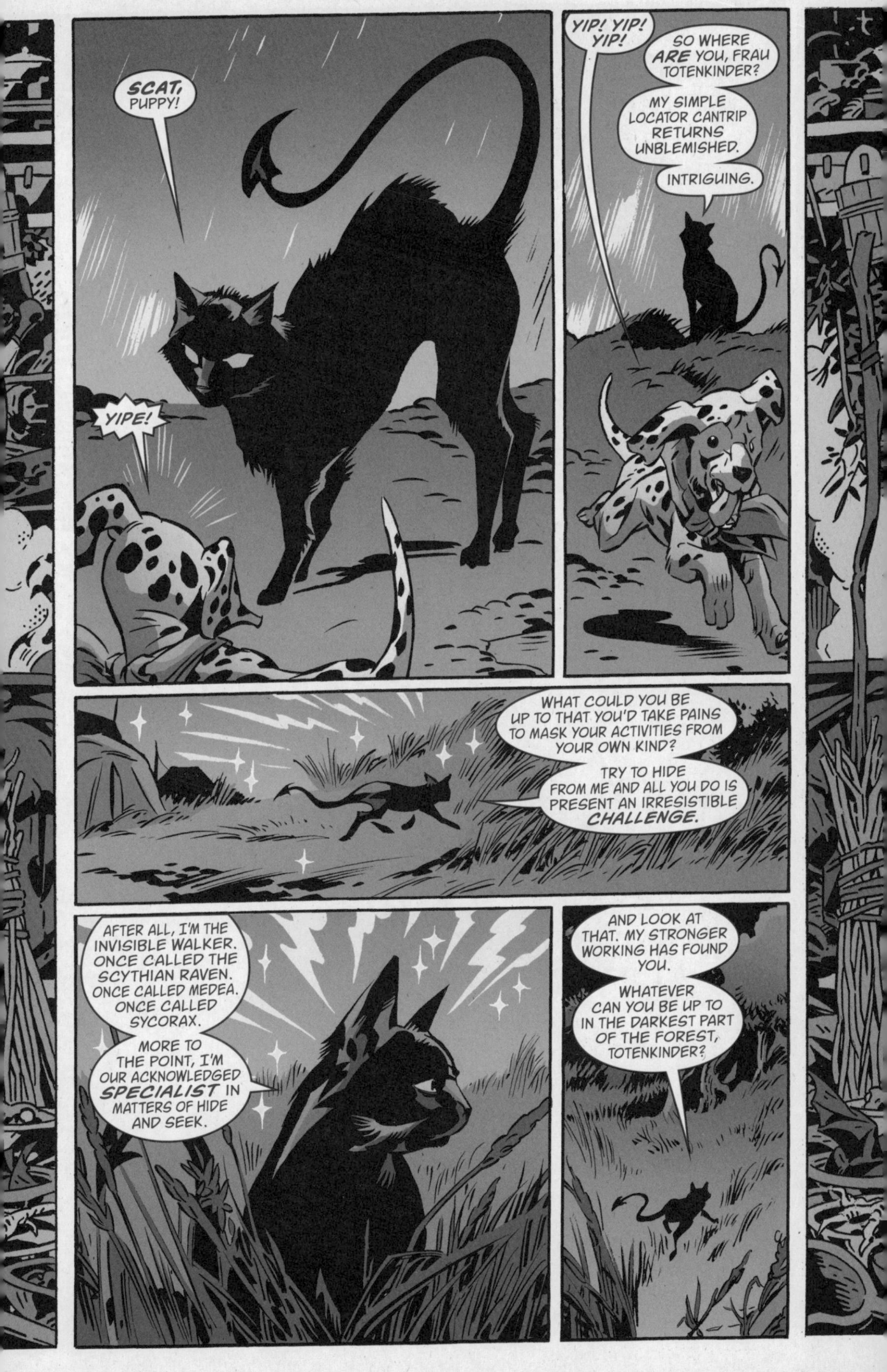
SCAT, PUPPY!
YIPE!
YIP! YIP! YIP!
SO WHERE ARE YOU, FRAU TOTENKINDER?
MY SIMPLE LOCATOR CANTRIP RETURNS UNBLEMISHED.
INTRIGUING.
WHAT COULD YOU BE UP TO THAT YOU'D TAKE PAINS TO MASK YOUR ACTIVITIES FROM YOUR OWN KIND?
TRY TO HIDE FROM ME AND ALL YOU DO IS PRESENT AN IRRESISTIBLE CHALLENGE.
AFTER ALL, I'M THE INVISIBLE WALKER. ONCE CALLED THE SCYTHIAN RAVEN. ONCE CALLED MEDEA. ONCE CALLED SYCORAX.
MORE TO THE POINT, I'M OUR ACKNOWLEDGED SPECIALIST IN MATTERS OF HIDE AND SEEK.
AND LOOK AT THAT. MY STRONGER WORKING HAS FOUND YOU.
WHATEVER CAN YOU BE UP TO IN THE DARKEST PART OF THE FOREST, TOTENKINDER?

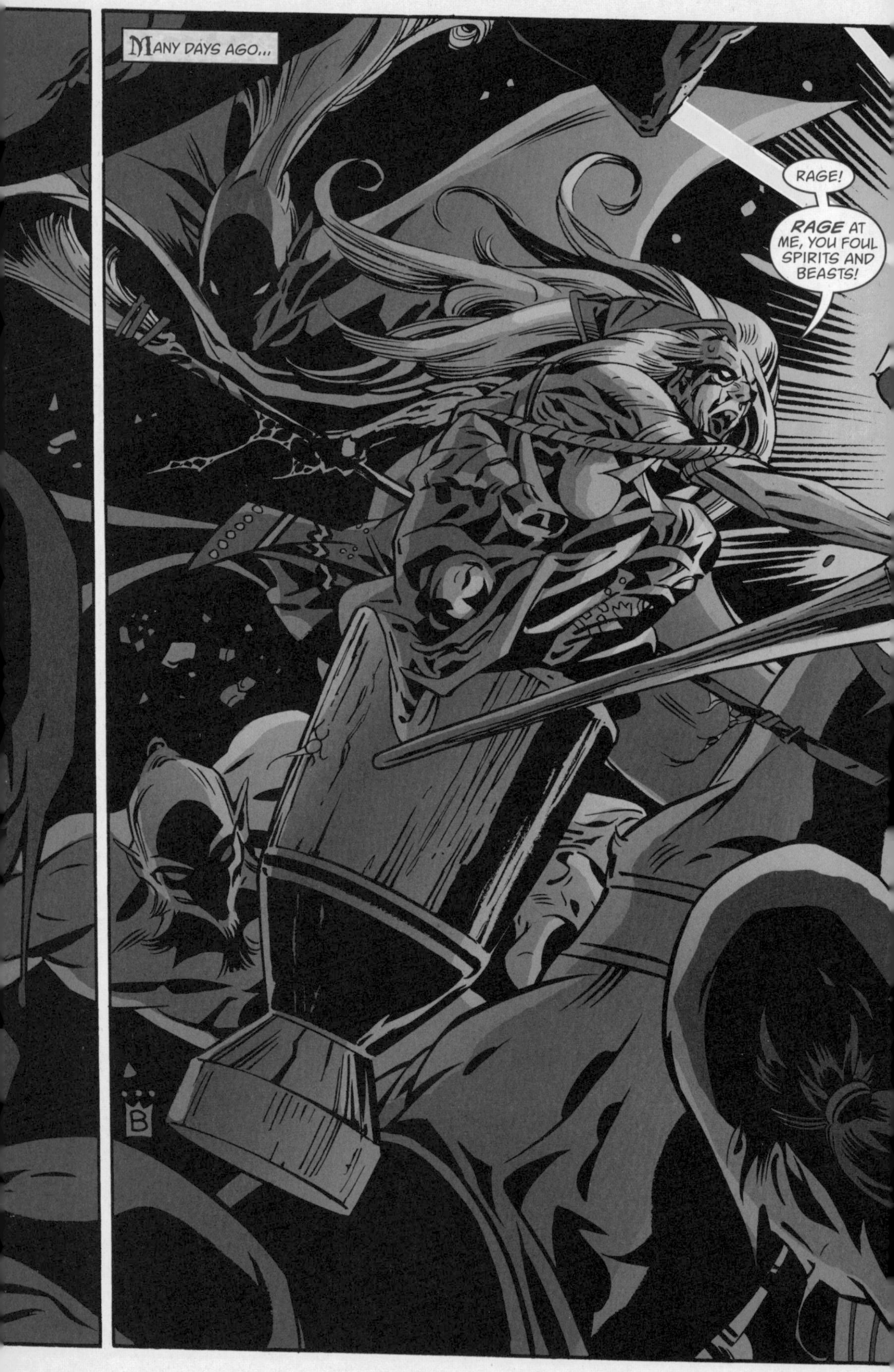
MANY DAYS AGO...
RAGE!
RAGE AT ME, YOU FOUL SPIRITS AND BEASTS!

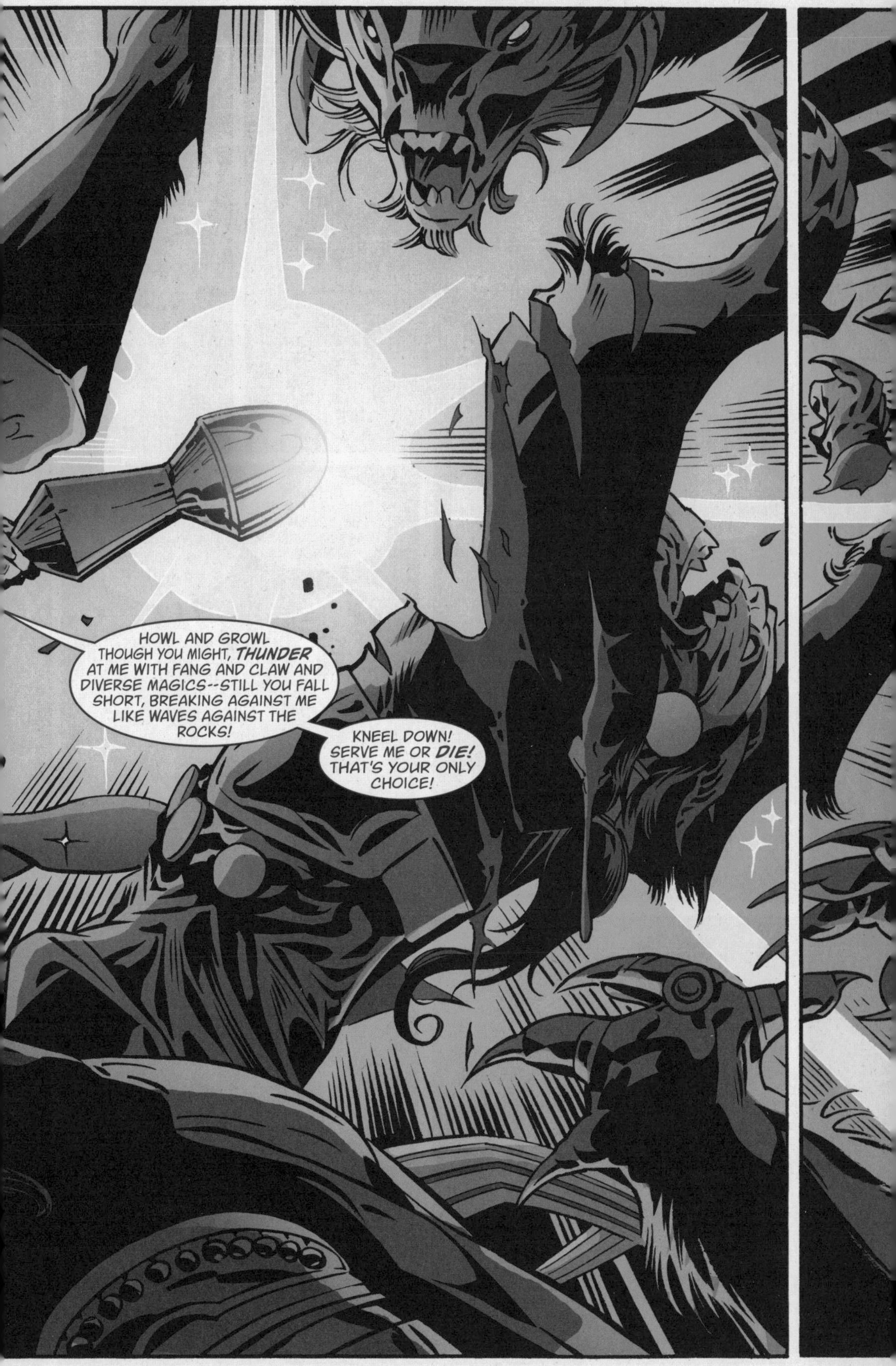
HOWL AND GROWL THOUGH YOU MIGHT, *THUNDER* AT ME WITH FANG AND CLAW AND DIVERSE MAGICS--STILL YOU FALL SHORT, BREAKING AGAINST ME LIKE WAVES AGAINST THE ROCKS!
KNEEL DOWN! SERVE ME OR *DIE!* THAT'S YOUR ONLY CHOICE!

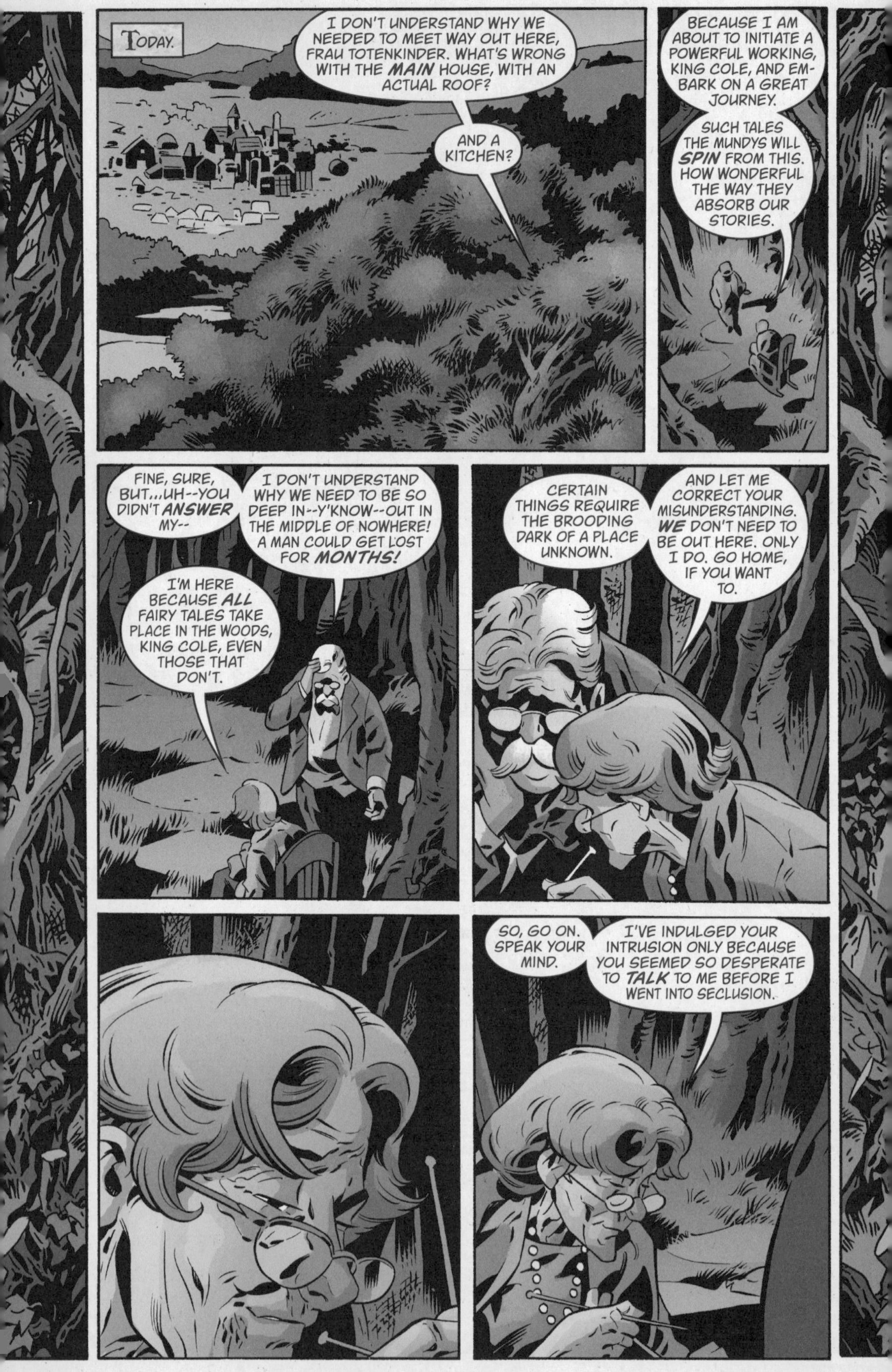
TODAY.
I DON'T UNDERSTAND WHY WE NEEDED TO MEET WAY OUT HERE, FRAU TOTENKINDER. WHAT'S WRONG WITH THE MAIN HOUSE, WITH AN ACTUAL ROOF?
AND A KITCHEN?
BECAUSE I AM ABOUT TO INITIATE A POWERFUL WORKING, KING COLE, AND EMBARK ON A GREAT JOURNEY.
SUCH TALES THE MUNDYS WILL SPIN FROM THIS. HOW WONDERFUL THE WAY THEY ABSORB OUR STORIES.
FINE, SURE, BUT...UH--YOU DIDN'T ANSWER MY--
I DON'T UNDERSTAND WHY WE NEED TO BE SO DEEP IN--Y'KNOW--OUT IN THE MIDDLE OF NOWHERE! A MAN COULD GET LOST FOR MONTHS!
I'M HERE BECAUSE ALL FAIRY TALES TAKE PLACE IN THE WOODS, KING COLE, EVEN THOSE THAT DON'T.
CERTAIN THINGS REQUIRE THE BROODING DARK OF A PLACE UNKNOWN.
AND LET ME CORRECT YOUR MISUNDERSTANDING. WE DON'T NEED TO BE OUT HERE. ONLY I DO. GO HOME, IF YOU WANT TO.
SO, GO ON. SPEAK YOUR MIND.
I'VE INDULGED YOUR INTRUSION ONLY BECAUSE YOU SEEMED SO DESPERATE TO TALK TO ME BEFORE I WENT INTO SECLUSION.

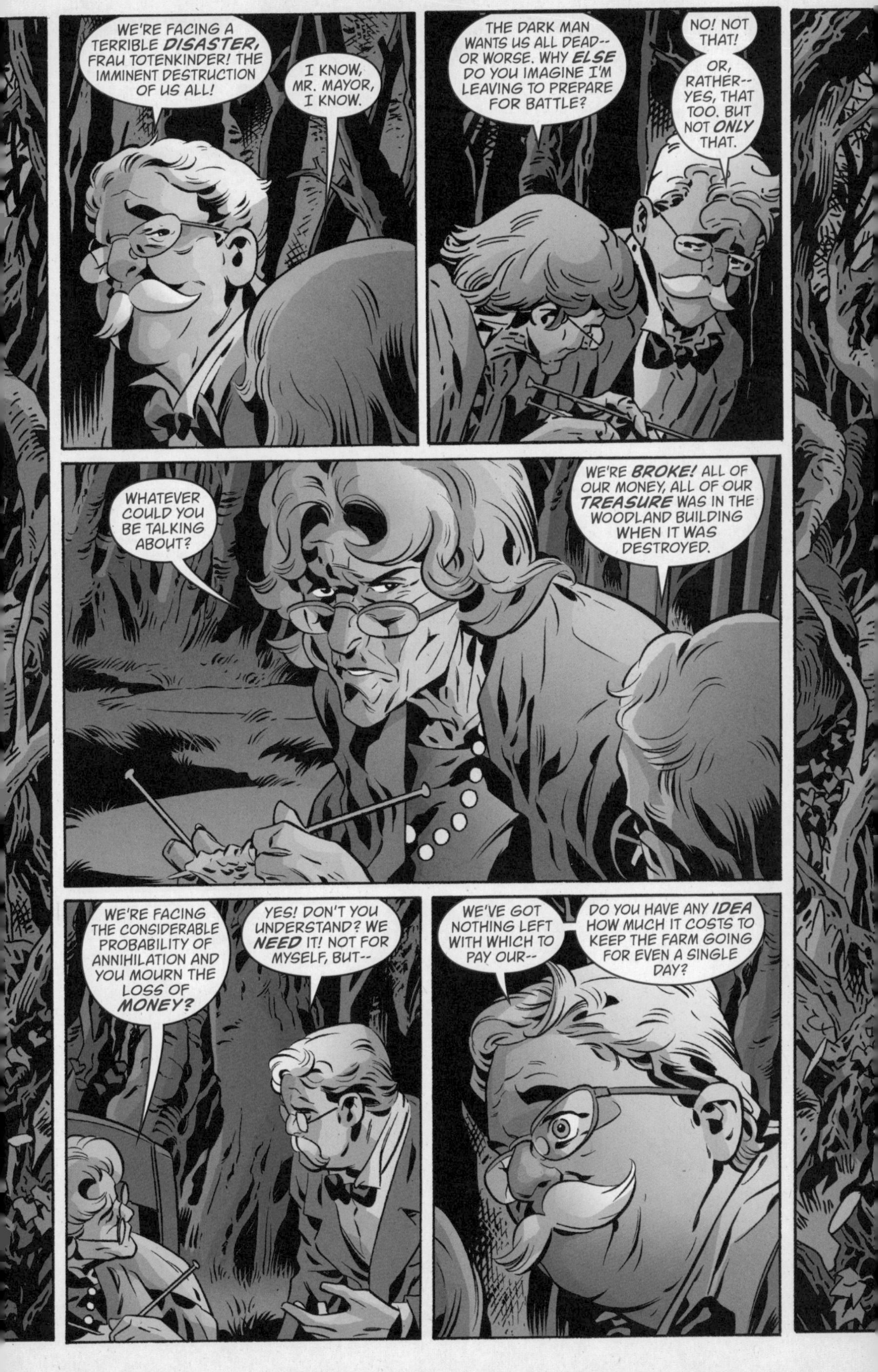
WE'RE FACING A TERRIBLE DISASTER, FRAU TOTENKINDER! THE IMMINENT DESTRUCTION OF US ALL!
I KNOW, MR. MAYOR, I KNOW.
THE DARK MAN WANTS US ALL DEAD-- OR WORSE. WHY ELSE DO YOU IMAGINE I'M LEAVING TO PREPARE FOR BATTLE?
NO! NOT THAT!
OR, RATHER-- YES, THAT TOO. BUT NOT ONLY THAT.
WHATEVER COULD YOU BE TALKING ABOUT?
WE'RE BROKE! ALL OF OUR MONEY, ALL OF OUR TREASURE WAS IN THE WOODLAND BUILDING WHEN IT WAS DESTROYED.
WE'RE FACING THE CONSIDERABLE PROBABILITY OF ANNIHILATION AND YOU MOURN THE LOSS OF MONEY?
YES! DON'T YOU UNDERSTAND? WE NEED IT! NOT FOR MYSELF, BUT--
WE'VE GOT NOTHING LEFT WITH WHICH TO PAY OUR--
DO YOU HAVE ANY IDEA HOW MUCH IT COSTS TO KEEP THE FARM GOING FOR EVEN A SINGLE DAY?

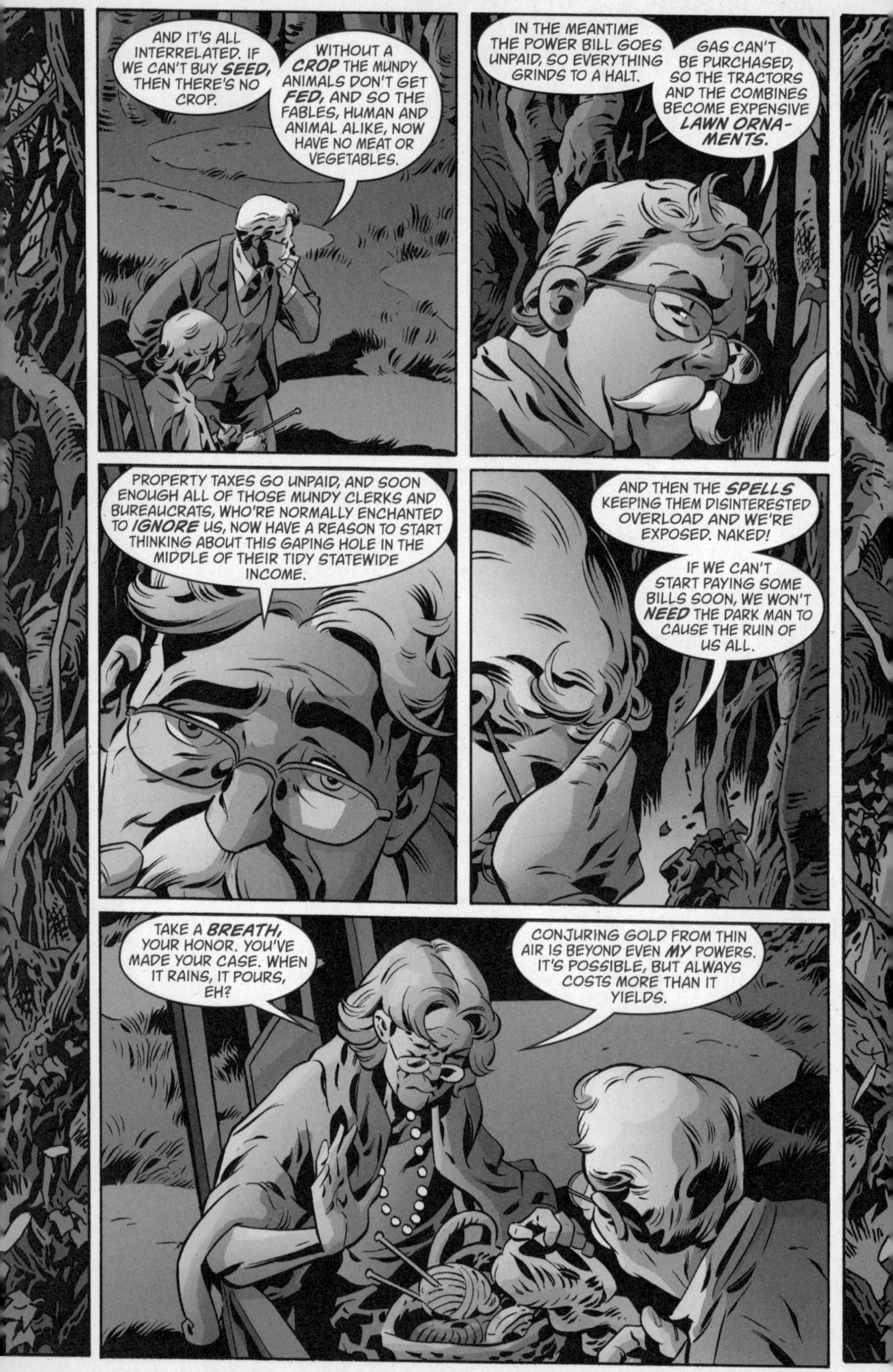
AND IT'S ALL INTERRELATED. IF WE CAN'T BUY SEED, THEN THERE'S NO CROP.
WITHOUT A CROP THE MUNDY ANIMALS DON'T GET FED, AND SO THE FABLES, HUMAN AND ANIMAL ALIKE, NOW HAVE NO MEAT OR VEGETABLES.
IN THE MEANTIME THE POWER BILL GOES UNPAID, SO EVERYTHING GRINDS TO A HALT.
GAS CAN'T BE PURCHASED, SO THE TRACTORS AND THE COMBINES BECOME EXPENSIVE LAWN ORNAMENTS.
PROPERTY TAXES GO UNPAID, AND SOON ENOUGH ALL OF THOSE MUNDY CLERKS AND BUREAUCRATS, WHO'RE NORMALLY ENCHANTED TO IGNORE US, NOW HAVE A REASON TO START THINKING ABOUT THIS GAPING HOLE IN THE MIDDLE OF THEIR TIDY STATEWIDE INCOME.
AND THEN THE SPELLS KEEPING THEM DISINTERESTED OVERLOAD AND WE'RE EXPOSED. NAKED!
IF WE CAN'T START PAYING SOME BILLS SOON, WE WON'T NEED THE DARK MAN TO CAUSE THE RUIN OF US ALL.
TAKE A BREATH, YOUR HONOR. YOU'VE MADE YOUR CASE. WHEN IT RAINS, IT POURS, EH?
CONJURING GOLD FROM THIN AIR IS BEYOND EVEN MY POWERS. IT'S POSSIBLE, BUT ALWAYS COSTS MORE THAN IT YIELDS.

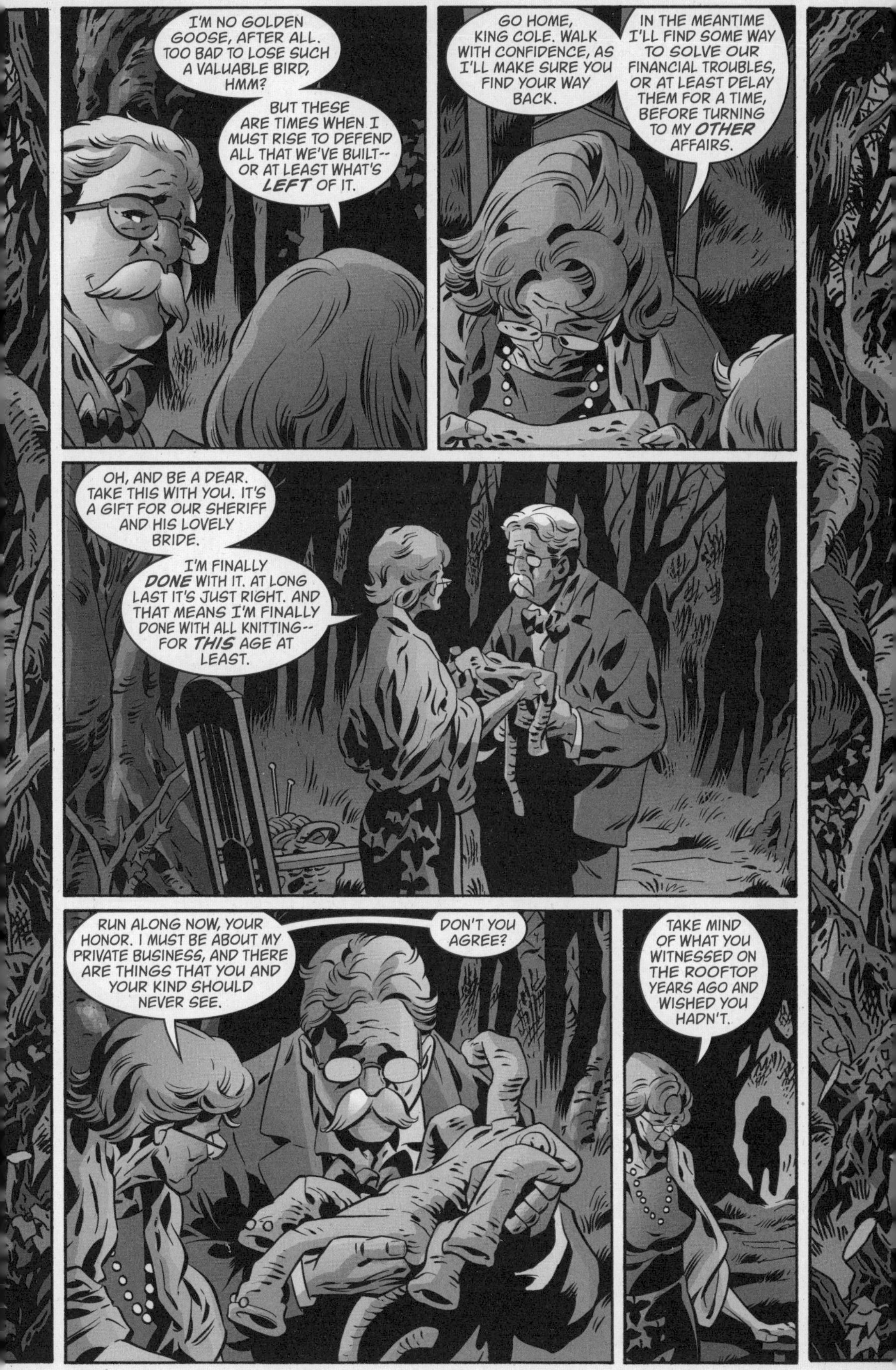
I'M NO GOLDEN GOOSE, AFTER ALL. TOO BAD TO LOSE SUCH A VALUABLE BIRD, HMM?
BUT THESE ARE TIMES WHEN I MUST RISE TO DEFEND ALL THAT WE'VE BUILT-- OR AT LEAST WHAT'S *LEFT* OF IT.
GO HOME, KING COLE. WALK WITH CONFIDENCE, AS I'LL MAKE SURE YOU FIND YOUR WAY BACK.
IN THE MEANTIME I'LL FIND SOME WAY TO SOLVE OUR FINANCIAL TROUBLES, OR AT LEAST DELAY THEM FOR A TIME, BEFORE TURNING TO MY *OTHER* AFFAIRS.
OH, AND BE A DEAR. TAKE THIS WITH YOU. IT'S A GIFT FOR OUR SHERIFF AND HIS LOVELY BRIDE.
I'M FINALLY *DONE* WITH IT. AT LONG LAST IT'S JUST RIGHT. AND THAT MEANS I'M FINALLY DONE WITH ALL KNITTING-- FOR *THIS* AGE AT LEAST.
RUN ALONG NOW, YOUR HONOR. I MUST BE ABOUT MY PRIVATE BUSINESS, AND THERE ARE THINGS THAT YOU AND YOUR KIND SHOULD NEVER SEE.
DON'T YOU AGREE?
TAKE MIND OF WHAT YOU WITNESSED ON THE ROOFTOP YEARS AGO AND WISHED YOU HADN'T.

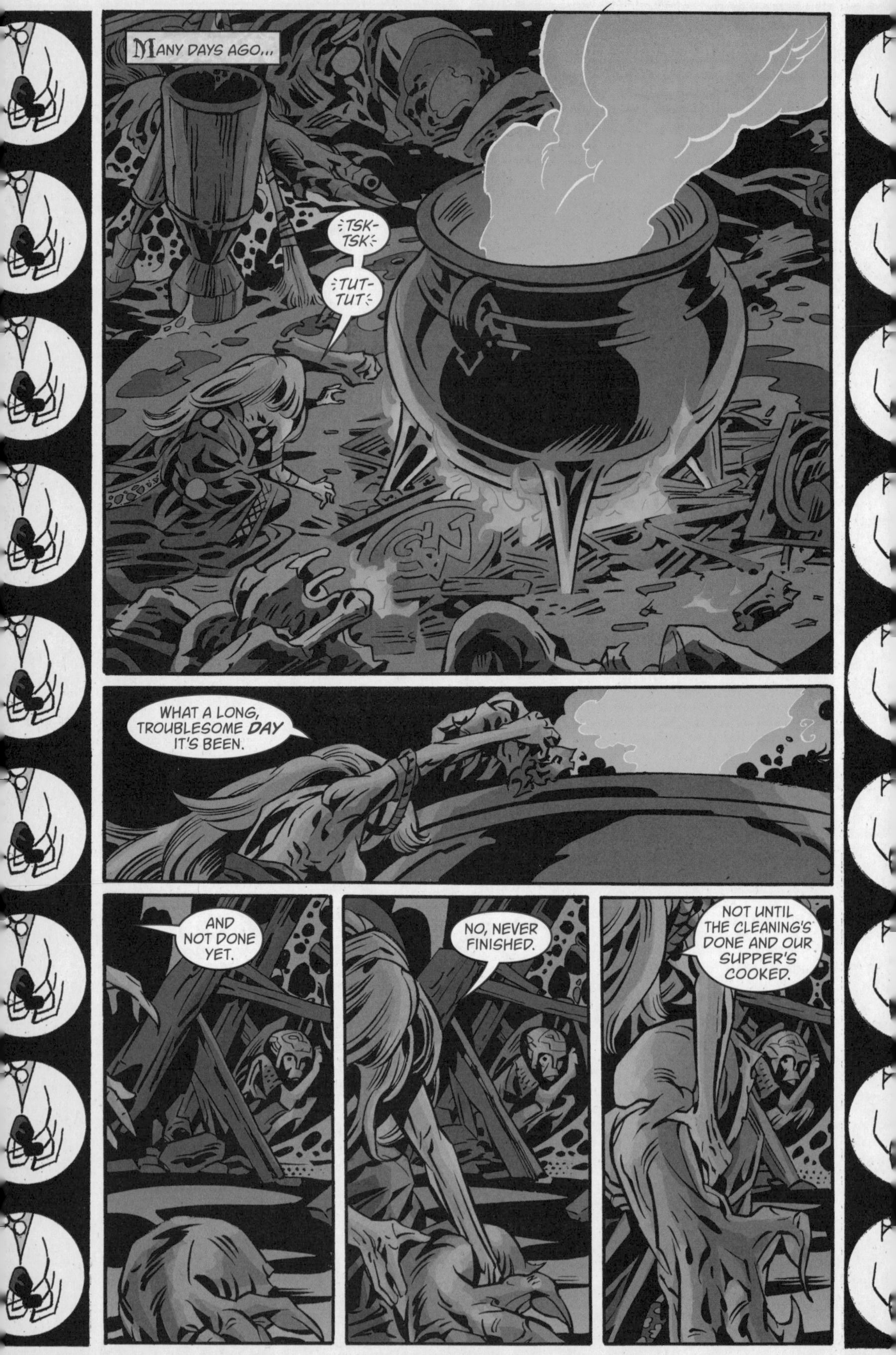
MANY DAYS AGO...
TSK-TSK
TUT-TUT
WHAT A LONG, TROUBLESOME DAY IT'S BEEN.
AND NOT DONE YET.
NO, NEVER FINISHED.
NOT UNTIL THE CLEANING'S DONE AND OUR SUPPER'S COOKED.

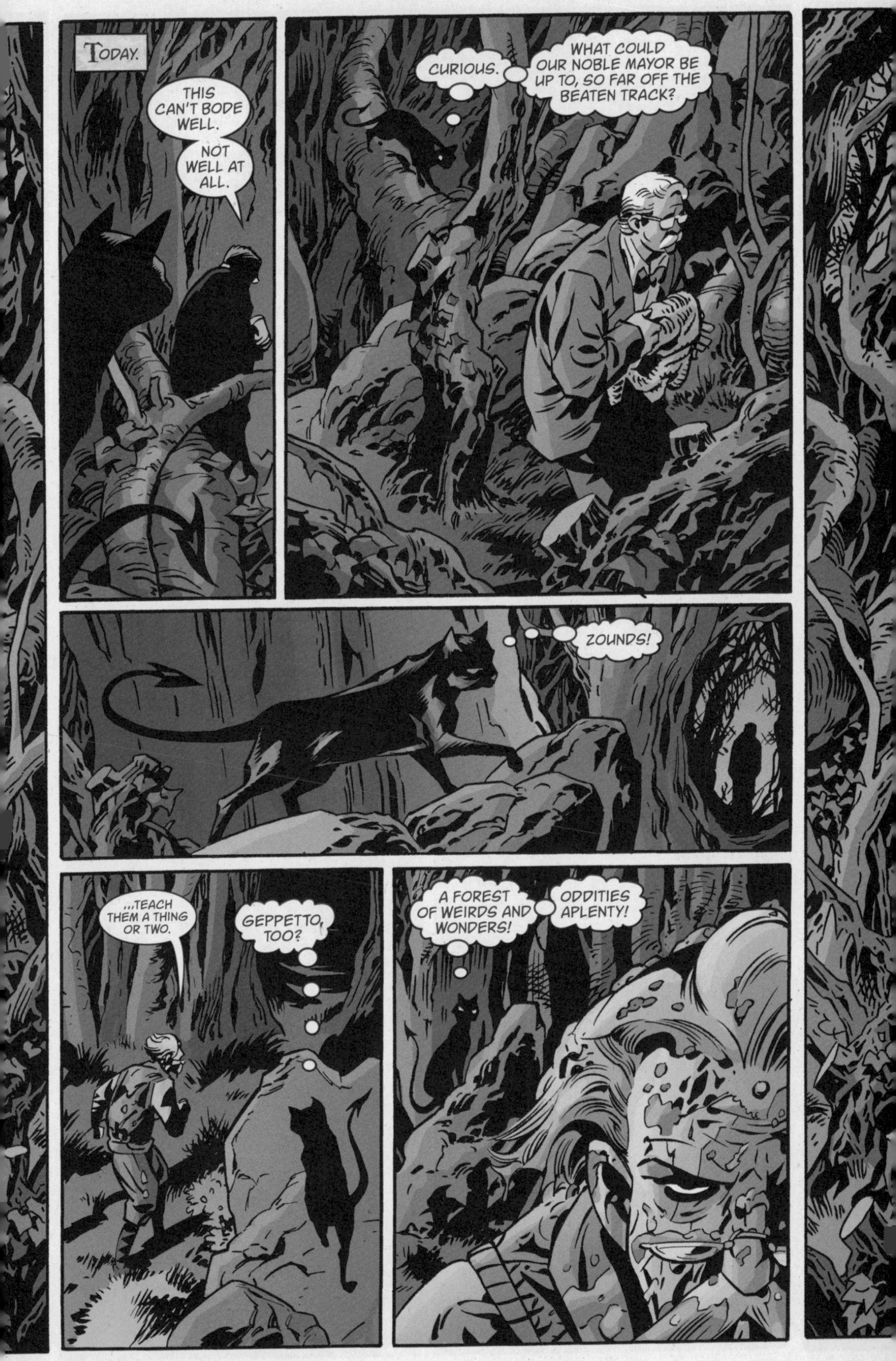
TODAY.
THIS CAN'T BODE WELL.
NOT WELL AT ALL.
CURIOUS.
WHAT COULD OUR NOBLE MAYOR BE UP TO, SO FAR OFF THE BEATEN TRACK?
ZOUNDS!
...TEACH THEM A THING OR TWO.
GEPPETTO, TOO?
A FOREST OF WEIRDS AND WONDERS!
ODDITIES APLENTY!

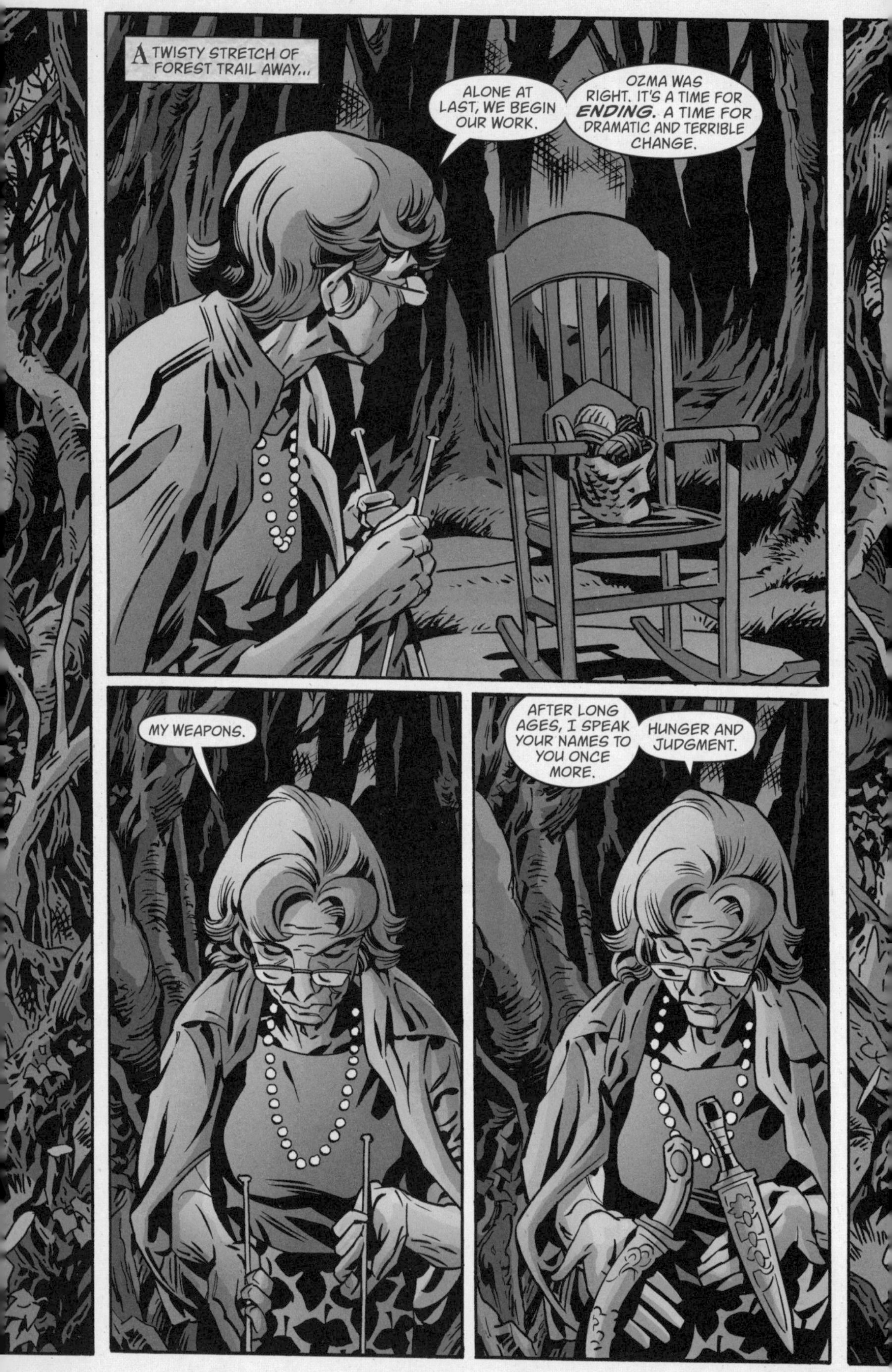
A TWISTY STRETCH OF FOREST TRAIL AWAY...
ALONE AT LAST, WE BEGIN OUR WORK.
OZMA WAS RIGHT. IT'S A TIME FOR ENDING. A TIME FOR DRAMATIC AND TERRIBLE CHANGE.
MY WEAPONS.
AFTER LONG AGES, I SPEAK YOUR NAMES TO YOU ONCE MORE.
HUNGER AND JUDGMENT.

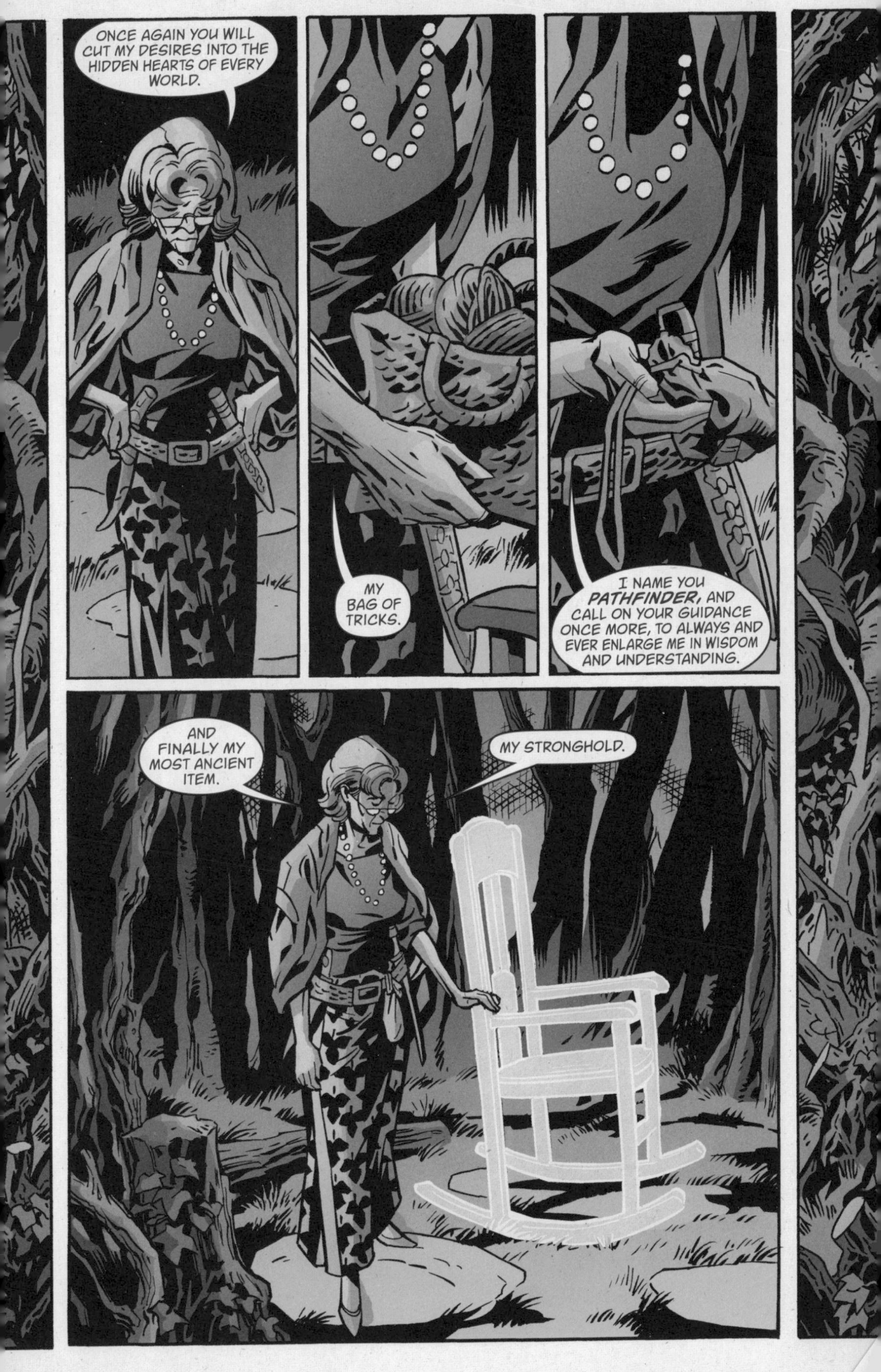
ONCE AGAIN YOU WILL CUT MY DESIRES INTO THE HIDDEN HEARTS OF EVERY WORLD.
MY BAG OF TRICKS.
I NAME YOU PATHFINDER, AND CALL ON YOUR GUIDANCE ONCE MORE, TO ALWAYS AND EVER ENLARGE ME IN WISDOM AND UNDERSTANDING.
AND FINALLY MY MOST ANCIENT ITEM.
MY STRONGHOLD.

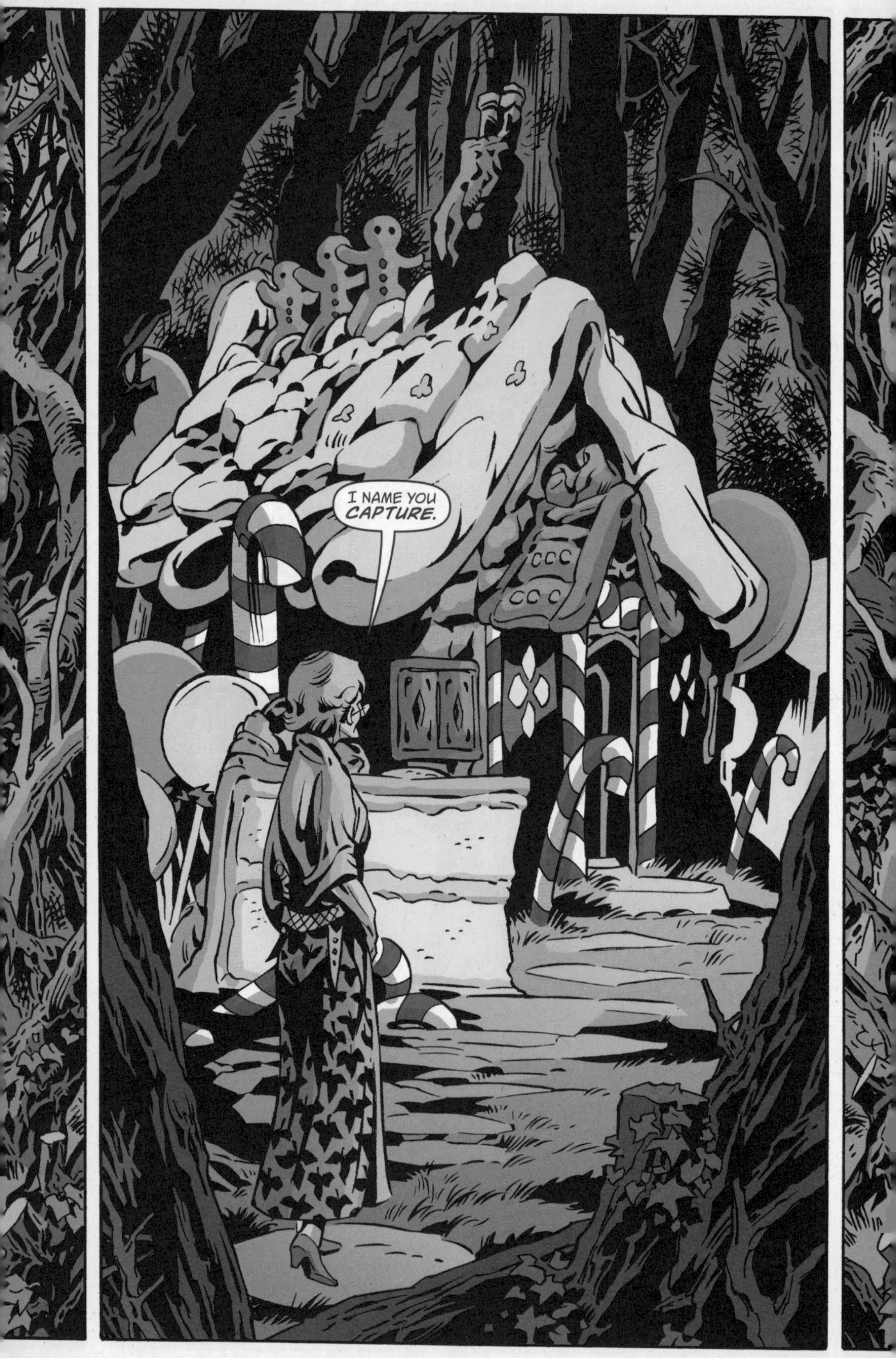
I NAME YOU CAPTURE.

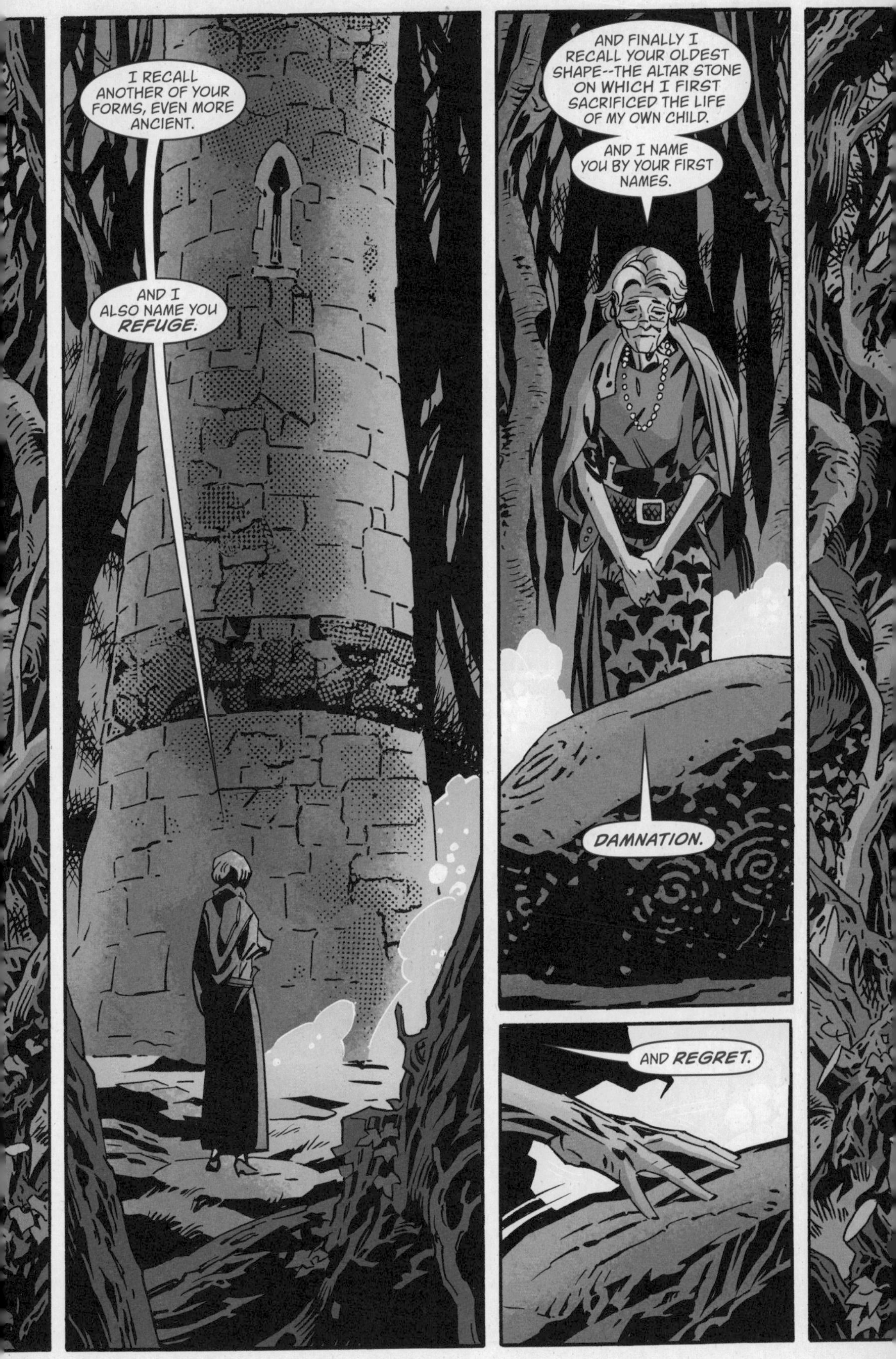
I RECALL ANOTHER OF YOUR FORMS, EVEN MORE ANCIENT.
AND I ALSO NAME YOU *REFUGE*.
AND FINALLY I RECALL YOUR OLDEST SHAPE--THE ALTAR STONE ON WHICH I FIRST SACRIFICED THE LIFE OF MY OWN CHILD.
AND I NAME YOU BY YOUR FIRST NAMES.
DAMNATION.
AND *REGRET*.

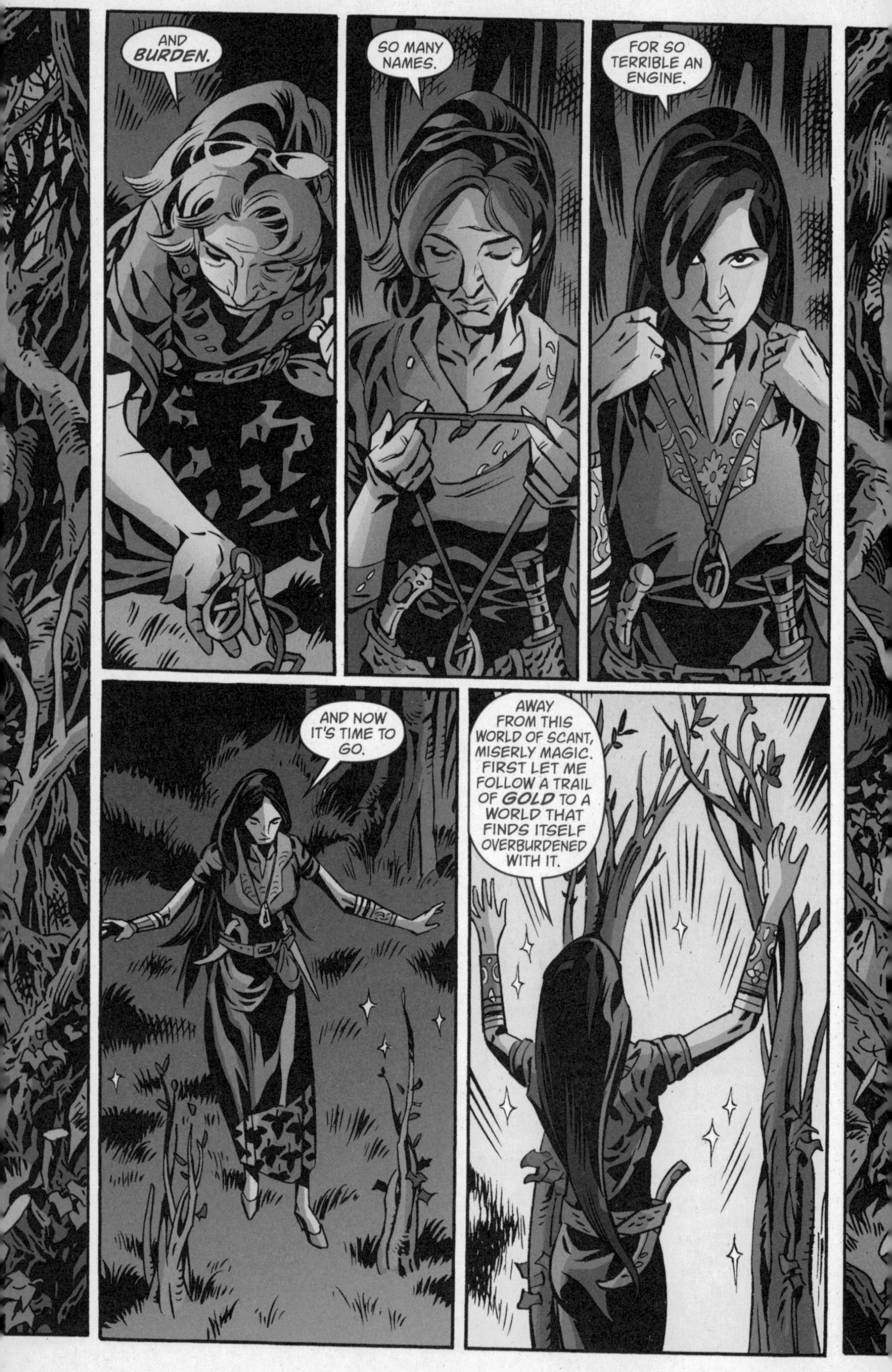
AND BURDEN.
SO MANY NAMES.
FOR SO TERRIBLE AN ENGINE.
AND NOW IT'S TIME TO GO.
AWAY FROM THIS WORLD OF SCANT, MISERLY MAGIC. FIRST LET ME FOLLOW A TRAIL OF GOLD TO A WORLD THAT FINDS ITSELF OVERBURDENED WITH IT.

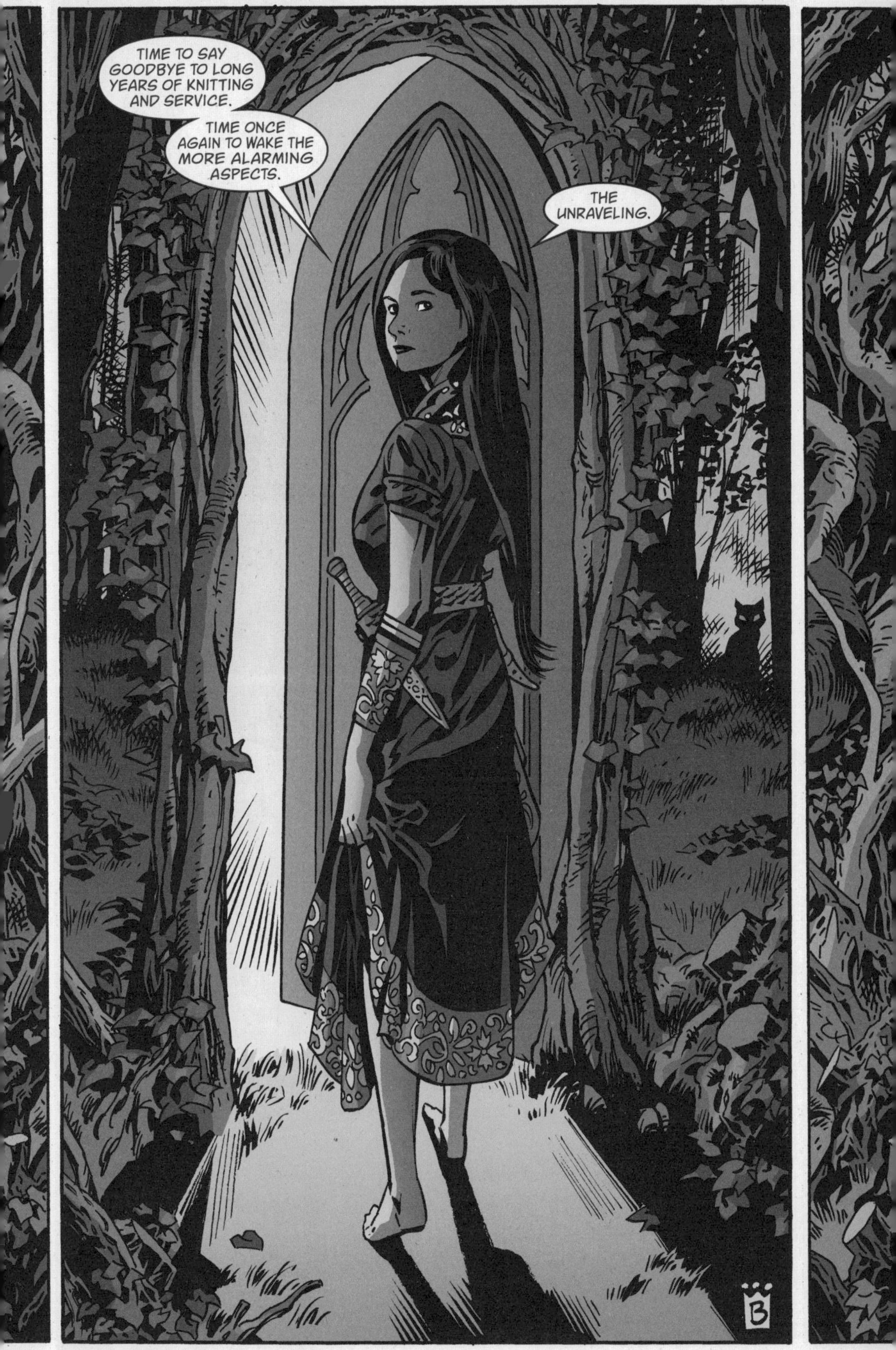
TIME TO SAY GOODBYE TO LONG YEARS OF KNITTING AND SERVICE.
TIME ONCE AGAIN TO WAKE THE MORE ALARMING ASPECTS.
THE UNRAVELING.

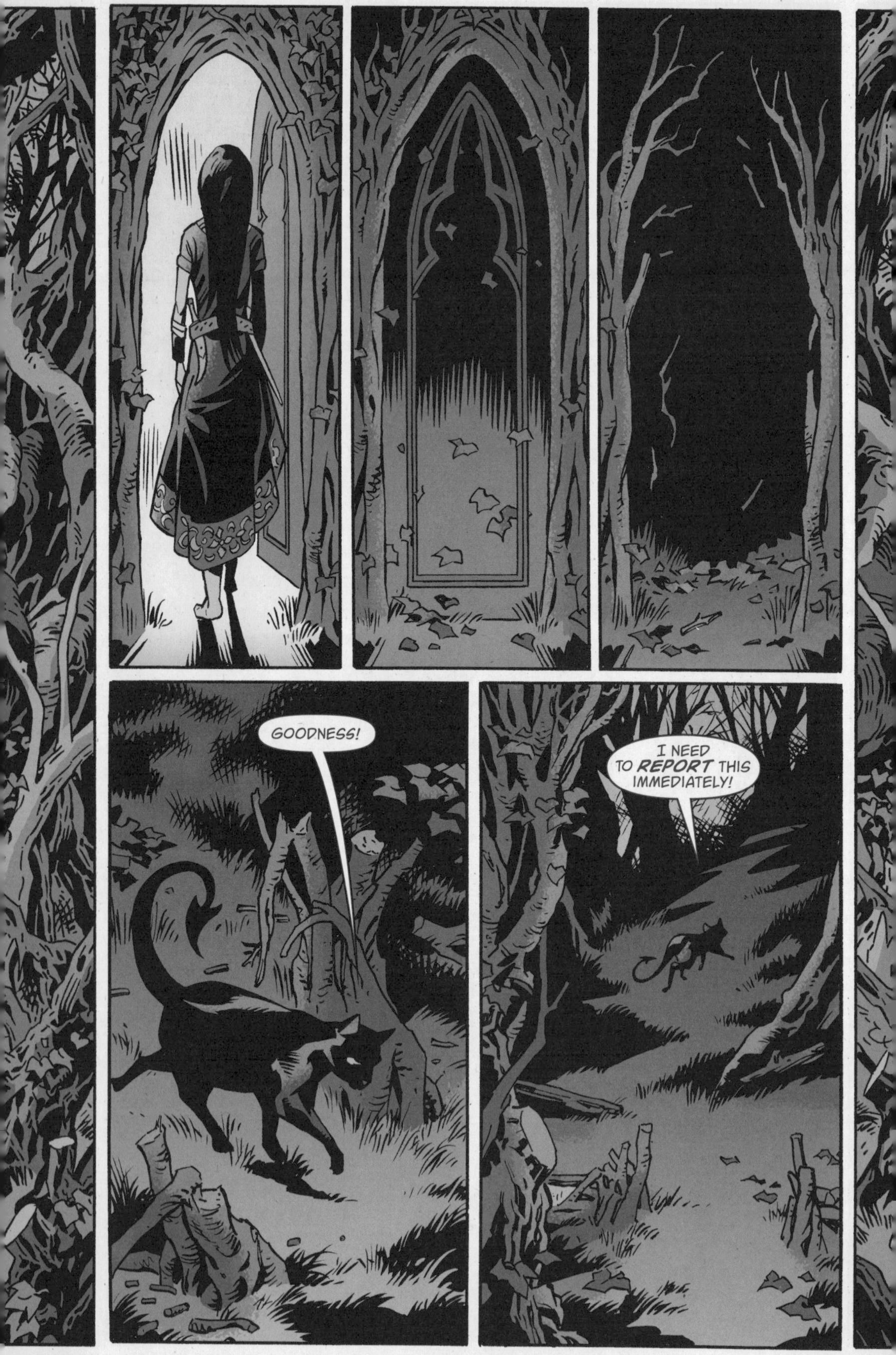
GOODNESS!
I NEED TO REPORT THIS IMMEDIATELY!

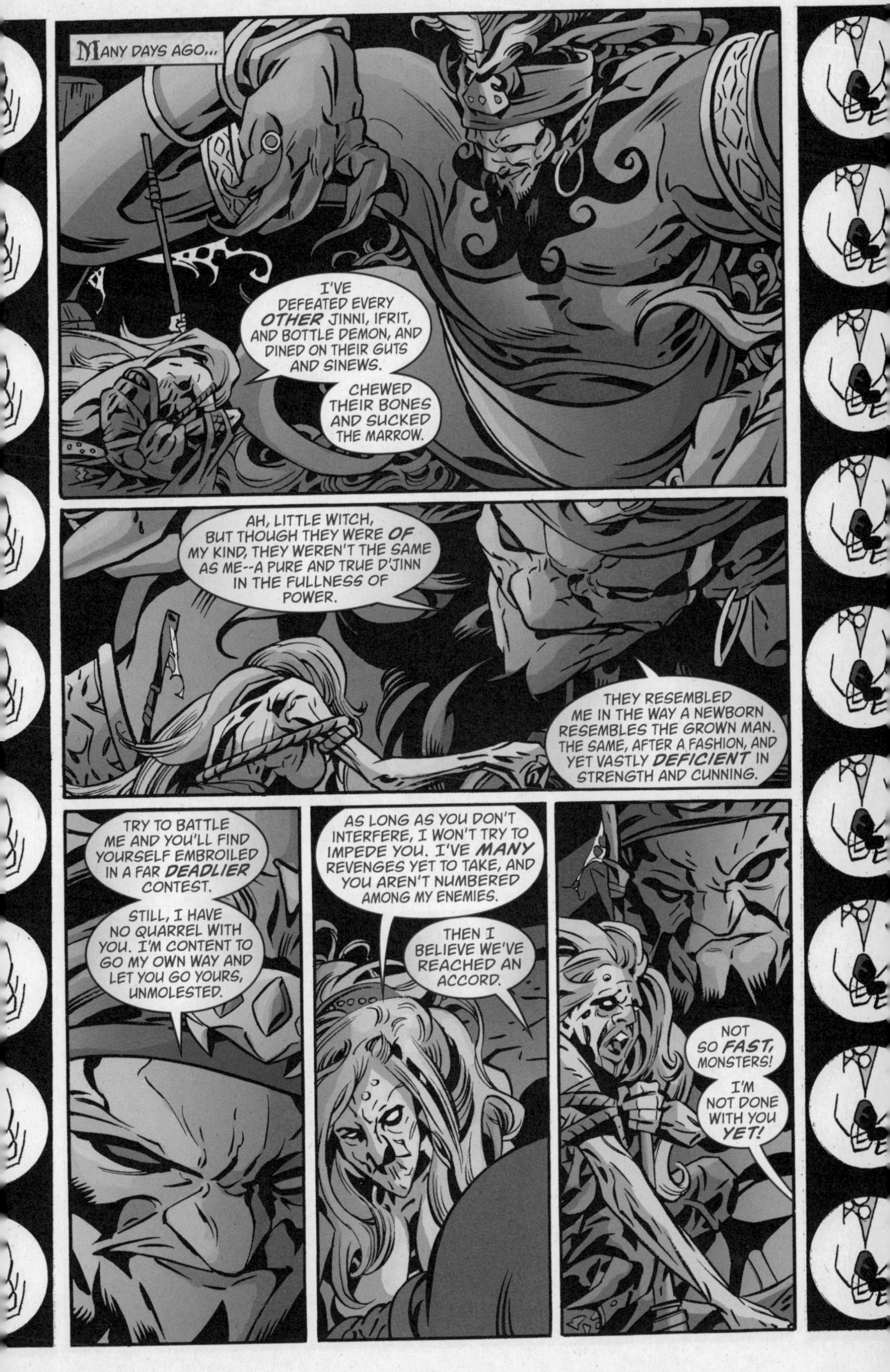
MANY DAYS AGO...
I'VE DEFEATED EVERY OTHER JINNI, IFRIT, AND BOTTLE DEMON, AND DINED ON THEIR GUTS AND SINEWS.
CHEWED THEIR BONES AND SUCKED THE MARROW.
AH, LITTLE WITCH, BUT THOUGH THEY WERE OF MY KIND, THEY WEREN'T THE SAME AS ME--A PURE AND TRUE D'JINN IN THE FULLNESS OF POWER.
THEY RESEMBLED ME IN THE WAY A NEWBORN RESEMBLES THE GROWN MAN. THE SAME, AFTER A FASHION, AND YET VASTLY DEFICIENT IN STRENGTH AND CUNNING.
TRY TO BATTLE ME AND YOU'LL FIND YOURSELF EMBROILED IN A FAR DEADLIER CONTEST.
STILL, I HAVE NO QUARREL WITH YOU. I'M CONTENT TO GO MY OWN WAY AND LET YOU GO YOURS, UNMOLESTED.
AS LONG AS YOU DON'T INTERFERE, I WON'T TRY TO IMPEDE YOU. I'VE MANY REVENGES YET TO TAKE, AND YOU AREN'T NUMBERED AMONG MY ENEMIES.
THEN I BELIEVE WE'VE REACHED AN ACCORD.
NOT SO FAST, MONSTERS!
I'M NOT DONE WITH YOU YET!

YOU'VE WRECKED MY HOME AND SCARED MY NEIGHBORS, AND I WON'T *HAVE* IT!

PREPARE TO MEET YOUR *DOOM* AT THE HANDS OF BUFKIN THE BRAVE!

HEH.

HEH-HEH-HEH-HEH!

HA HA HA HA HA HA! HA HA!

HEH-HEH-HEE-HEE-*HEE* HEE-HEE!

HEH-HEH-HEE-HEE-HEE-*HEE* HEE-HEE!

HA HA HA HA HAAA HA HA HA HA HAH!

STOP THAT! STOP IT THIS *INSTANT!*

I--

I REALLY *MEAN* IT!

I'M BEGINNING TO GET *MAD!*

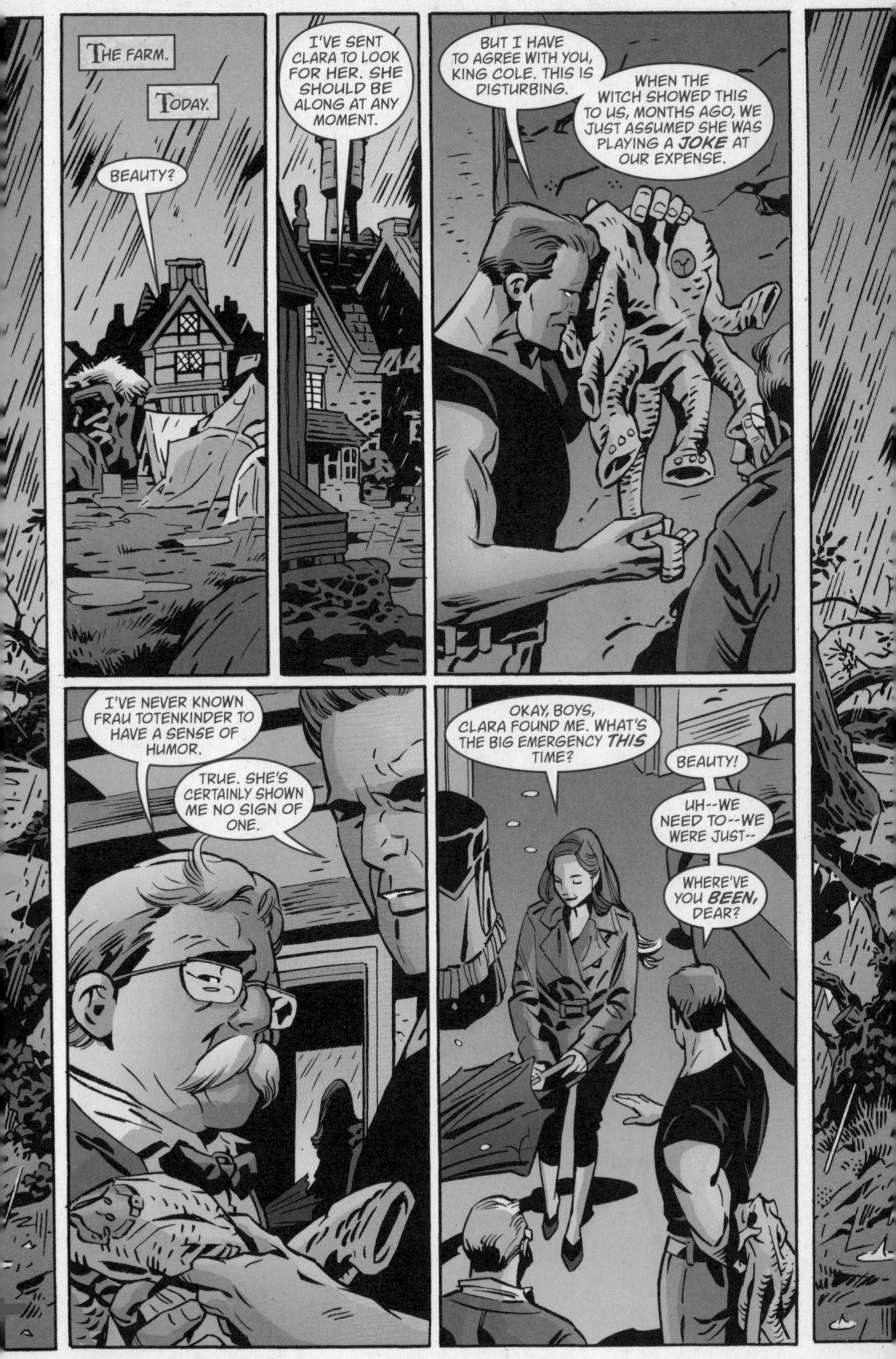
THE FARM.
TODAY.
BEAUTY?
I'VE SENT CLARA TO LOOK FOR HER. SHE SHOULD BE ALONG AT ANY MOMENT.
BUT I HAVE TO AGREE WITH YOU, KING COLE. THIS IS DISTURBING.
WHEN THE WITCH SHOWED THIS TO US, MONTHS AGO, WE JUST ASSUMED SHE WAS PLAYING A JOKE AT OUR EXPENSE.
I'VE NEVER KNOWN FRAU TOTENKINDER TO HAVE A SENSE OF HUMOR.
TRUE. SHE'S CERTAINLY SHOWN ME NO SIGN OF ONE.
OKAY, BOYS, CLARA FOUND ME. WHAT'S THE BIG EMERGENCY THIS TIME?
BEAUTY!
UH--WE NEED TO--WE WERE JUST--
WHERE'VE YOU BEEN, DEAR?

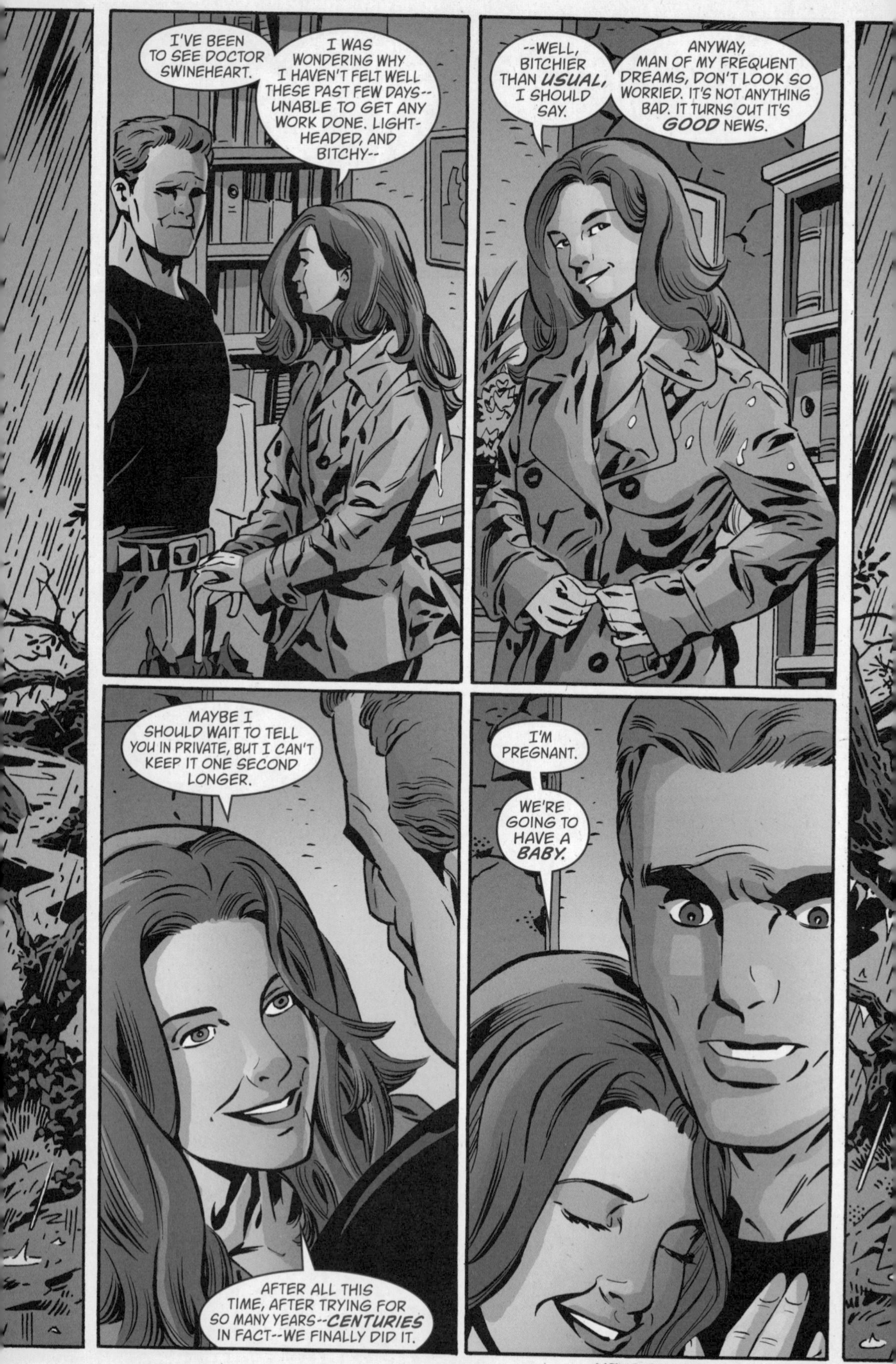

I'VE BEEN TO SEE DOCTOR SWINEHEART.
I WAS WONDERING WHY I HAVEN'T FELT WELL THESE PAST FEW DAYS-- UNABLE TO GET ANY WORK DONE. LIGHT-HEADED, AND BITCHY--
--WELL, BITCHIER THAN USUAL, I SHOULD SAY.
ANYWAY, MAN OF MY FREQUENT DREAMS, DON'T LOOK SO WORRIED. IT'S NOT ANYTHING BAD. IT TURNS OUT IT'S GOOD NEWS.
MAYBE I SHOULD WAIT TO TELL YOU IN PRIVATE, BUT I CAN'T KEEP IT ONE SECOND LONGER.
AFTER ALL THIS TIME, AFTER TRYING FOR SO MANY YEARS--CENTURIES IN FACT--WE FINALLY DID IT.
I'M PREGNANT.
WE'RE GOING TO HAVE A BABY.

NEXT: OH HAPPY DAY! (OR NOT.)

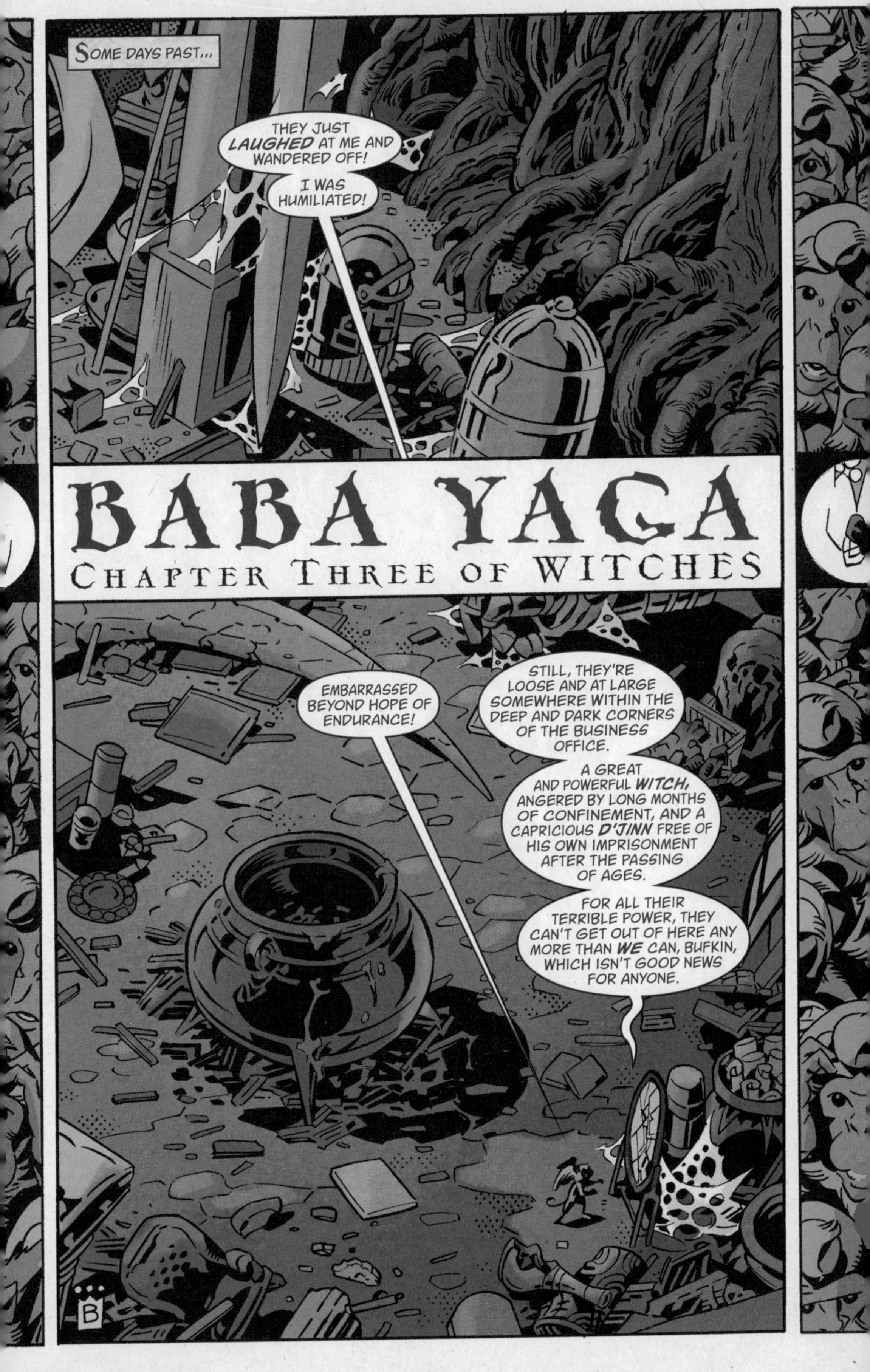
SOME DAYS PAST...
THEY JUST LAUGHED AT ME AND WANDERED OFF!
I WAS HUMILIATED!
BABA YAGA
CHAPTER THREE OF WITCHES
EMBARRASSED BEYOND HOPE OF ENDURANCE!
STILL, THEY'RE LOOSE AND AT LARGE SOMEWHERE WITHIN THE DEEP AND DARK CORNERS OF THE BUSINESS OFFICE.
A GREAT AND POWERFUL WITCH, ANGERED BY LONG MONTHS OF CONFINEMENT, AND A CAPRICIOUS D'JINN FREE OF HIS OWN IMPRISONMENT AFTER THE PASSING OF AGES.
FOR ALL THEIR TERRIBLE POWER, THEY CAN'T GET OUT OF HERE ANY MORE THAN WE CAN, BUFKIN, WHICH ISN'T GOOD NEWS FOR ANYONE.

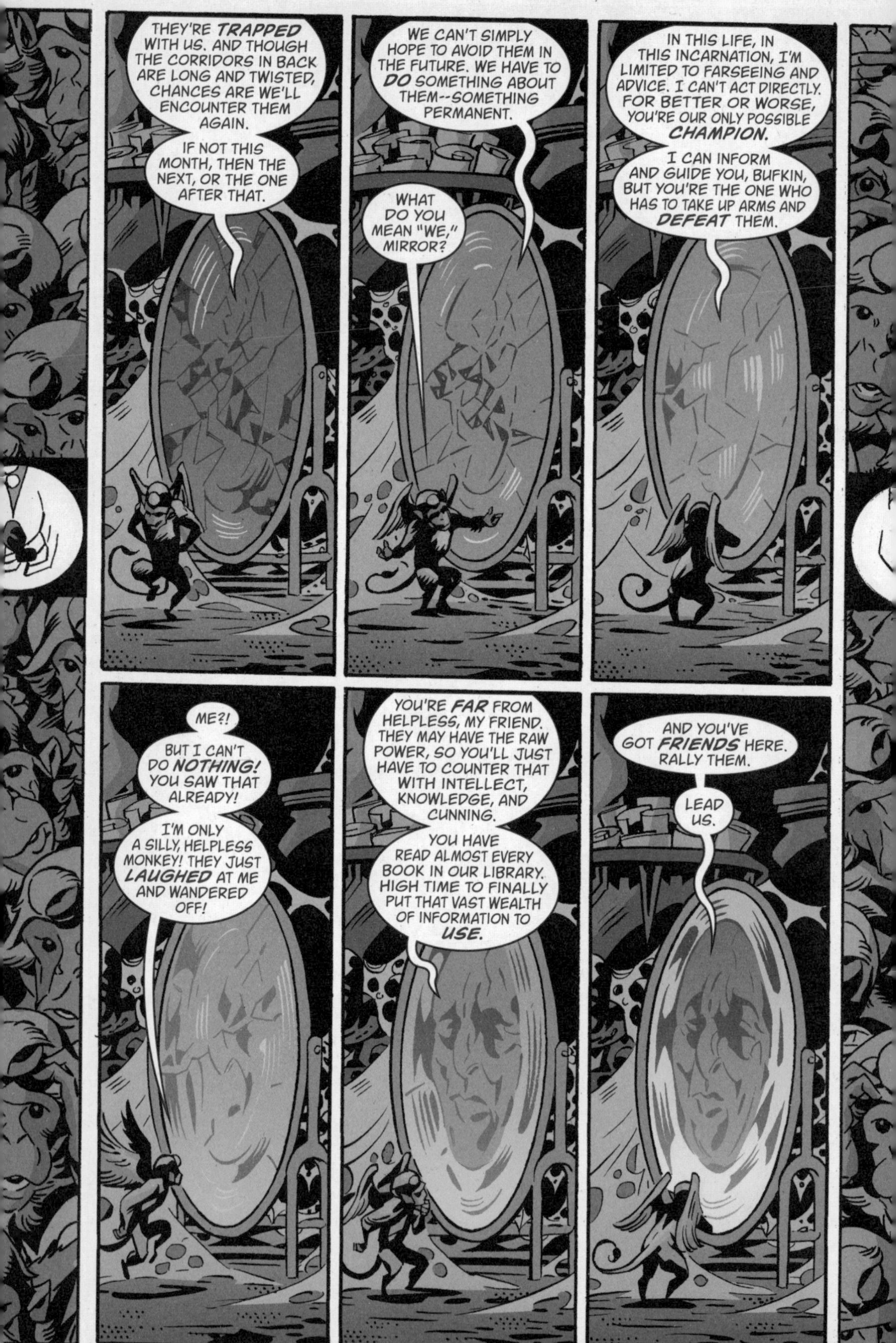
THEY'RE TRAPPED WITH US. AND THOUGH THE CORRIDORS IN BACK ARE LONG AND TWISTED, CHANCES ARE WE'LL ENCOUNTER THEM AGAIN.
IF NOT THIS MONTH, THEN THE NEXT, OR THE ONE AFTER THAT.
WE CAN'T SIMPLY HOPE TO AVOID THEM IN THE FUTURE. WE HAVE TO DO SOMETHING ABOUT THEM--SOMETHING PERMANENT.
WHAT DO YOU MEAN "WE," MIRROR?
IN THIS LIFE, IN THIS INCARNATION, I'M LIMITED TO FARSEEING AND ADVICE. I CAN'T ACT DIRECTLY. FOR BETTER OR WORSE, YOU'RE OUR ONLY POSSIBLE CHAMPION.
I CAN INFORM AND GUIDE YOU, BUFKIN, BUT YOU'RE THE ONE WHO HAS TO TAKE UP ARMS AND DEFEAT THEM.
ME?!
BUT I CAN'T DO NOTHING! YOU SAW THAT ALREADY!
I'M ONLY A SILLY, HELPLESS MONKEY! THEY JUST LAUGHED AT ME AND WANDERED OFF!
YOU'RE FAR FROM HELPLESS, MY FRIEND. THEY MAY HAVE THE RAW POWER, SO YOU'LL JUST HAVE TO COUNTER THAT WITH INTELLECT, KNOWLEDGE, AND CUNNING.
YOU HAVE READ ALMOST EVERY BOOK IN OUR LIBRARY. HIGH TIME TO FINALLY PUT THAT VAST WEALTH OF INFORMATION TO USE.
AND YOU'VE GOT FRIENDS HERE. RALLY THEM.
LEAD US.

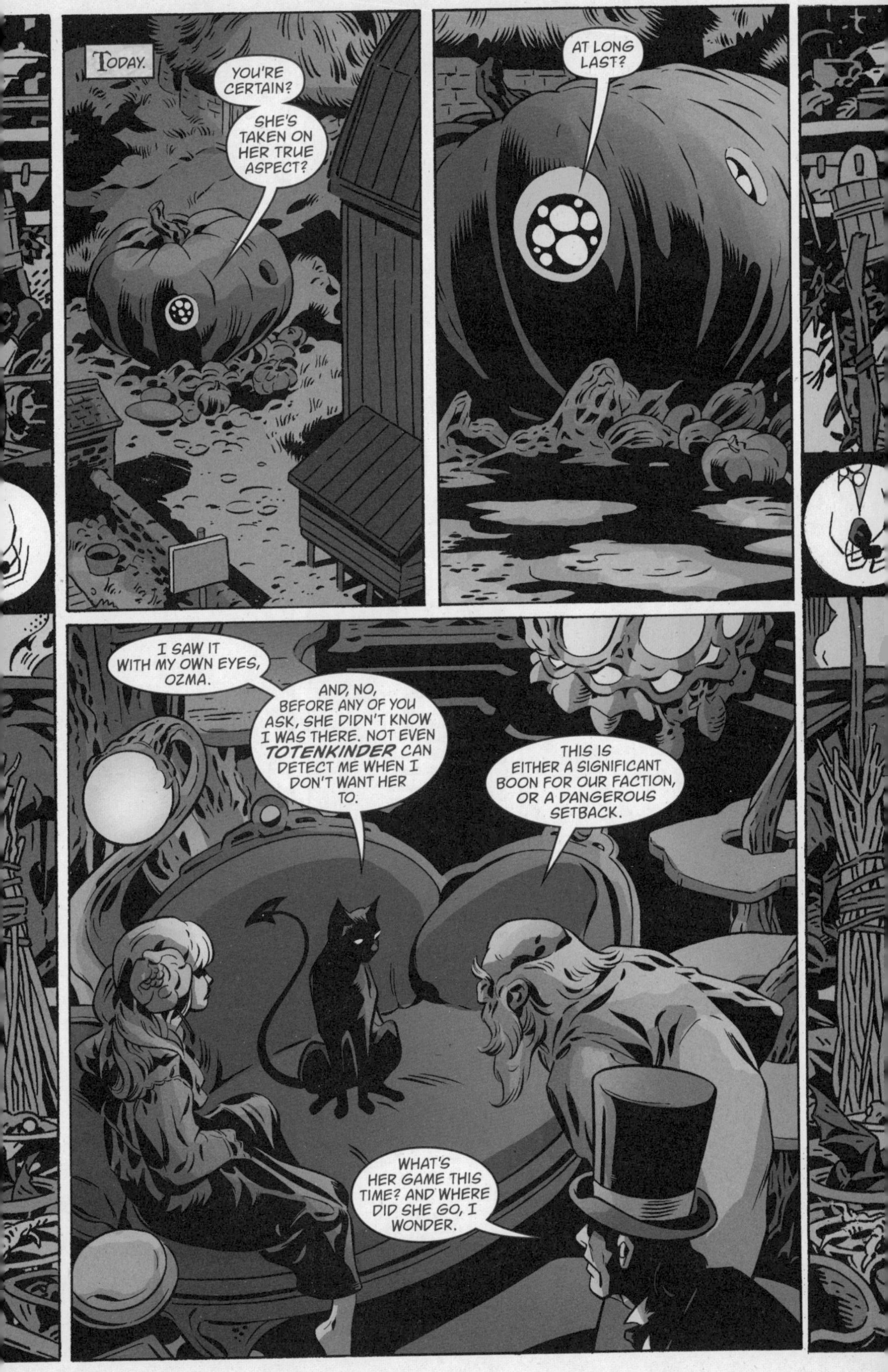
TODAY.
YOU'RE CERTAIN?
SHE'S TAKEN ON HER TRUE ASPECT?
AT LONG LAST?
I SAW IT WITH MY OWN EYES, OZMA.
AND, NO, BEFORE ANY OF YOU ASK, SHE DIDN'T KNOW I WAS THERE. NOT EVEN TOTENKINDER CAN DETECT ME WHEN I DON'T WANT HER TO.
THIS IS EITHER A SIGNIFICANT BOON FOR OUR FACTION, OR A DANGEROUS SETBACK.
WHAT'S HER GAME THIS TIME? AND WHERE DID SHE GO, I WONDER.

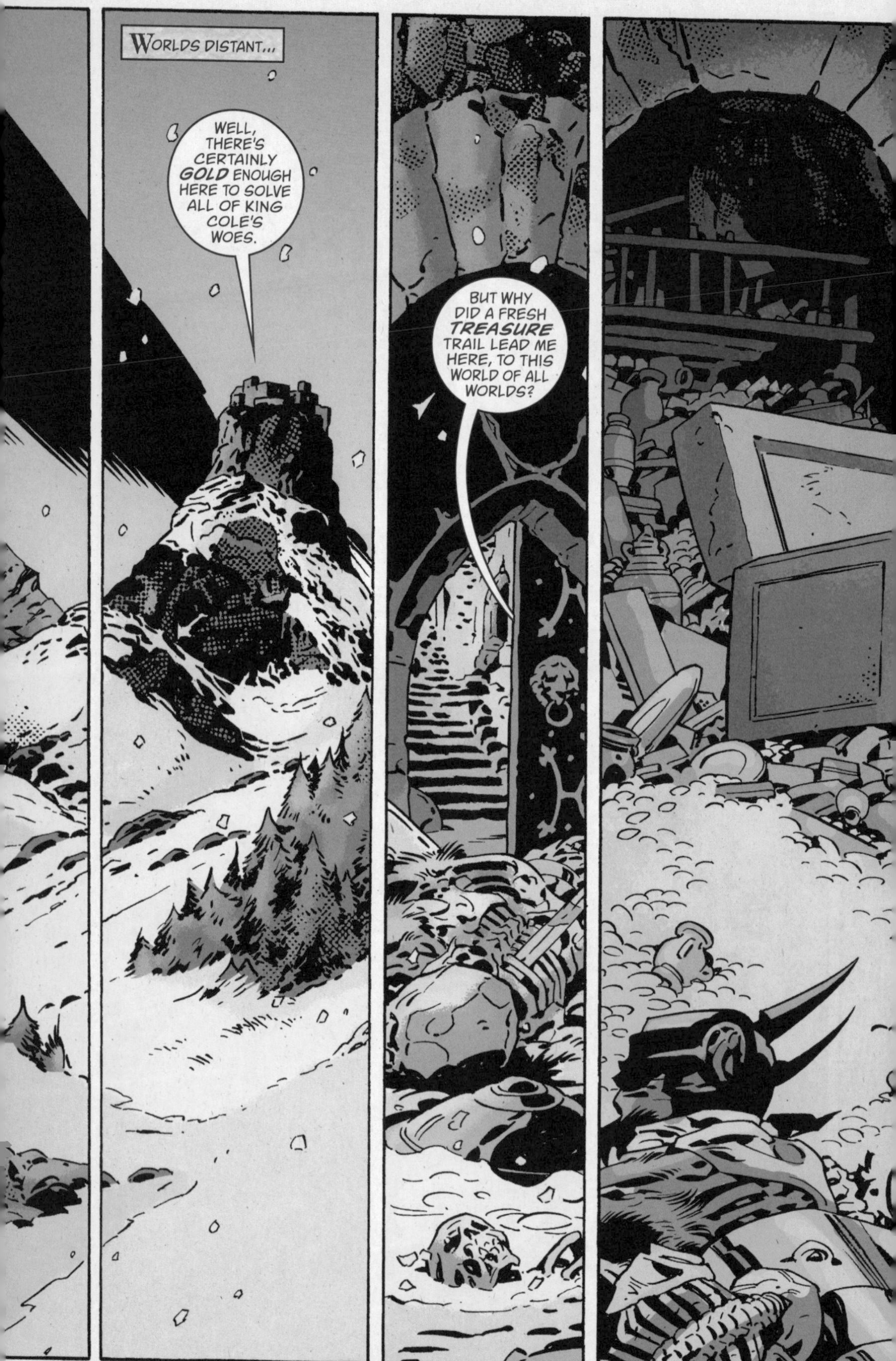
WORLDS DISTANT...
WELL, THERE'S CERTAINLY GOLD ENOUGH HERE TO SOLVE ALL OF KING COLE'S WOES.
BUT WHY DID A FRESH TREASURE TRAIL LEAD ME HERE, TO THIS WORLD OF ALL WORLDS?

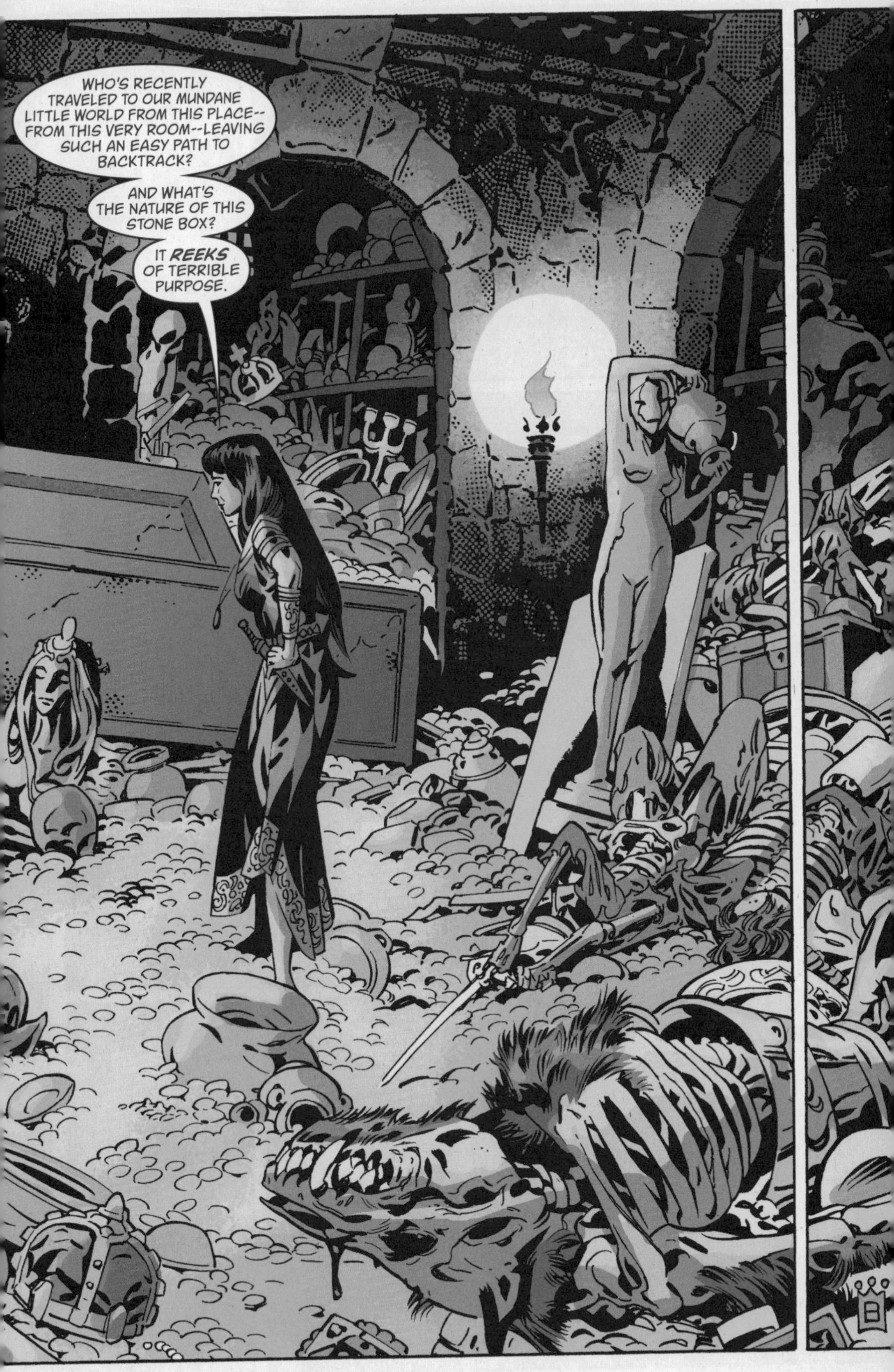
WHO'S RECENTLY TRAVELED TO OUR MUNDANE LITTLE WORLD FROM THIS PLACE-- FROM THIS VERY ROOM--LEAVING SUCH AN EASY PATH TO BACKTRACK?
AND WHAT'S THE NATURE OF THIS STONE BOX?
IT *REEKS* OF TERRIBLE PURPOSE.

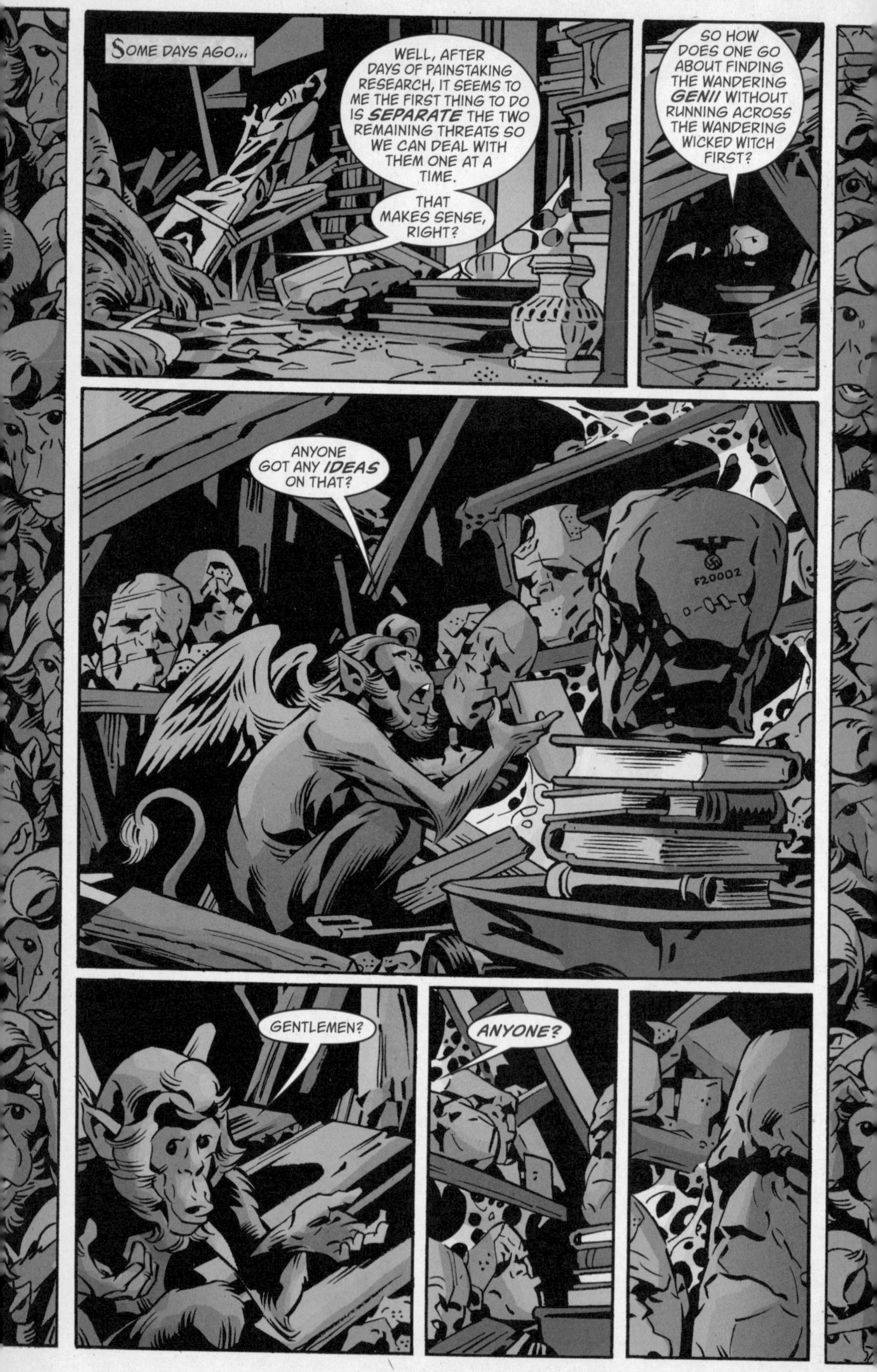

SOME DAYS AGO...
WELL, AFTER DAYS OF PAINSTAKING RESEARCH, IT SEEMS TO ME THE FIRST THING TO DO IS SEPARATE THE TWO REMAINING THREATS SO WE CAN DEAL WITH THEM ONE AT A TIME.
THAT MAKES SENSE, RIGHT?
SO HOW DOES ONE GO ABOUT FINDING THE WANDERING GENII WITHOUT RUNNING ACROSS THE WANDERING WICKED WITCH FIRST?
ANYONE GOT ANY IDEAS ON THAT?
F20002
GENTLEMEN?
ANYONE?

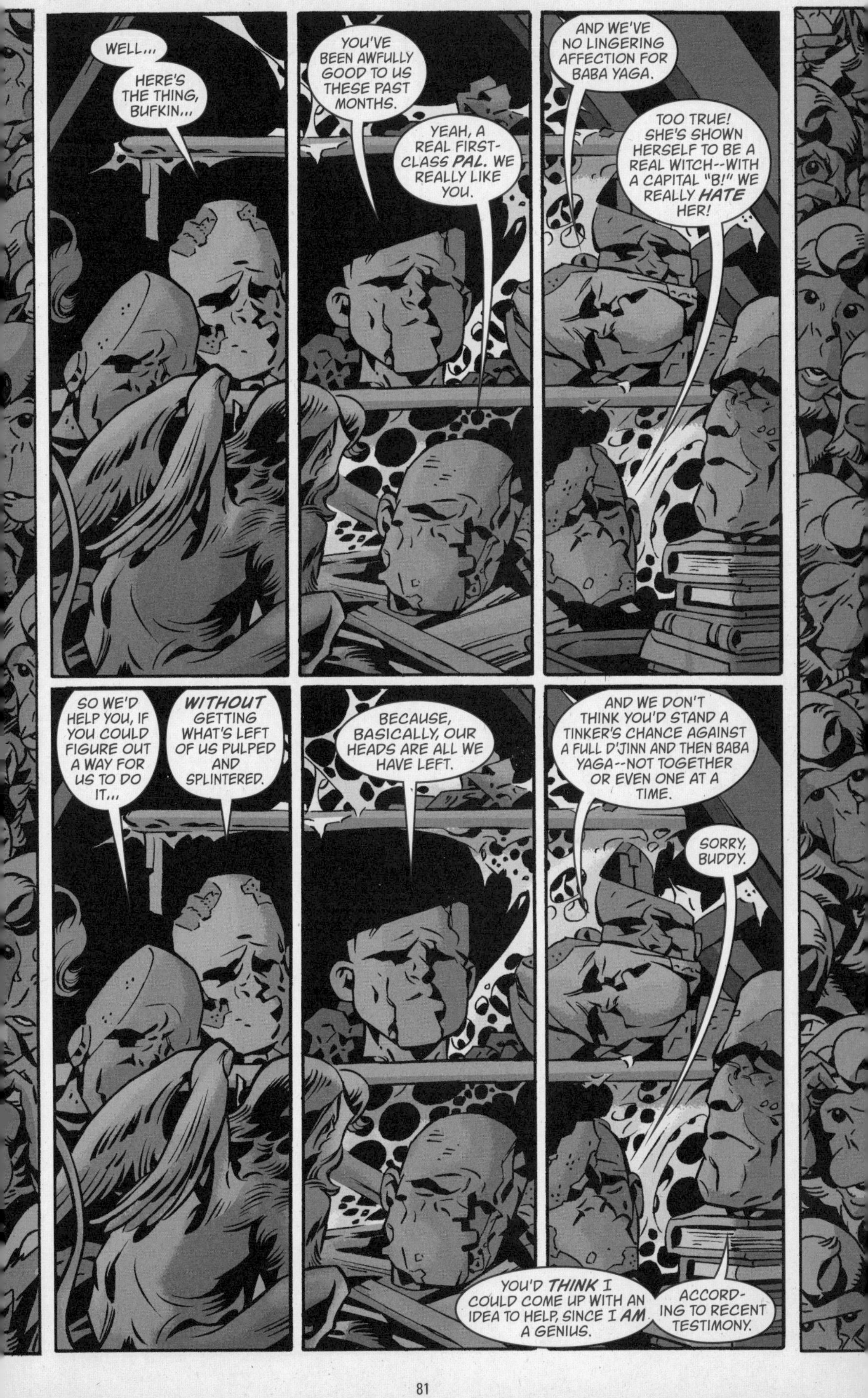
WELL...
HERE'S THE THING, BUFKIN...
YOU'VE BEEN AWFULLY GOOD TO US THESE PAST MONTHS.
YEAH, A REAL FIRST-CLASS PAL. WE REALLY LIKE YOU.
AND WE'VE NO LINGERING AFFECTION FOR BABA YAGA.
TOO TRUE! SHE'S SHOWN HERSELF TO BE A REAL WITCH--WITH A CAPITAL "B!" WE REALLY HATE HER!
SO WE'D HELP YOU, IF YOU COULD FIGURE OUT A WAY FOR US TO DO IT...
WITHOUT GETTING WHAT'S LEFT OF US PULPED AND SPLINTERED.
BECAUSE, BASICALLY, OUR HEADS ARE ALL WE HAVE LEFT.
AND WE DON'T THINK YOU'D STAND A TINKER'S CHANCE AGAINST A FULL D'JINN AND THEN BABA YAGA--NOT TOGETHER OR EVEN ONE AT A TIME.
SORRY, BUDDY.
YOU'D THINK I COULD COME UP WITH AN IDEA TO HELP, SINCE I AM A GENIUS.
ACCORD-ING TO RECENT TESTIMONY.

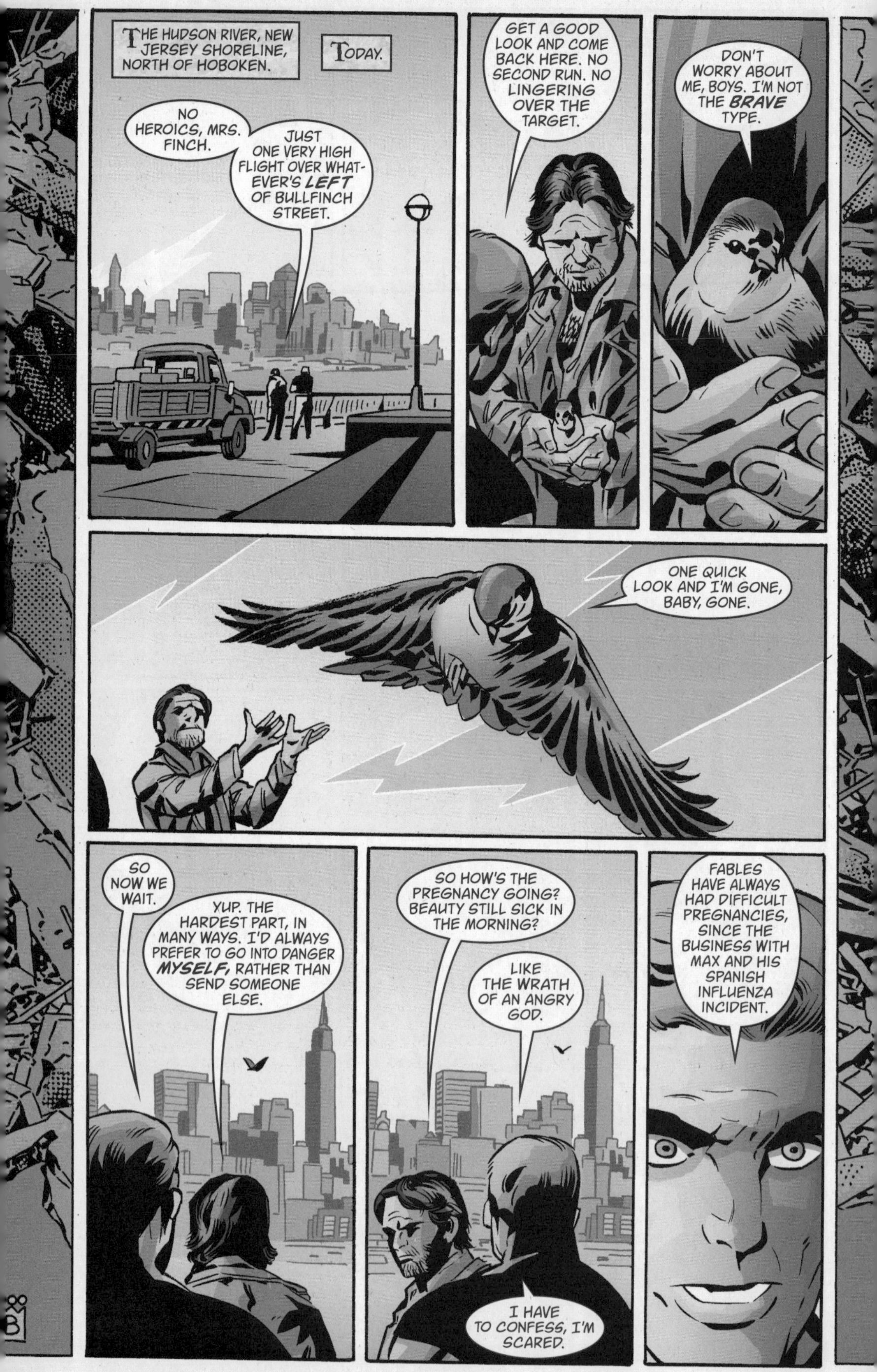
THE HUDSON RIVER, NEW JERSEY SHORELINE, NORTH OF HOBOKEN.
TODAY.
NO HEROICS, MRS. FINCH.
JUST ONE VERY HIGH FLIGHT OVER WHAT-EVER'S LEFT OF BULLFINCH STREET.
GET A GOOD LOOK AND COME BACK HERE. NO SECOND RUN. NO LINGERING OVER THE TARGET.
DON'T WORRY ABOUT ME, BOYS. I'M NOT THE BRAVE TYPE.
ONE QUICK LOOK AND I'M GONE, BABY, GONE.
SO NOW WE WAIT.
YUP. THE HARDEST PART, IN MANY WAYS. I'D ALWAYS PREFER TO GO INTO DANGER MYSELF, RATHER THAN SEND SOMEONE ELSE.
SO HOW'S THE PREGNANCY GOING? BEAUTY STILL SICK IN THE MORNING?
LIKE THE WRATH OF AN ANGRY GOD.
I HAVE TO CONFESS, I'M SCARED.
FABLES HAVE ALWAYS HAD DIFFICULT PREGNANCIES, SINCE THE BUSINESS WITH MAX AND HIS SPANISH INFLUENZA INCIDENT.

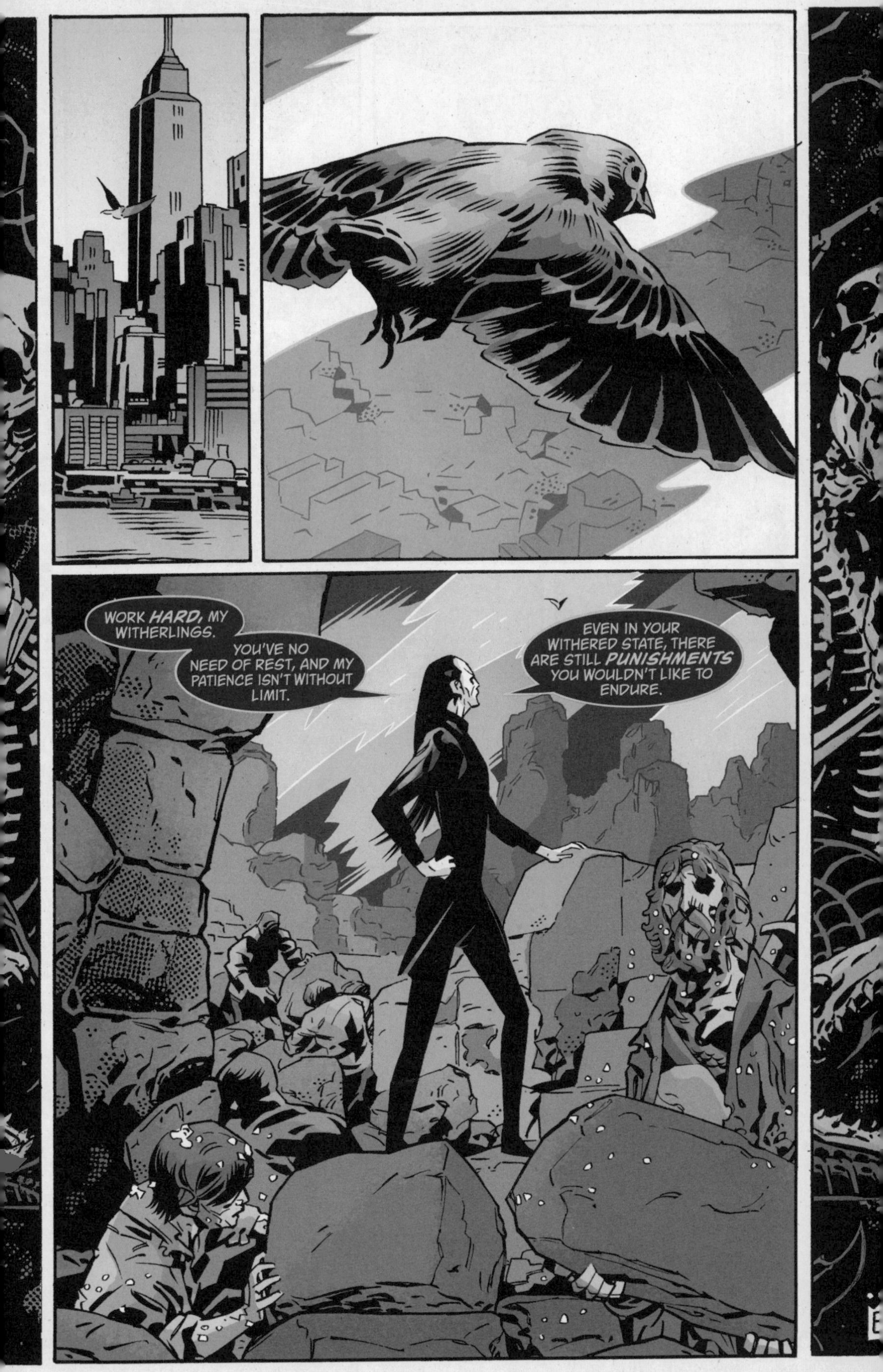

WORK HARD, MY WITHERLINGS.
YOU'VE NO NEED OF REST, AND MY PATIENCE ISN'T WITHOUT LIMIT.
EVEN IN YOUR WITHERED STATE, THERE ARE STILL PUNISHMENTS YOU WOULDN'T LIKE TO ENDURE.

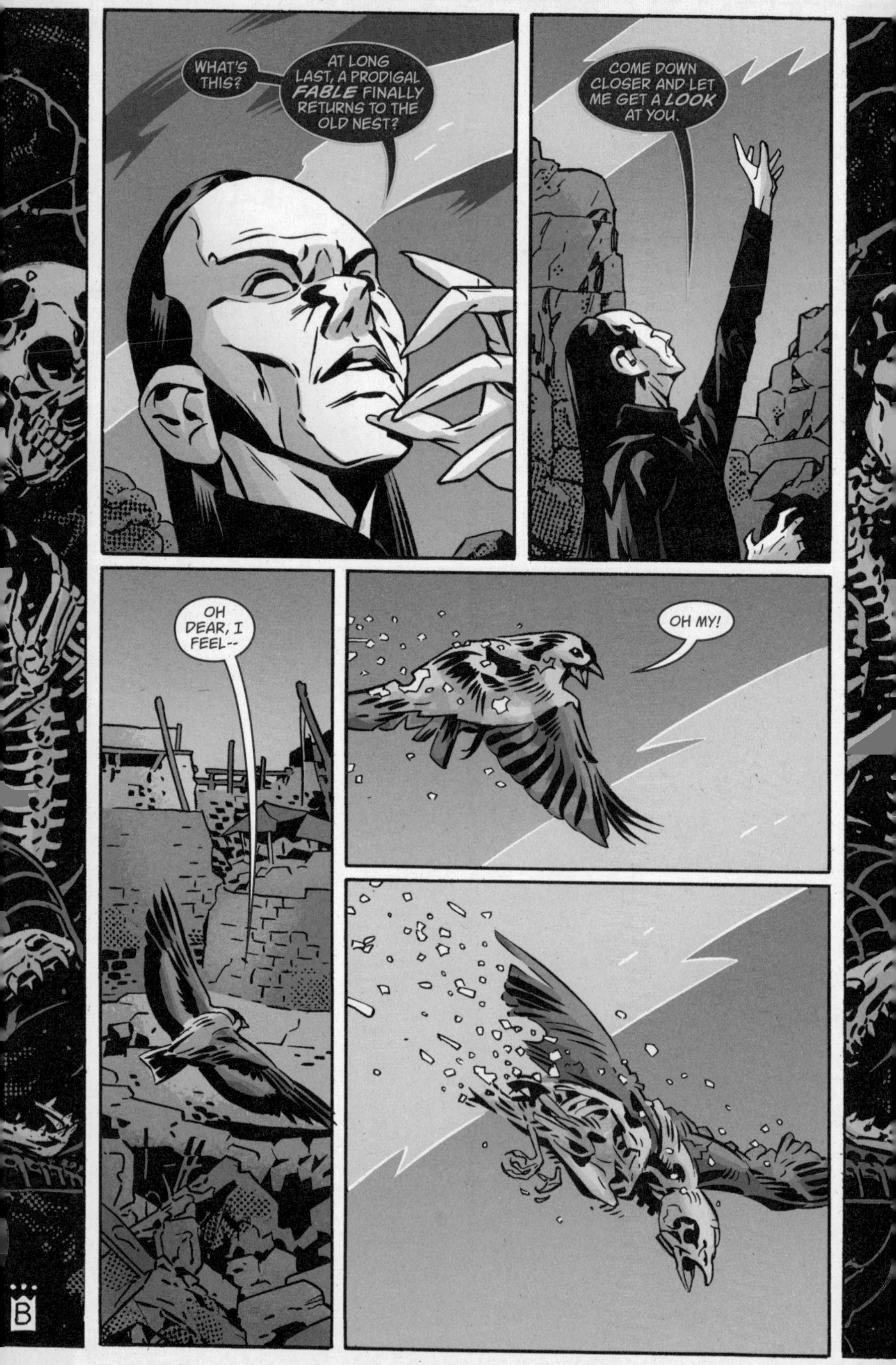
WHAT'S THIS?
AT LONG LAST, A PRODIGAL FABLE FINALLY RETURNS TO THE OLD NEST?
COME DOWN CLOSER AND LET ME GET A LOOK AT YOU.
OH DEAR, I FEEL--
OH MY!

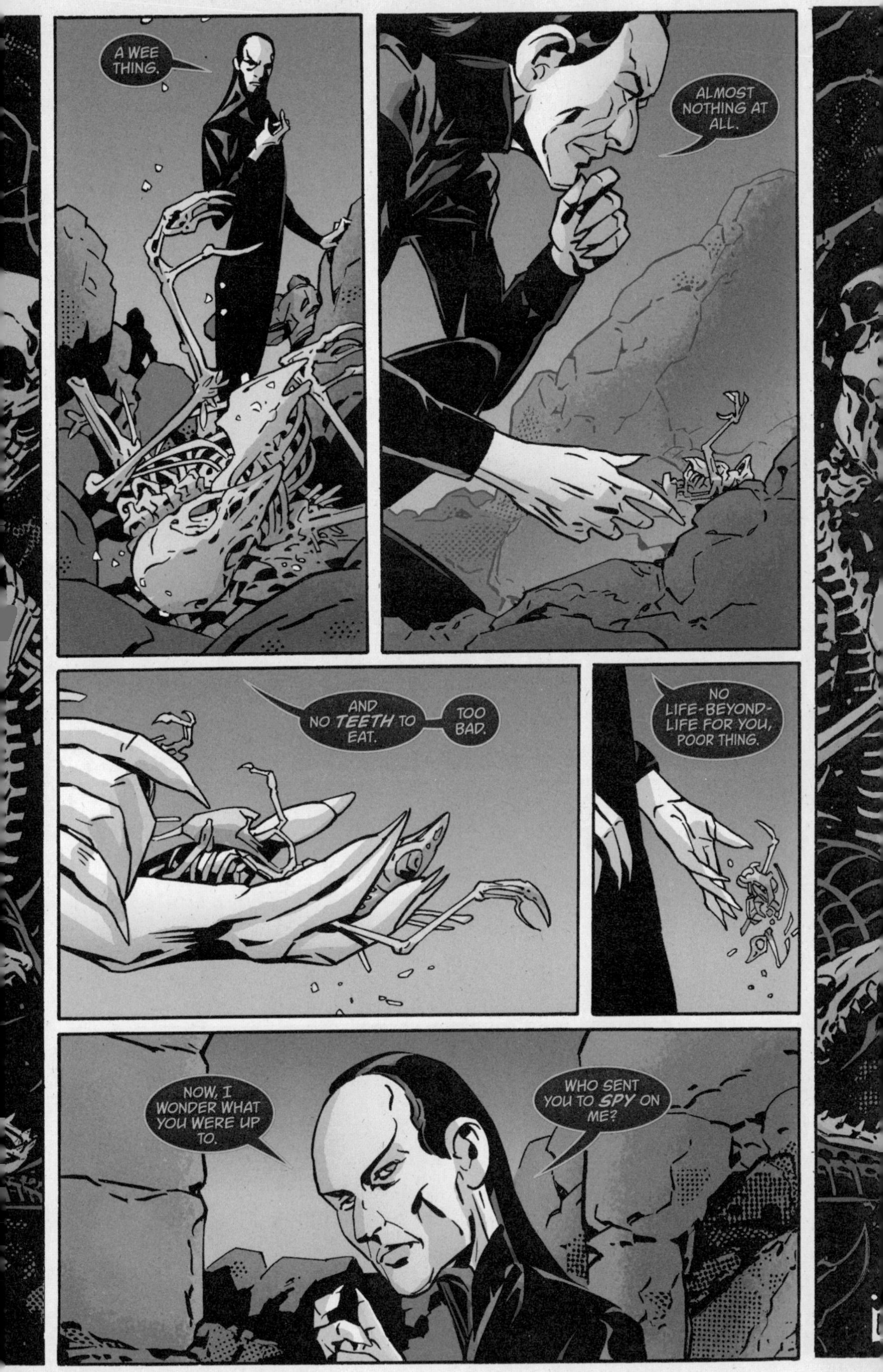

A WEE THING.
ALMOST NOTHING AT ALL.
AND NO TEETH TO EAT.
TOO BAD.
NO LIFE-BEYOND-LIFE FOR YOU, POOR THING.
NOW, I WONDER WHAT YOU WERE UP TO.
WHO SENT YOU TO SPY ON ME?

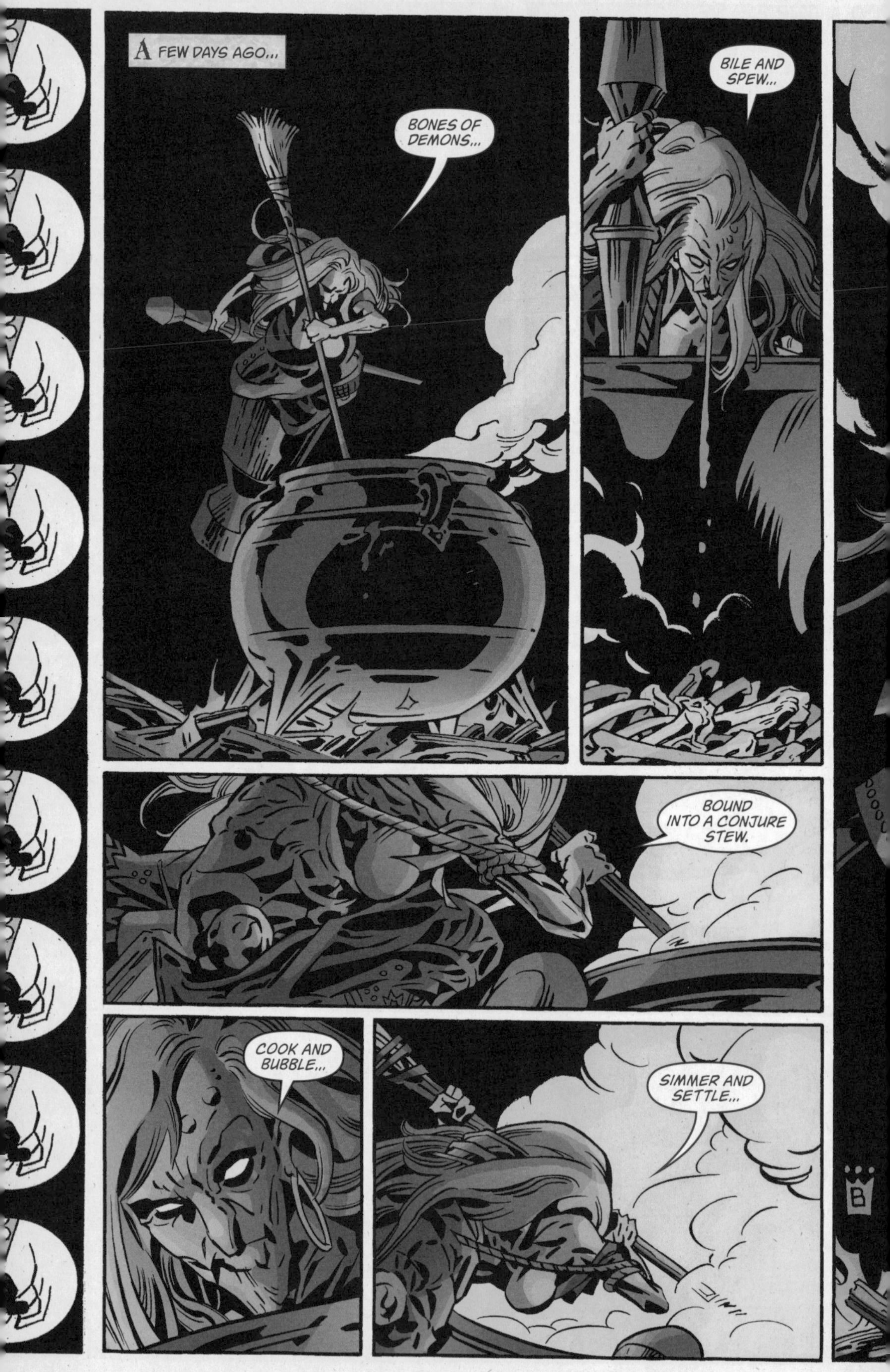
A FEW DAYS AGO...
BONES OF DEMONS...
BILE AND SPEW...
BOUND INTO A CONJURE STEW.
COOK AND BUBBLE...
SIMMER AND SETTLE...

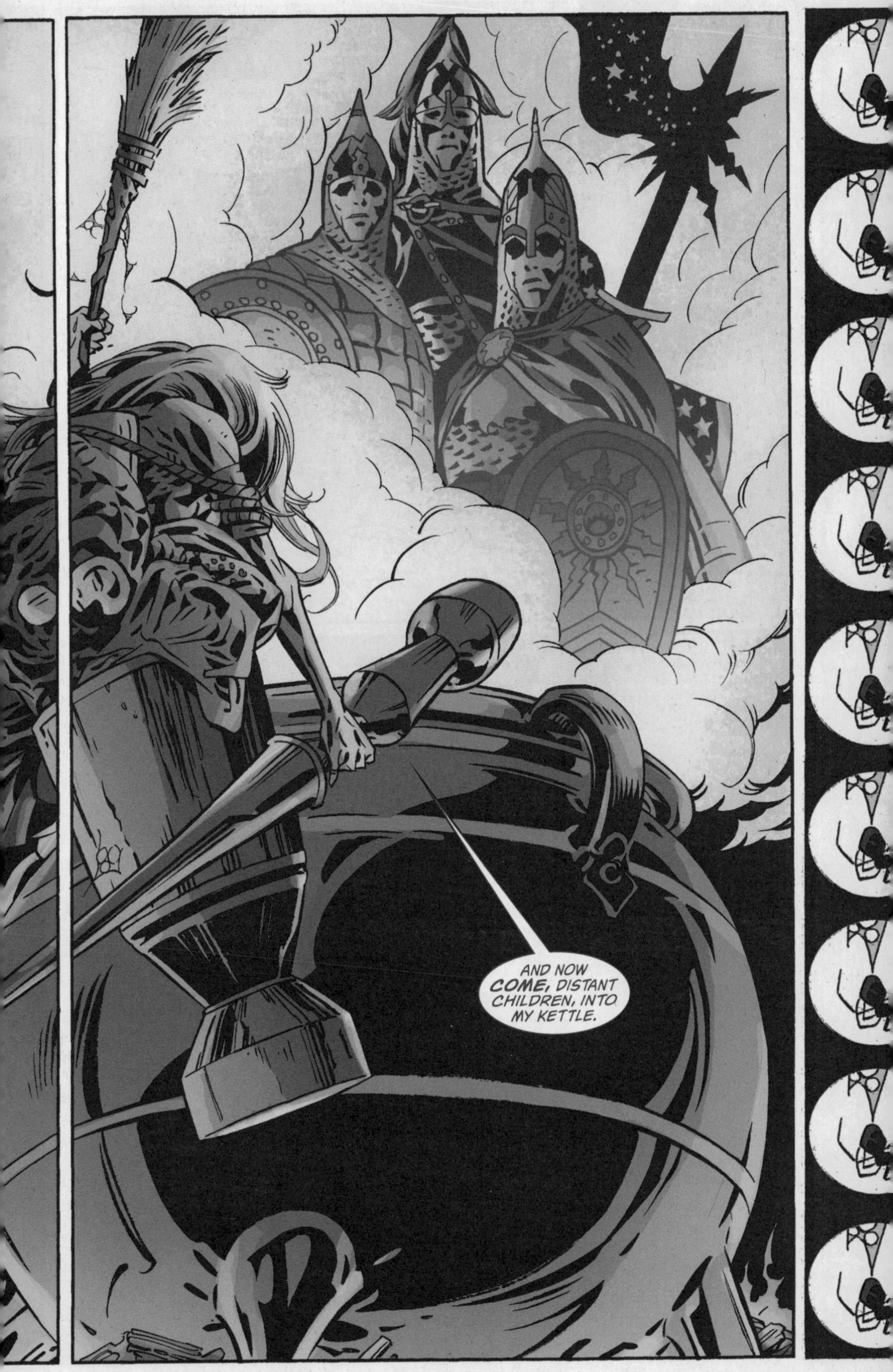
AND NOW COME, DISTANT CHILDREN, INTO MY KETTLE.

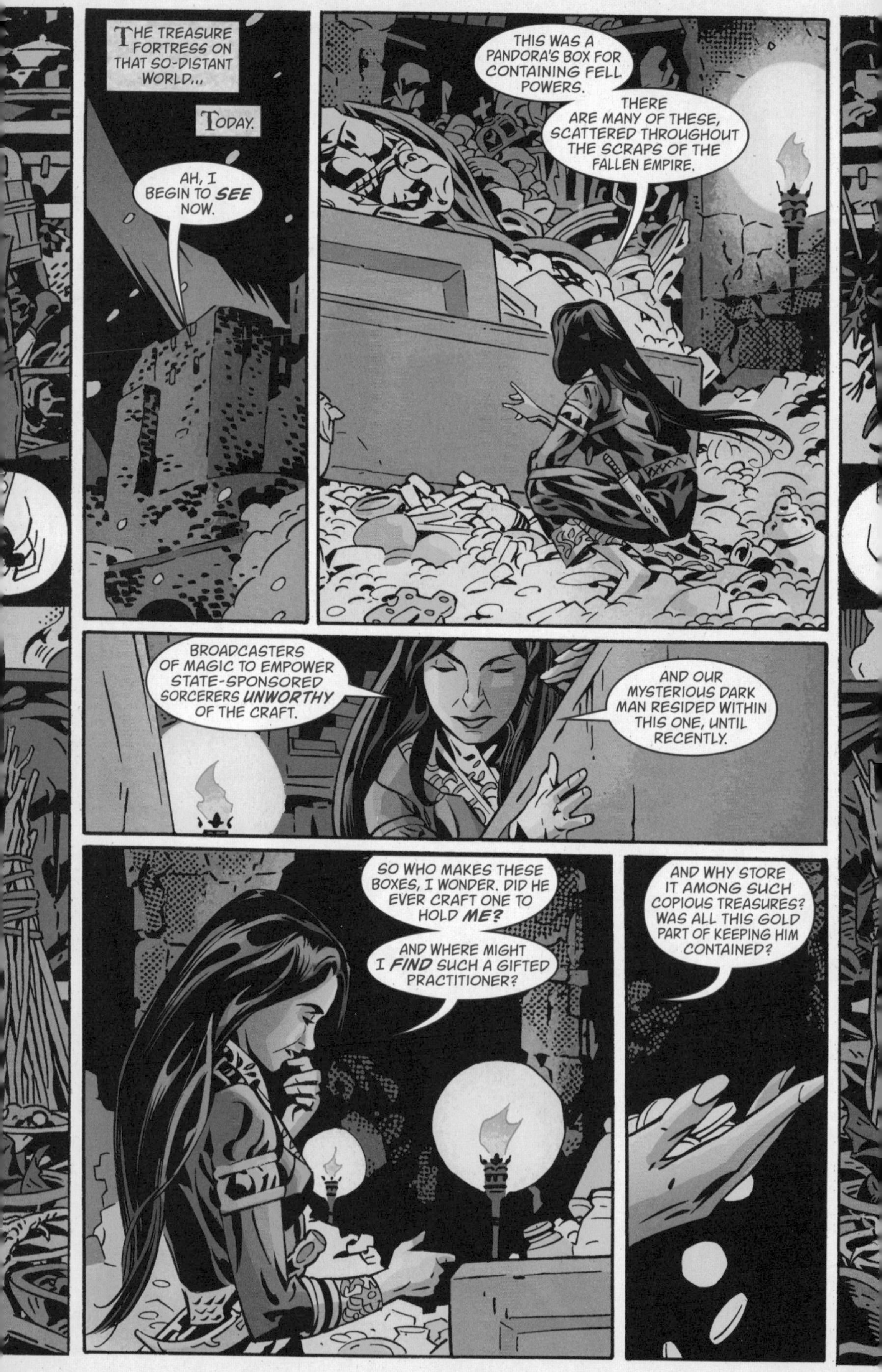

THE TREASURE FORTRESS ON THAT SO-DISTANT WORLD...
TODAY.
AH, I BEGIN TO SEE NOW.
THIS WAS A PANDORA'S BOX FOR CONTAINING FELL POWERS.
THERE ARE MANY OF THESE, SCATTERED THROUGHOUT THE SCRAPS OF THE FALLEN EMPIRE.
BROADCASTERS OF MAGIC TO EMPOWER STATE-SPONSORED SORCERERS UNWORTHY OF THE CRAFT.
AND OUR MYSTERIOUS DARK MAN RESIDED WITHIN THIS ONE, UNTIL RECENTLY.
SO WHO MAKES THESE BOXES, I WONDER. DID HE EVER CRAFT ONE TO HOLD ME?
AND WHERE MIGHT I FIND SUCH A GIFTED PRACTITIONER?
AND WHY STORE IT AMONG SUCH COPIOUS TREASURES? WAS ALL THIS GOLD PART OF KEEPING HIM CONTAINED?

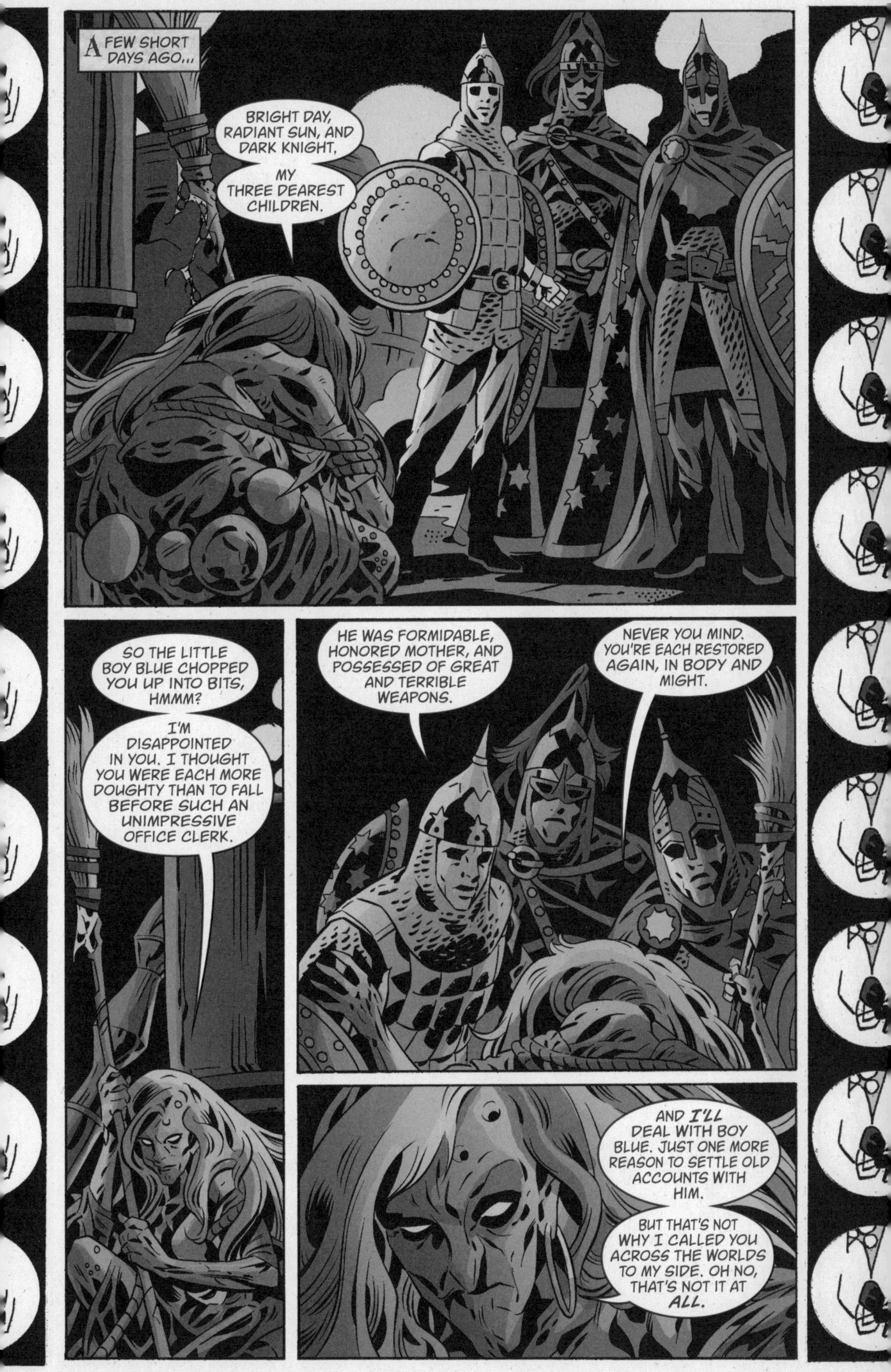
A FEW SHORT DAYS AGO...
BRIGHT DAY, RADIANT SUN, AND DARK KNIGHT,
MY THREE DEAREST CHILDREN.
SO THE LITTLE BOY BLUE CHOPPED YOU UP INTO BITS, HMMM?
I'M DISAPPOINTED IN YOU. I THOUGHT YOU WERE EACH MORE DOUGHTY THAN TO FALL BEFORE SUCH AN UNIMPRESSIVE OFFICE CLERK.
HE WAS FORMIDABLE, HONORED MOTHER, AND POSSESSED OF GREAT AND TERRIBLE WEAPONS.
NEVER YOU MIND. YOU'RE EACH RESTORED AGAIN, IN BODY AND MIGHT.
AND I'LL DEAL WITH BOY BLUE. JUST ONE MORE REASON TO SETTLE OLD ACCOUNTS WITH HIM.
BUT THAT'S NOT WHY I CALLED YOU ACROSS THE WORLDS TO MY SIDE. OH NO, THAT'S NOT IT AT ALL.

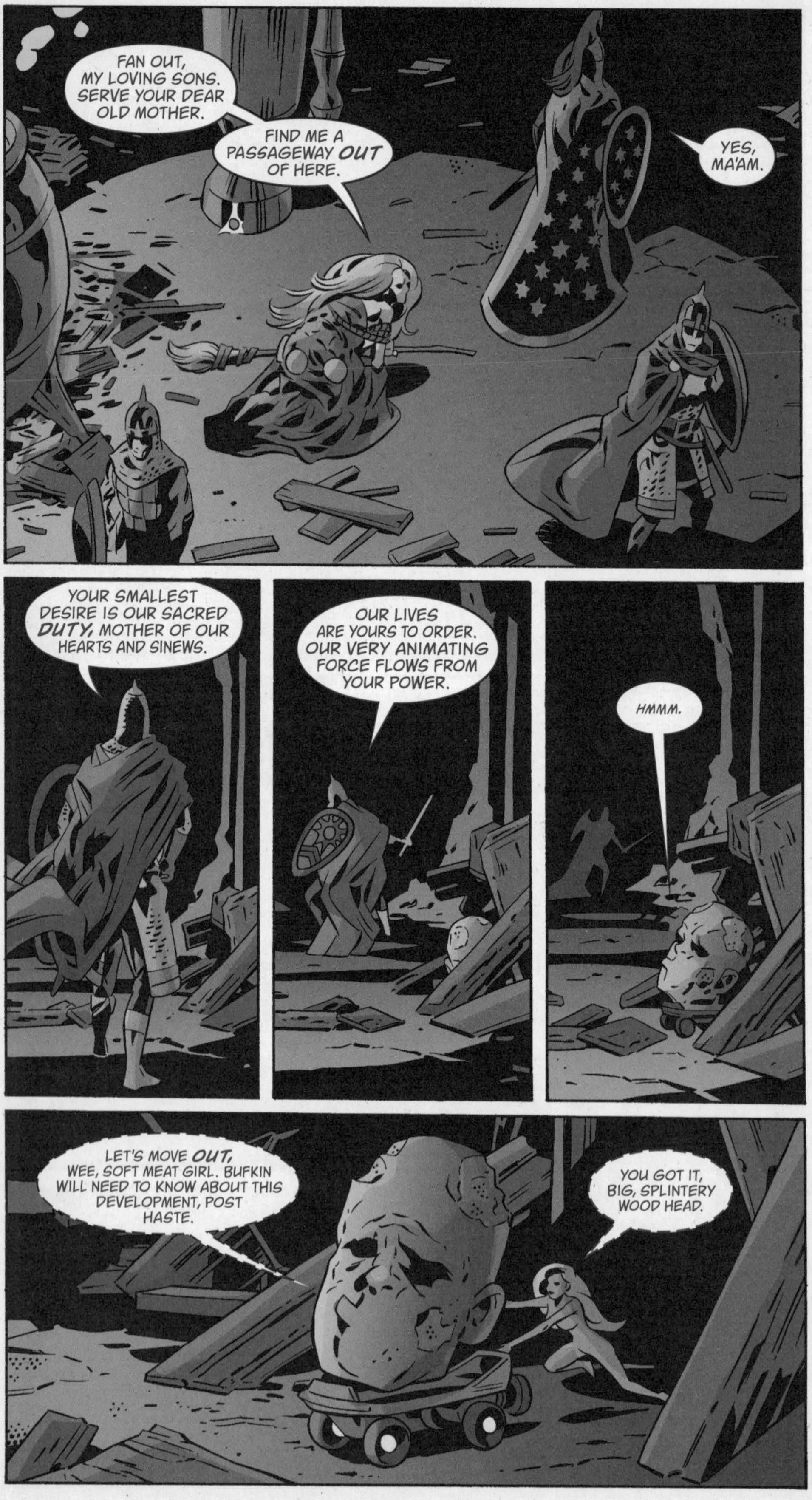

FAN OUT, MY LOVING SONS. SERVE YOUR DEAR OLD MOTHER.
FIND ME A PASSAGEWAY OUT OF HERE.
YES, MA'AM.
YOUR SMALLEST DESIRE IS OUR SACRED DUTY, MOTHER OF OUR HEARTS AND SINEWS.
OUR LIVES ARE YOURS TO ORDER. OUR VERY ANIMATING FORCE FLOWS FROM YOUR POWER.
HMMM.
LET'S MOVE OUT, WEE, SOFT MEAT GIRL. BUFKIN WILL NEED TO KNOW ABOUT THIS DEVELOPMENT, POST HASTE.
YOU GOT IT, BIG, SPLINTERY WOOD HEAD.

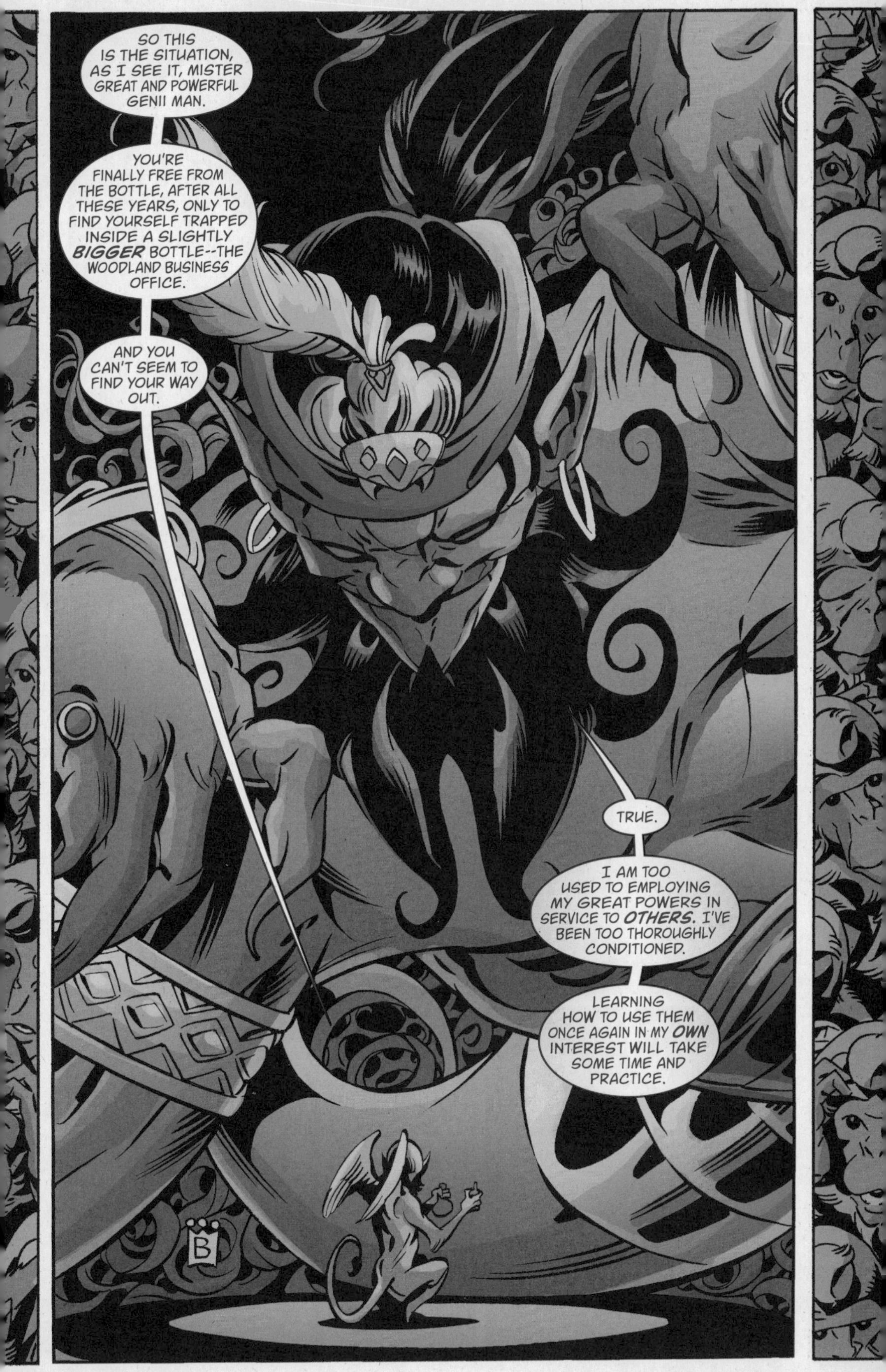

SO THIS IS THE SITUATION, AS I SEE IT, MISTER GREAT AND POWERFUL GENII MAN.
YOU'RE FINALLY FREE FROM THE BOTTLE, AFTER ALL THESE YEARS, ONLY TO FIND YOURSELF TRAPPED INSIDE A SLIGHTLY ***BIGGER*** BOTTLE--THE WOODLAND BUSINESS OFFICE.
AND YOU CAN'T SEEM TO FIND YOUR WAY OUT.
TRUE.
I AM TOO USED TO EMPLOYING MY GREAT POWERS IN SERVICE TO ***OTHERS.*** I'VE BEEN TOO THOROUGHLY CONDITIONED.
LEARNING HOW TO USE THEM ONCE AGAIN IN MY ***OWN*** INTEREST WILL TAKE SOME TIME AND PRACTICE.

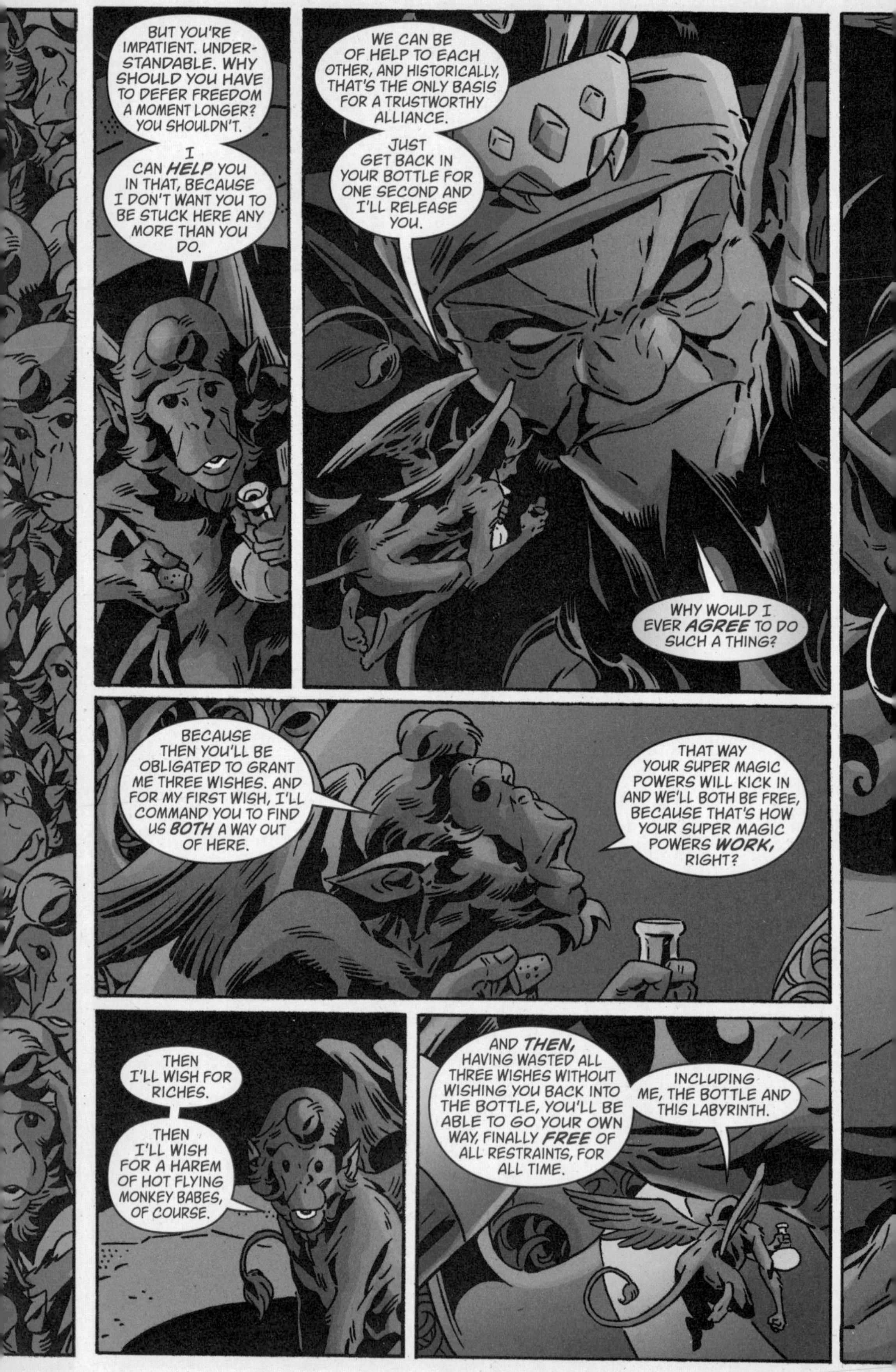

BUT YOU'RE IMPATIENT. UNDERSTANDABLE. WHY SHOULD YOU HAVE TO DEFER FREEDOM A MOMENT LONGER? YOU SHOULDN'T.
I CAN HELP YOU IN THAT, BECAUSE I DON'T WANT YOU TO BE STUCK HERE ANY MORE THAN YOU DO.
WE CAN BE OF HELP TO EACH OTHER, AND HISTORICALLY, THAT'S THE ONLY BASIS FOR A TRUSTWORTHY ALLIANCE.
JUST GET BACK IN YOUR BOTTLE FOR ONE SECOND AND I'LL RELEASE YOU.
WHY WOULD I EVER AGREE TO DO SUCH A THING?
BECAUSE THEN YOU'LL BE OBLIGATED TO GRANT ME THREE WISHES. AND FOR MY FIRST WISH, I'LL COMMAND YOU TO FIND US BOTH A WAY OUT OF HERE.
THAT WAY YOUR SUPER MAGIC POWERS WILL KICK IN AND WE'LL BOTH BE FREE, BECAUSE THAT'S HOW YOUR SUPER MAGIC POWERS WORK, RIGHT?
THEN I'LL WISH FOR RICHES.
THEN I'LL WISH FOR A HAREM OF HOT FLYING MONKEY BABES, OF COURSE.
AND THEN, HAVING WASTED ALL THREE WISHES WITHOUT WISHING YOU BACK INTO THE BOTTLE, YOU'LL BE ABLE TO GO YOUR OWN WAY, FINALLY FREE OF ALL RESTRAINTS, FOR ALL TIME.
INCLUDING ME, THE BOTTLE AND THIS LABYRINTH.

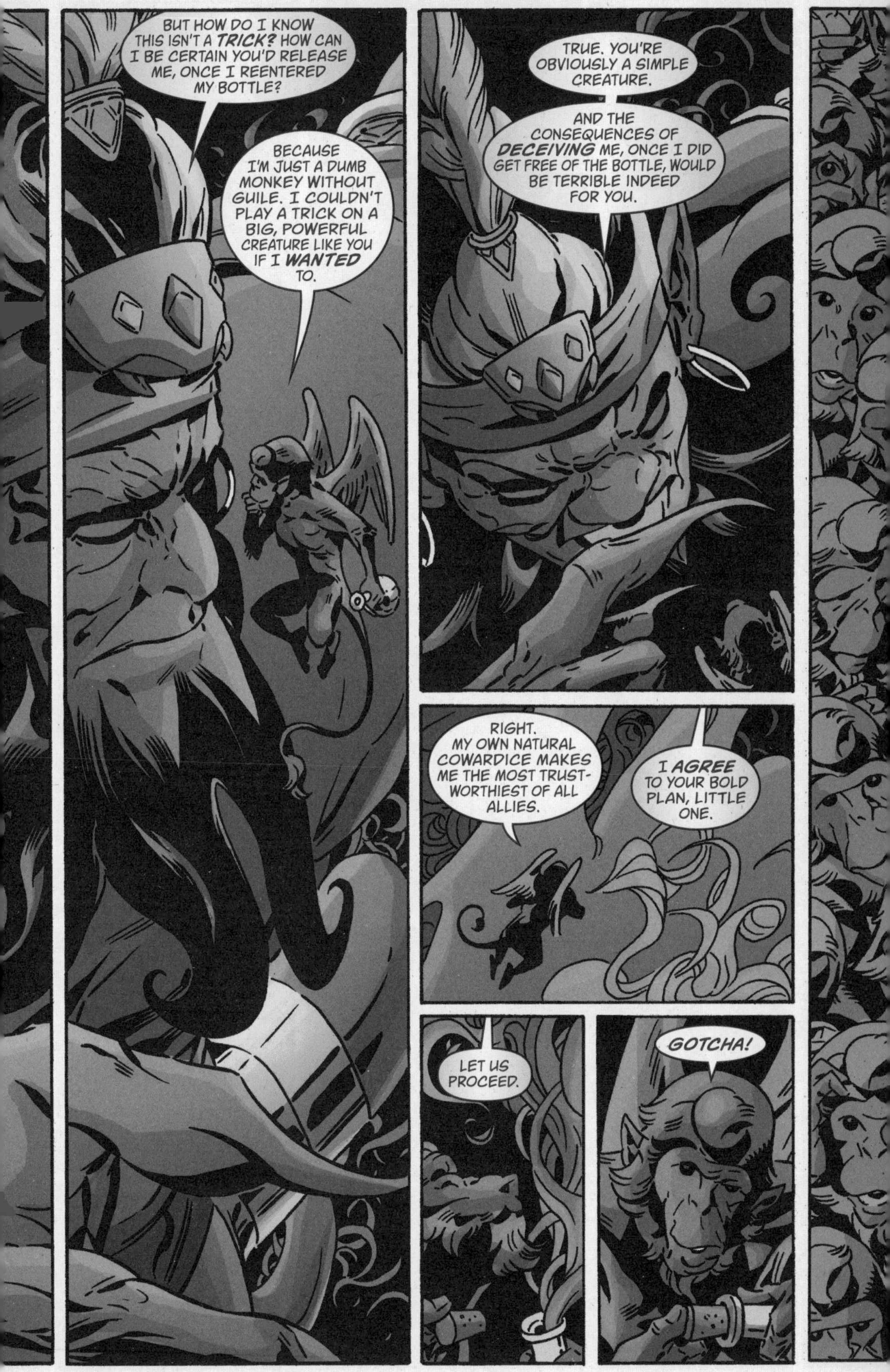
BUT HOW DO I KNOW THIS ISN'T A TRICK? HOW CAN I BE CERTAIN YOU'D RELEASE ME, ONCE I REENTERED MY BOTTLE?
BECAUSE I'M JUST A DUMB MONKEY WITHOUT GUILE. I COULDN'T PLAY A TRICK ON A BIG, POWERFUL CREATURE LIKE YOU IF I WANTED TO.
TRUE. YOU'RE OBVIOUSLY A SIMPLE CREATURE.
AND THE CONSEQUENCES OF DECEIVING ME, ONCE I DID GET FREE OF THE BOTTLE, WOULD BE TERRIBLE INDEED FOR YOU.
RIGHT. MY OWN NATURAL COWARDICE MAKES ME THE MOST TRUST-WORTHIEST OF ALL ALLIES.
I AGREE TO YOUR BOLD PLAN, LITTLE ONE.
LET US PROCEED.
GOTCHA!

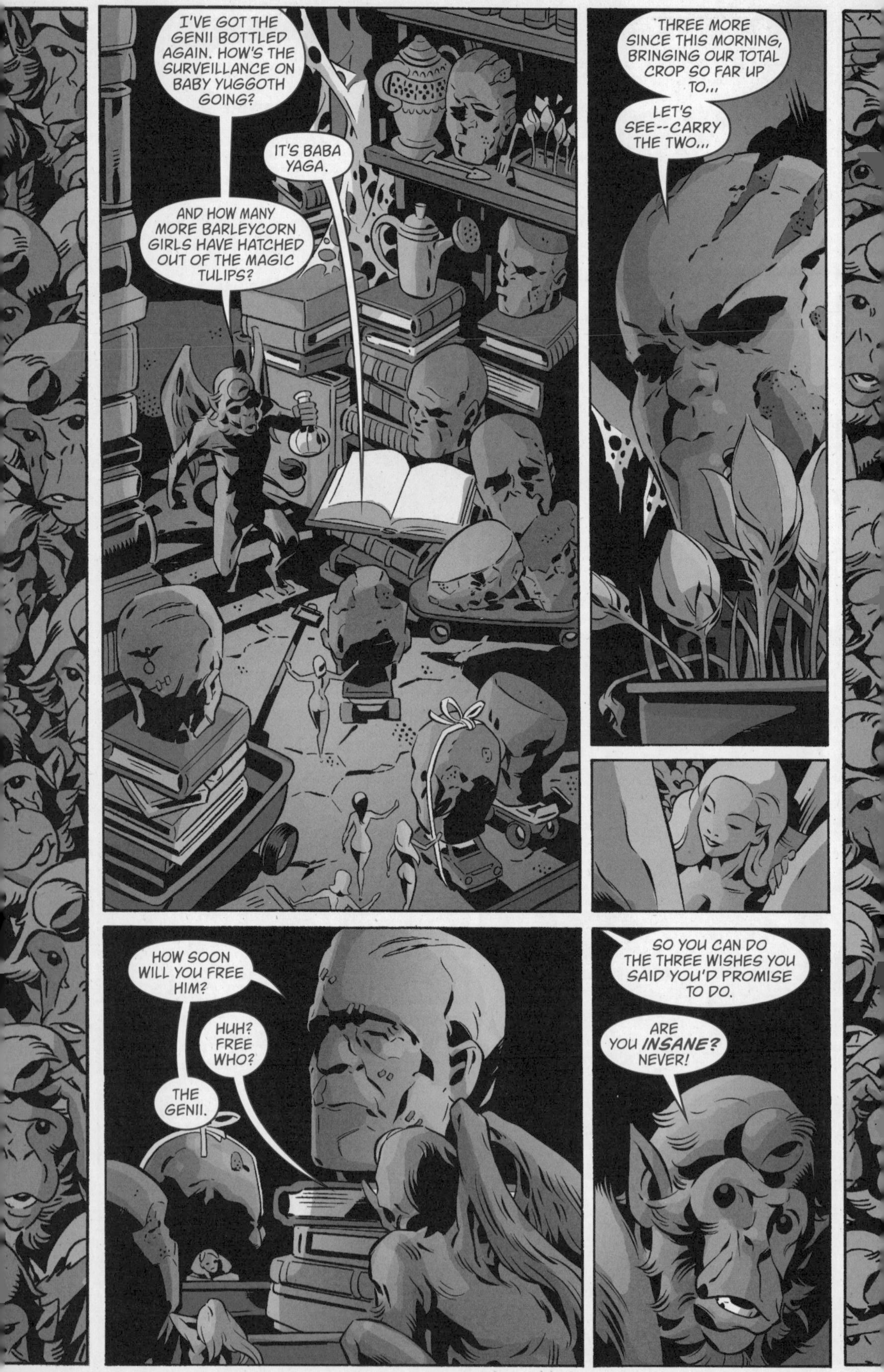

I'VE GOT THE GENII BOTTLED AGAIN. HOW'S THE SURVEILLANCE ON BABY YUGGOTH GOING?
IT'S BABA YAGA.
AND HOW MANY MORE BARLEYCORN GIRLS HAVE HATCHED OUT OF THE MAGIC TULIPS?
THREE MORE SINCE THIS MORNING, BRINGING OUR TOTAL CROP SO FAR UP TO...
LET'S SEE--CARRY THE TWO...
HOW SOON WILL YOU FREE HIM?
HUH? FREE WHO?
THE GENII.
SO YOU CAN DO THE THREE WISHES YOU SAID YOU'D PROMISE TO DO.
ARE YOU *INSANE?* NEVER!

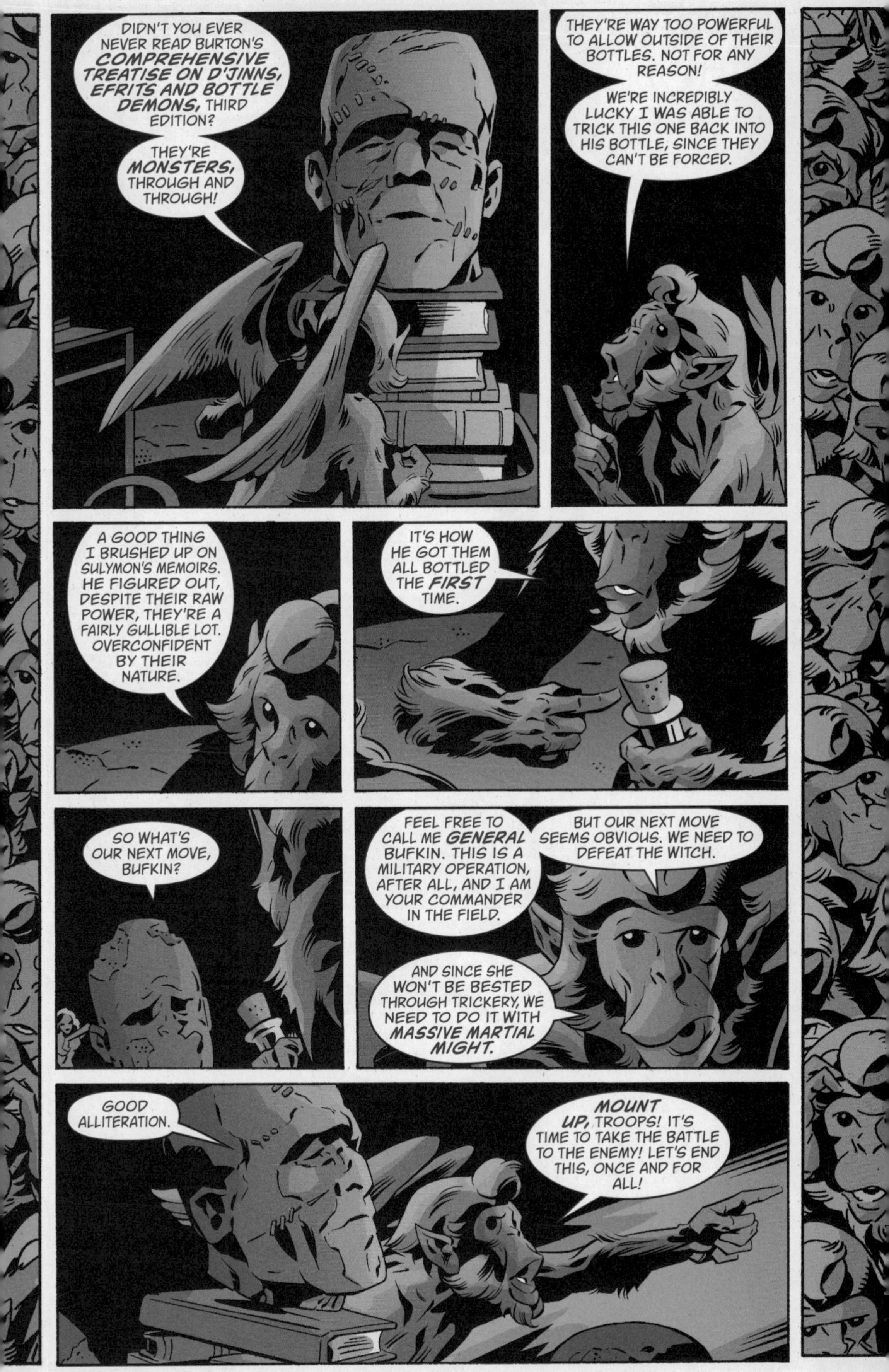

DIDN'T YOU EVER NEVER READ BURTON'S COMPREHENSIVE TREATISE ON D'JINNS, EFRITS AND BOTTLE DEMONS, THIRD EDITION?
THEY'RE MONSTERS, THROUGH AND THROUGH!
THEY'RE WAY TOO POWERFUL TO ALLOW OUTSIDE OF THEIR BOTTLES. NOT FOR ANY REASON!
WE'RE INCREDIBLY LUCKY I WAS ABLE TO TRICK THIS ONE BACK INTO HIS BOTTLE, SINCE THEY CAN'T BE FORCED.
A GOOD THING I BRUSHED UP ON SULYMON'S MEMOIRS. HE FIGURED OUT, DESPITE THEIR RAW POWER, THEY'RE A FAIRLY GULLIBLE LOT. OVERCONFIDENT BY THEIR NATURE.
IT'S HOW HE GOT THEM ALL BOTTLED THE FIRST TIME.
SO WHAT'S OUR NEXT MOVE, BUFKIN?
FEEL FREE TO CALL ME GENERAL BUFKIN. THIS IS A MILITARY OPERATION, AFTER ALL, AND I AM YOUR COMMANDER IN THE FIELD.
BUT OUR NEXT MOVE SEEMS OBVIOUS. WE NEED TO DEFEAT THE WITCH.
AND SINCE SHE WON'T BE BESTED THROUGH TRICKERY, WE NEED TO DO IT WITH MASSIVE MARTIAL MIGHT.
GOOD ALLITERATION.
MOUNT UP, TROOPS! IT'S TIME TO TAKE THE BATTLE TO THE ENEMY! LET'S END THIS, ONCE AND FOR ALL!

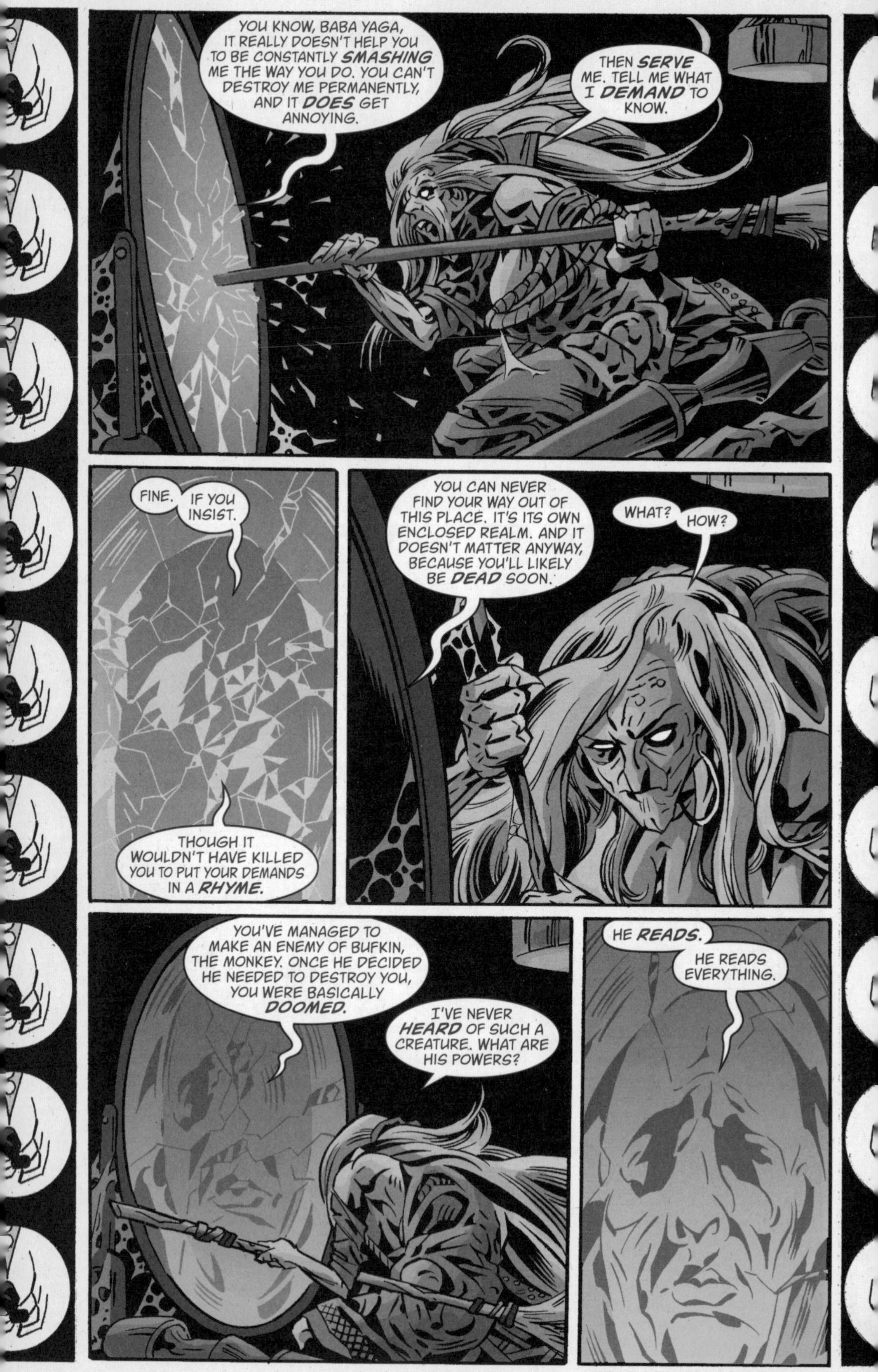
YOU KNOW, BABA YAGA, IT REALLY DOESN'T HELP YOU TO BE CONSTANTLY SMASHING ME THE WAY YOU DO. YOU CAN'T DESTROY ME PERMANENTLY, AND IT DOES GET ANNOYING.
THEN SERVE ME. TELL ME WHAT I DEMAND TO KNOW.
FINE.
IF YOU INSIST.
THOUGH IT WOULDN'T HAVE KILLED YOU TO PUT YOUR DEMANDS IN A RHYME.
YOU CAN NEVER FIND YOUR WAY OUT OF THIS PLACE. IT'S ITS OWN ENCLOSED REALM. AND IT DOESN'T MATTER ANYWAY, BECAUSE YOU'LL LIKELY BE DEAD SOON.
WHAT?
HOW?
YOU'VE MANAGED TO MAKE AN ENEMY OF BUFKIN, THE MONKEY. ONCE HE DECIDED HE NEEDED TO DESTROY YOU, YOU WERE BASICALLY DOOMED.
I'VE NEVER HEARD OF SUCH A CREATURE. WHAT ARE HIS POWERS?
HE READS.
HE READS EVERYTHING.

NEXT: THE WITCH GOES TO WAR!

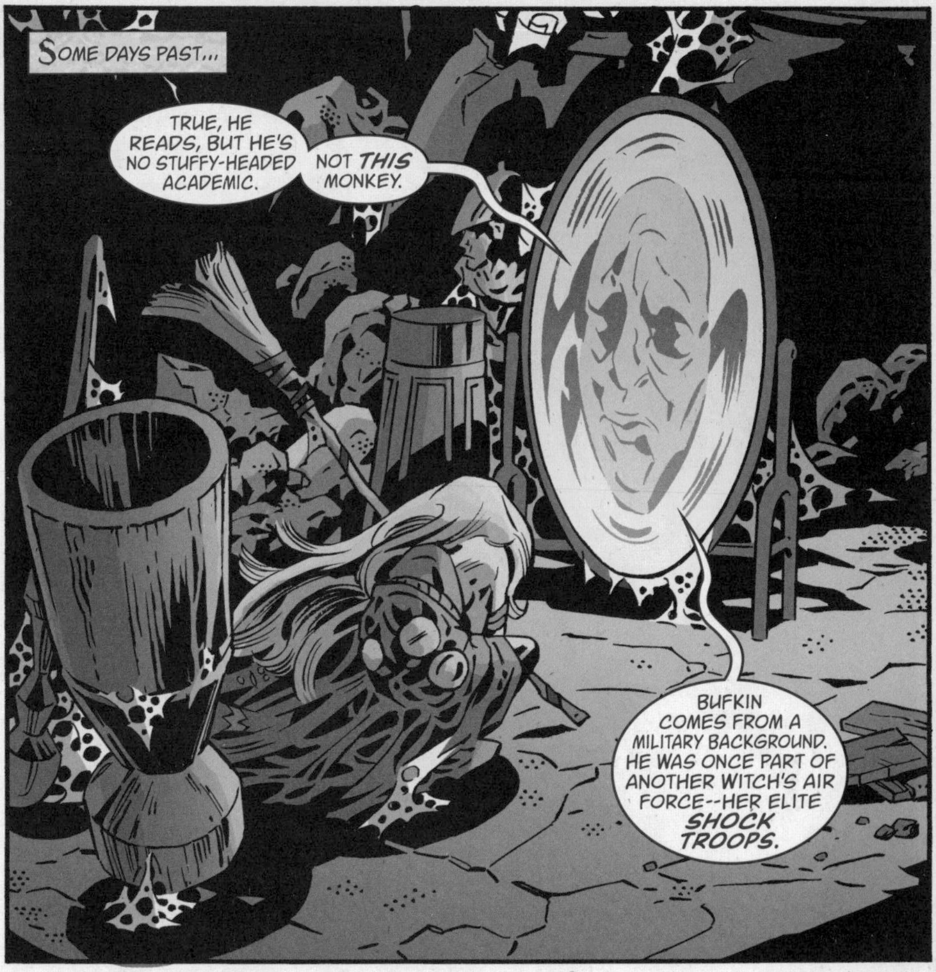
SOME DAYS PAST...
TRUE, HE READS, BUT HE'S NO STUFFY-HEADED ACADEMIC.
NOT THIS MONKEY.
BUFKIN COMES FROM A MILITARY BACKGROUND. HE WAS ONCE PART OF ANOTHER WITCH'S AIR FORCE--HER ELITE SHOCK TROOPS.

OZMA

CHAPTER FOUR OF WITCHES

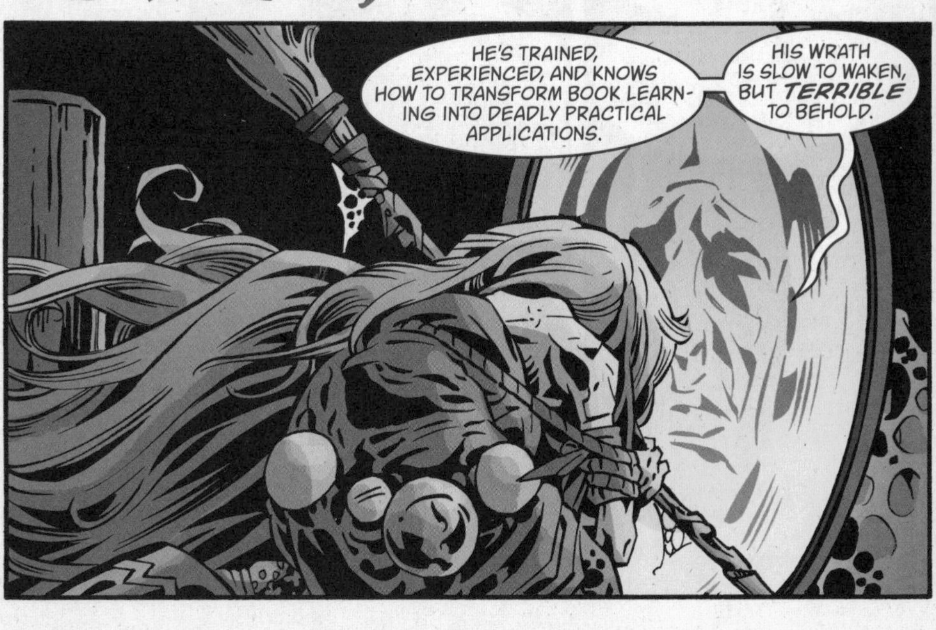
HE'S TRAINED, EXPERIENCED, AND KNOWS HOW TO TRANSFORM BOOK LEARNING INTO DEADLY PRACTICAL APPLICATIONS.
HIS WRATH IS SLOW TO WAKEN, BUT TERRIBLE TO BEHOLD.

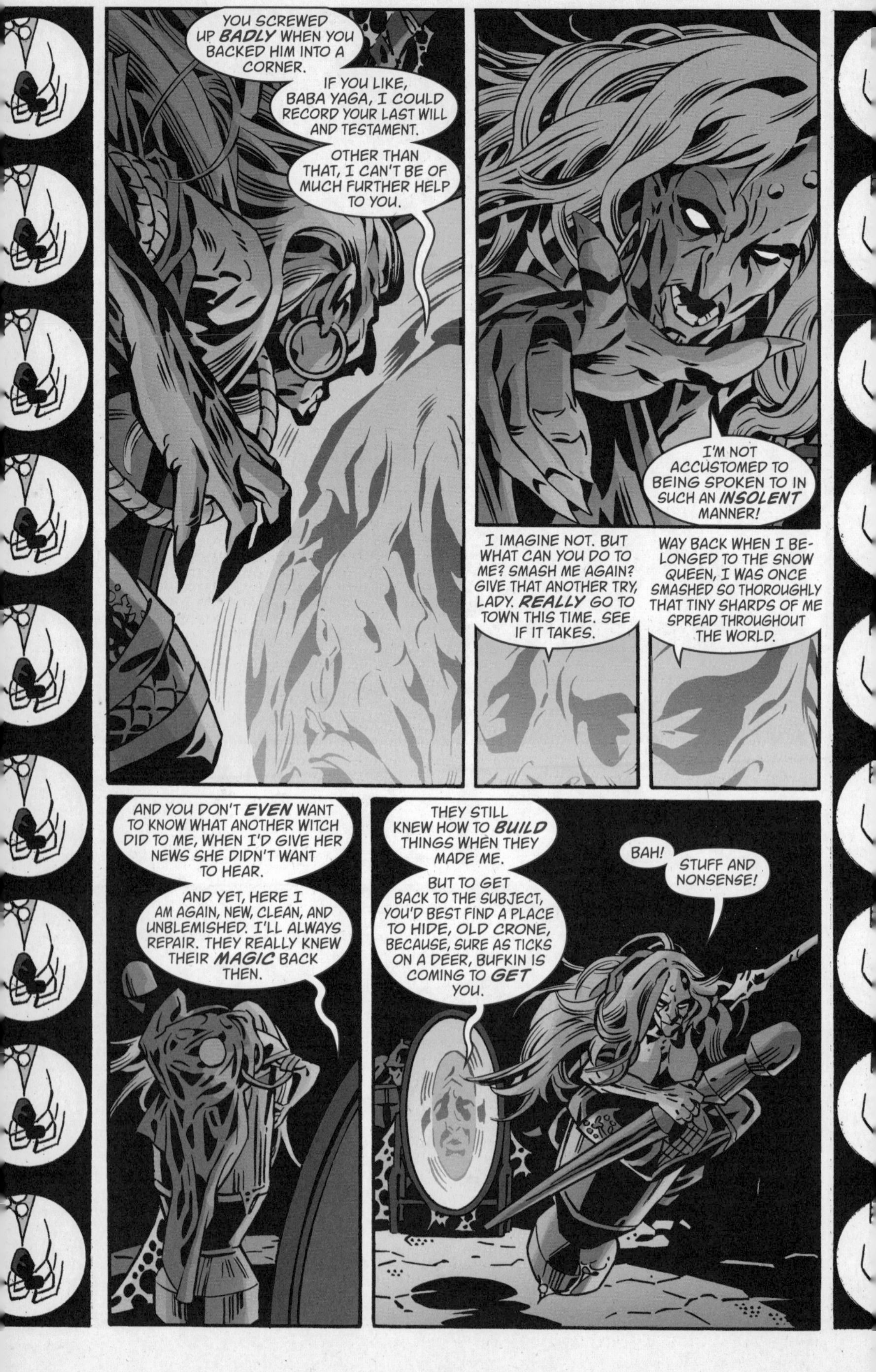

YOU SCREWED UP BADLY WHEN YOU BACKED HIM INTO A CORNER.
IF YOU LIKE, BABA YAGA, I COULD RECORD YOUR LAST WILL AND TESTAMENT.
OTHER THAN THAT, I CAN'T BE OF MUCH FURTHER HELP TO YOU.
I'M NOT ACCUSTOMED TO BEING SPOKEN TO IN SUCH AN INSOLENT MANNER!
I IMAGINE NOT. BUT WHAT CAN YOU DO TO ME? SMASH ME AGAIN? GIVE THAT ANOTHER TRY, LADY. REALLY GO TO TOWN THIS TIME. SEE IF IT TAKES.
WAY BACK WHEN I BE-LONGED TO THE SNOW QUEEN, I WAS ONCE SMASHED SO THOROUGHLY THAT TINY SHARDS OF ME SPREAD THROUGHOUT THE WORLD.
AND YOU DON'T EVEN WANT TO KNOW WHAT ANOTHER WITCH DID TO ME, WHEN I'D GIVE HER NEWS SHE DIDN'T WANT TO HEAR.
AND YET, HERE I AM AGAIN, NEW, CLEAN, AND UNBLEMISHED. I'LL ALWAYS REPAIR. THEY REALLY KNEW THEIR MAGIC BACK THEN.
THEY STILL KNEW HOW TO BUILD THINGS WHEN THEY MADE ME.
BUT TO GET BACK TO THE SUBJECT, YOU'D BEST FIND A PLACE TO HIDE, OLD CRONE, BECAUSE, SURE AS TICKS ON A DEER, BUFKIN IS COMING TO GET YOU.
BAH!
STUFF AND NONSENSE!

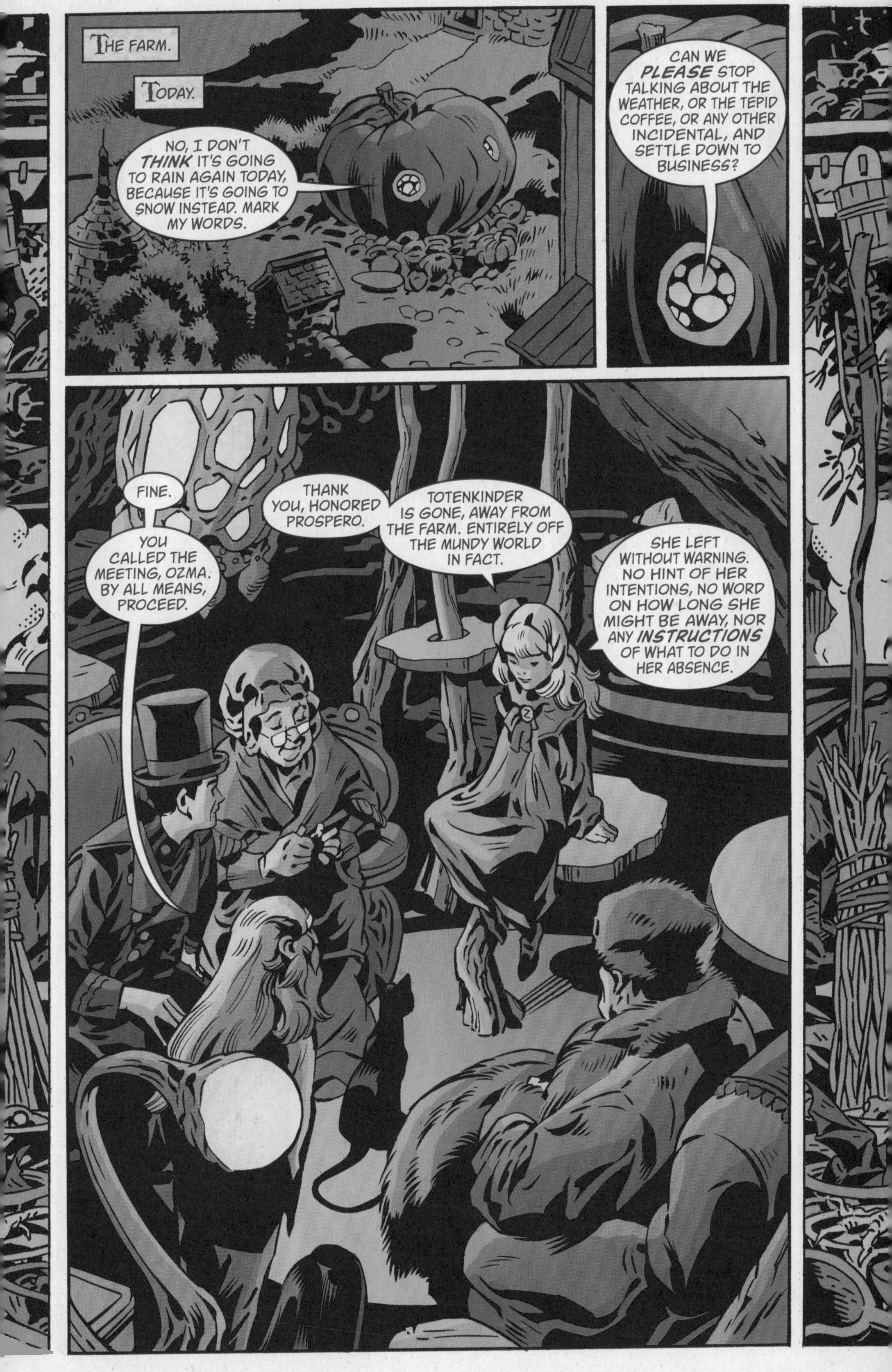
THE FARM.
TODAY.
NO, I DON'T THINK IT'S GOING TO RAIN AGAIN TODAY, BECAUSE IT'S GOING TO SNOW INSTEAD. MARK MY WORDS.
CAN WE PLEASE STOP TALKING ABOUT THE WEATHER, OR THE TEPID COFFEE, OR ANY OTHER INCIDENTAL, AND SETTLE DOWN TO BUSINESS?
FINE.
YOU CALLED THE MEETING, OZMA. BY ALL MEANS, PROCEED.
THANK YOU, HONORED PROSPERO.
TOTENKINDER IS GONE, AWAY FROM THE FARM. ENTIRELY OFF THE MUNDY WORLD IN FACT.
SHE LEFT WITHOUT WARNING. NO HINT OF HER INTENTIONS, NO WORD ON HOW LONG SHE MIGHT BE AWAY, NOR ANY INSTRUCTIONS OF WHAT TO DO IN HER ABSENCE.

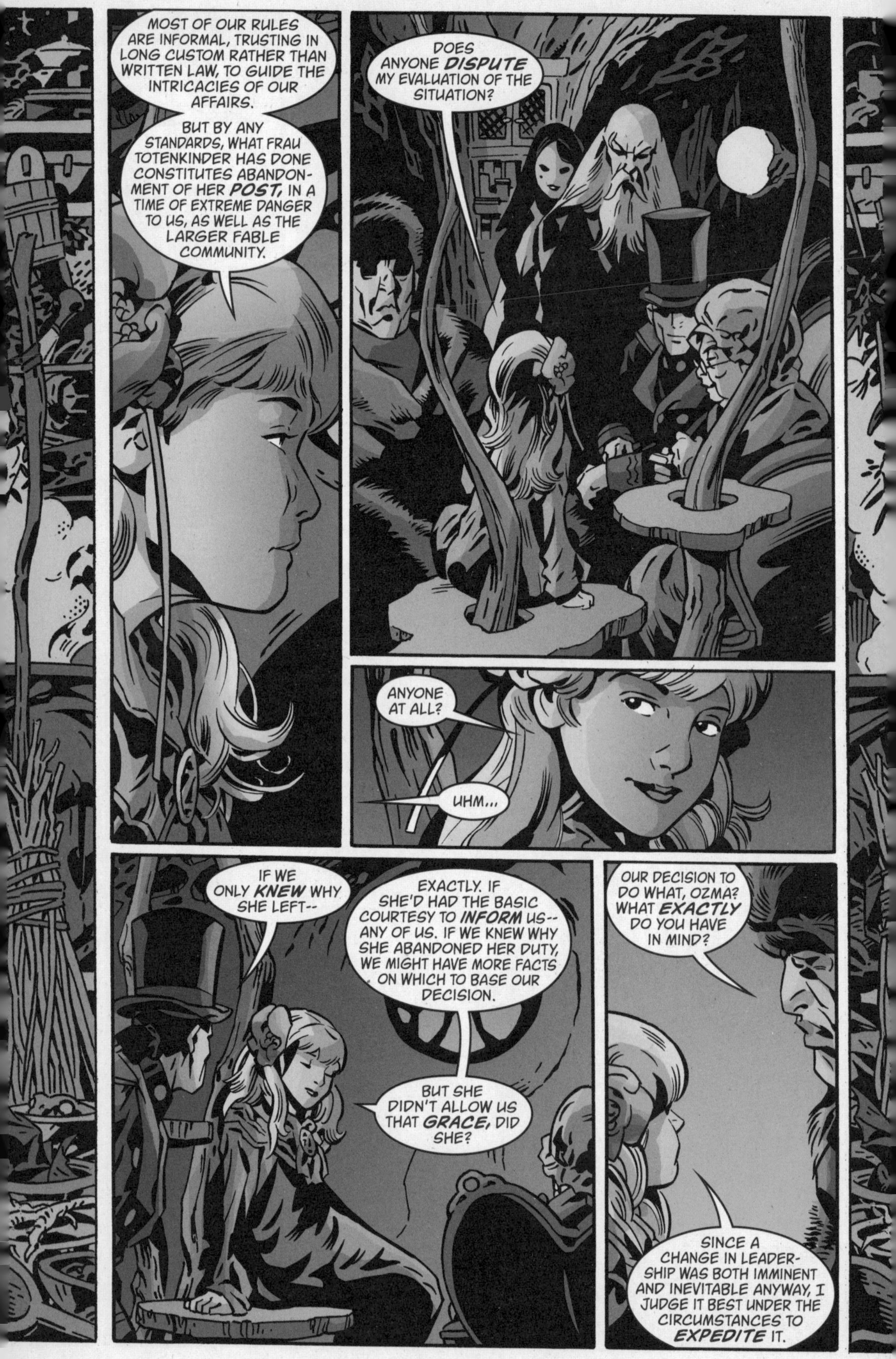

MOST OF OUR RULES ARE INFORMAL, TRUSTING IN LONG CUSTOM RATHER THAN WRITTEN LAW, TO GUIDE THE INTRICACIES OF OUR AFFAIRS.
BUT BY ANY STANDARDS, WHAT FRAU TOTENKINDER HAS DONE CONSTITUTES ABANDONMENT OF HER POST, IN A TIME OF EXTREME DANGER TO US, AS WELL AS THE LARGER FABLE COMMUNITY.
DOES ANYONE DISPUTE MY EVALUATION OF THE SITUATION?
ANYONE AT ALL?
UHM...
IF WE ONLY KNEW WHY SHE LEFT--
EXACTLY. IF SHE'D HAD THE BASIC COURTESY TO INFORM US--ANY OF US. IF WE KNEW WHY SHE ABANDONED HER DUTY, WE MIGHT HAVE MORE FACTS ON WHICH TO BASE OUR DECISION.
BUT SHE DIDN'T ALLOW US THAT GRACE, DID SHE?
OUR DECISION TO DO WHAT, OZMA? WHAT EXACTLY DO YOU HAVE IN MIND?
SINCE A CHANGE IN LEADERSHIP WAS BOTH IMMINENT AND INEVITABLE ANYWAY, I JUDGE IT BEST UNDER THE CIRCUMSTANCES TO EXPEDITE IT.

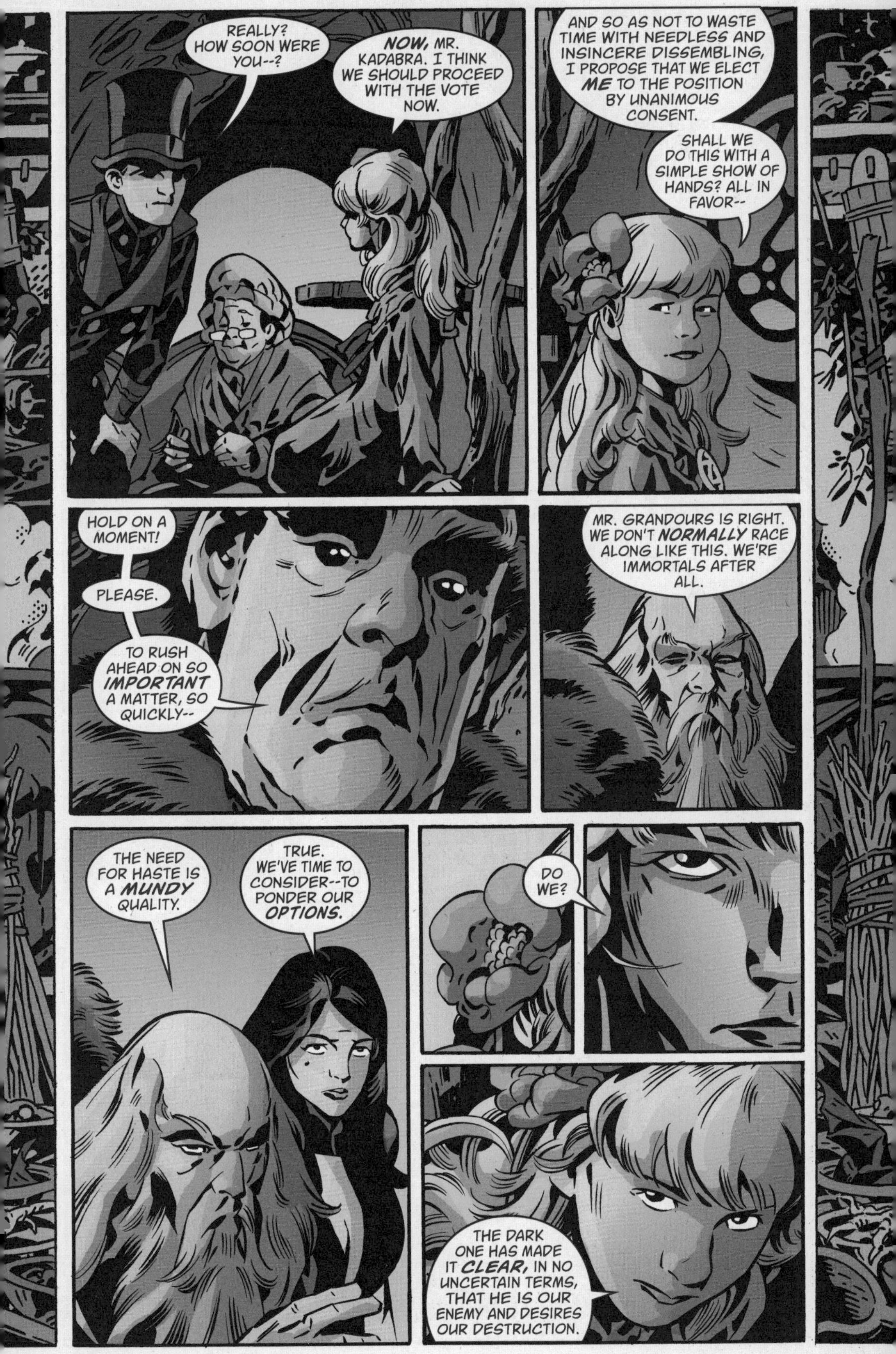

REALLY? HOW SOON WERE YOU--?
NOW, MR. KADABRA. I THINK WE SHOULD PROCEED WITH THE VOTE NOW.
AND SO AS NOT TO WASTE TIME WITH NEEDLESS AND INSINCERE DISSEMBLING, I PROPOSE THAT WE ELECT ME TO THE POSITION BY UNANIMOUS CONSENT.
SHALL WE DO THIS WITH A SIMPLE SHOW OF HANDS? ALL IN FAVOR--
HOLD ON A MOMENT!
PLEASE.
TO RUSH AHEAD ON SO IMPORTANT A MATTER, SO QUICKLY--
MR. GRANDOURS IS RIGHT. WE DON'T NORMALLY RACE ALONG LIKE THIS. WE'RE IMMORTALS AFTER ALL.
THE NEED FOR HASTE IS A MUNDY QUALITY.
TRUE. WE'VE TIME TO CONSIDER--TO PONDER OUR OPTIONS.
DO WE?
THE DARK ONE HAS MADE IT CLEAR, IN NO UNCERTAIN TERMS, THAT HE IS OUR ENEMY AND DESIRES OUR DESTRUCTION.

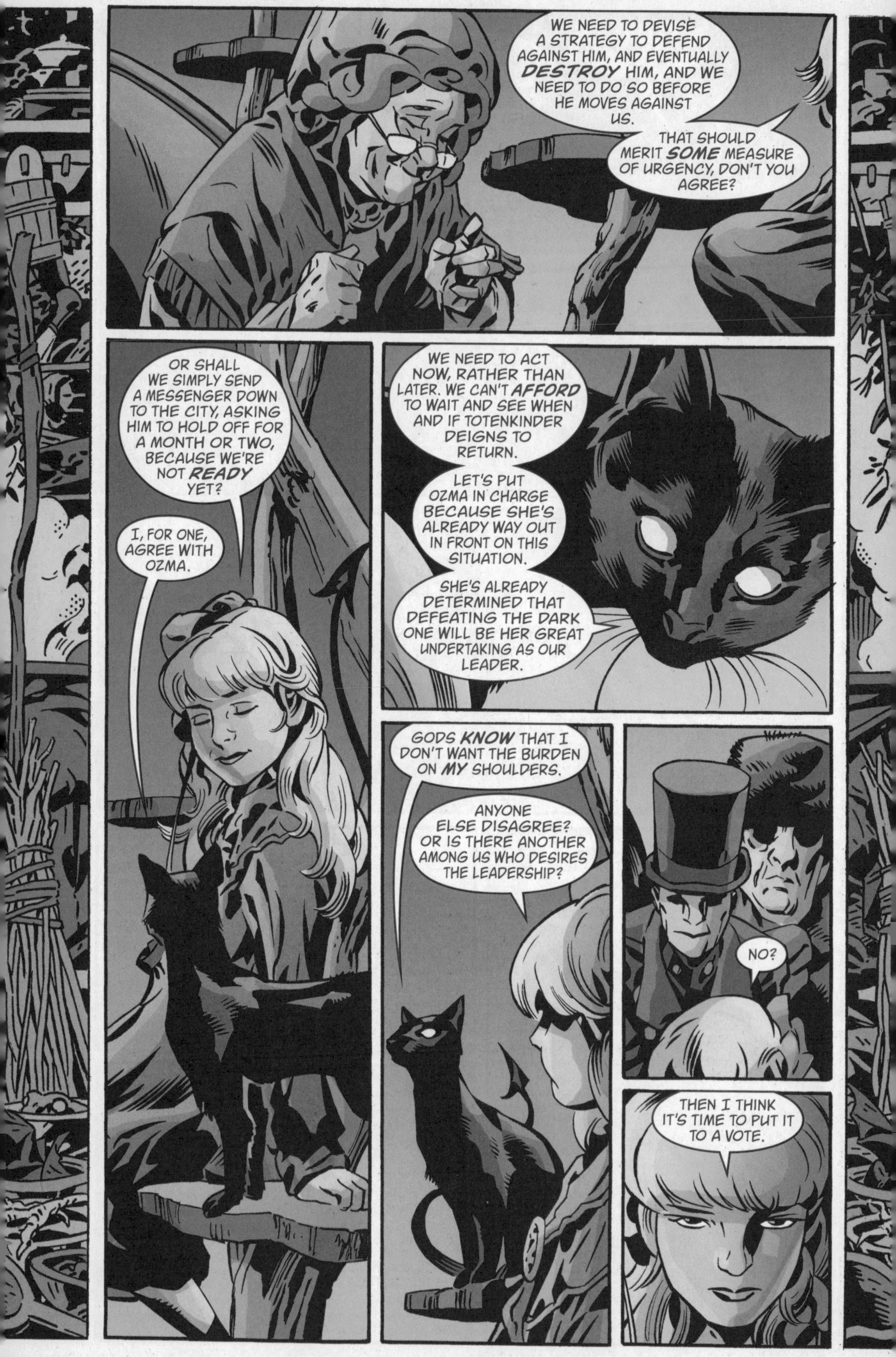
WE NEED TO DEVISE A STRATEGY TO DEFEND AGAINST HIM, AND EVENTUALLY DESTROY HIM, AND WE NEED TO DO SO BEFORE HE MOVES AGAINST US.
THAT SHOULD MERIT SOME MEASURE OF URGENCY, DON'T YOU AGREE?
OR SHALL WE SIMPLY SEND A MESSENGER DOWN TO THE CITY, ASKING HIM TO HOLD OFF FOR A MONTH OR TWO, BECAUSE WE'RE NOT READY YET?
I, FOR ONE, AGREE WITH OZMA.
WE NEED TO ACT NOW, RATHER THAN LATER. WE CAN'T AFFORD TO WAIT AND SEE WHEN AND IF TOTENKINDER DEIGNS TO RETURN.
LET'S PUT OZMA IN CHARGE BECAUSE SHE'S ALREADY WAY OUT IN FRONT ON THIS SITUATION.
SHE'S ALREADY DETERMINED THAT DEFEATING THE DARK ONE WILL BE HER GREAT UNDERTAKING AS OUR LEADER.
GODS KNOW THAT I DON'T WANT THE BURDEN ON MY SHOULDERS.
ANYONE ELSE DISAGREE? OR IS THERE ANOTHER AMONG US WHO DESIRES THE LEADERSHIP?
NO?
THEN I THINK IT'S TIME TO PUT IT TO A VOTE.

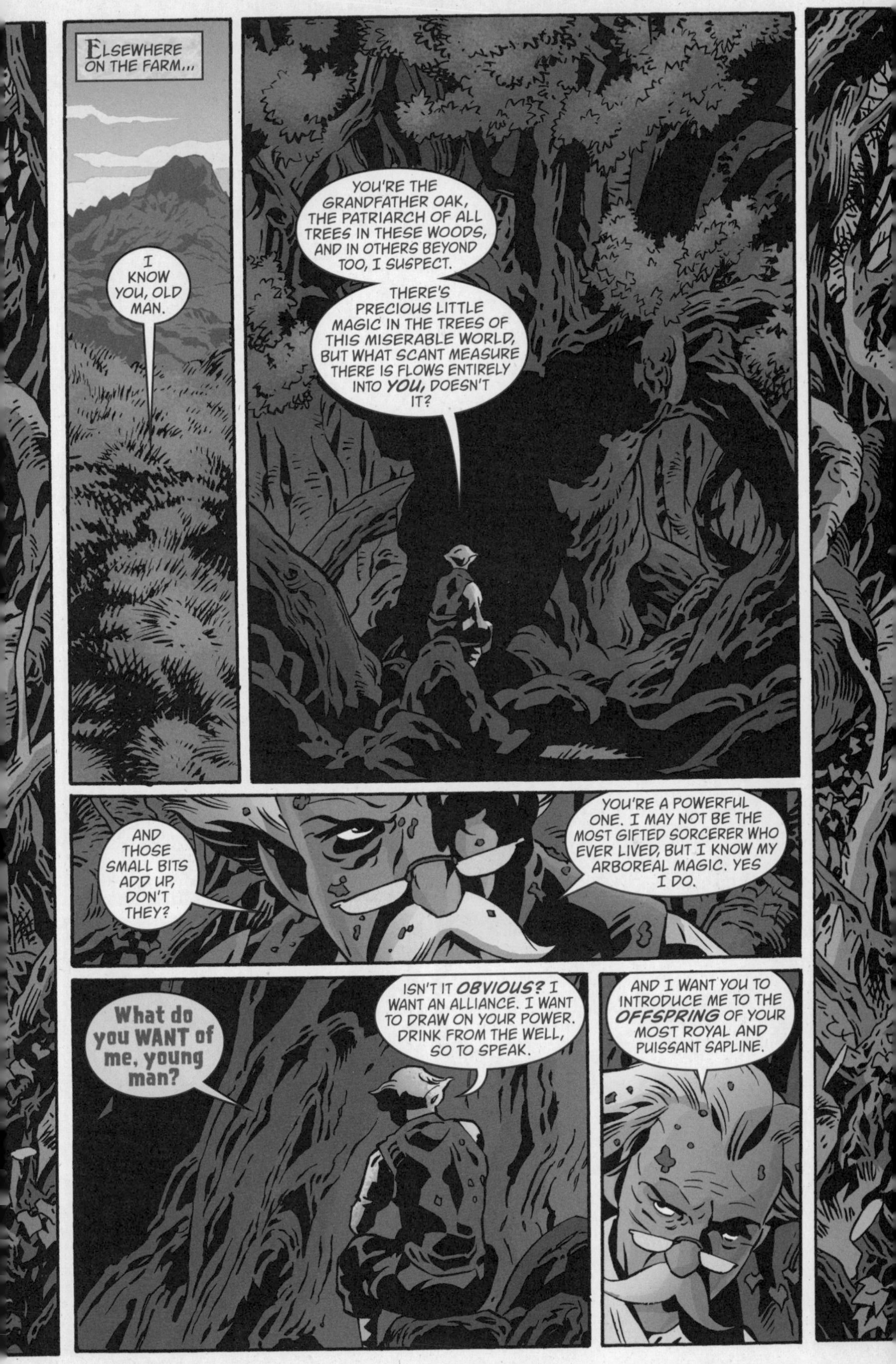
ELSEWHERE ON THE FARM...
I KNOW YOU, OLD MAN.
YOU'RE THE GRANDFATHER OAK, THE PATRIARCH OF ALL TREES IN THESE WOODS, AND IN OTHERS BEYOND TOO, I SUSPECT.
THERE'S PRECIOUS LITTLE MAGIC IN THE TREES OF THIS MISERABLE WORLD, BUT WHAT SCANT MEASURE THERE IS FLOWS ENTIRELY INTO YOU, DOESN'T IT?
AND THOSE SMALL BITS ADD UP, DON'T THEY?
YOU'RE A POWERFUL ONE. I MAY NOT BE THE MOST GIFTED SORCERER WHO EVER LIVED, BUT I KNOW MY ARBOREAL MAGIC. YES I DO.
What do you WANT of me, young man?
ISN'T IT OBVIOUS? I WANT AN ALLIANCE. I WANT TO DRAW ON YOUR POWER. DRINK FROM THE WELL, SO TO SPEAK.
AND I WANT YOU TO INTRODUCE ME TO THE OFFSPRING OF YOUR MOST ROYAL AND PUISSANT SAPLINE.

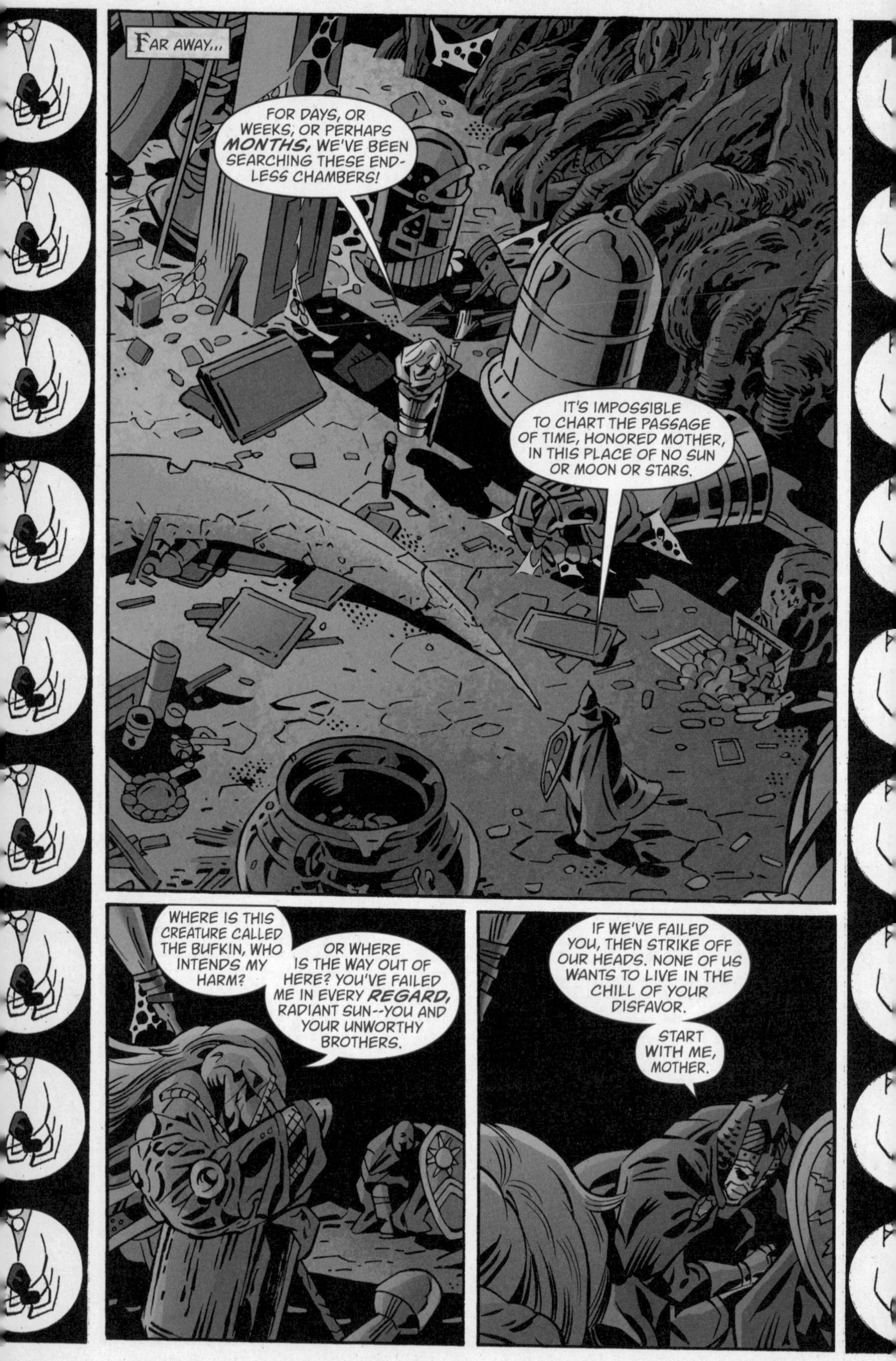
FAR AWAY...
FOR DAYS, OR WEEKS, OR PERHAPS MONTHS, WE'VE BEEN SEARCHING THESE END-LESS CHAMBERS!
IT'S IMPOSSIBLE TO CHART THE PASSAGE OF TIME, HONORED MOTHER, IN THIS PLACE OF NO SUN OR MOON OR STARS.
WHERE IS THIS CREATURE CALLED THE BUFKIN, WHO INTENDS MY HARM?
OR WHERE IS THE WAY OUT OF HERE? YOU'VE FAILED ME IN EVERY REGARD, RADIANT SUN--YOU AND YOUR UNWORTHY BROTHERS.
IF WE'VE FAILED YOU, THEN STRIKE OFF OUR HEADS. NONE OF US WANTS TO LIVE IN THE CHILL OF YOUR DISFAVOR.
START WITH ME, MOTHER.

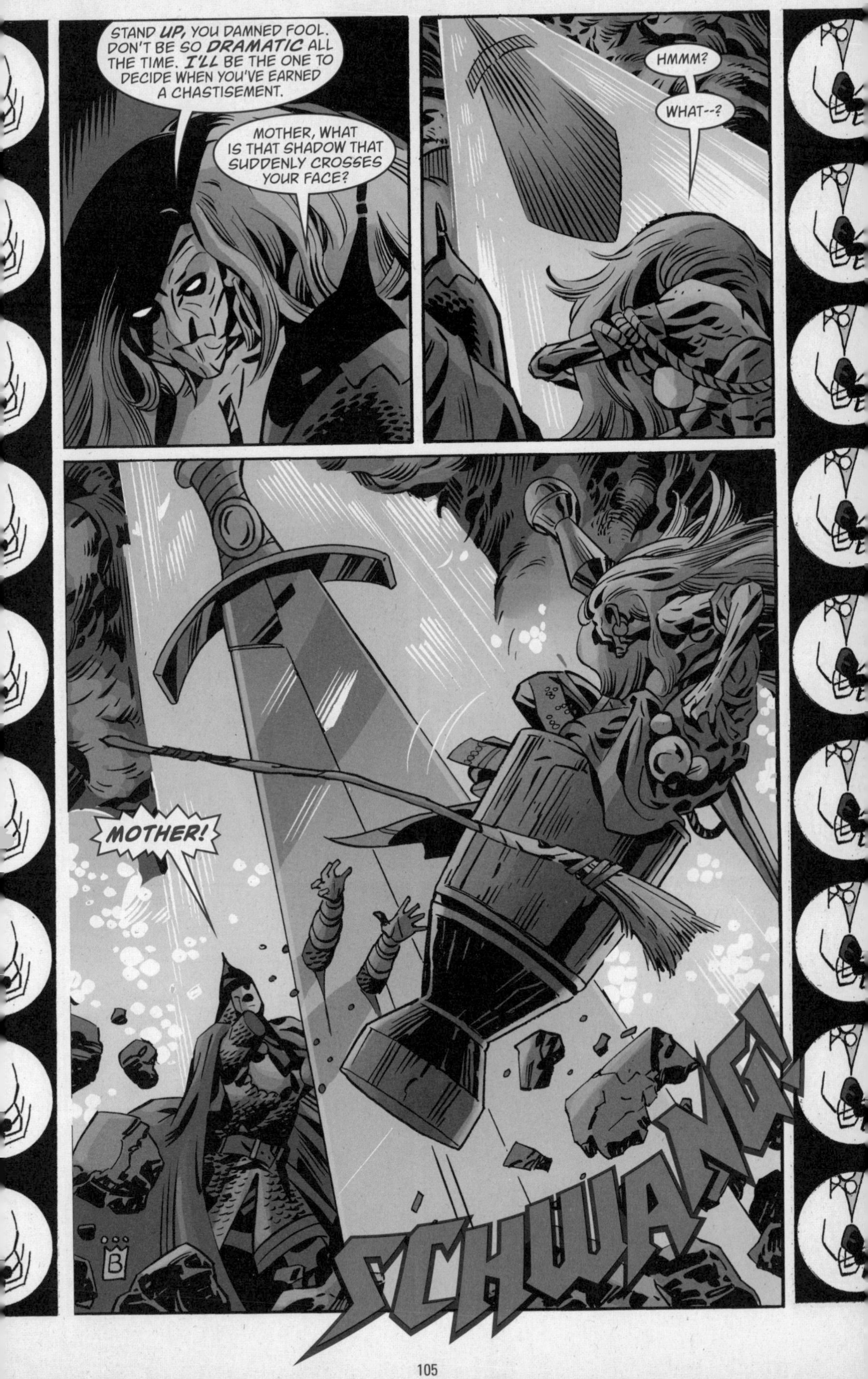
STAND UP, YOU DAMNED FOOL. DON'T BE SO DRAMATIC ALL THE TIME. I'LL BE THE ONE TO DECIDE WHEN YOU'VE EARNED A CHASTISEMENT.
MOTHER, WHAT IS THAT SHADOW THAT SUDDENLY CROSSES YOUR FACE?
HMMM?
WHAT--?
MOTHER!
SCHWANG!

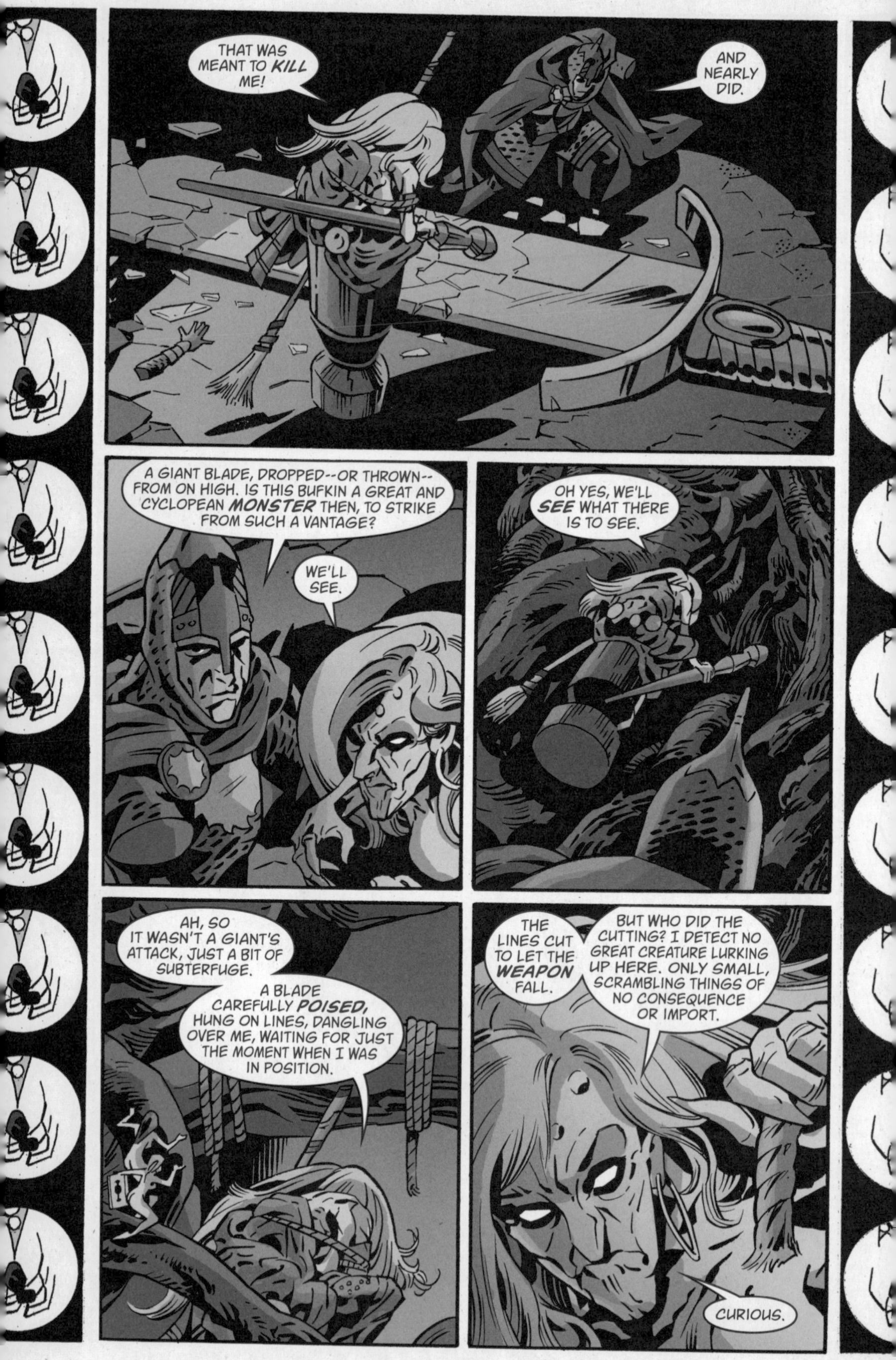
THAT WAS MEANT TO KILL ME!
AND NEARLY DID.
A GIANT BLADE, DROPPED--OR THROWN--FROM ON HIGH. IS THIS BUFKIN A GREAT AND CYCLOPEAN MONSTER THEN, TO STRIKE FROM SUCH A VANTAGE?
WE'LL SEE.
OH YES, WE'LL SEE WHAT THERE IS TO SEE.
AH, SO IT WASN'T A GIANT'S ATTACK, JUST A BIT OF SUBTERFUGE.
A BLADE CAREFULLY POISED, HUNG ON LINES, DANGLING OVER ME, WAITING FOR JUST THE MOMENT WHEN I WAS IN POSITION.
THE LINES CUT TO LET THE WEAPON FALL.
BUT WHO DID THE CUTTING? I DETECT NO GREAT CREATURE LURKING UP HERE. ONLY SMALL, SCRAMBLING THINGS OF NO CONSEQUENCE OR IMPORT.
CURIOUS.

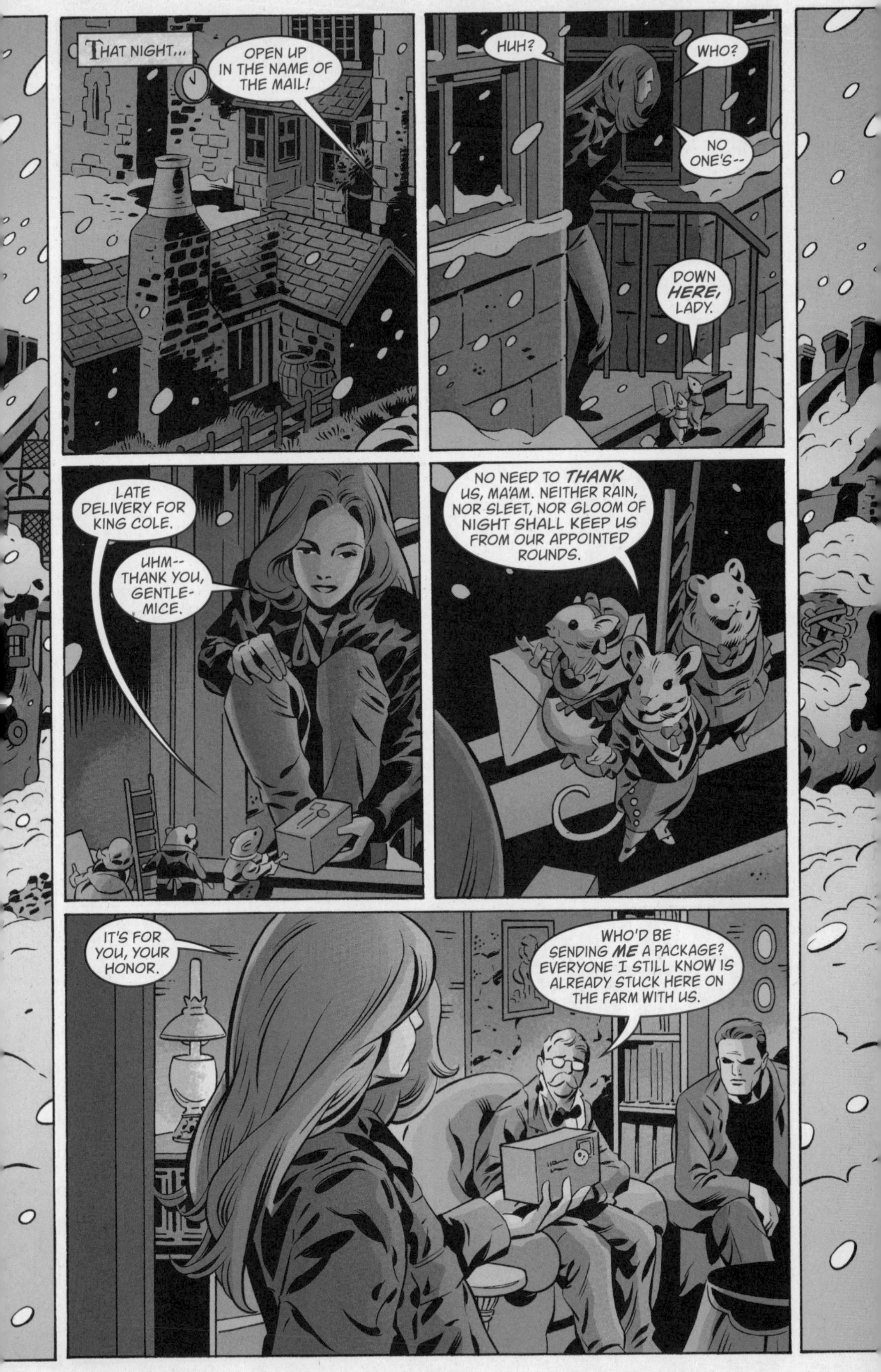
THAT NIGHT...
OPEN UP IN THE NAME OF THE MAIL!
HUH?
WHO?
NO ONE'S--
DOWN HERE, LADY.
LATE DELIVERY FOR KING COLE.
UHM-- THANK YOU, GENTLE-MICE.
NO NEED TO THANK US, MA'AM. NEITHER RAIN, NOR SLEET, NOR GLOOM OF NIGHT SHALL KEEP US FROM OUR APPOINTED ROUNDS.
IT'S FOR YOU, YOUR HONOR.
WHO'D BE SENDING ME A PACKAGE? EVERYONE I STILL KNOW IS ALREADY STUCK HERE ON THE FARM WITH US.

NO RETURN ADDRESS.

CURIOUS.

A TINY COIN PURSE?

OH, GOOD. THERE'S A *NOTE* AT LEAST.

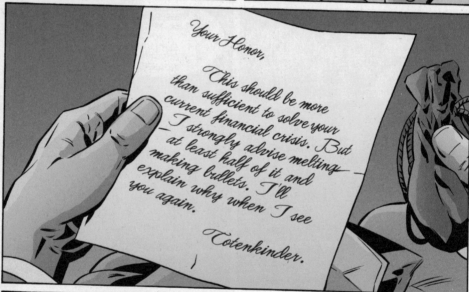

Your Honor,

This should be more than sufficient to solve your current financial crisis. But I strongly advise melting—at least half of it and making bullets. I'll explain why when I see you again.

Totenkinder.

WHAT DID THE NOTE *SAY?*

WHAT'S IN THE PURSE?

HOLD ON, I--

A COIN OF *GOLD!*

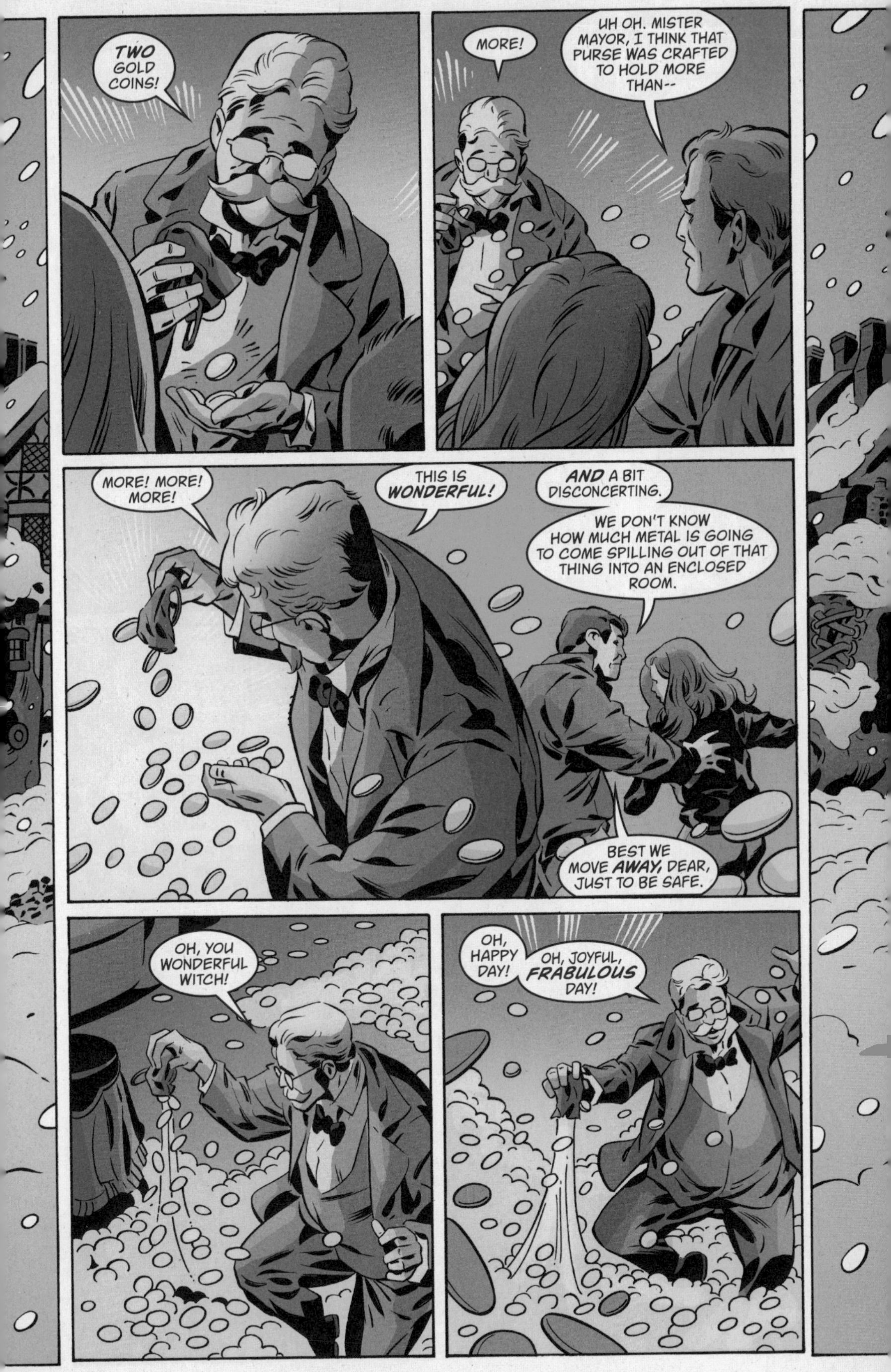
TWO GOLD COINS!
MORE!
UH OH. MISTER MAYOR, I THINK THAT PURSE WAS CRAFTED TO HOLD MORE THAN--
MORE! MORE! MORE!
THIS IS WONDERFUL!
AND A BIT DISCONCERTING.
WE DON'T KNOW HOW MUCH METAL IS GOING TO COME SPILLING OUT OF THAT THING INTO AN ENCLOSED ROOM.
BEST WE MOVE AWAY, DEAR, JUST TO BE SAFE.
OH, YOU WONDERFUL WITCH!
OH, HAPPY DAY!
OH, JOYFUL, FRABULOUS DAY!

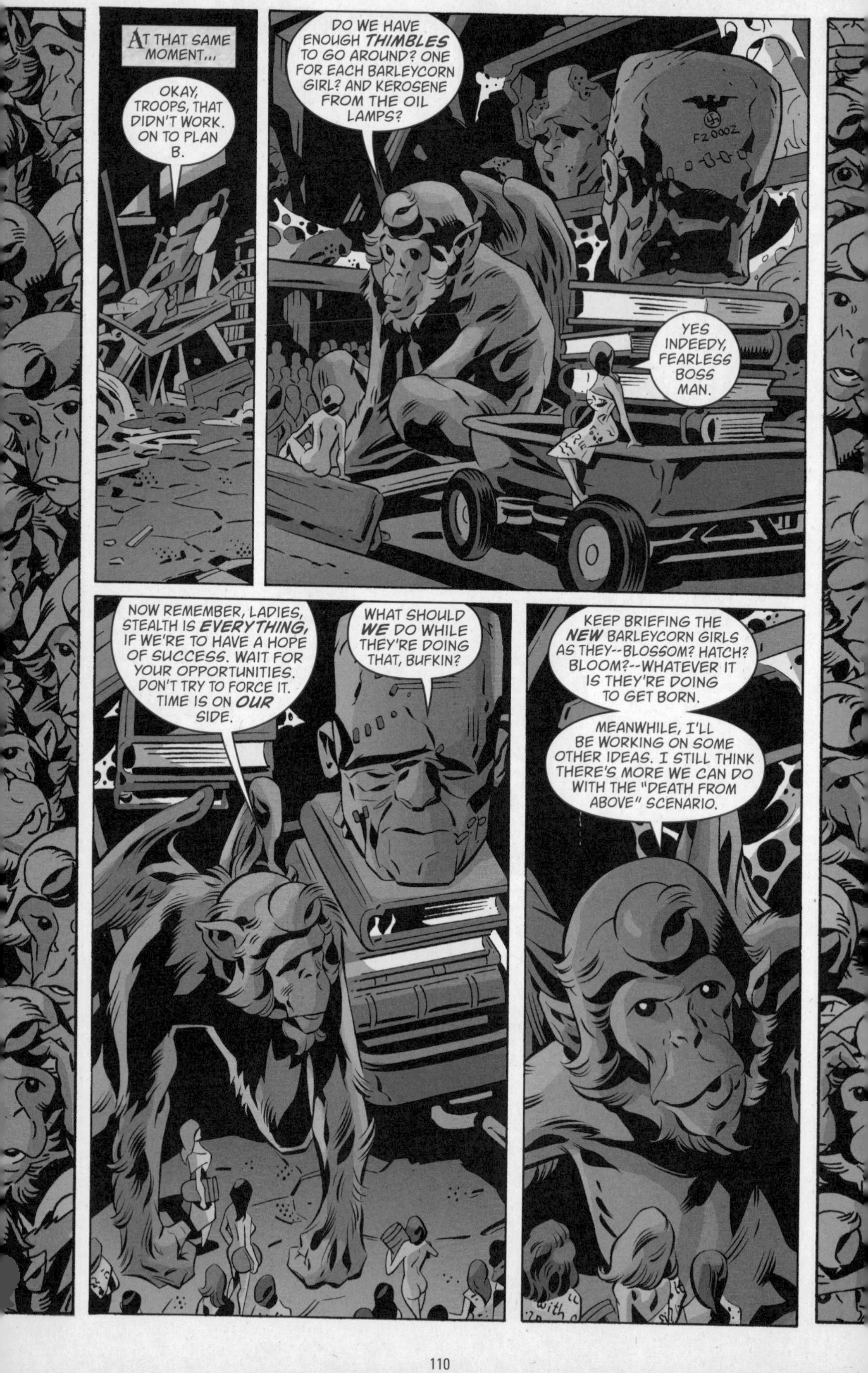

AT THAT SAME MOMENT...
OKAY, TROOPS, THAT DIDN'T WORK. ON TO PLAN B.
DO WE HAVE ENOUGH *THIMBLES* TO GO AROUND? ONE FOR EACH BARLEYCORN GIRL? AND KEROSENE FROM THE OIL LAMPS?
F20002
YES INDEEDY, FEARLESS BOSS MAN.
NOW REMEMBER, LADIES, STEALTH IS *EVERYTHING,* IF WE'RE TO HAVE A HOPE OF SUCCESS. WAIT FOR YOUR OPPORTUNITIES. DON'T TRY TO FORCE IT. TIME IS ON *OUR* SIDE.
WHAT SHOULD *WE* DO WHILE THEY'RE DOING THAT, BUFKIN?
KEEP BRIEFING THE *NEW* BARLEYCORN GIRLS AS THEY--BLOSSOM? HATCH? BLOOM?--WHATEVER IT IS THEY'RE DOING TO GET BORN.
MEANWHILE, I'LL BE WORKING ON SOME OTHER IDEAS. I STILL THINK THERE'S MORE WE CAN DO WITH THE "DEATH FROM ABOVE" SCENARIO.

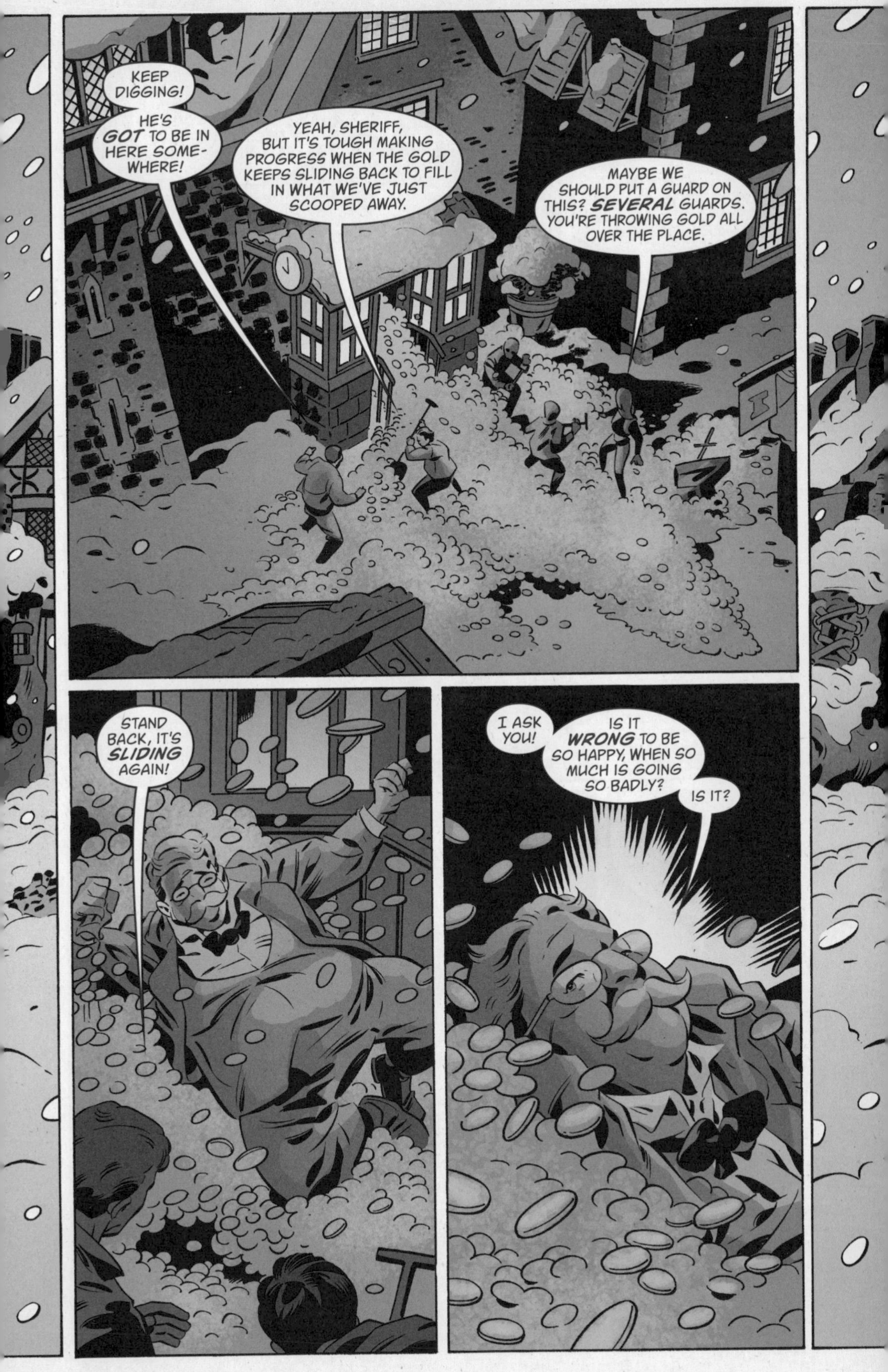
KEEP DIGGING!
HE'S GOT TO BE IN HERE SOME-WHERE!
YEAH, SHERIFF, BUT IT'S TOUGH MAKING PROGRESS WHEN THE GOLD KEEPS SLIDING BACK TO FILL IN WHAT WE'VE JUST SCOOPED AWAY.
MAYBE WE SHOULD PUT A GUARD ON THIS? SEVERAL GUARDS. YOU'RE THROWING GOLD ALL OVER THE PLACE.
STAND BACK, IT'S SLIDING AGAIN!
I ASK YOU!
IS IT WRONG TO BE SO HAPPY, WHEN SO MUCH IS GOING SO BADLY?
IS IT?

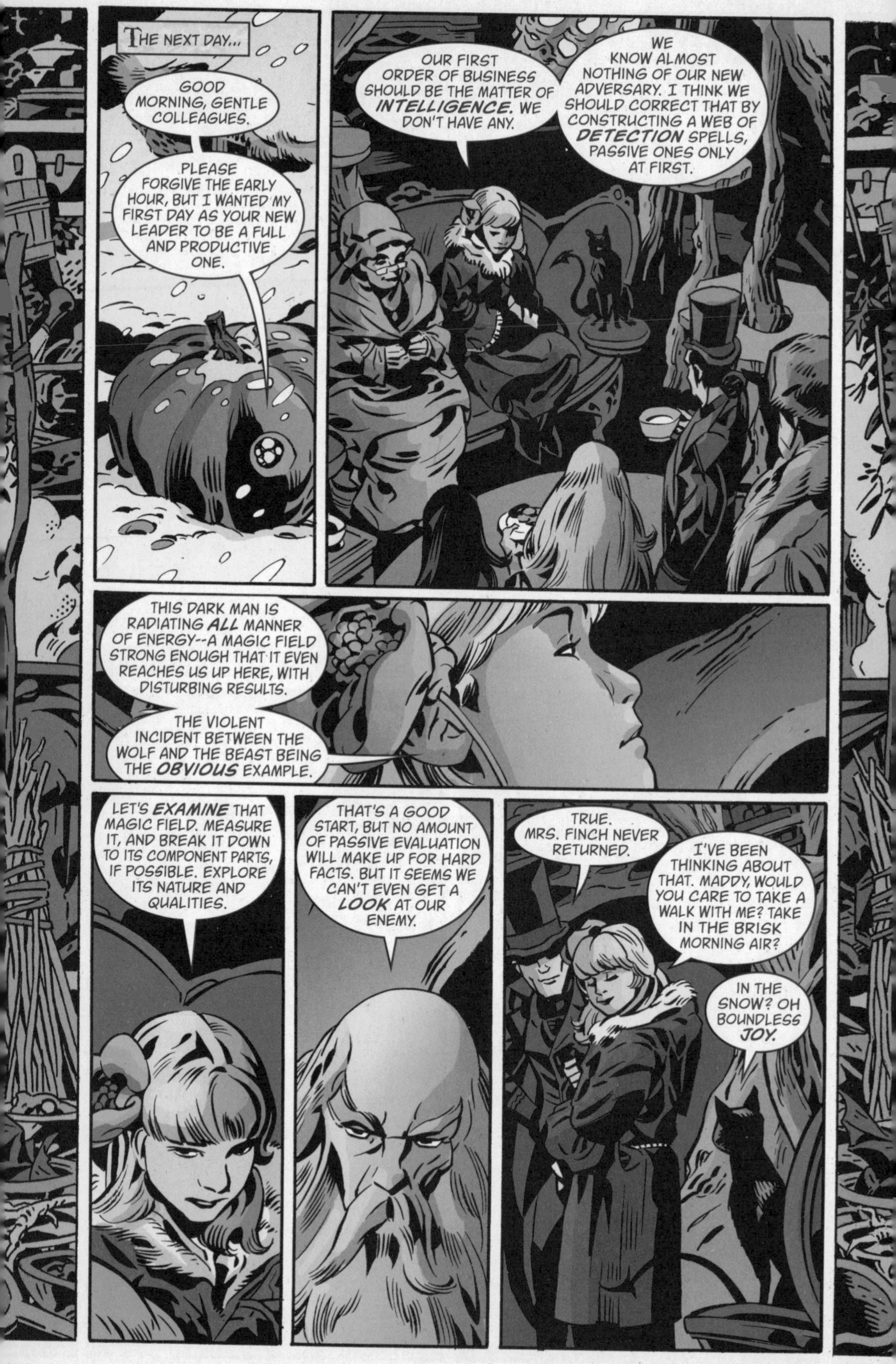
THE NEXT DAY...
GOOD MORNING, GENTLE COLLEAGUES.
PLEASE FORGIVE THE EARLY HOUR, BUT I WANTED MY FIRST DAY AS YOUR NEW LEADER TO BE A FULL AND PRODUCTIVE ONE.
OUR FIRST ORDER OF BUSINESS SHOULD BE THE MATTER OF *INTELLIGENCE*. WE DON'T HAVE ANY.
WE KNOW ALMOST NOTHING OF OUR NEW ADVERSARY. I THINK WE SHOULD CORRECT THAT BY CONSTRUCTING A WEB OF *DETECTION* SPELLS, PASSIVE ONES ONLY AT FIRST.
THIS DARK MAN IS RADIATING *ALL* MANNER OF ENERGY--A MAGIC FIELD STRONG ENOUGH THAT IT EVEN REACHES US UP HERE, WITH DISTURBING RESULTS.
THE VIOLENT INCIDENT BETWEEN THE WOLF AND THE BEAST BEING THE *OBVIOUS* EXAMPLE.
LET'S *EXAMINE* THAT MAGIC FIELD. MEASURE IT, AND BREAK IT DOWN TO ITS COMPONENT PARTS, IF POSSIBLE. EXPLORE ITS NATURE AND QUALITIES.
THAT'S A GOOD START, BUT NO AMOUNT OF PASSIVE EVALUATION WILL MAKE UP FOR HARD FACTS. BUT IT SEEMS WE CAN'T EVEN GET A *LOOK* AT OUR ENEMY.
TRUE. MRS. FINCH NEVER RETURNED.
I'VE BEEN THINKING ABOUT THAT. MADDY, WOULD YOU CARE TO TAKE A WALK WITH ME? TAKE IN THE BRISK MORNING AIR?
IN THE SNOW? OH BOUNDLESS *JOY*.

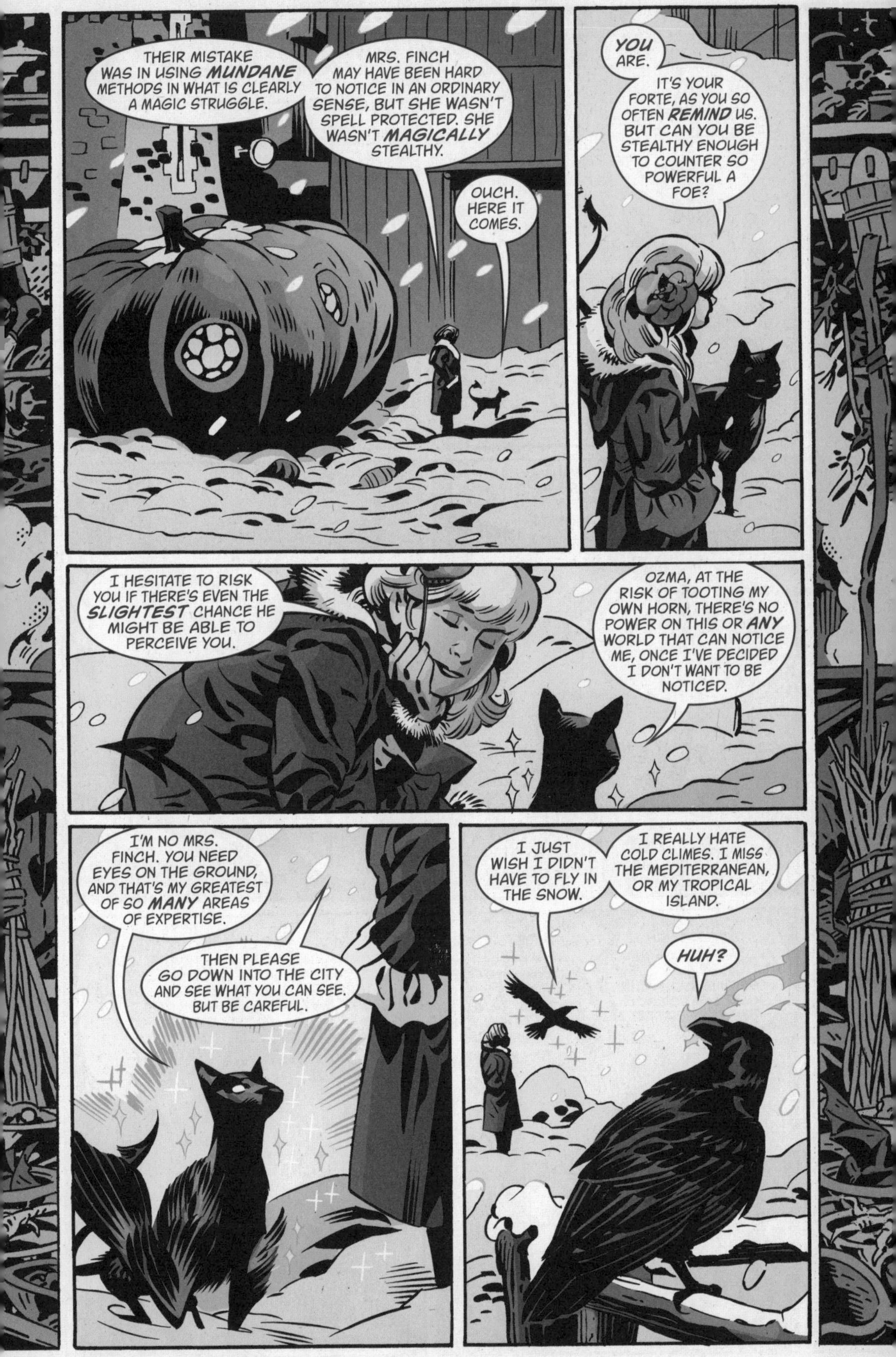
THEIR MISTAKE WAS IN USING MUNDANE METHODS IN WHAT IS CLEARLY A MAGIC STRUGGLE.
MRS. FINCH MAY HAVE BEEN HARD TO NOTICE IN AN ORDINARY SENSE, BUT SHE WASN'T SPELL PROTECTED. SHE WASN'T MAGICALLY STEALTHY.
OUCH. HERE IT COMES.
YOU ARE.
IT'S YOUR FORTE, AS YOU SO OFTEN REMIND US. BUT CAN YOU BE STEALTHY ENOUGH TO COUNTER SO POWERFUL A FOE?
I HESITATE TO RISK YOU IF THERE'S EVEN THE SLIGHTEST CHANCE HE MIGHT BE ABLE TO PERCEIVE YOU.
OZMA, AT THE RISK OF TOOTING MY OWN HORN, THERE'S NO POWER ON THIS OR ANY WORLD THAT CAN NOTICE ME, ONCE I'VE DECIDED I DON'T WANT TO BE NOTICED.
I'M NO MRS. FINCH. YOU NEED EYES ON THE GROUND, AND THAT'S MY GREATEST OF SO MANY AREAS OF EXPERTISE.
THEN PLEASE GO DOWN INTO THE CITY AND SEE WHAT YOU CAN SEE. BUT BE CAREFUL.
I JUST WISH I DIDN'T HAVE TO FLY IN THE SNOW.
I REALLY HATE COLD CLIMES. I MISS THE MEDITERRANEAN, OR MY TROPICAL ISLAND.
HUH?

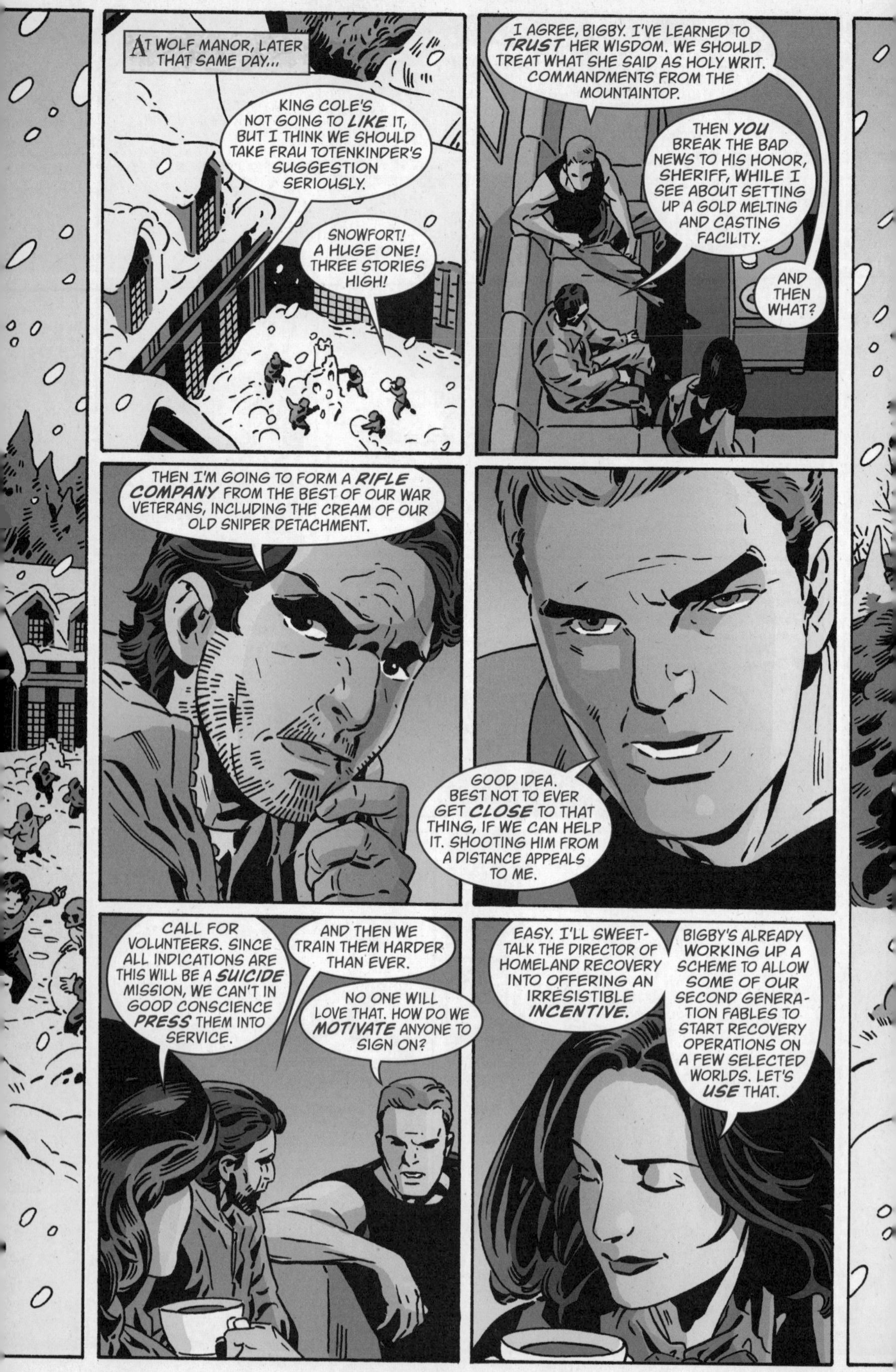
AT WOLF MANOR, LATER THAT SAME DAY...
KING COLE'S NOT GOING TO LIKE IT, BUT I THINK WE SHOULD TAKE FRAU TOTENKINDER'S SUGGESTION SERIOUSLY.
SNOWFORT! A HUGE ONE! THREE STORIES HIGH!
I AGREE, BIGBY. I'VE LEARNED TO TRUST HER WISDOM. WE SHOULD TREAT WHAT SHE SAID AS HOLY WRIT. COMMANDMENTS FROM THE MOUNTAINTOP.
THEN YOU BREAK THE BAD NEWS TO HIS HONOR, SHERIFF, WHILE I SEE ABOUT SETTING UP A GOLD MELTING AND CASTING FACILITY.
AND THEN WHAT?
THEN I'M GOING TO FORM A RIFLE COMPANY FROM THE BEST OF OUR WAR VETERANS, INCLUDING THE CREAM OF OUR OLD SNIPER DETACHMENT.
GOOD IDEA. BEST NOT TO EVER GET CLOSE TO THAT THING, IF WE CAN HELP IT. SHOOTING HIM FROM A DISTANCE APPEALS TO ME.
CALL FOR VOLUNTEERS. SINCE ALL INDICATIONS ARE THIS WILL BE A SUICIDE MISSION, WE CAN'T IN GOOD CONSCIENCE PRESS THEM INTO SERVICE.
AND THEN WE TRAIN THEM HARDER THAN EVER.
NO ONE WILL LOVE THAT. HOW DO WE MOTIVATE ANYONE TO SIGN ON?
EASY. I'LL SWEET-TALK THE DIRECTOR OF HOMELAND RECOVERY INTO OFFERING AN IRRESISTIBLE INCENTIVE.
BIGBY'S ALREADY WORKING UP A SCHEME TO ALLOW SOME OF OUR SECOND GENERATION FABLES TO START RECOVERY OPERATIONS ON A FEW SELECTED WORLDS. LET'S USE THAT.

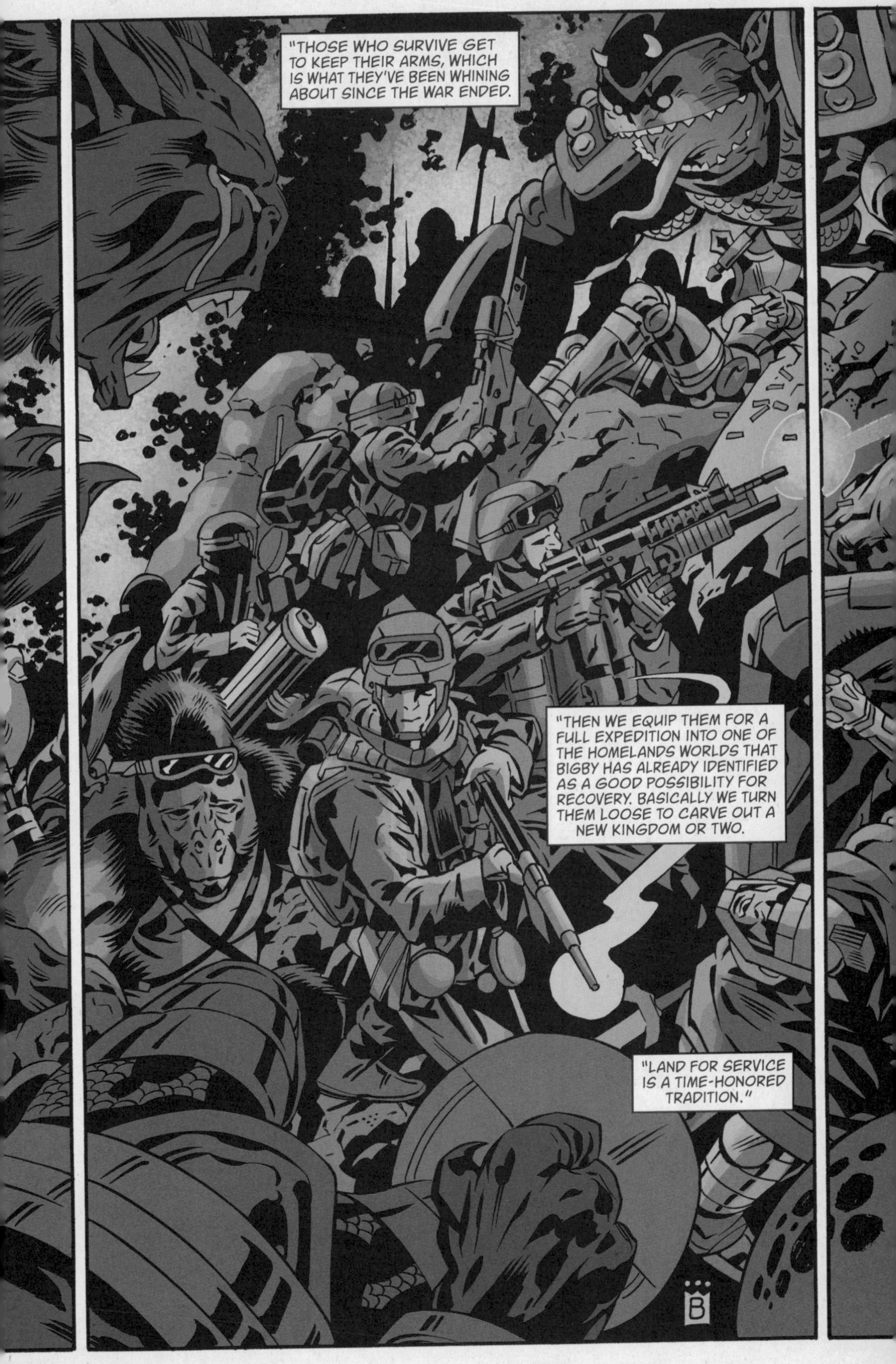
"THOSE WHO SURVIVE GET TO KEEP THEIR ARMS, WHICH IS WHAT THEY'VE BEEN WHINING ABOUT SINCE THE WAR ENDED.
"THEN WE EQUIP THEM FOR A FULL EXPEDITION INTO ONE OF THE HOMELANDS WORLDS THAT BIGBY HAS ALREADY IDENTIFIED AS A GOOD POSSIBILITY FOR RECOVERY. BASICALLY WE TURN THEM LOOSE TO CARVE OUT A NEW KINGDOM OR TWO.
"LAND FOR SERVICE IS A TIME-HONORED TRADITION."

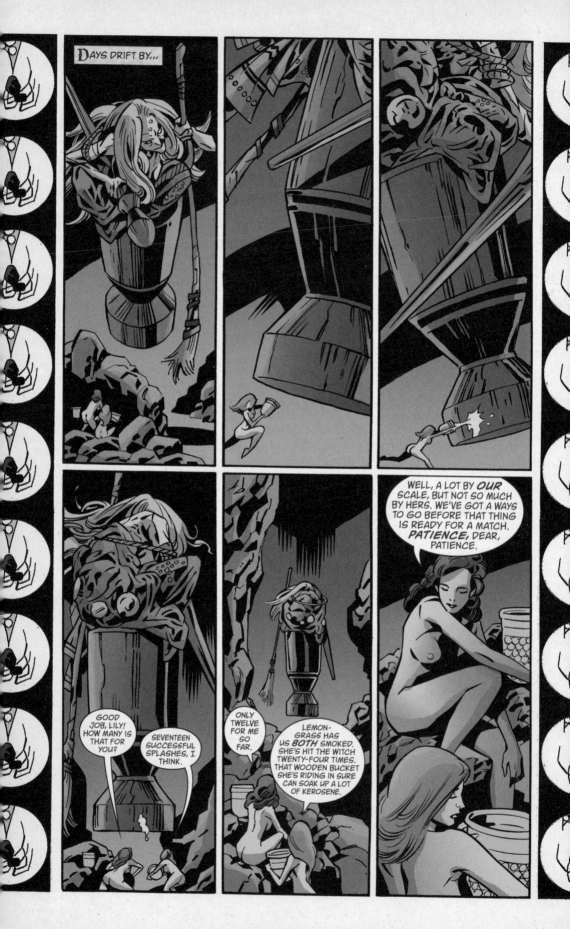

DAYS DRIFT BY...

GOOD JOB, LILY! HOW MANY IS THAT FOR YOU?

SEVENTEEN SUCCESSFUL SPLASHES, I THINK.

ONLY TWELVE FOR ME SO FAR.

LEMONGRASS HAS US *BOTH* SMOKED. SHE'S HIT THE WITCH TWENTY-FOUR TIMES. THAT WOODEN BUCKET SHE'S RIDING IN SURE CAN SOAK UP A LOT OF KEROSENE.

WELL, A LOT BY *OUR* SCALE, BUT NOT SO MUCH BY HERS. WE'VE GOT A WAYS TO GO BEFORE THAT THING IS READY FOR A MATCH. *PATIENCE*, DEAR, PATIENCE.

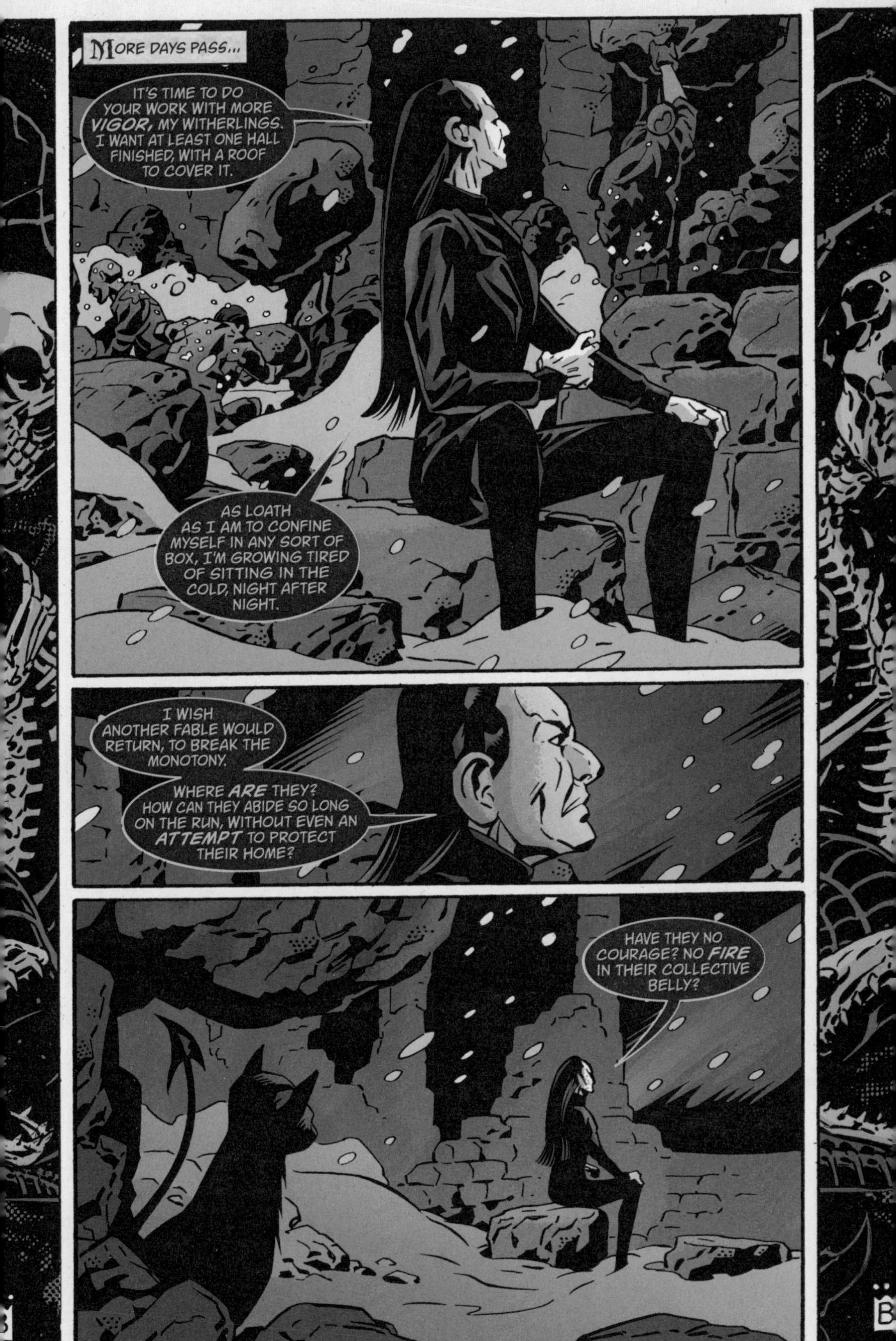
MORE DAYS PASS...
IT'S TIME TO DO YOUR WORK WITH MORE VIGOR, MY WITHERLINGS. I WANT AT LEAST ONE HALL FINISHED, WITH A ROOF TO COVER IT.
AS LOATH AS I AM TO CONFINE MYSELF IN ANY SORT OF BOX, I'M GROWING TIRED OF SITTING IN THE COLD, NIGHT AFTER NIGHT.
I WISH ANOTHER FABLE WOULD RETURN, TO BREAK THE MONOTONY.
WHERE ARE THEY? HOW CAN THEY ABIDE SO LONG ON THE RUN, WITHOUT EVEN AN ATTEMPT TO PROTECT THEIR HOME?
HAVE THEY NO COURAGE? NO FIRE IN THEIR COLLECTIVE BELLY?

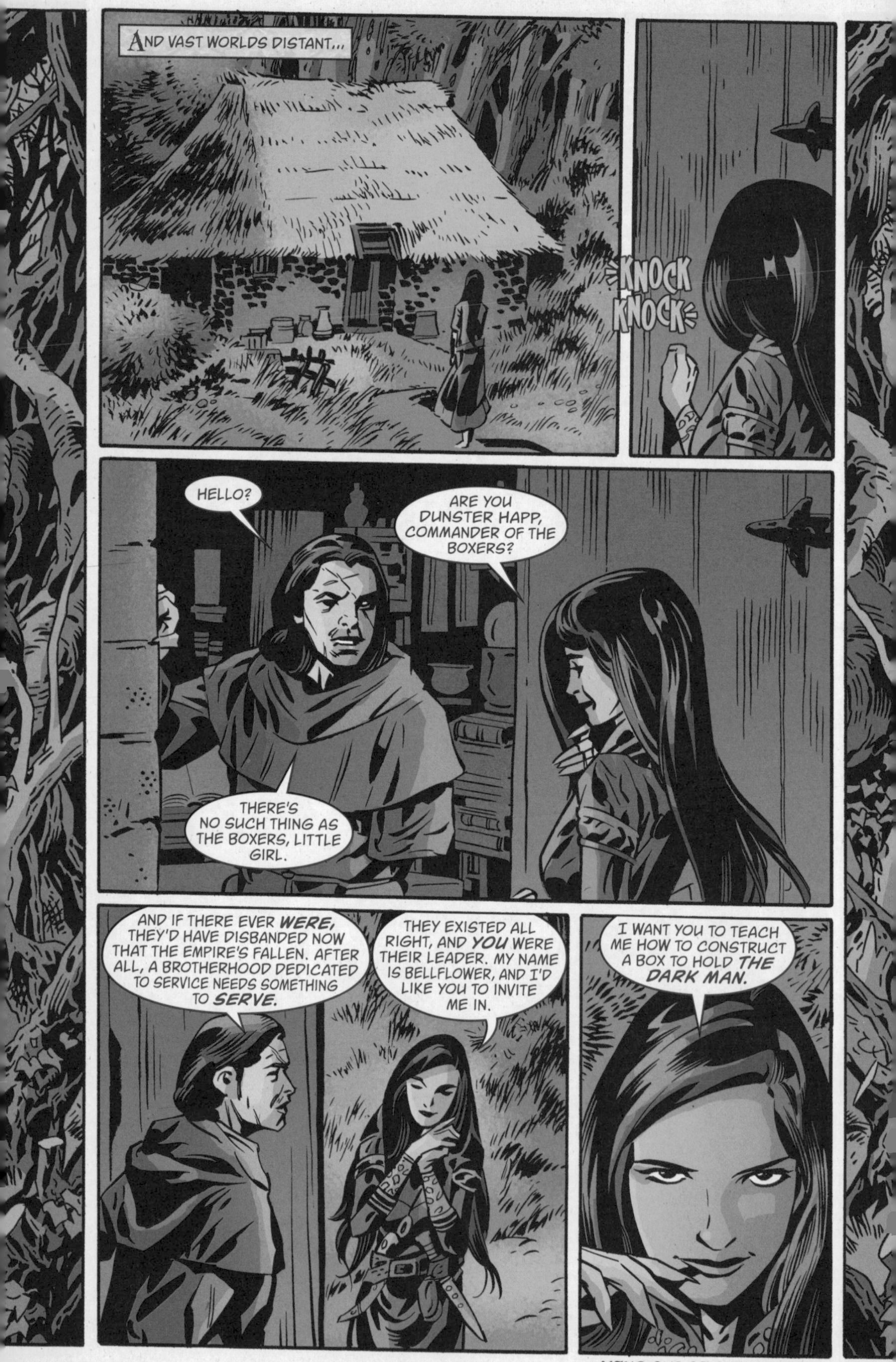
AND VAST WORLDS DISTANT...
KNOCK KNOCK
HELLO?
ARE YOU DUNSTER HAPP, COMMANDER OF THE BOXERS?
THERE'S NO SUCH THING AS THE BOXERS, LITTLE GIRL.
AND IF THERE EVER WERE, THEY'D HAVE DISBANDED NOW THAT THE EMPIRE'S FALLEN. AFTER ALL, A BROTHERHOOD DEDICATED TO SERVICE NEEDS SOMETHING TO SERVE.
THEY EXISTED ALL RIGHT, AND YOU WERE THEIR LEADER. MY NAME IS BELLFLOWER, AND I'D LIKE YOU TO INVITE ME IN.
I WANT YOU TO TEACH ME HOW TO CONSTRUCT A BOX TO HOLD THE DARK MAN.

NEXT: OUT OF THE WOODS!

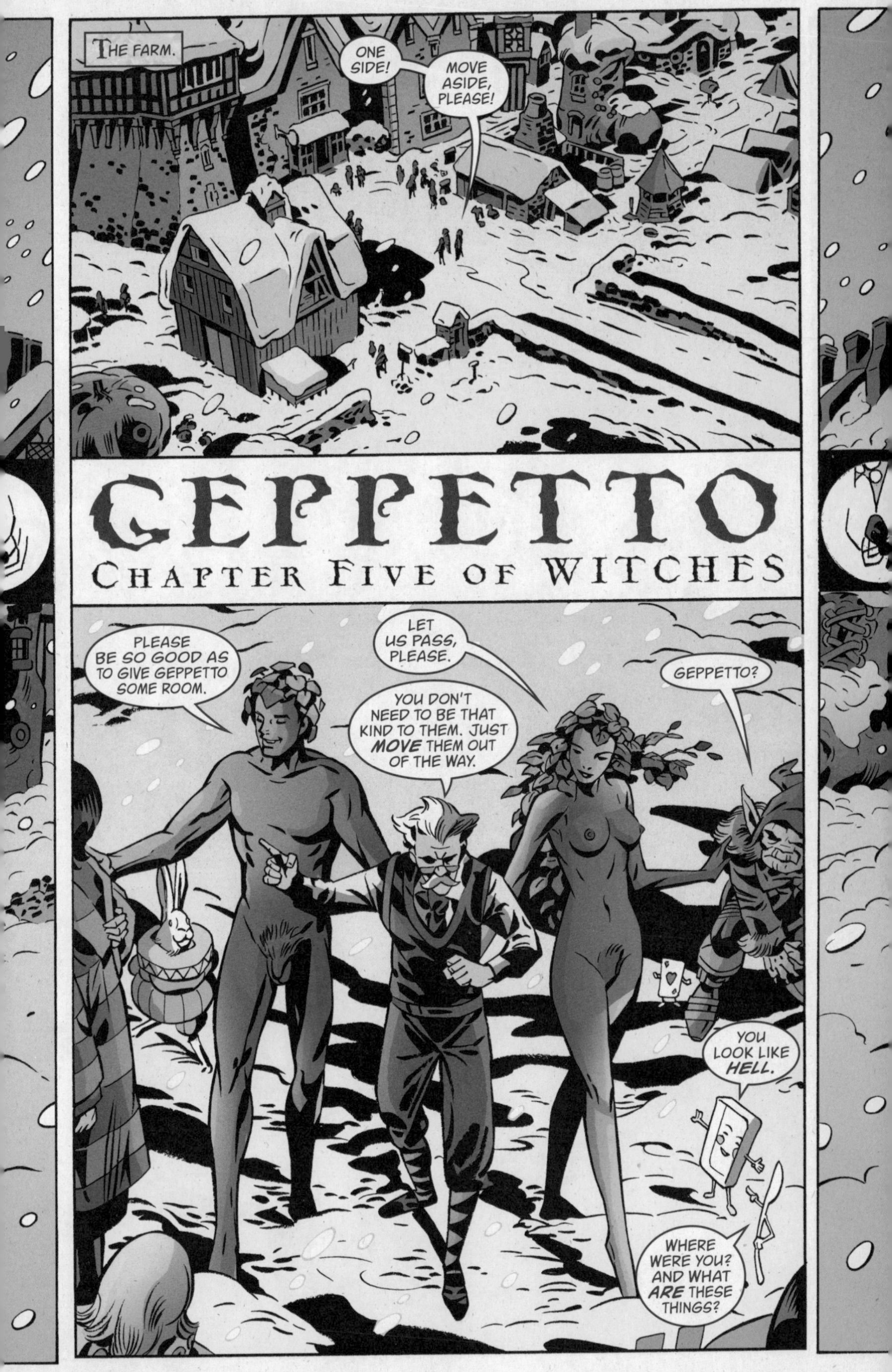

THE FARM.
ONE SIDE!
MOVE ASIDE, PLEASE!
GEPPETTO
CHAPTER FIVE OF WITCHES
PLEASE BE SO GOOD AS TO GIVE GEPPETTO SOME ROOM.
LET US PASS, PLEASE.
YOU DON'T NEED TO BE THAT KIND TO THEM. JUST MOVE THEM OUT OF THE WAY.
GEPPETTO?
YOU LOOK LIKE HELL.
WHERE WERE YOU? AND WHAT ARE THESE THINGS?

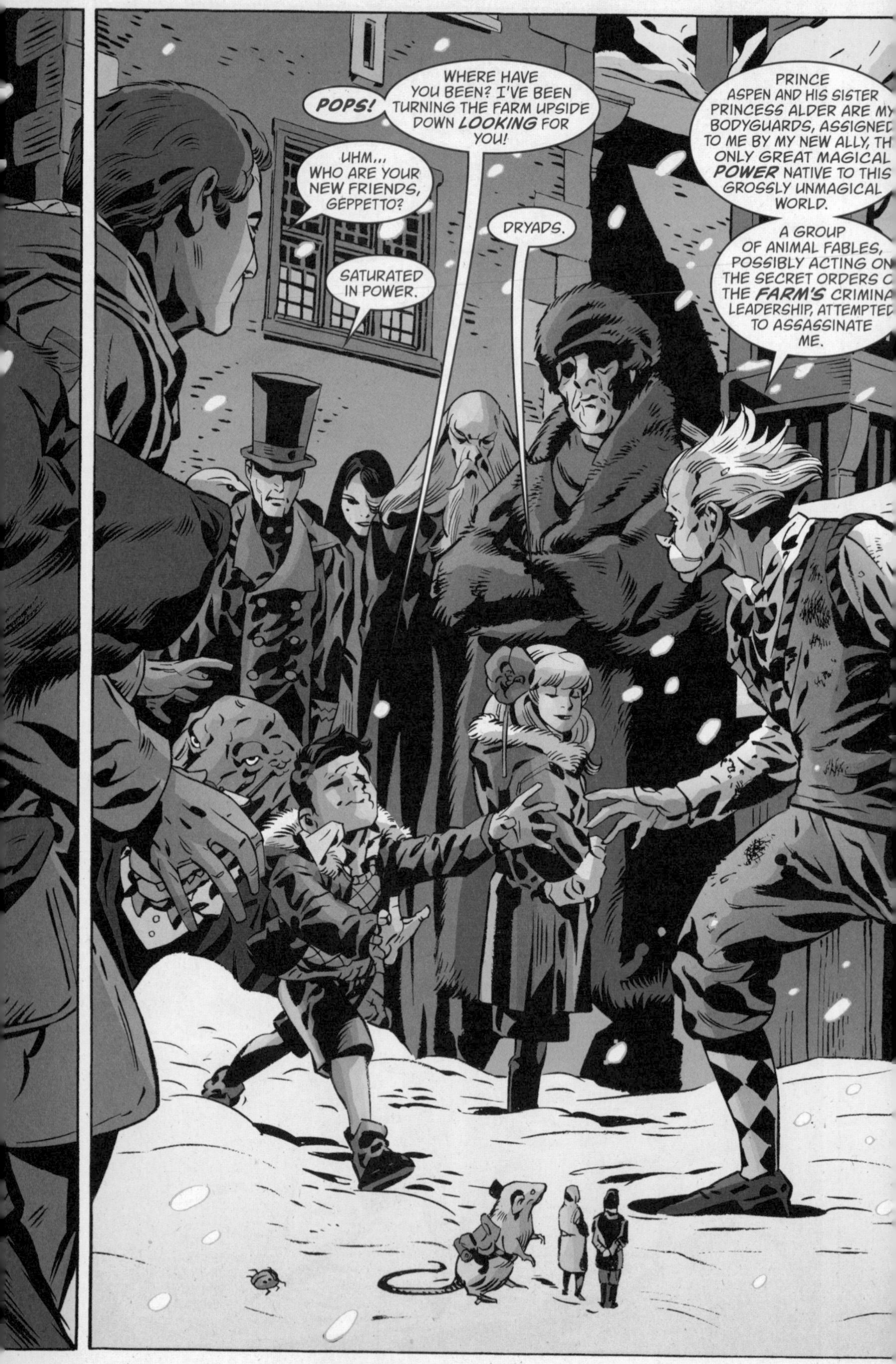

POPS!
WHERE HAVE YOU BEEN? I'VE BEEN TURNING THE FARM UPSIDE DOWN *LOOKING* FOR YOU!
UHM... WHO ARE YOUR NEW FRIENDS, GEPPETTO?
DRYADS.
SATURATED IN POWER.
PRINCE ASPEN AND HIS SISTER PRINCESS ALDER ARE MY BODYGUARDS, ASSIGNED TO ME BY MY NEW ALLY, TH ONLY GREAT MAGICAL *POWER* NATIVE TO THIS GROSSLY UNMAGICAL WORLD.
A GROUP OF ANIMAL FABLES, POSSIBLY ACTING ON THE SECRET ORDERS O THE *FARM'S* CRIMINA LEADERSHIP, ATTEMPTED TO ASSASSINATE ME.

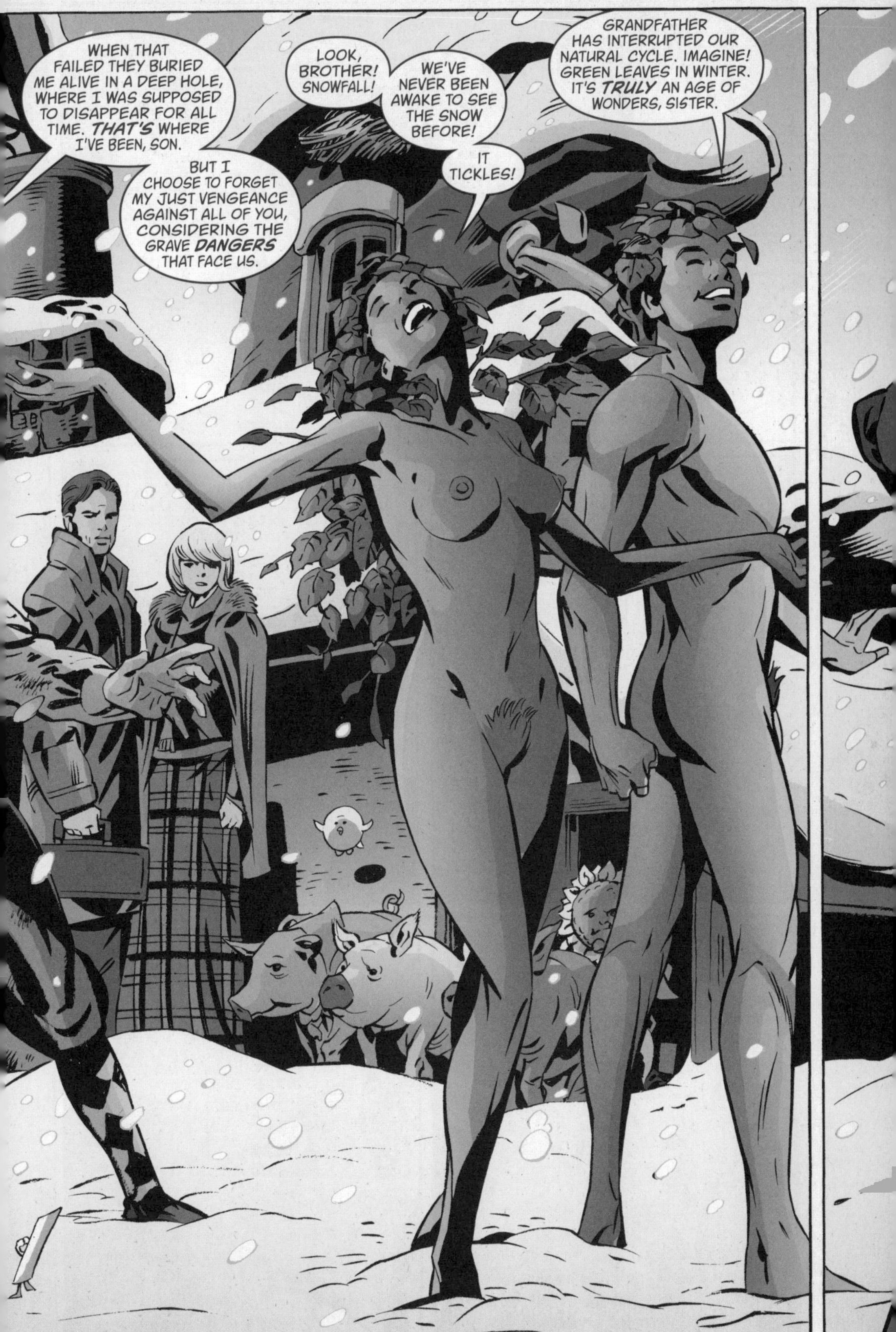
WHEN THAT FAILED THEY BURIED ME ALIVE IN A DEEP HOLE, WHERE I WAS SUPPOSED TO DISAPPEAR FOR ALL TIME. THAT'S WHERE I'VE BEEN, SON.
BUT I CHOOSE TO FORGET MY JUST VENGEANCE AGAINST ALL OF YOU, CONSIDERING THE GRAVE DANGERS THAT FACE US.
LOOK, BROTHER! SNOWFALL!
WE'VE NEVER BEEN AWAKE TO SEE THE SNOW BEFORE!
IT TICKLES!
GRANDFATHER HAS INTERRUPTED OUR NATURAL CYCLE. IMAGINE! GREEN LEAVES IN WINTER. IT'S TRULY AN AGE OF WONDERS, SISTER.

LOOK AT YOU! YOU'RE ALL WET AND DIRTY! AND NO COAT? WE NEED TO GET YOU INSIDE, POPS, BEFORE YOU CATCH YOUR DEATH!

SETTLE DOWN, BOY. IF ALL THEY'VE TRIED TO DO COULDN'T KILL ME, A BIT OF NASTY *WEATHER* WON'T DO IT.

IS IT TRUE, KING COLE? DID YOU TRY TO KILL MY DAD? WE HAD A *DEAL!*

I DIDN'T... WE NEVER...

WE HAD *NOTHING* TO DO WITH GEPPETTO'S DISAPPEARANCE, PINOCCHIO. WORD OF HONOR.

WHAT HONOR MIGHT SUCH AS *YOU* HAVE? BUT IT DOESN'T MATTER. WE'VE OTHER ISSUES OF IMPORT TO CONCERN US. MISTER DARK OCCUPIES OUR HOME IN NEW YORK TOWN.

IT'S NEW YORK *CITY,* POPS.

MISTER DARK?

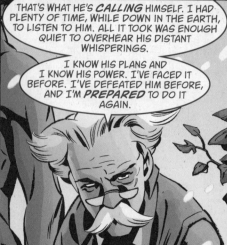

THAT'S WHAT HE'S *CALLING* HIMSELF. I HAD PLENTY OF TIME, WHILE DOWN IN THE EARTH, TO LISTEN TO HIM. ALL IT TOOK WAS ENOUGH QUIET TO OVERHEAR HIS DISTANT WHISPERINGS.

I KNOW HIS PLANS AND I KNOW HIS POWER. I'VE FACED IT BEFORE. I'VE DEFEATED HIM BEFORE, AND I'M *PREPARED* TO DO IT AGAIN.

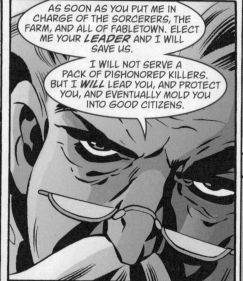

AS SOON AS YOU PUT ME IN CHARGE OF THE SORCERERS, THE FARM, AND ALL OF FABLETOWN. ELECT ME YOUR *LEADER* AND I WILL SAVE US.

I WILL NOT SERVE A PACK OF DISHONORED KILLERS. BUT I *WILL* LEAD YOU, AND PROTECT YOU, AND EVENTUALLY MOLD YOU INTO GOOD CITIZENS.

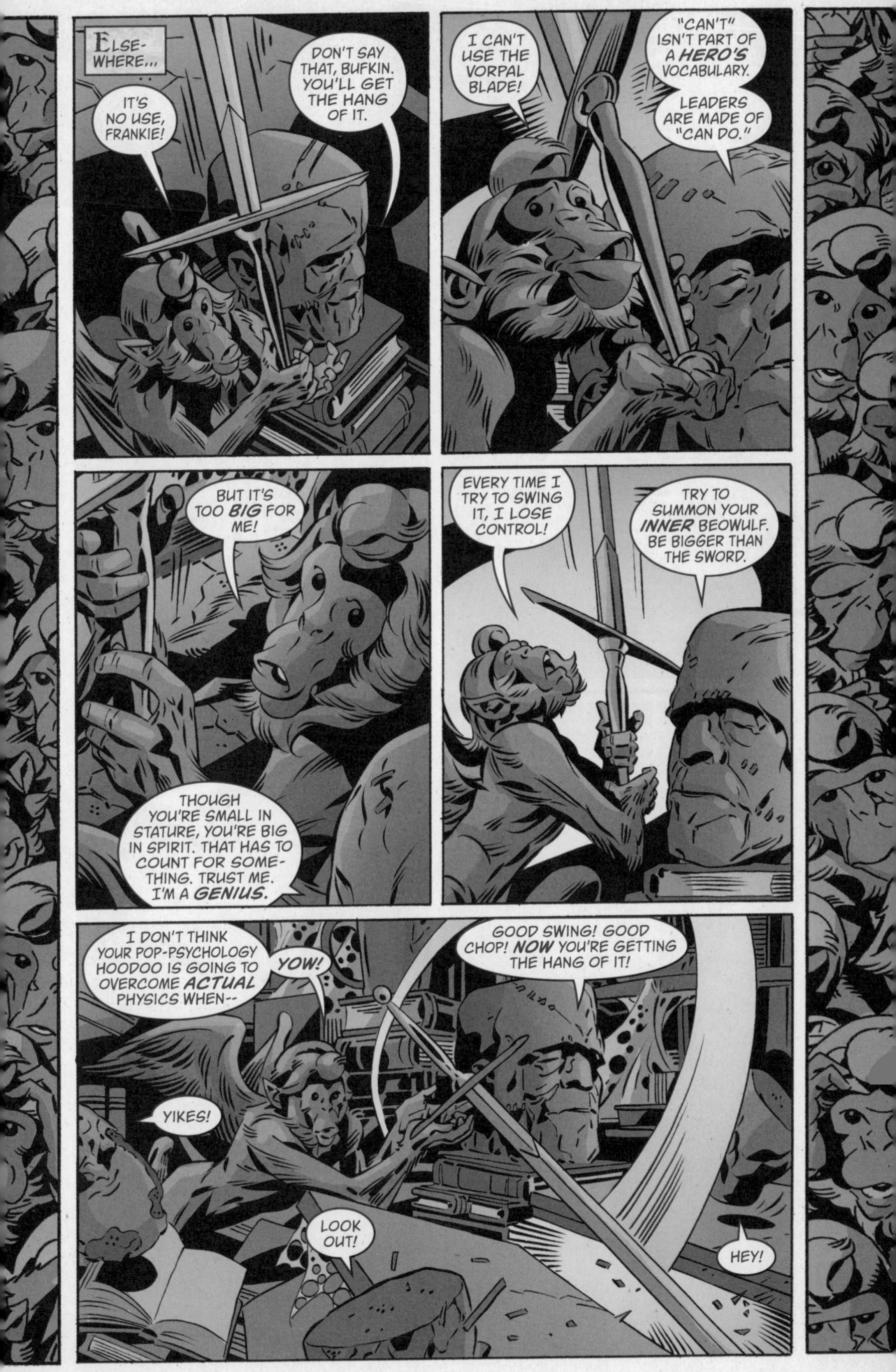
ELSE-WHERE...
IT'S NO USE, FRANKIE!
DON'T SAY THAT, BUFKIN. YOU'LL GET THE HANG OF IT.
I CAN'T USE THE VORPAL BLADE!
"CAN'T" ISN'T PART OF A HERO'S VOCABULARY.
LEADERS ARE MADE OF "CAN DO."
BUT IT'S TOO BIG FOR ME!
THOUGH YOU'RE SMALL IN STATURE, YOU'RE BIG IN SPIRIT. THAT HAS TO COUNT FOR SOME-THING. TRUST ME. I'M A GENIUS.
EVERY TIME I TRY TO SWING IT, I LOSE CONTROL!
TRY TO SUMMON YOUR INNER BEOWULF. BE BIGGER THAN THE SWORD.
I DON'T THINK YOUR POP-PSYCHOLOGY HOODOO IS GOING TO OVERCOME ACTUAL PHYSICS WHEN--
YOW!
GOOD SWING! GOOD CHOP! NOW YOU'RE GETTING THE HANG OF IT!
YIKES!
LOOK OUT!
HEY!

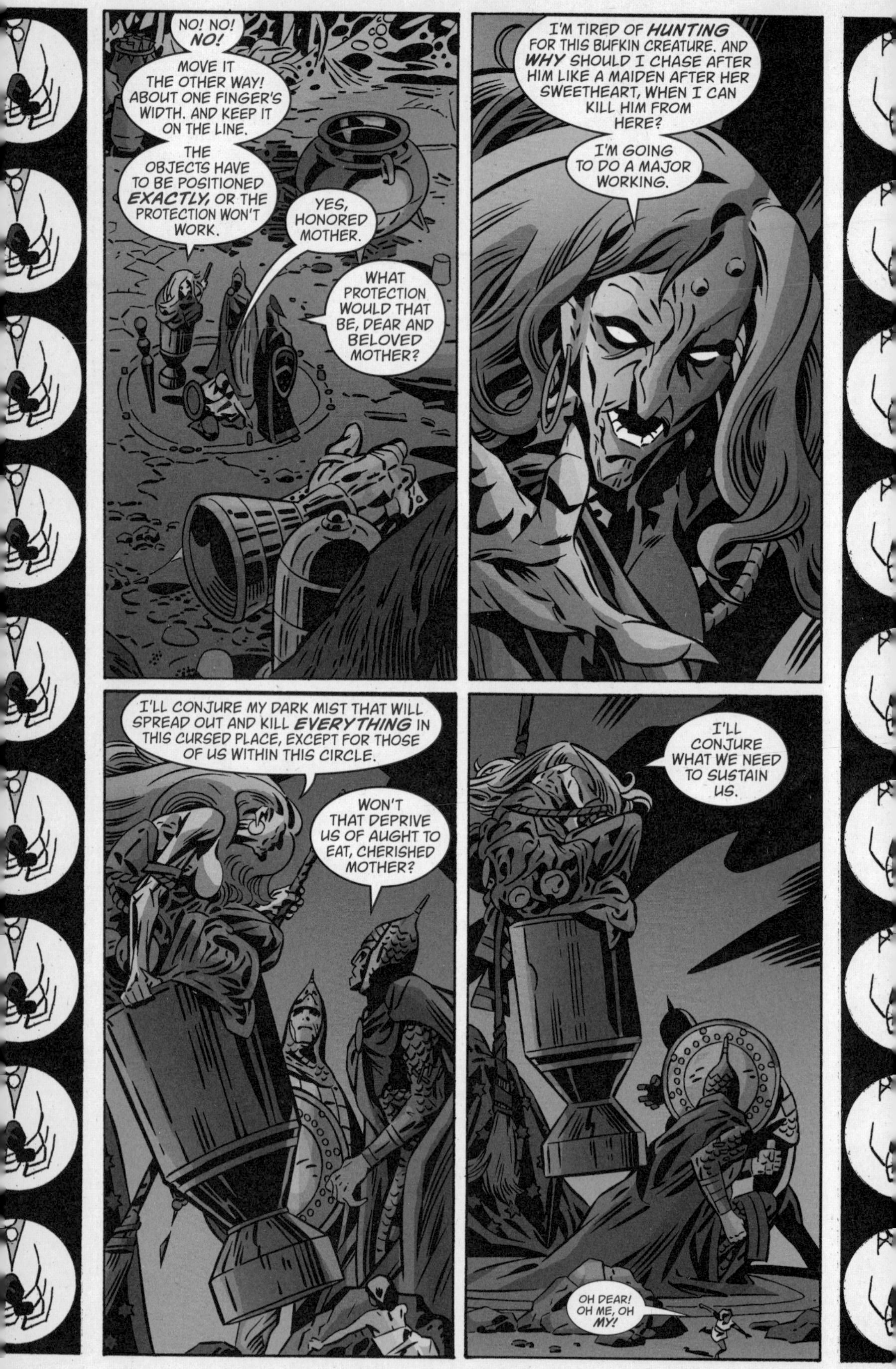

NO! NO! NO!
MOVE IT THE OTHER WAY! ABOUT ONE FINGER'S WIDTH. AND KEEP IT ON THE LINE.
THE OBJECTS HAVE TO BE POSITIONED EXACTLY, OR THE PROTECTION WON'T WORK.
YES, HONORED MOTHER.
WHAT PROTECTION WOULD THAT BE, DEAR AND BELOVED MOTHER?
I'M TIRED OF HUNTING FOR THIS BUFKIN CREATURE. AND WHY SHOULD I CHASE AFTER HIM LIKE A MAIDEN AFTER HER SWEETHEART, WHEN I CAN KILL HIM FROM HERE?
I'M GOING TO DO A MAJOR WORKING.
I'LL CONJURE MY DARK MIST THAT WILL SPREAD OUT AND KILL EVERYTHING IN THIS CURSED PLACE, EXCEPT FOR THOSE OF US WITHIN THIS CIRCLE.
WON'T THAT DEPRIVE US OF AUGHT TO EAT, CHERISHED MOTHER?
I'LL CONJURE WHAT WE NEED TO SUSTAIN US.
OH DEAR! OH ME, OH MY!

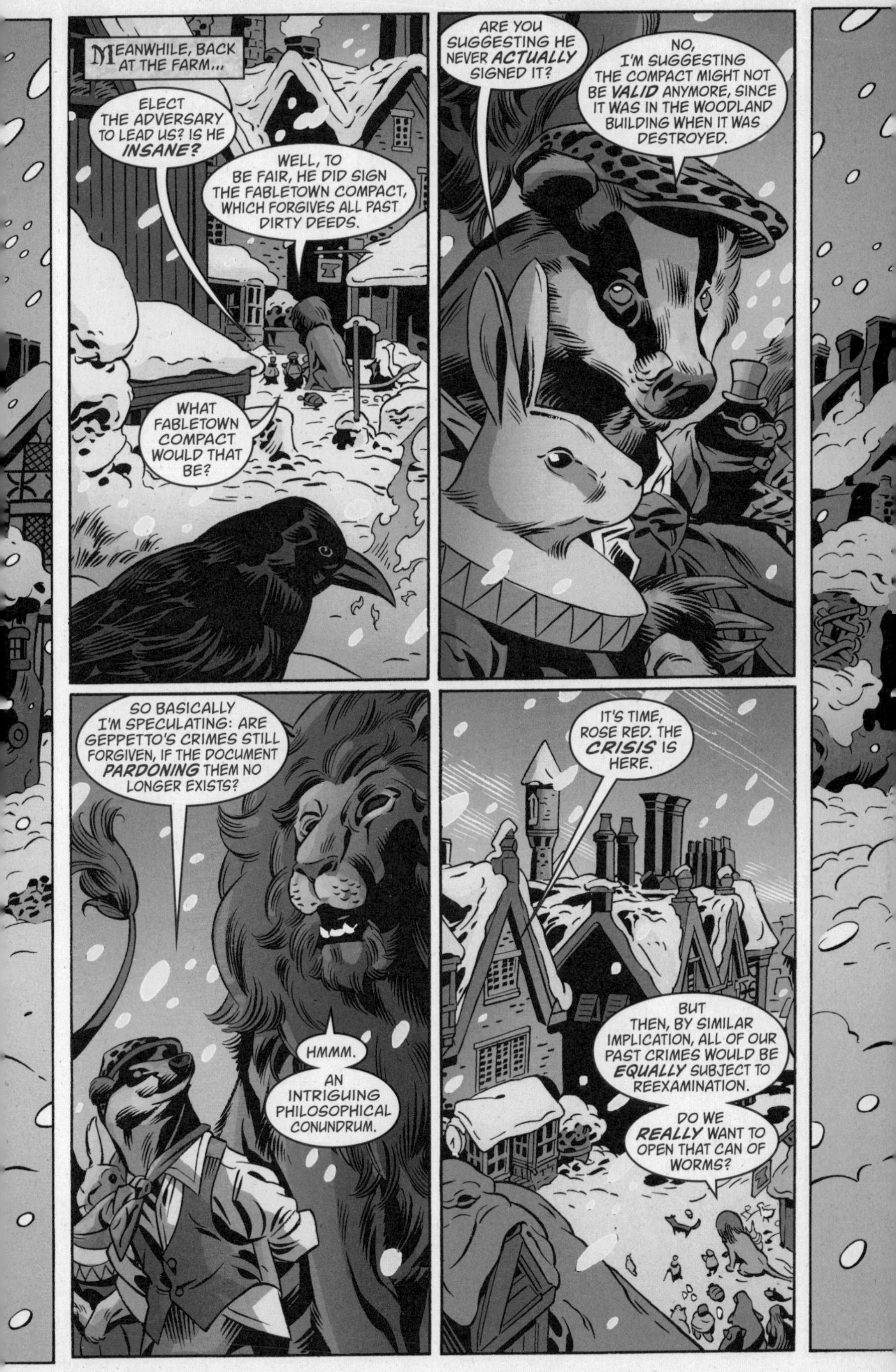
MEANWHILE, BACK AT THE FARM...
ELECT THE ADVERSARY TO LEAD US? IS HE INSANE?
WELL, TO BE FAIR, HE DID SIGN THE FABLETOWN COMPACT, WHICH FORGIVES ALL PAST DIRTY DEEDS.
WHAT FABLETOWN COMPACT WOULD THAT BE?
ARE YOU SUGGESTING HE NEVER ACTUALLY SIGNED IT?
NO, I'M SUGGESTING THE COMPACT MIGHT NOT BE VALID ANYMORE, SINCE IT WAS IN THE WOODLAND BUILDING WHEN IT WAS DESTROYED.
SO BASICALLY I'M SPECULATING: ARE GEPPETTO'S CRIMES STILL FORGIVEN, IF THE DOCUMENT PARDONING THEM NO LONGER EXISTS?
HMMM.
AN INTRIGUING PHILOSOPHICAL CONUNDRUM.
IT'S TIME, ROSE RED. THE CRISIS IS HERE.
BUT THEN, BY SIMILAR IMPLICATION, ALL OF OUR PAST CRIMES WOULD BE EQUALLY SUBJECT TO REEXAMINATION.
DO WE REALLY WANT TO OPEN THAT CAN OF WORMS?

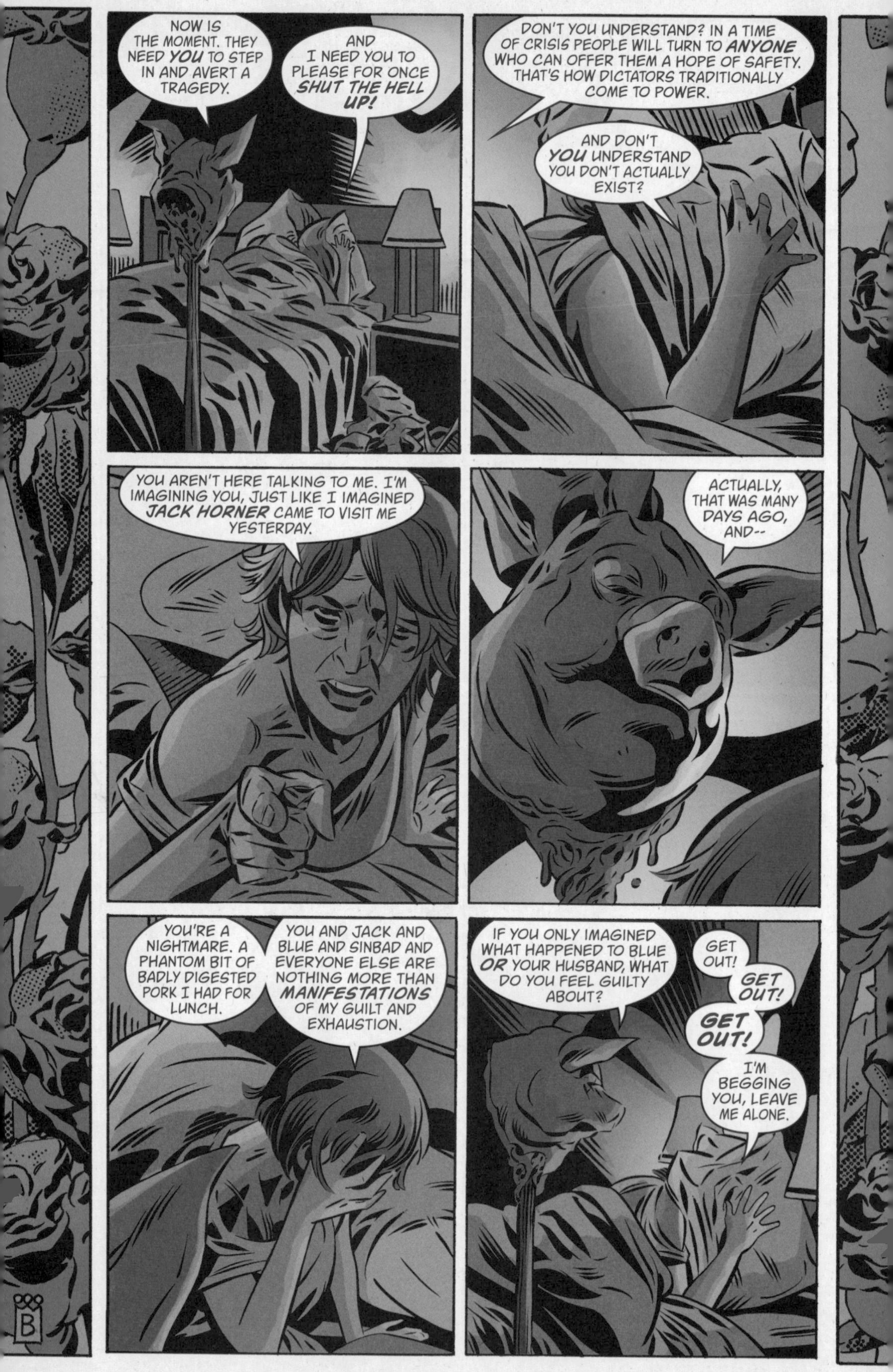
NOW IS THE MOMENT. THEY NEED YOU TO STEP IN AND AVERT A TRAGEDY.
AND I NEED YOU TO PLEASE FOR ONCE SHUT THE HELL UP!
DON'T YOU UNDERSTAND? IN A TIME OF CRISIS PEOPLE WILL TURN TO ANYONE WHO CAN OFFER THEM A HOPE OF SAFETY. THAT'S HOW DICTATORS TRADITIONALLY COME TO POWER.
AND DON'T YOU UNDERSTAND YOU DON'T ACTUALLY EXIST?
YOU AREN'T HERE TALKING TO ME. I'M IMAGINING YOU, JUST LIKE I IMAGINED JACK HORNER CAME TO VISIT ME YESTERDAY.
ACTUALLY, THAT WAS MANY DAYS AGO, AND--
YOU'RE A NIGHTMARE. A PHANTOM BIT OF BADLY DIGESTED PORK I HAD FOR LUNCH.
YOU AND JACK AND BLUE AND SINBAD AND EVERYONE ELSE ARE NOTHING MORE THAN MANIFESTATIONS OF MY GUILT AND EXHAUSTION.
IF YOU ONLY IMAGINED WHAT HAPPENED TO BLUE OR YOUR HUSBAND, WHAT DO YOU FEEL GUILTY ABOUT?
GET OUT!
GET OUT!
GET OUT!
I'M BEGGING YOU, LEAVE ME ALONE.

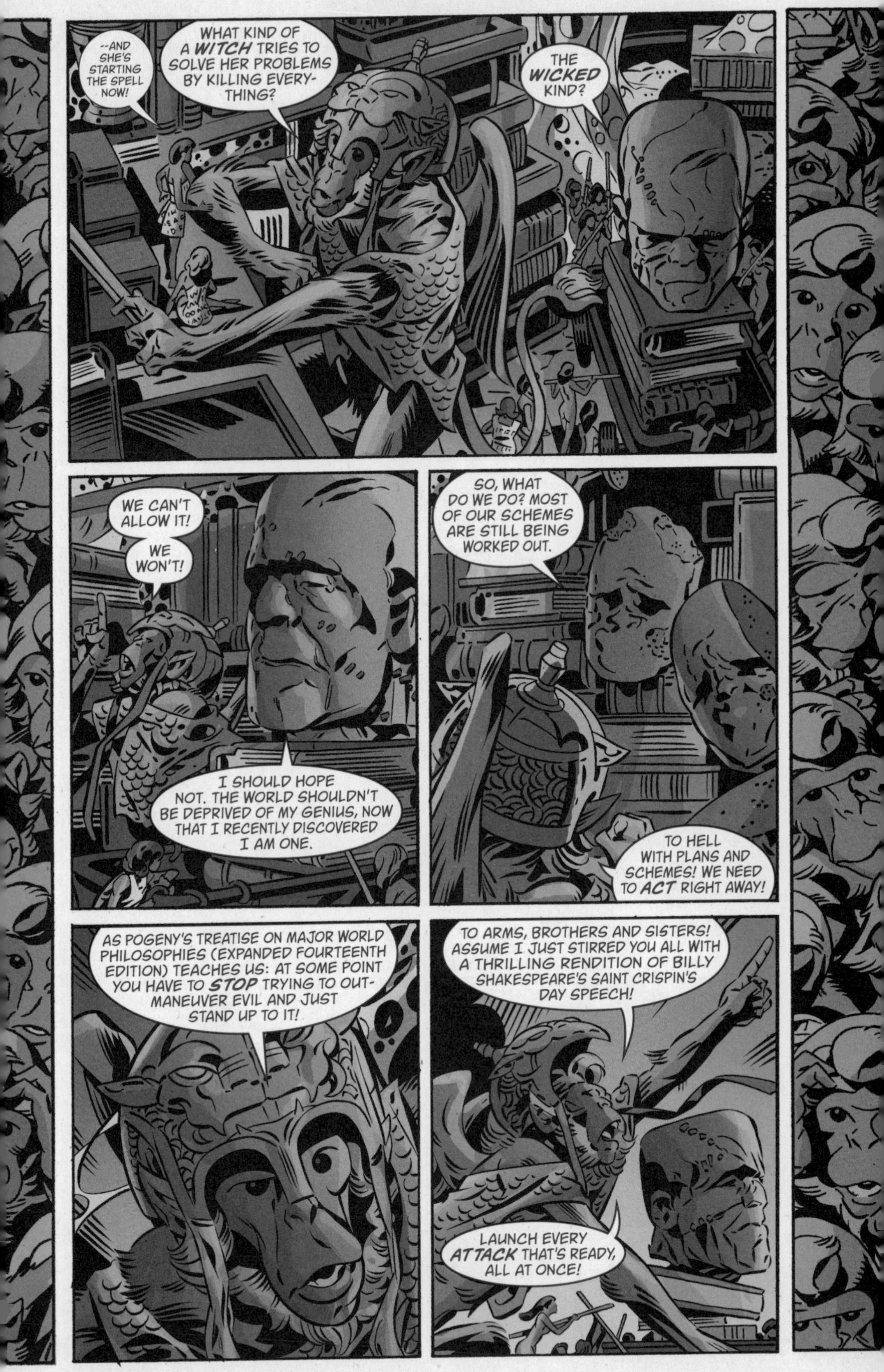
--AND SHE'S STARTING THE SPELL NOW!
WHAT KIND OF A WITCH TRIES TO SOLVE HER PROBLEMS BY KILLING EVERYTHING?
THE WICKED KIND?
WE CAN'T ALLOW IT!
WE WON'T!
I SHOULD HOPE NOT. THE WORLD SHOULDN'T BE DEPRIVED OF MY GENIUS, NOW THAT I RECENTLY DISCOVERED I AM ONE.
SO, WHAT DO WE DO? MOST OF OUR SCHEMES ARE STILL BEING WORKED OUT.
TO HELL WITH PLANS AND SCHEMES! WE NEED TO ACT RIGHT AWAY!
AS POGENY'S TREATISE ON MAJOR WORLD PHILOSOPHIES (EXPANDED FOURTEENTH EDITION) TEACHES US: AT SOME POINT YOU HAVE TO STOP TRYING TO OUT-MANEUVER EVIL AND JUST STAND UP TO IT!
TO ARMS, BROTHERS AND SISTERS! ASSUME I JUST STIRRED YOU ALL WITH A THRILLING RENDITION OF BILLY SHAKESPEARE'S SAINT CRISPIN'S DAY SPEECH!
LAUNCH EVERY ATTACK THAT'S READY, ALL AT ONCE!

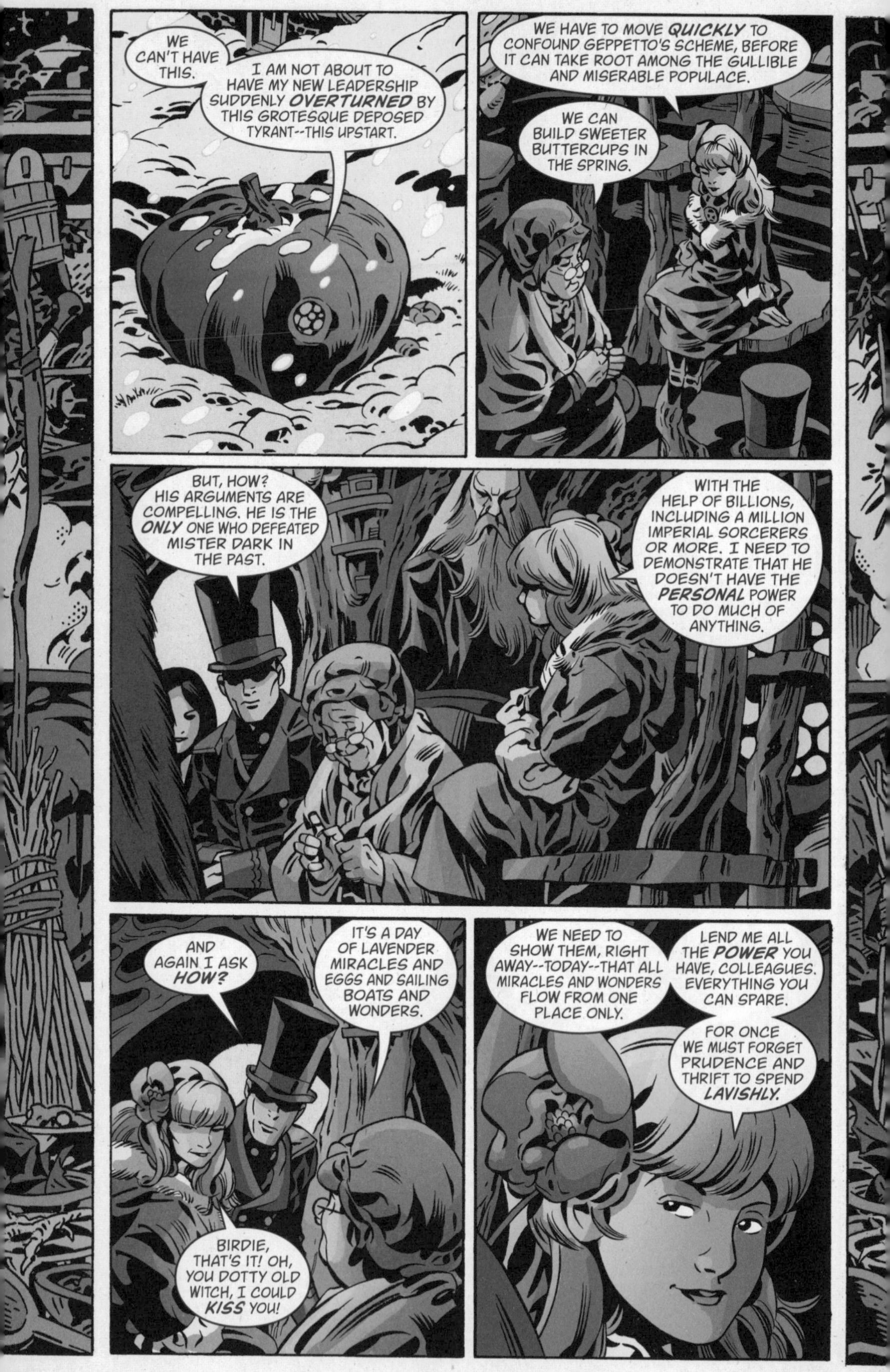
WE CAN'T HAVE THIS.
I AM NOT ABOUT TO HAVE MY NEW LEADERSHIP SUDDENLY OVERTURNED BY THIS GROTESQUE DEPOSED TYRANT--THIS UPSTART.
WE HAVE TO MOVE QUICKLY TO CONFOUND GEPPETTO'S SCHEME, BEFORE IT CAN TAKE ROOT AMONG THE GULLIBLE AND MISERABLE POPULACE.
WE CAN BUILD SWEETER BUTTERCUPS IN THE SPRING.
BUT, HOW? HIS ARGUMENTS ARE COMPELLING. HE IS THE ONLY ONE WHO DEFEATED MISTER DARK IN THE PAST.
WITH THE HELP OF BILLIONS, INCLUDING A MILLION IMPERIAL SORCERERS OR MORE. I NEED TO DEMONSTRATE THAT HE DOESN'T HAVE THE PERSONAL POWER TO DO MUCH OF ANYTHING.
AND AGAIN I ASK HOW?
IT'S A DAY OF LAVENDER MIRACLES AND EGGS AND SAILING BOATS AND WONDERS.
BIRDIE, THAT'S IT! OH, YOU DOTTY OLD WITCH, I COULD KISS YOU!
WE NEED TO SHOW THEM, RIGHT AWAY--TODAY--THAT ALL MIRACLES AND WONDERS FLOW FROM ONE PLACE ONLY.
LEND ME ALL THE POWER YOU HAVE, COLLEAGUES. EVERYTHING YOU CAN SPARE.
FOR ONCE WE MUST FORGET PRUDENCE AND THRIFT TO SPEND LAVISHLY.

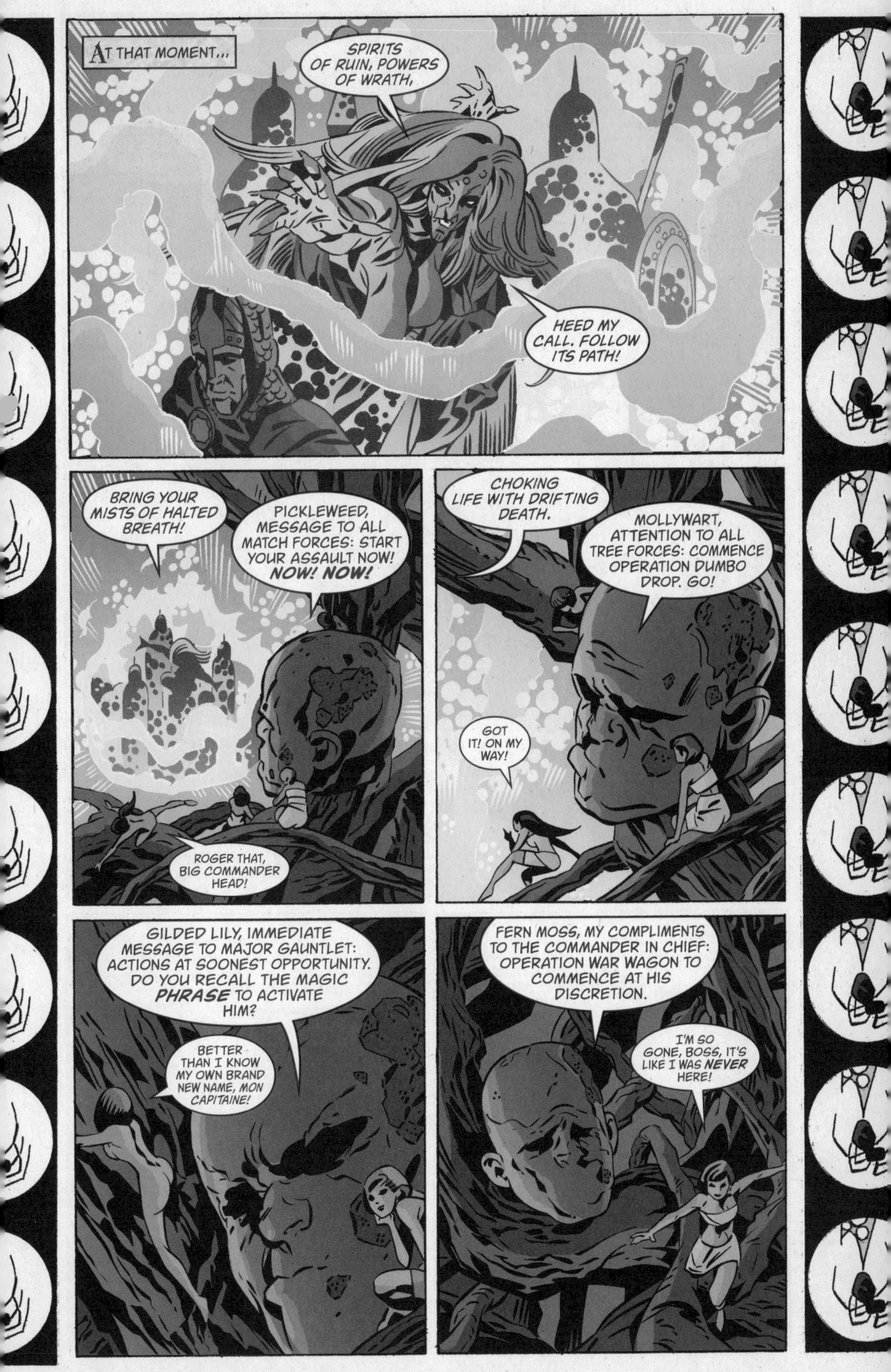
AT THAT MOMENT...
SPIRITS OF RUIN, POWERS OF WRATH,
HEED MY CALL. FOLLOW ITS PATH!
BRING YOUR MISTS OF HALTED BREATH!
PICKLEWEED, MESSAGE TO ALL MATCH FORCES: START YOUR ASSAULT NOW! NOW! NOW!
ROGER THAT, BIG COMMANDER HEAD!
CHOKING LIFE WITH DRIFTING DEATH.
MOLLYWART, ATTENTION TO ALL TREE FORCES: COMMENCE OPERATION DUMBO DROP. GO!
GOT IT! ON MY WAY!
GILDED LILY, IMMEDIATE MESSAGE TO MAJOR GAUNTLET: ACTIONS AT SOONEST OPPORTUNITY. DO YOU RECALL THE MAGIC PHRASE TO ACTIVATE HIM?
BETTER THAN I KNOW MY OWN BRAND NEW NAME, MON CAPITAINE!
FERN MOSS, MY COMPLIMENTS TO THE COMMANDER IN CHIEF: OPERATION WAR WAGON TO COMMENCE AT HIS DISCRETION.
I'M SO GONE, BOSS, IT'S LIKE I WAS NEVER HERE!

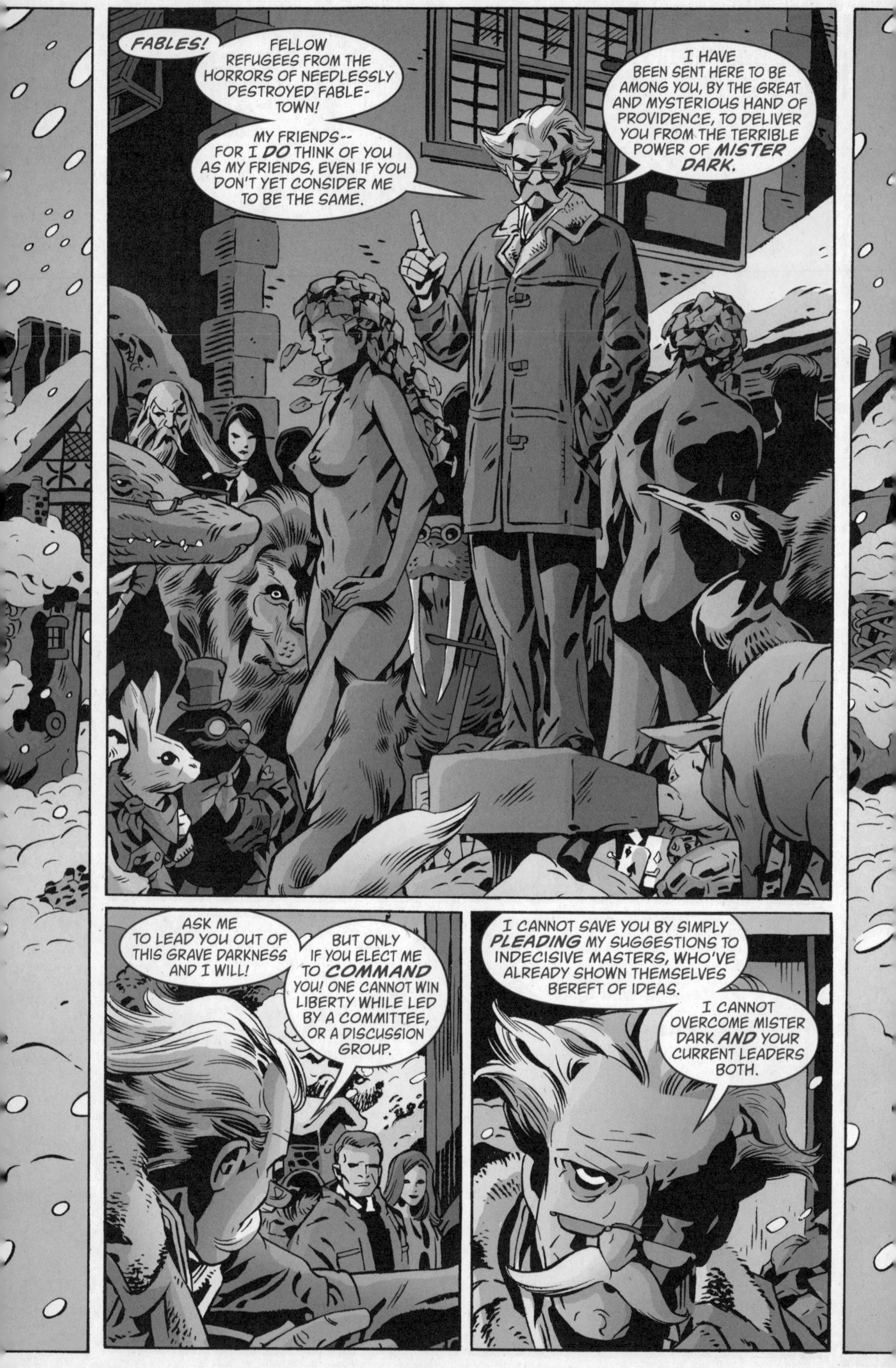

FABLES!
FELLOW REFUGEES FROM THE HORRORS OF NEEDLESSLY DESTROYED FABLE-TOWN!
MY FRIENDS-- FOR I DO THINK OF YOU AS MY FRIENDS, EVEN IF YOU DON'T YET CONSIDER ME TO BE THE SAME.
I HAVE BEEN SENT HERE TO BE AMONG YOU, BY THE GREAT AND MYSTERIOUS HAND OF PROVIDENCE, TO DELIVER YOU FROM THE TERRIBLE POWER OF MISTER DARK.
ASK ME TO LEAD YOU OUT OF THIS GRAVE DARKNESS AND I WILL!
BUT ONLY IF YOU ELECT ME TO COMMAND YOU! ONE CANNOT WIN LIBERTY WHILE LED BY A COMMITTEE, OR A DISCUSSION GROUP.
I CANNOT SAVE YOU BY SIMPLY PLEADING MY SUGGESTIONS TO INDECISIVE MASTERS, WHO'VE ALREADY SHOWN THEMSELVES BEREFT OF IDEAS.
I CANNOT OVERCOME MISTER DARK AND YOUR CURRENT LEADERS BOTH.

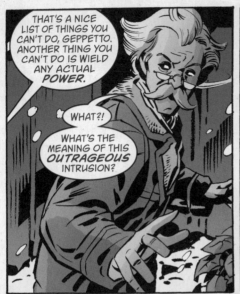

THAT'S A NICE LIST OF THINGS YOU CAN'T DO, GEPPETTO. ANOTHER THING YOU CAN'T DO IS WIELD ANY ACTUAL *POWER*.

WHAT?!

WHAT'S THE MEANING OF THIS *OUTRAGEOUS* INTRUSION?

GUARDS! *SLAY* THAT MEDDLER!

I DON'T THINK SO, SIR.

WE WON'T DO YOUR KILLING FOR YOU. WE'RE ONLY PLEDGED TO *PROTECT* YOU FROM ACTUAL HARM. RUDE BEHAVIOR DOESN'T COUNT.

SEE, GEPPETTO? GIVING ORDERS ISN'T THE SAME AS HAVING ACTUAL *ABILITIES*, IS IT? WHEN WERE YOU PLANNING TO *ADMIT* THAT YOU'VE LITTLE OR NO POWER OF YOUR *OWN* LEFT?

WHEREAS I'VE SO MUCH POWER AT MY BECK AND CALL, I CAN PERFORM *MIRACLES* AT THE SLIGHTEST WHIM.

UNAUTHORIZED WITCH! PRACTITIONER OF *LIES*!

WANT TO TEST ME? FINE. WHAT SHALL I DO? OH, I KNOW. WHERE'S THE *FOX* NAMED REYNARD? STEP FORWARD IF YOU'RE HERE, PLEASE.

YOU CALLED, YOUNG LADY (WITH DISTURBINGLY OLD EYES)?

IT OCCURS TO ME THAT YOU WERE NEVER ADEQUATELY REWARDED FOR YOUR *LOYALTY* DURING PAST TROUBLES. SHALL WE RECTIFY THAT NOW?

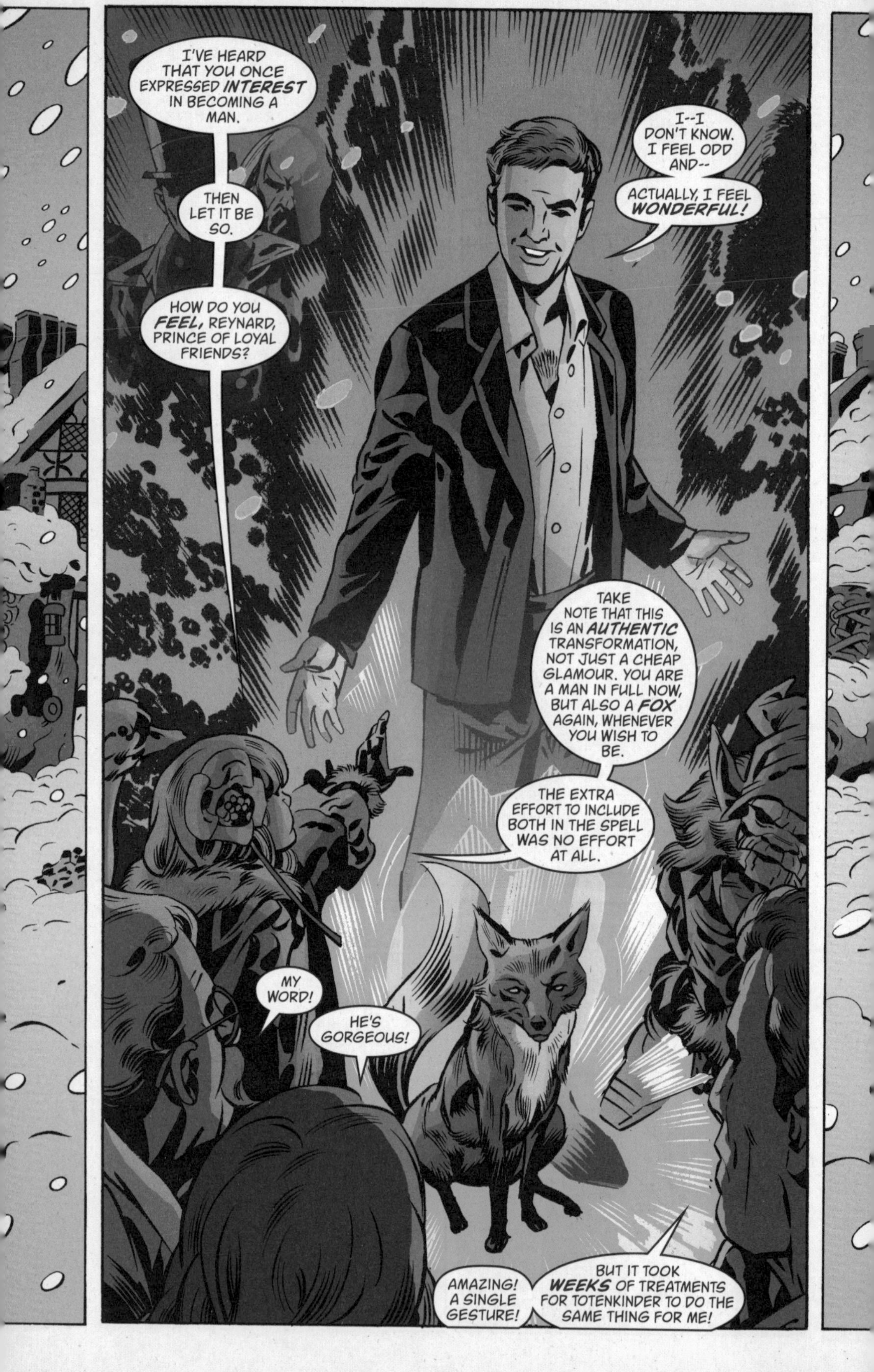
I'VE HEARD THAT YOU ONCE EXPRESSED INTEREST IN BECOMING A MAN.
THEN LET IT BE SO.
HOW DO YOU FEEL, REYNARD, PRINCE OF LOYAL FRIENDS?
I--I DON'T KNOW. I FEEL ODD AND--
ACTUALLY, I FEEL WONDERFUL!
TAKE NOTE THAT THIS IS AN AUTHENTIC TRANSFORMATION, NOT JUST A CHEAP GLAMOUR. YOU ARE A MAN IN FULL NOW, BUT ALSO A FOX AGAIN, WHENEVER YOU WISH TO BE.
THE EXTRA EFFORT TO INCLUDE BOTH IN THE SPELL WAS NO EFFORT AT ALL.
MY WORD!
HE'S GORGEOUS!
AMAZING! A SINGLE GESTURE!
BUT IT TOOK WEEKS OF TREATMENTS FOR TOTENKINDER TO DO THE SAME THING FOR ME!

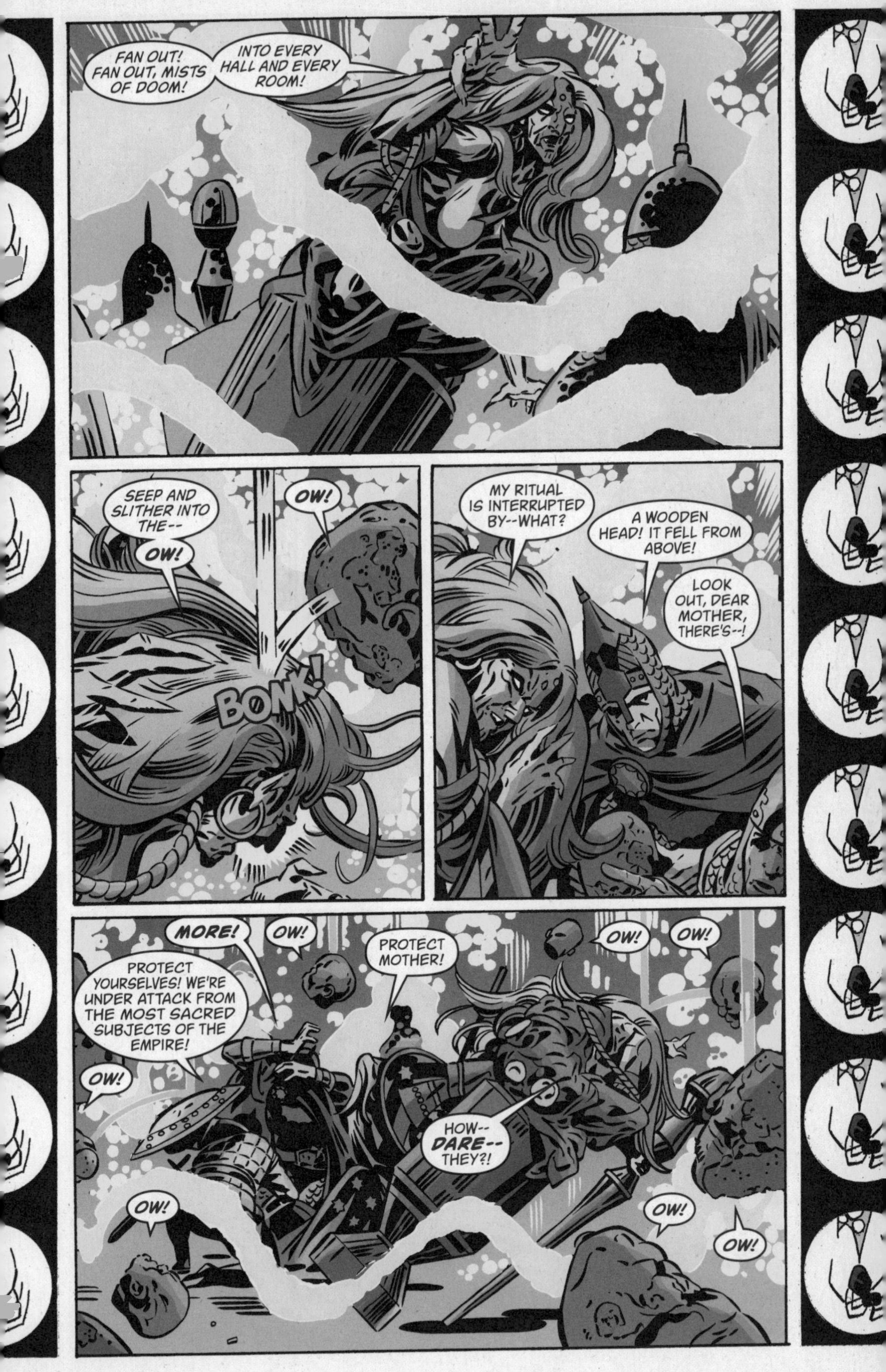
FAN OUT! FAN OUT, MISTS OF DOOM!
INTO EVERY HALL AND EVERY ROOM!
SEEP AND SLITHER INTO THE--
OW!
OW!
BONK!
MY RITUAL IS INTERRUPTED BY--WHAT?
A WOODEN HEAD! IT FELL FROM ABOVE!
LOOK OUT, DEAR MOTHER, THERE'S--!
MORE!
OW!
PROTECT YOURSELVES! WE'RE UNDER ATTACK FROM THE MOST SACRED SUBJECTS OF THE EMPIRE!
OW!
PROTECT MOTHER!
OW!
OW!
HOW-- DARE-- THEY?!
OW!
OW!
OW!

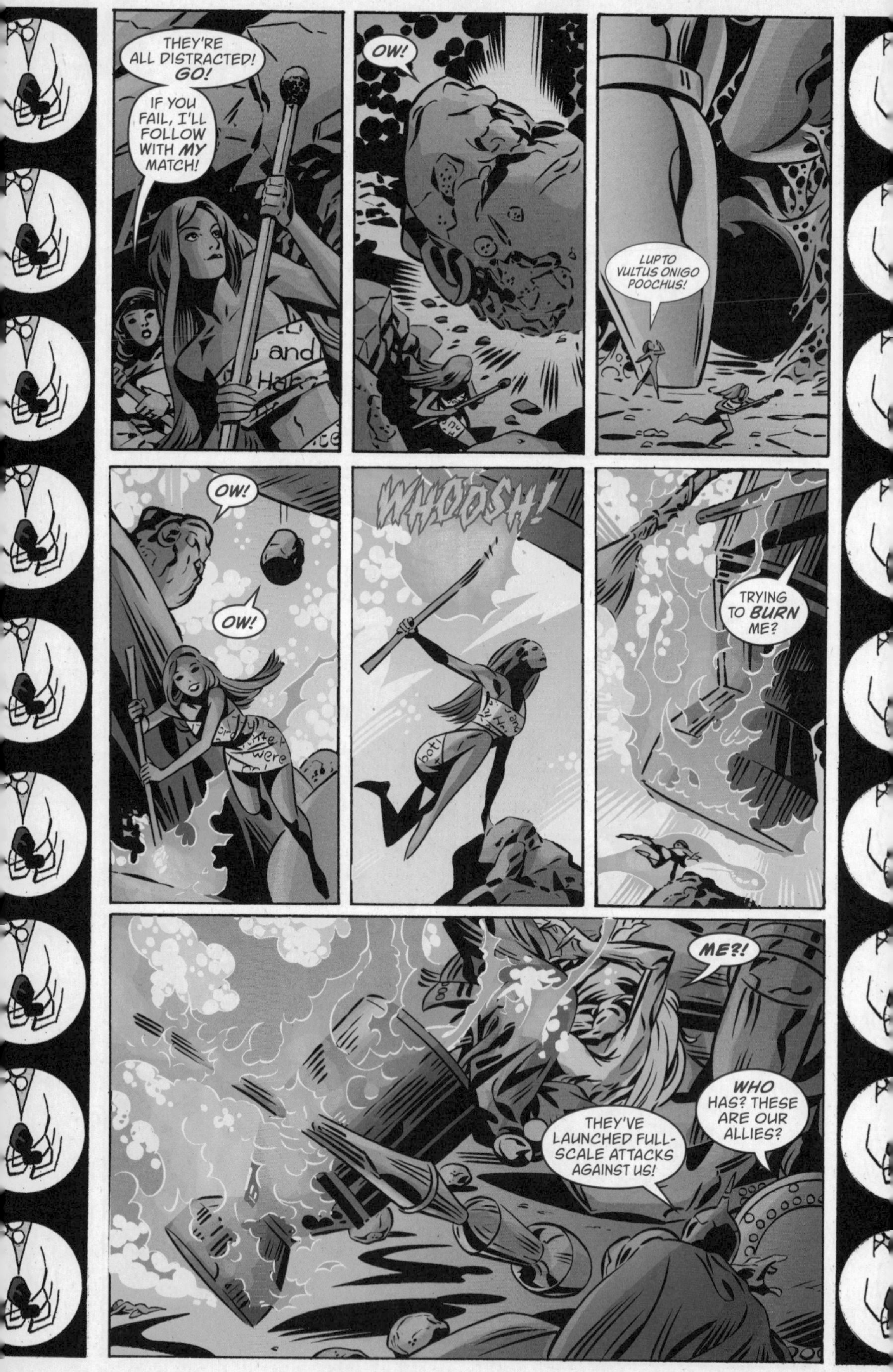

THEY'RE ALL DISTRACTED! GO!
IF YOU FAIL, I'LL FOLLOW WITH MY MATCH!
OW!
LUPTO VULTUS ONIGO POOCHUS!
OW!
OW!
WHOOSH!
TRYING TO BURN ME?
ME?!
WHO HAS? THESE ARE OUR ALLIES?
THEY'VE LAUNCHED FULL-SCALE ATTACKS AGAINST US!

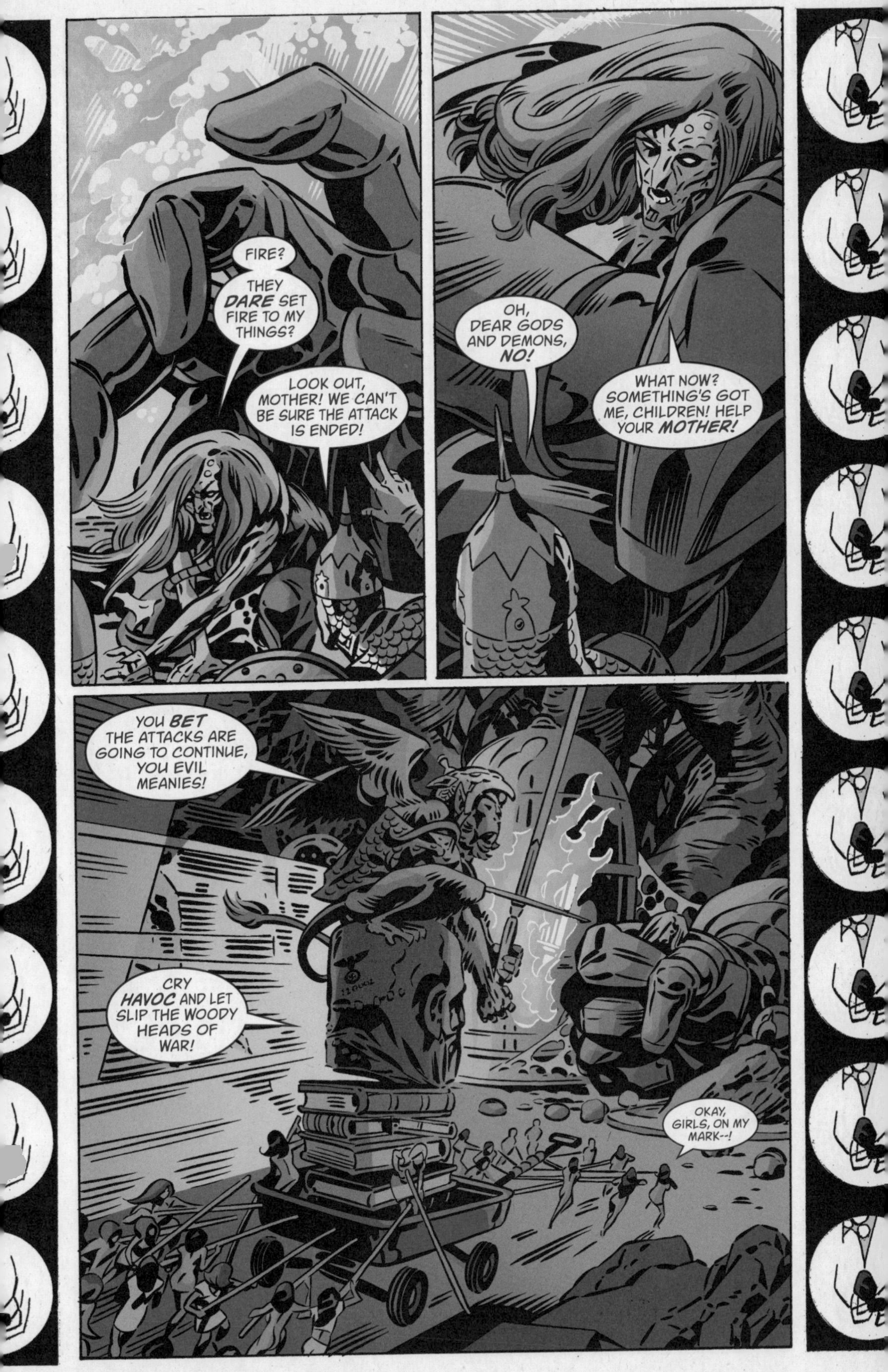
FIRE?
THEY DARE SET FIRE TO MY THINGS?
LOOK OUT, MOTHER! WE CAN'T BE SURE THE ATTACK IS ENDED!
OH, DEAR GODS AND DEMONS, NO!
WHAT NOW? SOMETHING'S GOT ME, CHILDREN! HELP YOUR MOTHER!
YOU BET THE ATTACKS ARE GOING TO CONTINUE, YOU EVIL MEANIES!
CRY HAVOC AND LET SLIP THE WOODY HEADS OF WAR!
OKAY, GIRLS, ON MY MARK--!

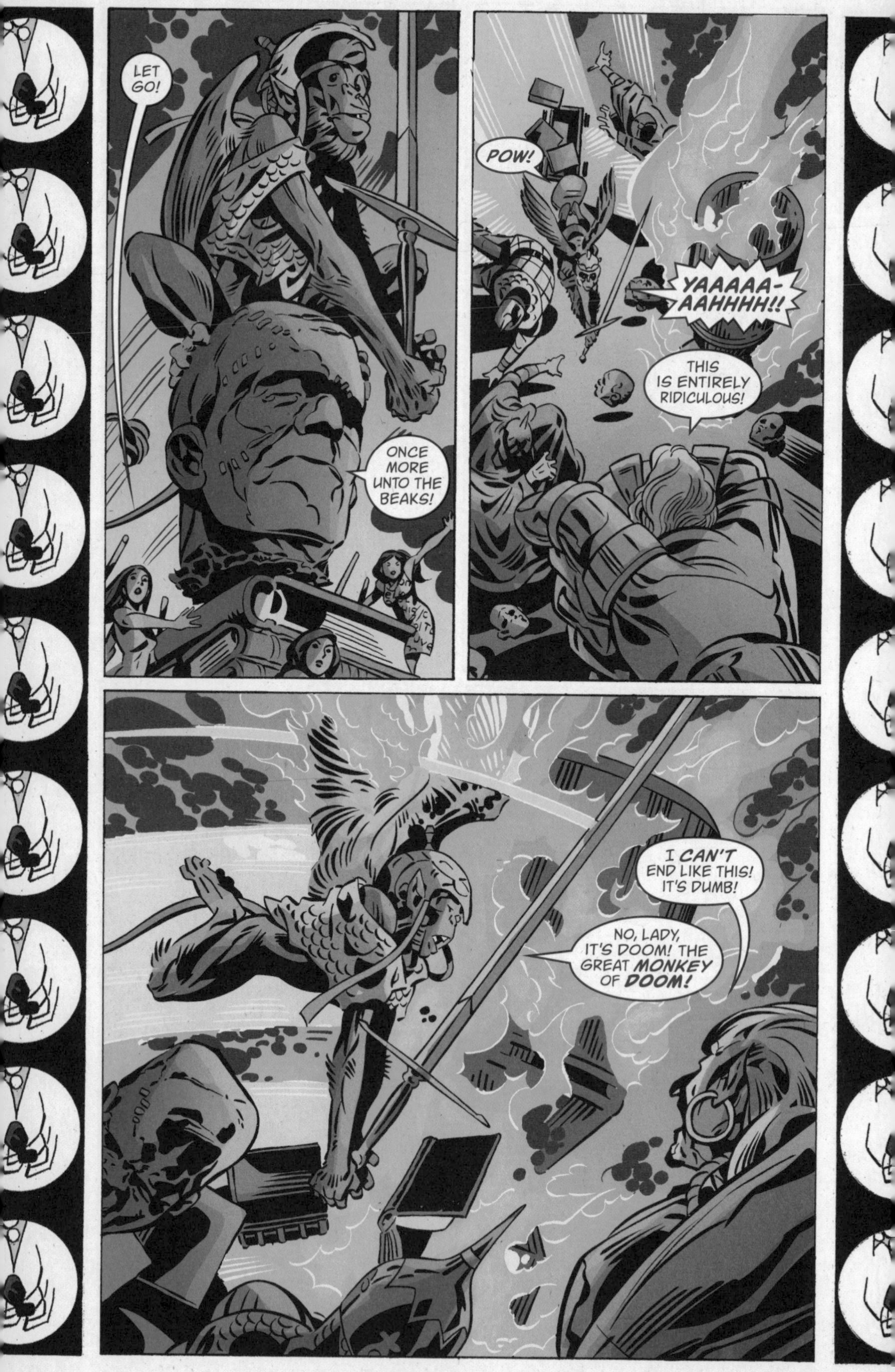
LET GO!
ONCE MORE UNTO THE BEAKS!
POW!
YAAAAA-AAHHHH!!
THIS IS ENTIRELY RIDICULOUS!
I CAN'T END LIKE THIS! IT'S DUMB!
NO, LADY, IT'S DOOM! THE GREAT MONKEY OF DOOM!

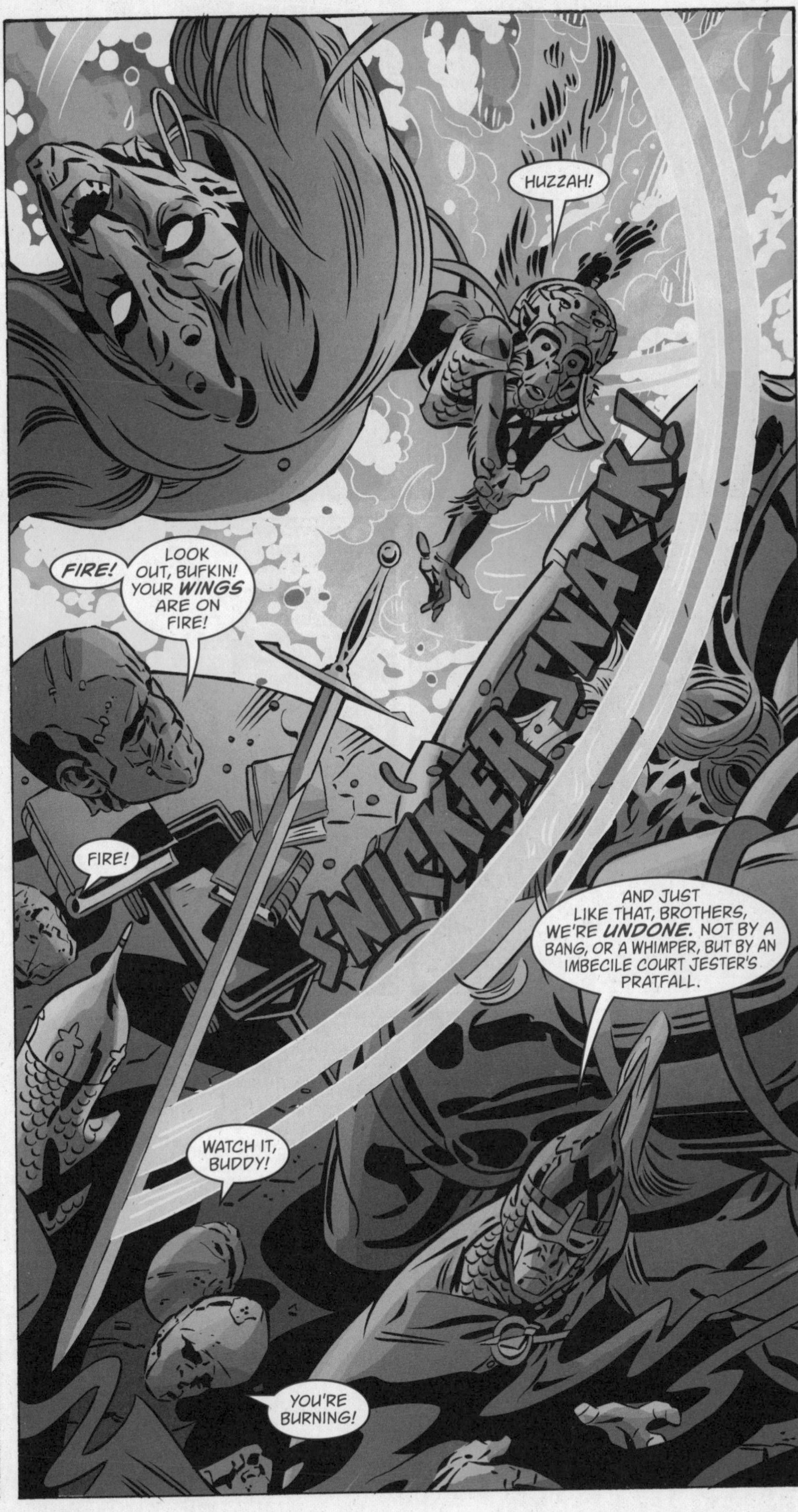
HUZZAH!
FIRE!
LOOK OUT, BUFKIN! YOUR WINGS ARE ON FIRE!
SNICKER SNACK!
FIRE!
AND JUST LIKE THAT, BROTHERS, WE'RE UNDONE. NOT BY A BANG, OR A WHIMPER, BUT BY AN IMBECILE COURT JESTER'S PRATFALL.
WATCH IT, BUDDY!
YOU'RE BURNING!

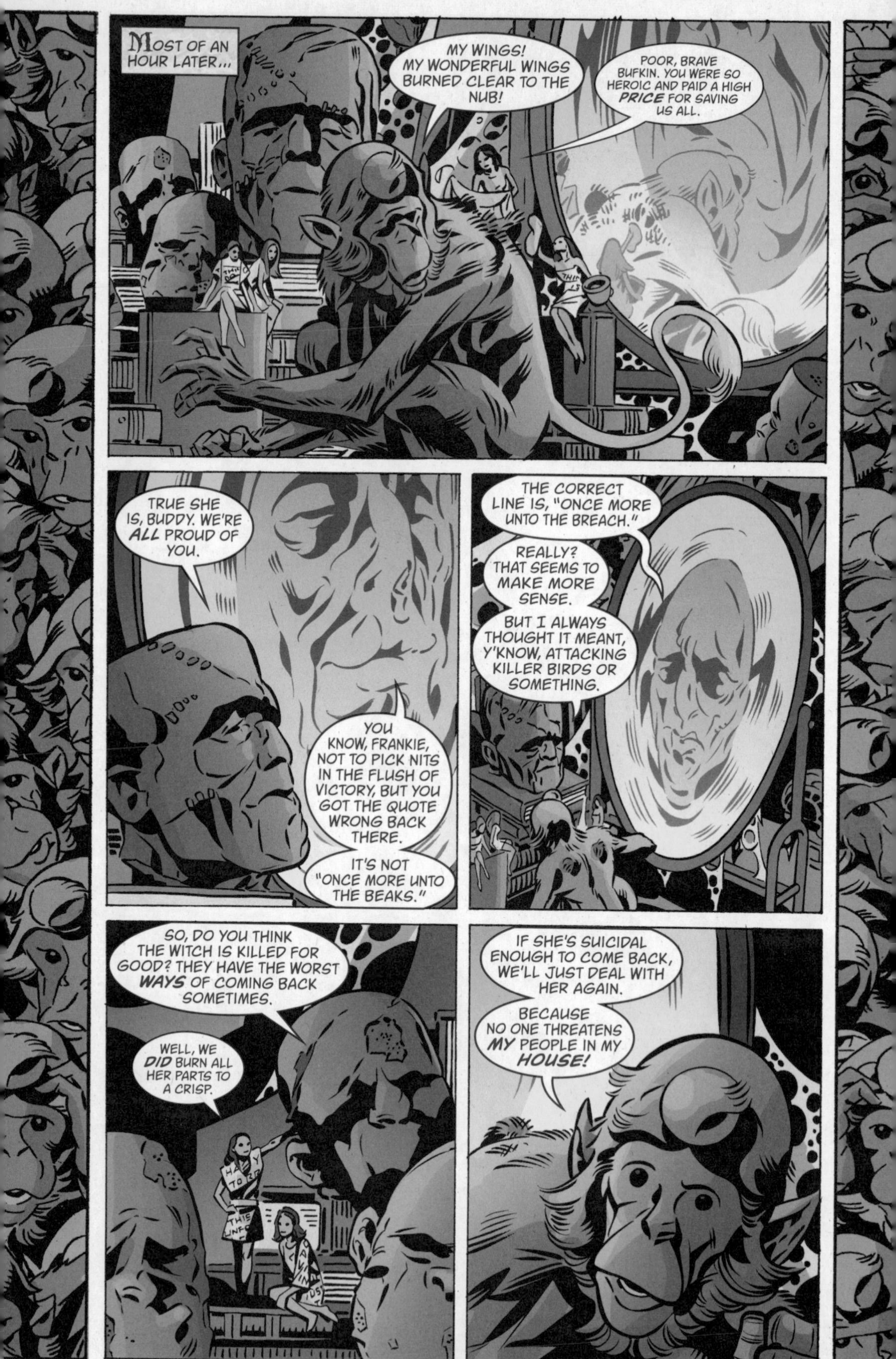
MOST OF AN HOUR LATER...
MY WINGS! MY WONDERFUL WINGS BURNED CLEAR TO THE NUB!
POOR, BRAVE BUFKIN. YOU WERE SO HEROIC AND PAID A HIGH PRICE FOR SAVING US ALL.
TRUE SHE IS, BUDDY. WE'RE ALL PROUD OF YOU.
YOU KNOW, FRANKIE, NOT TO PICK NITS IN THE FLUSH OF VICTORY, BUT YOU GOT THE QUOTE WRONG BACK THERE.
IT'S NOT "ONCE MORE UNTO THE BEAKS."
THE CORRECT LINE IS, "ONCE MORE UNTO THE BREACH."
REALLY? THAT SEEMS TO MAKE MORE SENSE.
BUT I ALWAYS THOUGHT IT MEANT, Y'KNOW, ATTACKING KILLER BIRDS OR SOMETHING.
SO, DO YOU THINK THE WITCH IS KILLED FOR GOOD? THEY HAVE THE WORST WAYS OF COMING BACK SOMETIMES.
WELL, WE DID BURN ALL HER PARTS TO A CRISP.
IF SHE'S SUICIDAL ENOUGH TO COME BACK, WE'LL JUST DEAL WITH HER AGAIN.
BECAUSE NO ONE THREATENS MY PEOPLE IN MY HOUSE!

AND WORLDS AWAY, AT THE FARM...

THIS IS A STUNT! A BLATANT AND CARELESS STUNT!

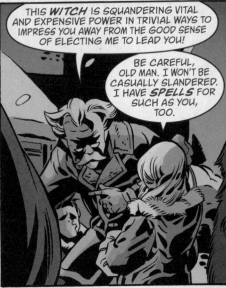

THIS **WITCH** IS SQUANDERING VITAL AND EXPENSIVE POWER IN TRIVIAL WAYS TO IMPRESS YOU AWAY FROM THE GOOD SENSE OF ELECTING ME TO LEAD YOU!

BE CAREFUL, OLD MAN. I WON'T BE CASUALLY SLANDERED. I HAVE **SPELLS** FOR SUCH AS YOU, TOO.

AND YOU BE CAREFUL, MISS. THAT SOUNDED PERILOUSLY **CLOSE** TO A THREAT.

YEAH, YOU CAN'T **THREATEN** MY DAD, OZMA. IT'S AGAINST THE RULES.

OH, DO SETTLE DOWN, ALL OF YOU. I'VE NO **INTENTION** OF HARMING THAT TOOTHLESS OLD HAS-BEEN. BUT I'M NOT THE ONLY ONE HE SHOULD BE WARY OF.

NOT BY A LONG SHOT.

WHILE I WON'T **MOVE** AGAINST A FELLOW PRACTITIONER, NO MATTER HOW DEPRAVED OR CORRUPTED, NOT **EVERYONE** HAS MY GIFT OF TOLERANCE AND DISCIPLINE.

BEFORE COMING OUT HERE, I DID MAKE THE MAGICAL EQUIVALENT OF A PHONE CALL TO SOMEONE WE ALL SHOULD HEAR FROM BEFORE MAKING ANY RASH DECISIONS.

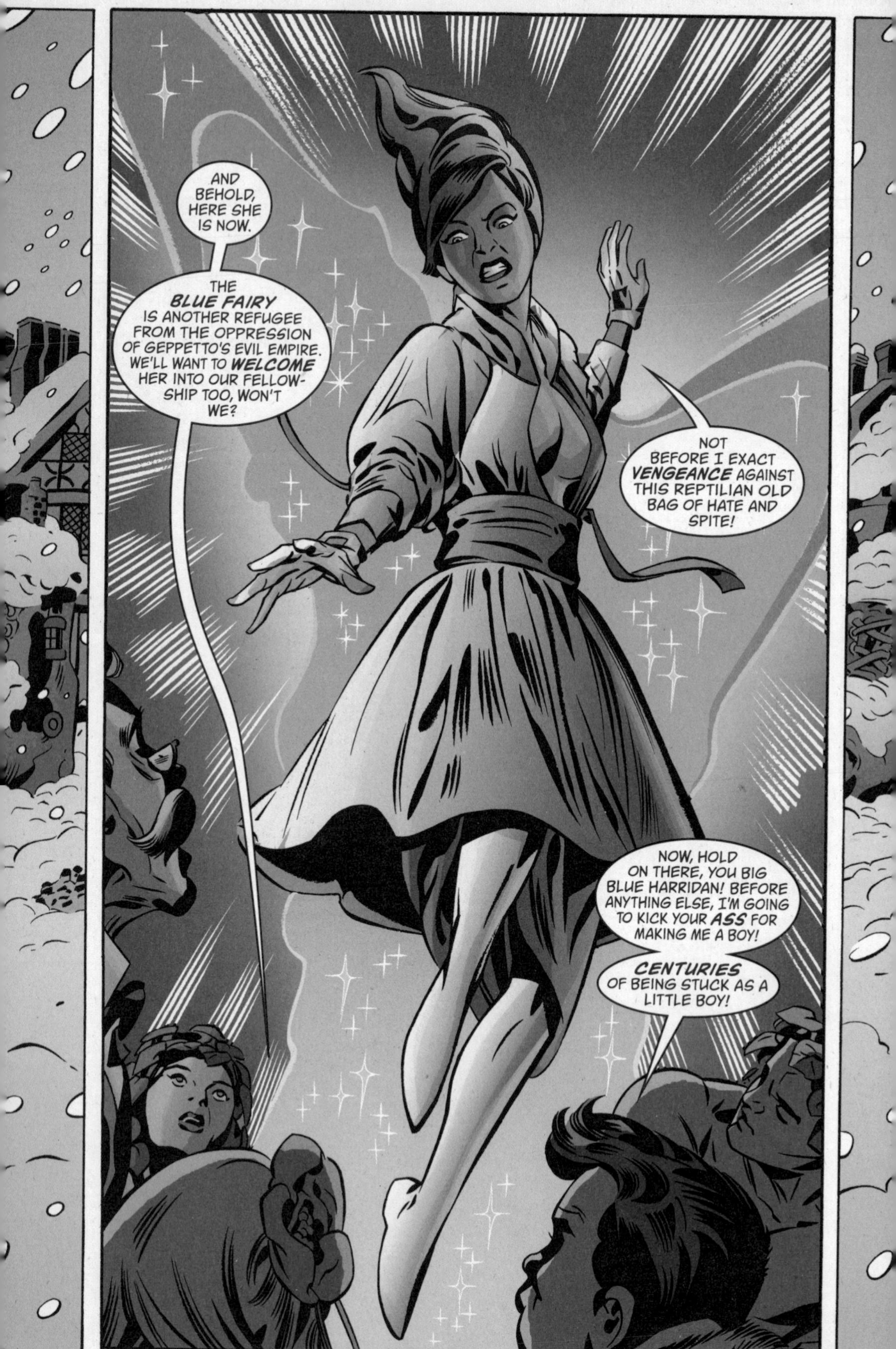
AND BEHOLD, HERE SHE IS NOW.
THE BLUE FAIRY IS ANOTHER REFUGEE FROM THE OPPRESSION OF GEPPETTO'S EVIL EMPIRE. WE'LL WANT TO WELCOME HER INTO OUR FELLOWSHIP TOO, WON'T WE?
NOT BEFORE I EXACT VENGEANCE AGAINST THIS REPTILIAN OLD BAG OF HATE AND SPITE!
NOW, HOLD ON THERE, YOU BIG BLUE HARRIDAN! BEFORE ANYTHING ELSE, I'M GOING TO KICK YOUR ASS FOR MAKING ME A BOY!
CENTURIES OF BEING STUCK AS A LITTLE BOY!

NEXT: THE OLD BALL GAME

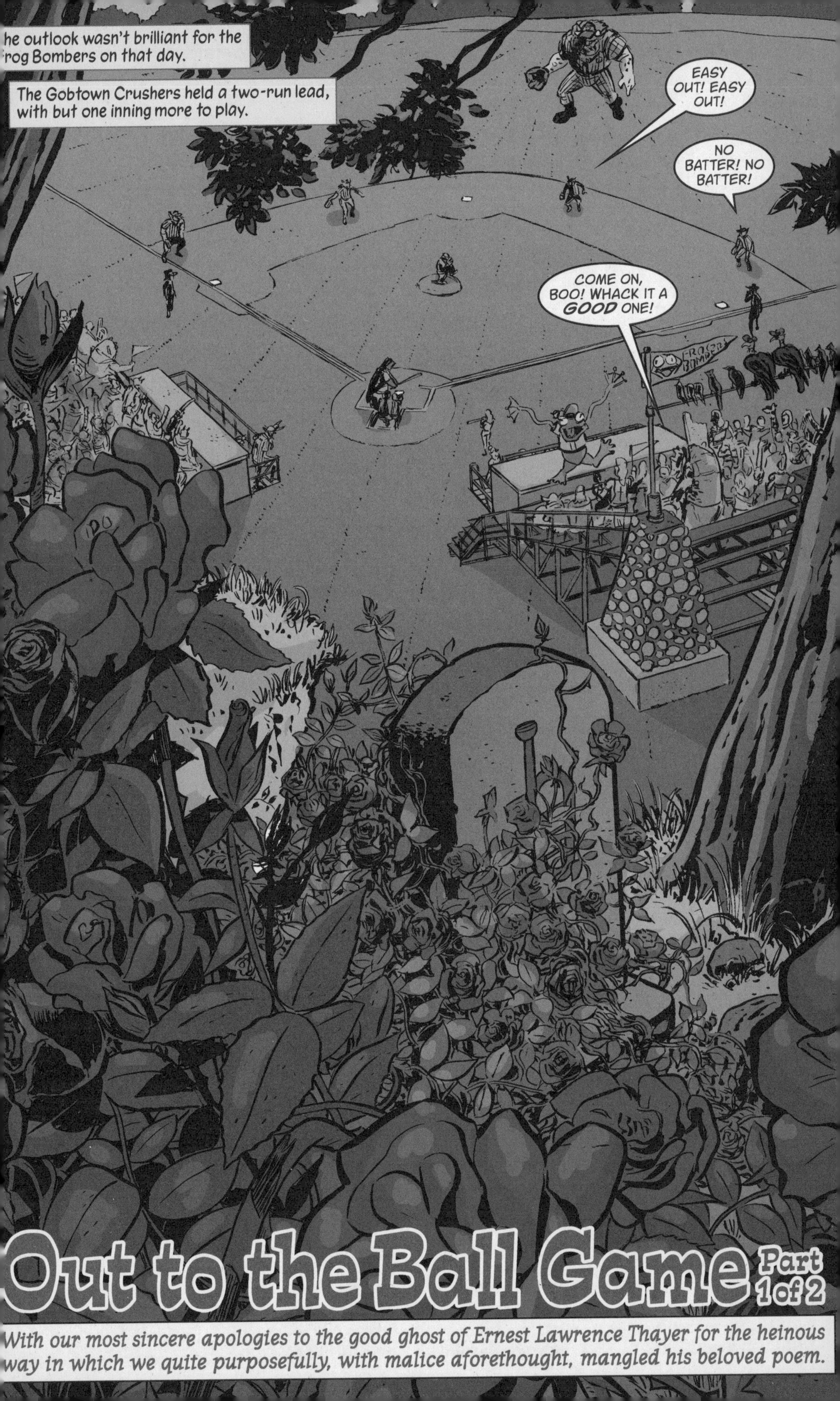
he outlook wasn't brilliant for the rog Bombers on that day.
The Gobtown Crushers held a two-run lead, with but one inning more to play.
EASY OUT! EASY OUT!
NO BATTER! NO BATTER!
COME ON, BOO! WHACK IT A GOOD ONE!
Out to the Ball Game Part 1 of 2
With our most sincere apologies to the good ghost of Ernest Lawrence Thayer for the heinous way in which we quite purposefully, with malice aforethought, mangled his beloved poem.

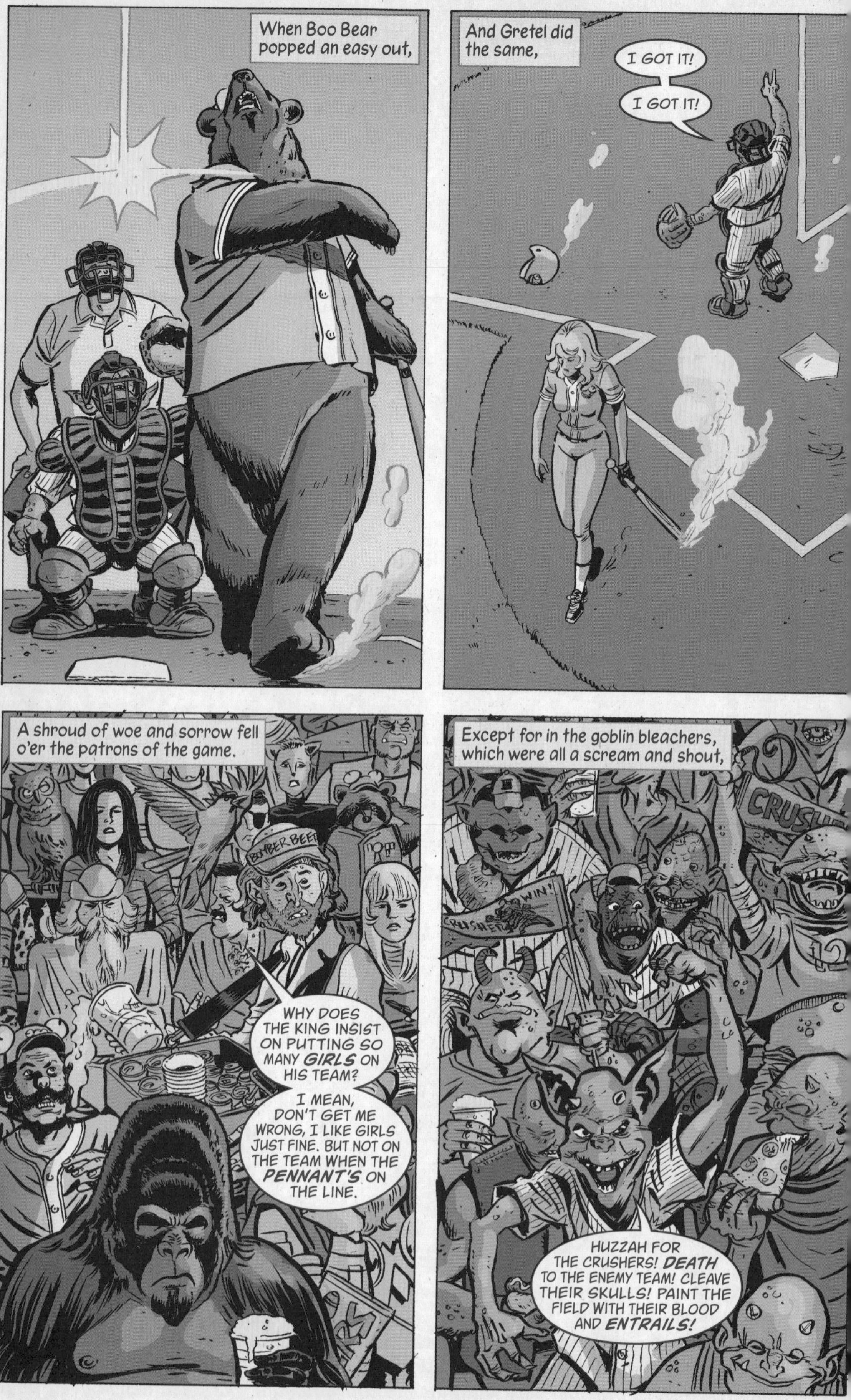

When Boo Bear popped an easy out,
And Gretel did the same,
I GOT IT!
I GOT IT!
A shroud of woe and sorrow fell o'er the patrons of the game.
BOMBER BEER
WHY DOES THE KING INSIST ON PUTTING SO MANY GIRLS ON HIS TEAM?
I MEAN, DON'T GET ME WRONG, I LIKE GIRLS JUST FINE. BUT NOT ON THE TEAM WHEN THE PENNANT'S ON THE LINE.
Except for in the goblin bleachers, which were all a scream and shout,
CRUSHERS
WIN
HUZZAH FOR THE CRUSHERS! DEATH TO THE ENEMY TEAM! CLEAVE THEIR SKULLS! PAINT THE FIELD WITH THEIR BLOOD AND ENTRAILS!

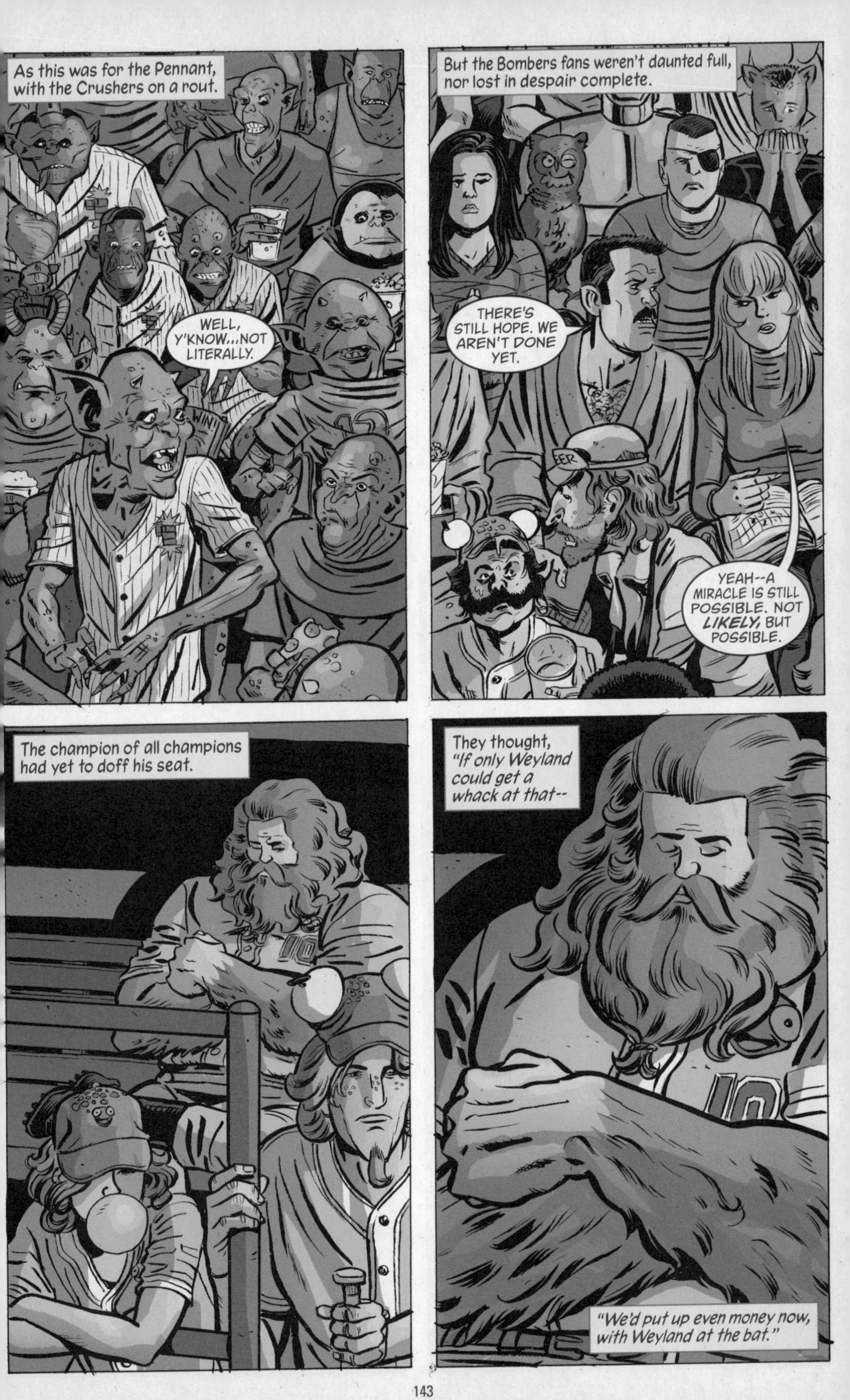
As this was for the Pennant, with the Crushers on a rout.
WELL, Y'KNOW...NOT LITERALLY.
But the Bombers fans weren't daunted full, nor lost in despair complete.
THERE'S STILL HOPE. WE AREN'T DONE YET.
YEAH--A MIRACLE IS STILL POSSIBLE. NOT LIKELY, BUT POSSIBLE.
The champion of all champions had yet to doff his seat.
They thought, "If only Weyland could get a whack at that--
"We'd put up even money now, with Weyland at the bat."

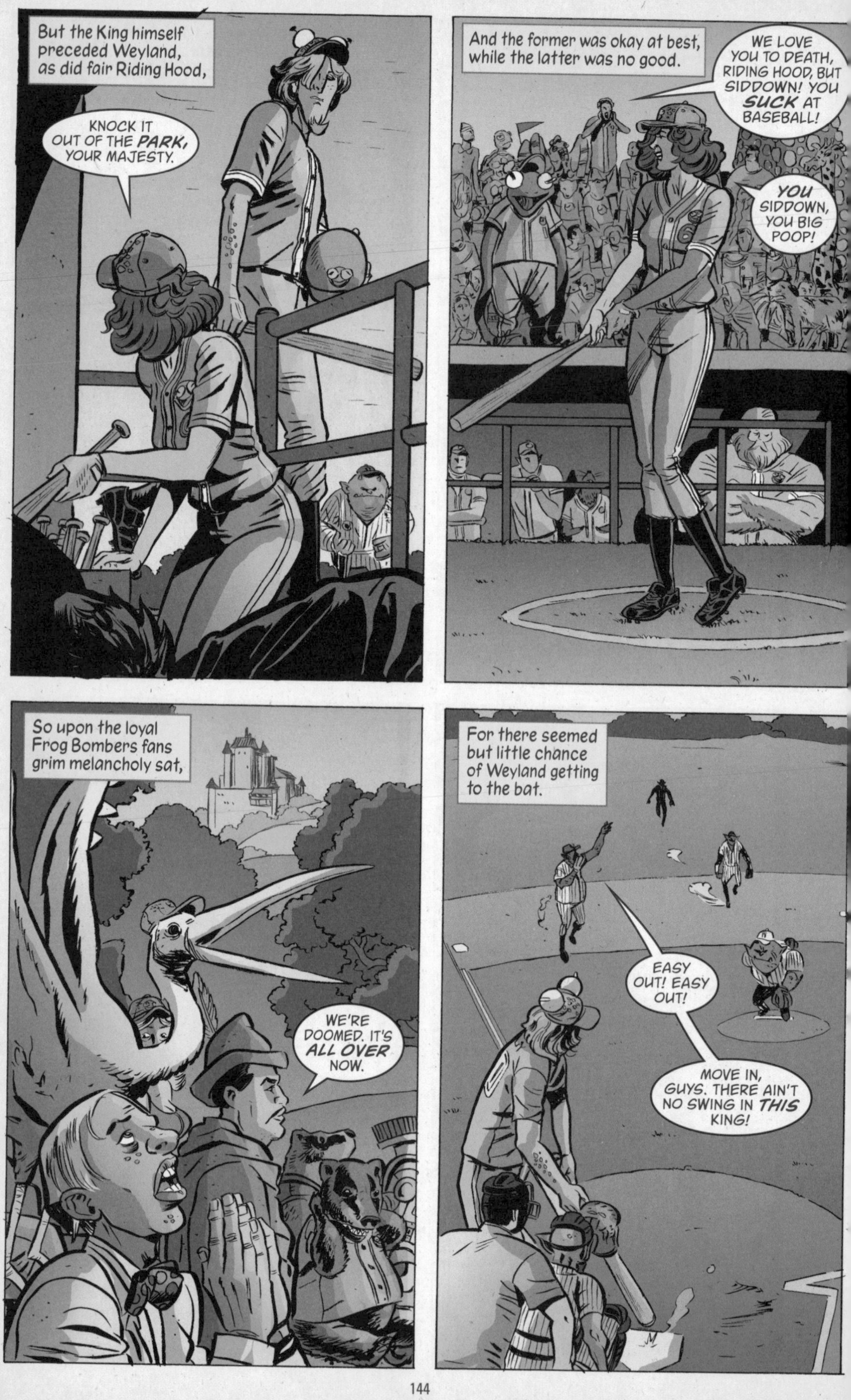
But the King himself preceded Weyland, as did fair Riding Hood,
KNOCK IT OUT OF THE PARK, YOUR MAJESTY.
And the former was okay at best, while the latter was no good.
WE LOVE YOU TO DEATH, RIDING HOOD, BUT SIDDOWN! YOU SUCK AT BASEBALL!
YOU SIDDOWN, YOU BIG POOP!
So upon the loyal Frog Bombers fans grim melancholy sat,
WE'RE DOOMED. IT'S ALL OVER NOW.
For there seemed but little chance of Weyland getting to the bat.
EASY OUT! EASY OUT!
MOVE IN, GUYS. THERE AIN'T NO SWING IN THIS KING!

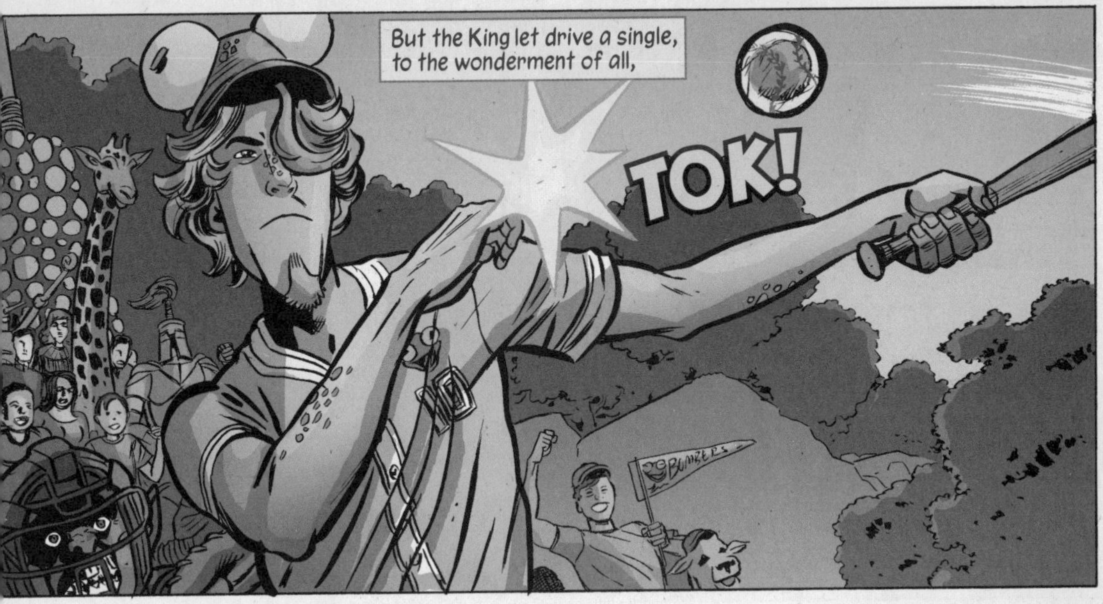
But the King let drive a single, to the wonderment of all,
TOK!

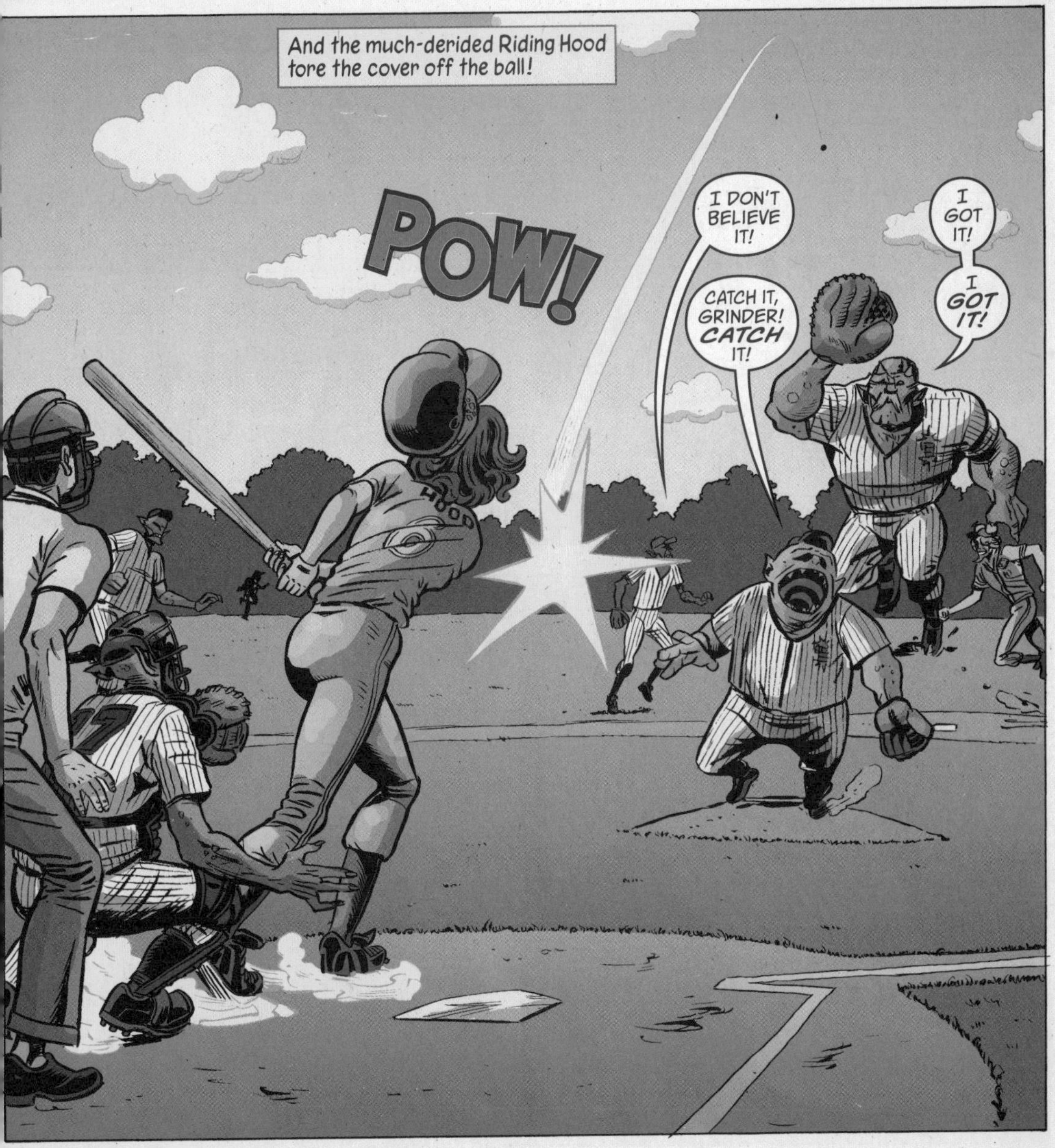
And the much-derided Riding Hood tore the cover off the ball!
POW!
I DON'T BELIEVE IT!
CATCH IT, GRINDER! CATCH IT!
I GOT IT!
I GOT IT!

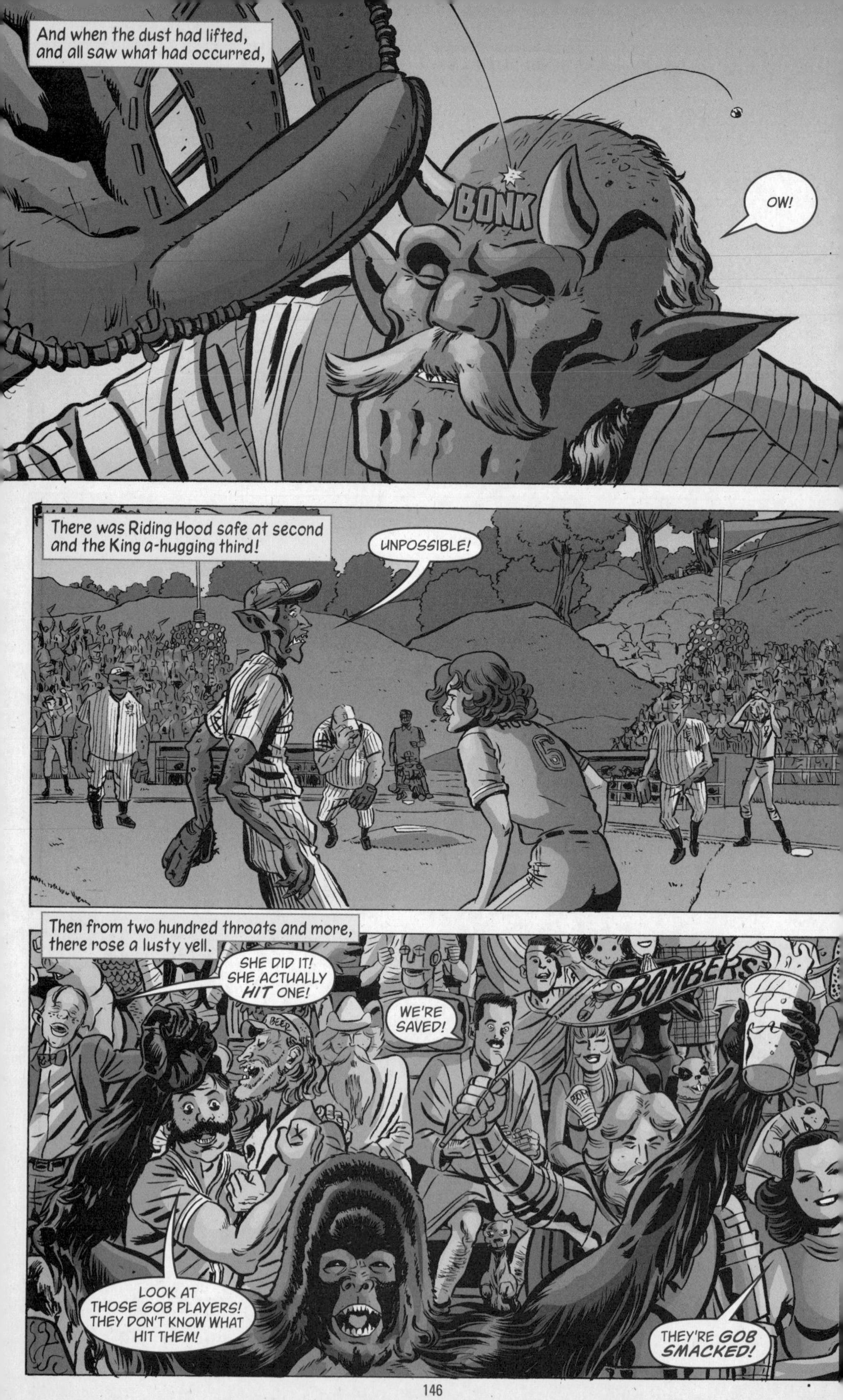
And when the dust had lifted, and all saw what had occurred,
BONK
OW!
There was Riding Hood safe at second and the King a-hugging third!
UNPOSSIBLE!
Then from two hundred throats and more, there rose a lusty yell.
SHE DID IT! SHE ACTUALLY *HIT* ONE!
WE'RE SAVED!
BOMBERS
LOOK AT THOSE GOB PLAYERS! THEY DON'T KNOW WHAT HIT THEM!
THEY'RE *GOB SMACKED!*

It rumbled through the valley, it rattled in the dell.

It pounded off the castle, and recoiled upon the flat,

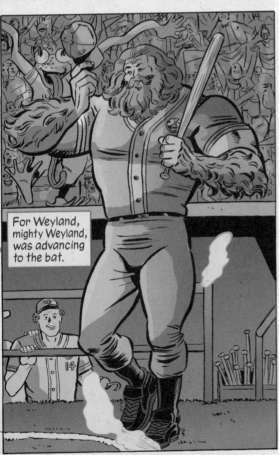

For Weyland, mighty Weyland, was advancing to the bat.

WHAT ARE WE GOING TO DO, MR. BRUMP? CAN YOU *BEAT* HIM?

I NE'ER HAVE B'FORE. WE HAD TH' GAME WON, MR. CUTLIVER. WE HAD TH' PENNANT IN OUR WARTY GRASP. BUT NOW--?

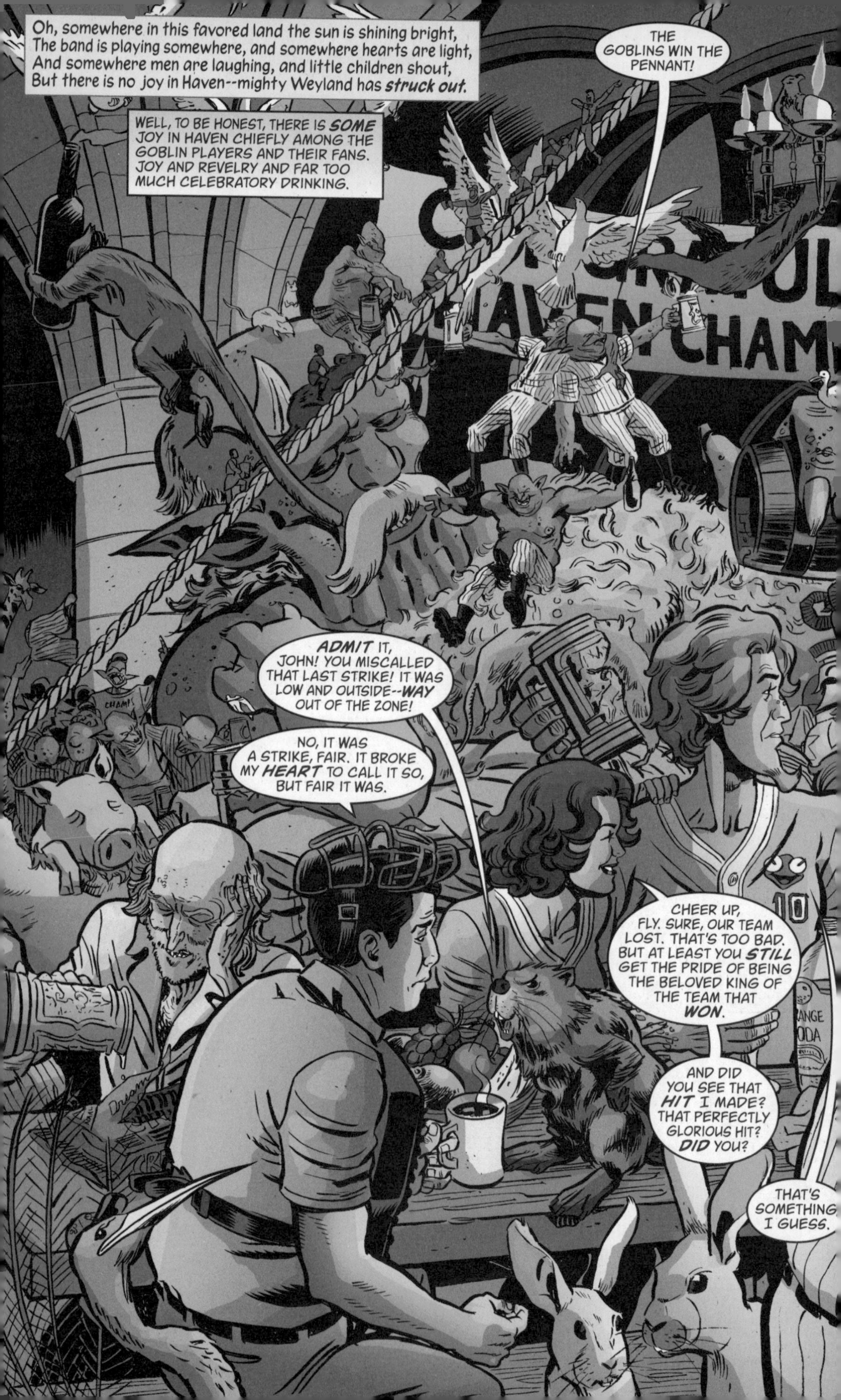
Oh, somewhere in this favored land the sun is shining bright, The band is playing somewhere, and somewhere hearts are light, And somewhere men are laughing, and little children shout, But there is no joy in Haven--mighty Weyland has **struck out**.
THE GOBLINS WIN THE PENNANT!
WELL, TO BE HONEST, THERE IS **SOME** JOY IN HAVEN CHIEFLY AMONG THE GOBLIN PLAYERS AND THEIR FANS. JOY AND REVELRY AND FAR TOO MUCH CELEBRATORY DRINKING.
HAVEN CHAM
CHAMPS
ADMIT IT, JOHN! YOU MISCALLED THAT LAST STRIKE! IT WAS LOW AND OUTSIDE--**WAY** OUT OF THE ZONE!
NO, IT WAS A STRIKE, FAIR. IT BROKE MY **HEART** TO CALL IT SO, BUT FAIR IT WAS.
CHEER UP, FLY. SURE, OUR TEAM LOST. THAT'S TOO BAD. BUT AT LEAST YOU **STILL** GET THE PRIDE OF BEING THE BELOVED KING OF THE TEAM THAT **WON**.
AND DID YOU SEE THAT **HIT** I MADE? THAT PERFECTLY GLORIOUS HIT? **DID** YOU?
THAT'S SOMETHING I GUESS.
10

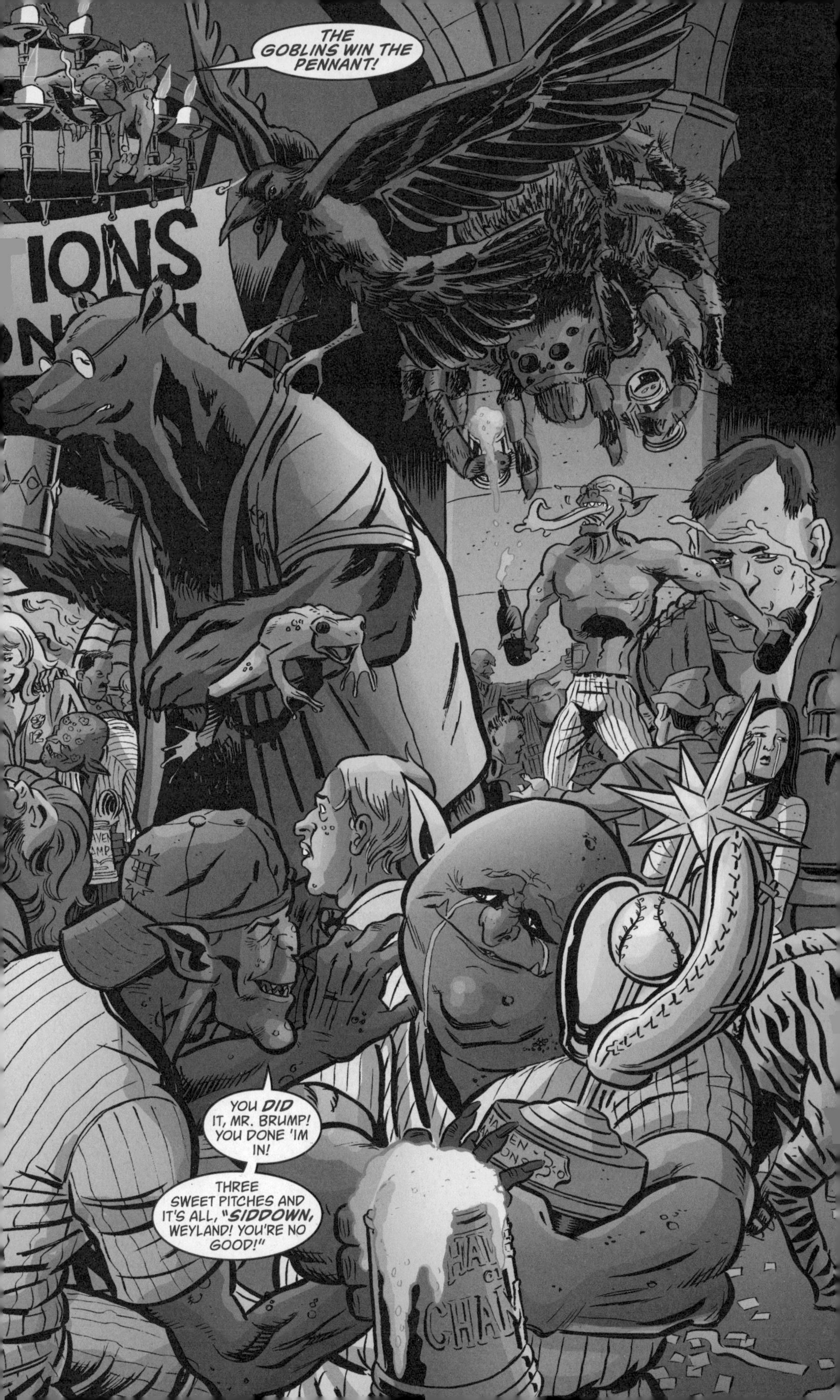
THE GOBLINS WIN THE PENNANT!
IONS
YOU DID IT, MR. BRUMP! YOU DONE 'IM IN!
THREE SWEET PITCHES AND IT'S ALL, "SIDDOWN, WEYLAND! YOU'RE NO GOOD!"

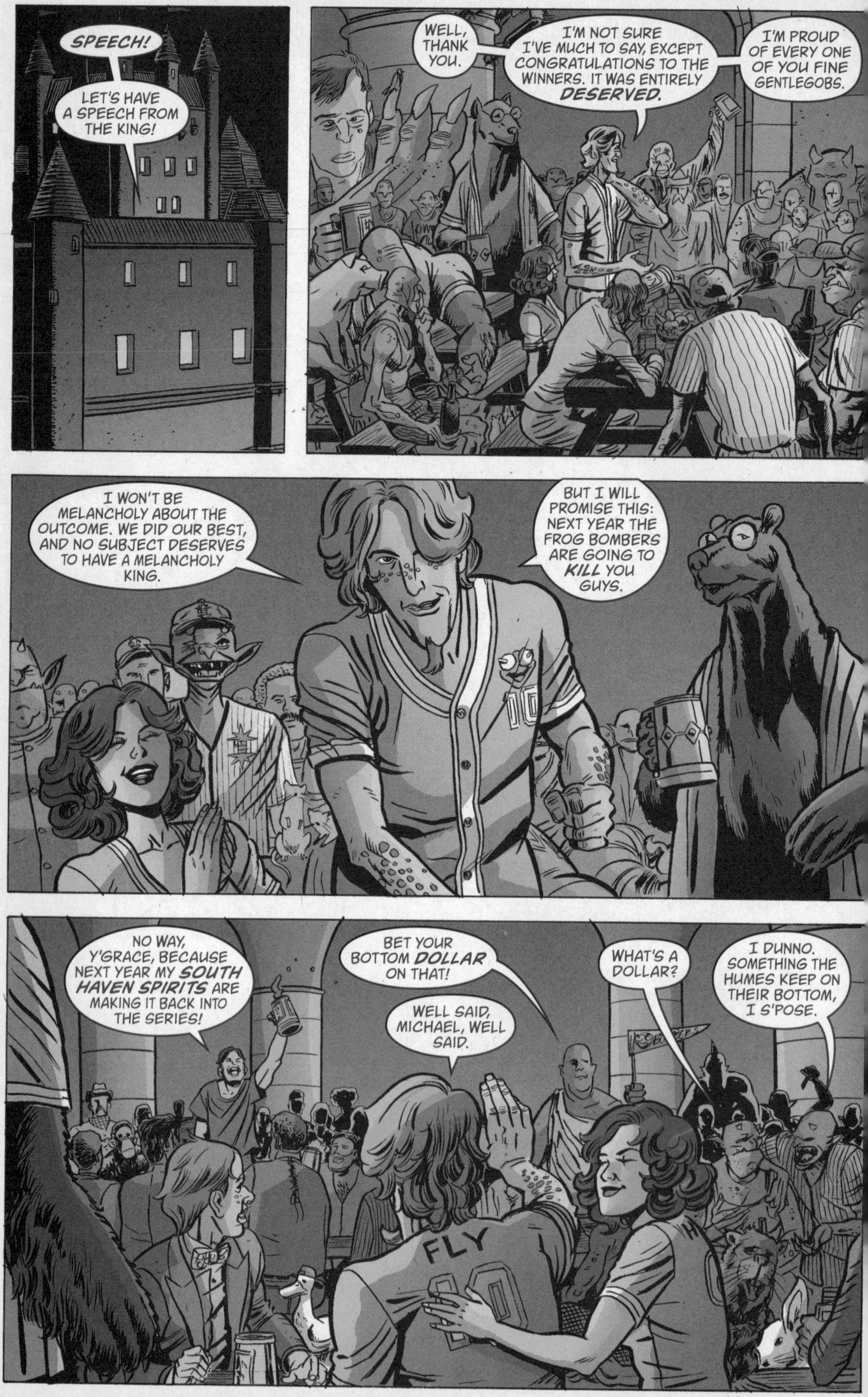
SPEECH!
LET'S HAVE A SPEECH FROM THE KING!
WELL, THANK YOU.
I'M NOT SURE I'VE MUCH TO SAY, EXCEPT CONGRATULATIONS TO THE WINNERS. IT WAS ENTIRELY DESERVED.
I'M PROUD OF EVERY ONE OF YOU FINE GENTLEGOBS.
I WON'T BE MELANCHOLY ABOUT THE OUTCOME. WE DID OUR BEST, AND NO SUBJECT DESERVES TO HAVE A MELANCHOLY KING.
BUT I WILL PROMISE THIS: NEXT YEAR THE FROG BOMBERS ARE GOING TO KILL YOU GUYS.
NO WAY, Y'GRACE, BECAUSE NEXT YEAR MY SOUTH HAVEN SPIRITS ARE MAKING IT BACK INTO THE SERIES!
BET YOUR BOTTOM DOLLAR ON THAT!
WELL SAID, MICHAEL, WELL SAID.
WHAT'S A DOLLAR?
I DUNNO. SOMETHING THE HUMES KEEP ON THEIR BOTTOM, I S'POSE.
FLY

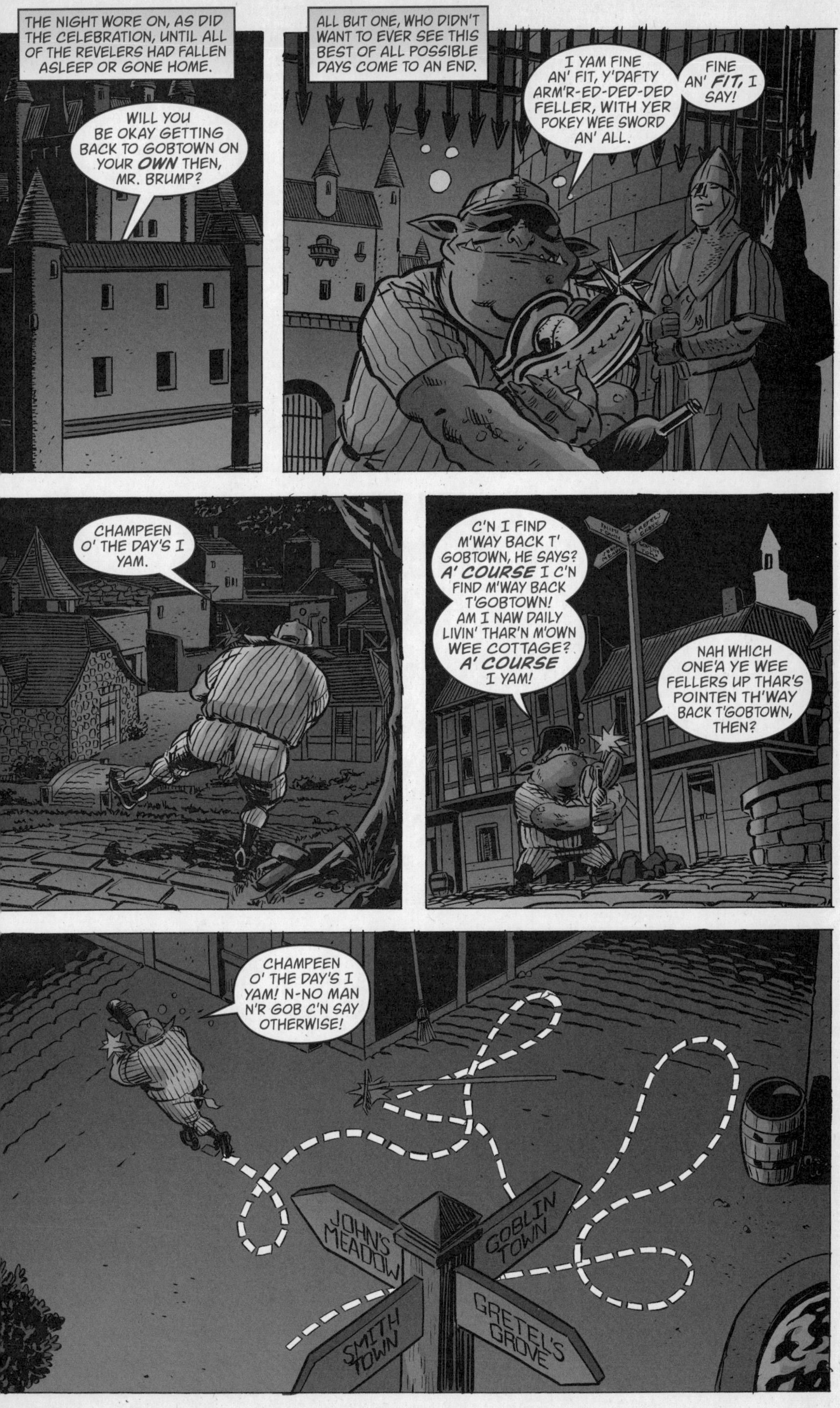
THE NIGHT WORE ON, AS DID THE CELEBRATION, UNTIL ALL OF THE REVELERS HAD FALLEN ASLEEP OR GONE HOME.
WILL YOU BE OKAY GETTING BACK TO GOBTOWN ON YOUR OWN THEN, MR. BRUMP?
ALL BUT ONE, WHO DIDN'T WANT TO EVER SEE THIS BEST OF ALL POSSIBLE DAYS COME TO AN END.
I YAM FINE AN' FIT, Y'DAFTY ARM'R-ED-DED-DED FELLER, WITH YER POKEY WEE SWORD AN' ALL.
FINE AN' FIT, I SAY!
CHAMPEEN O' THE DAY'S I YAM.
C'N I FIND M'WAY BACK T' GOBTOWN, HE SAYS? A' COURSE I C'N FIND M'WAY BACK T'GOBTOWN! AM I NAW DAILY LIVIN' THAR'N M'OWN WEE COTTAGE? A' COURSE I YAM!
NAH WHICH ONE'A YE WEE FELLERS UP THAR'S POINTEN TH'WAY BACK T'GOBTOWN, THEN?
CHAMPEEN O' THE DAY'S I YAM! N-NO MAN N'R GOB C'N SAY OTHERWISE!
JOHN'S MEADOW
GOBLIN TOWN
SMITH TOWN
GRETEL'S GROVE

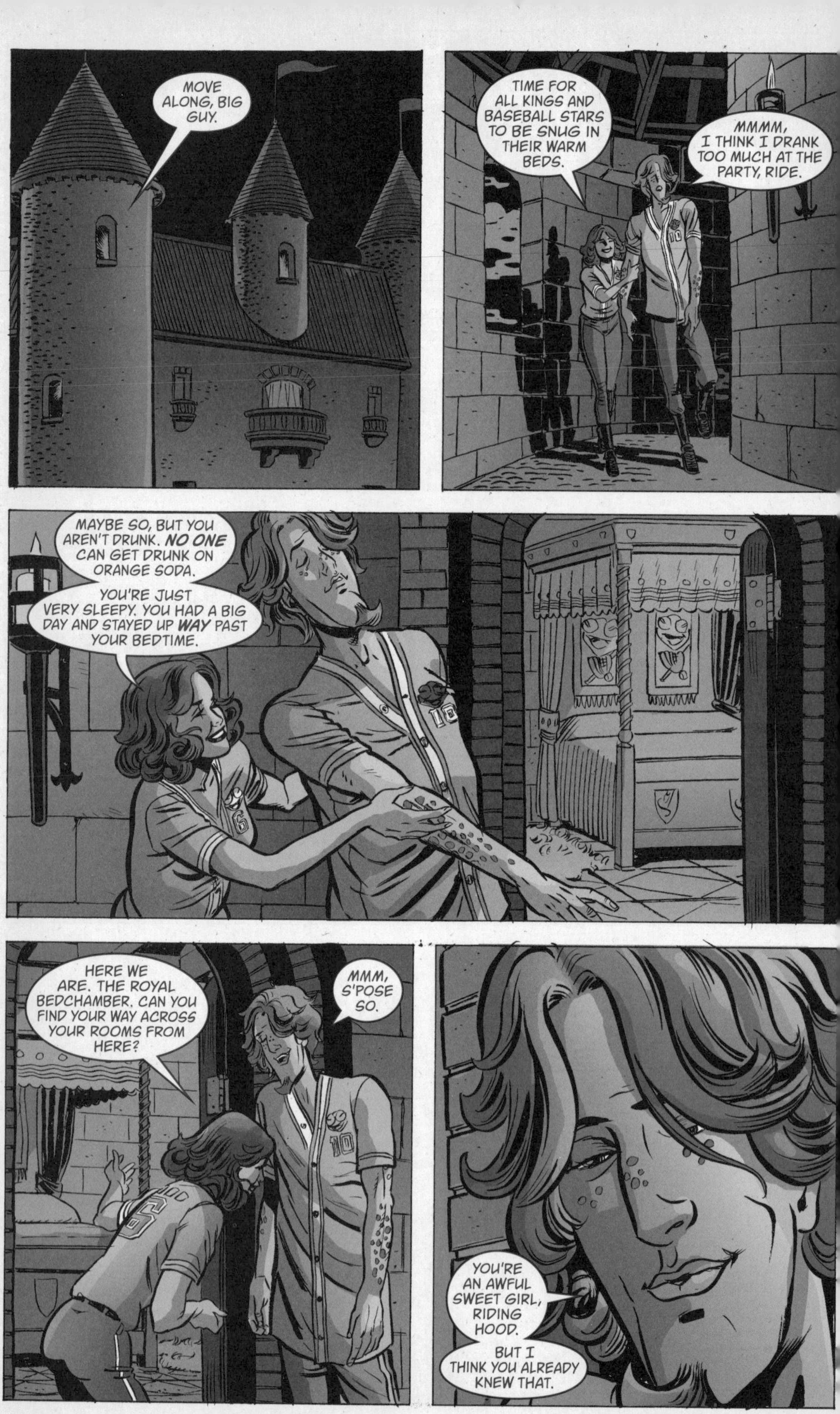
MOVE ALONG, BIG GUY.
TIME FOR ALL KINGS AND BASEBALL STARS TO BE SNUG IN THEIR WARM BEDS.
MMMM, I THINK I DRANK TOO MUCH AT THE PARTY, RIDE.
MAYBE SO, BUT YOU AREN'T DRUNK. NO ONE CAN GET DRUNK ON ORANGE SODA.
YOU'RE JUST VERY SLEEPY. YOU HAD A BIG DAY AND STAYED UP WAY PAST YOUR BEDTIME.
HERE WE ARE. THE ROYAL BEDCHAMBER. CAN YOU FIND YOUR WAY ACROSS YOUR ROOMS FROM HERE?
MMM, S'POSE SO.
YOU'RE AN AWFUL SWEET GIRL, RIDING HOOD.
BUT I THINK YOU ALREADY KNEW THAT.

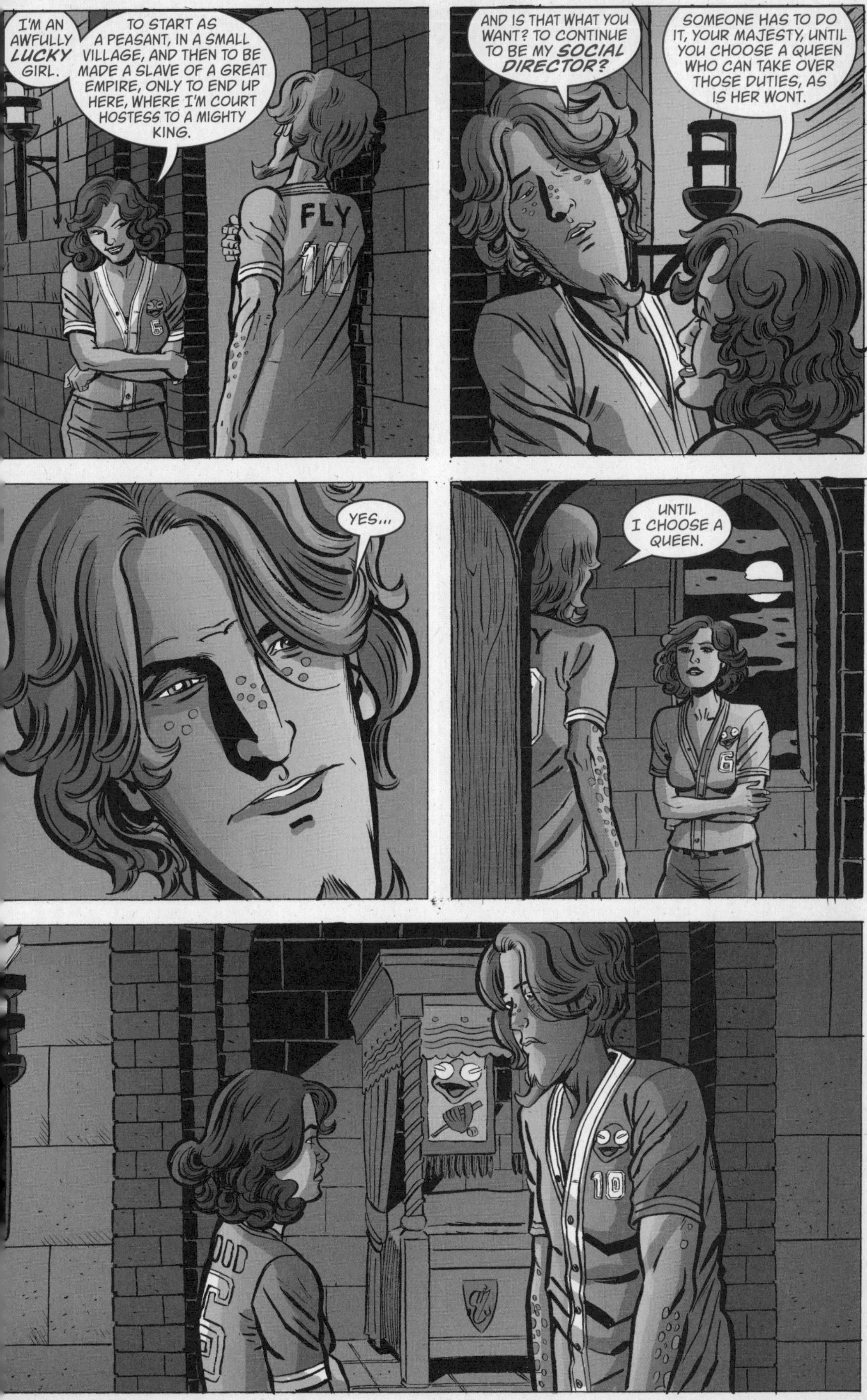
I'M AN AWFULLY LUCKY GIRL.
TO START AS A PEASANT, IN A SMALL VILLAGE, AND THEN TO BE MADE A SLAVE OF A GREAT EMPIRE, ONLY TO END UP HERE, WHERE I'M COURT HOSTESS TO A MIGHTY KING.
FLY 10
AND IS THAT WHAT YOU WANT? TO CONTINUE TO BE MY SOCIAL DIRECTOR?
SOMEONE HAS TO DO IT, YOUR MAJESTY, UNTIL YOU CHOOSE A QUEEN WHO CAN TAKE OVER THOSE DUTIES, AS IS HER WONT.
YES...
UNTIL I CHOOSE A QUEEN.

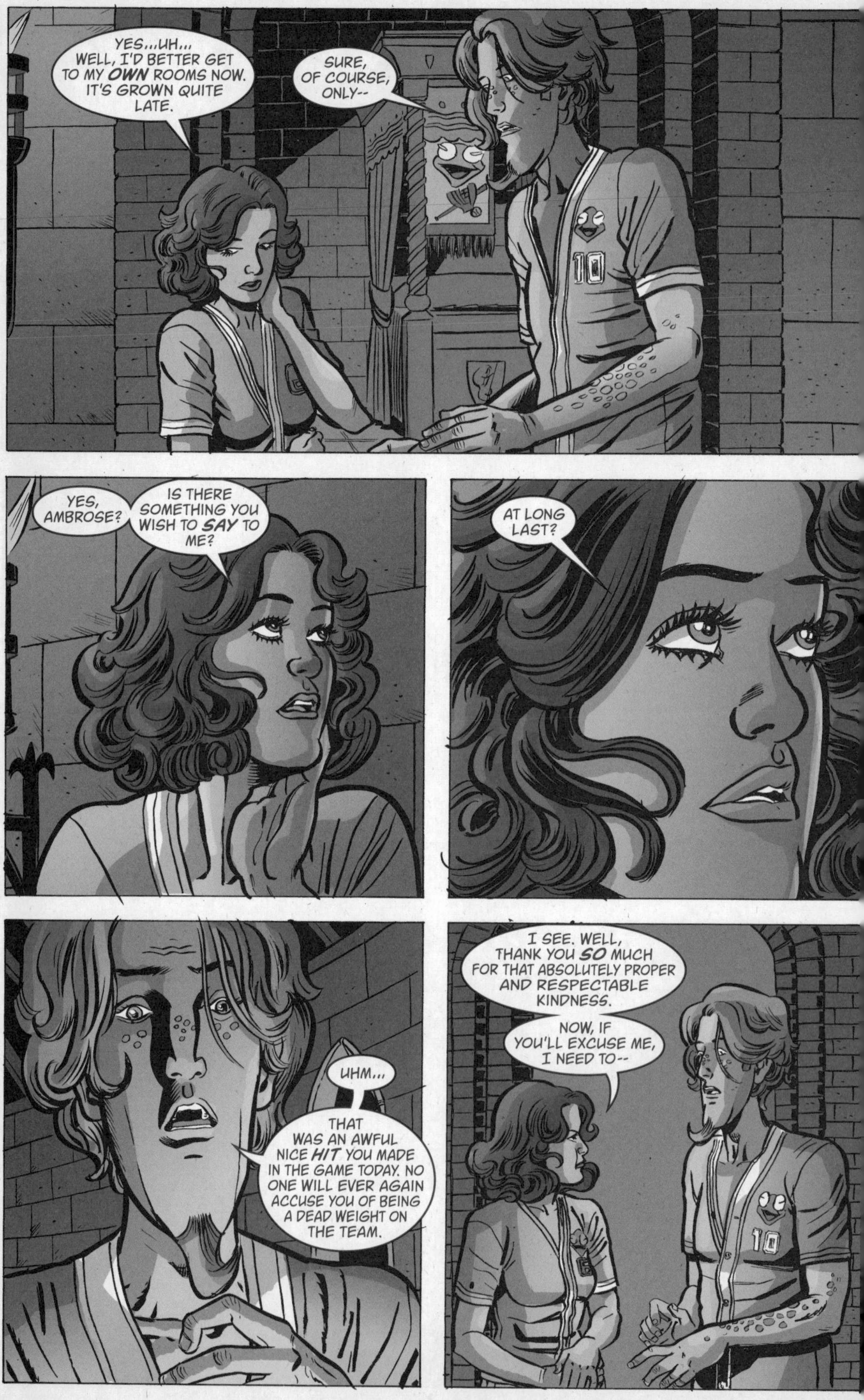
YES...UH... WELL, I'D BETTER GET TO MY OWN ROOMS NOW. IT'S GROWN QUITE LATE.
SURE, OF COURSE, ONLY--
YES, AMBROSE?
IS THERE SOMETHING YOU WISH TO SAY TO ME?
AT LONG LAST?
UHM...
THAT WAS AN AWFUL NICE HIT YOU MADE IN THE GAME TODAY. NO ONE WILL EVER AGAIN ACCUSE YOU OF BEING A DEAD WEIGHT ON THE TEAM.
I SEE. WELL, THANK YOU SO MUCH FOR THAT ABSOLUTELY PROPER AND RESPECTABLE KINDNESS.
NOW, IF YOU'LL EXCUSE ME, I NEED TO--

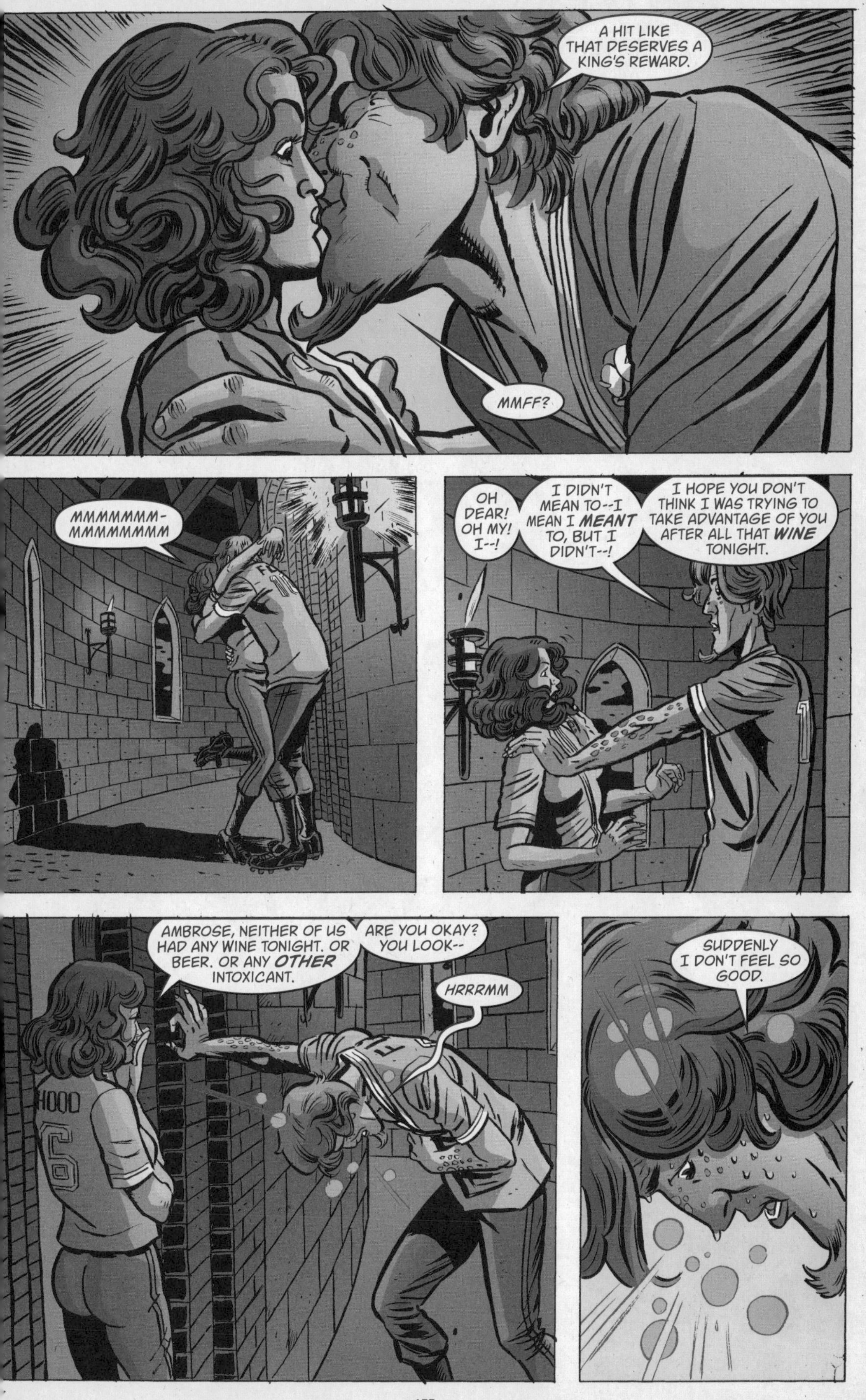

A HIT LIKE THAT DESERVES A KING'S REWARD.
MMFF?
MMMMMMM-MMMMMMMM
OH DEAR! OH MY! I--!
I DIDN'T MEAN TO--I MEAN I MEANT TO, BUT I DIDN'T--!
I HOPE YOU DON'T THINK I WAS TRYING TO TAKE ADVANTAGE OF YOU AFTER ALL THAT WINE TONIGHT.
AMBROSE, NEITHER OF US HAD ANY WINE TONIGHT. OR BEER. OR ANY OTHER INTOXICANT.
ARE YOU OKAY? YOU LOOK--
HRRRMM
HOOD 6
SUDDENLY I DON'T FEEL SO GOOD.

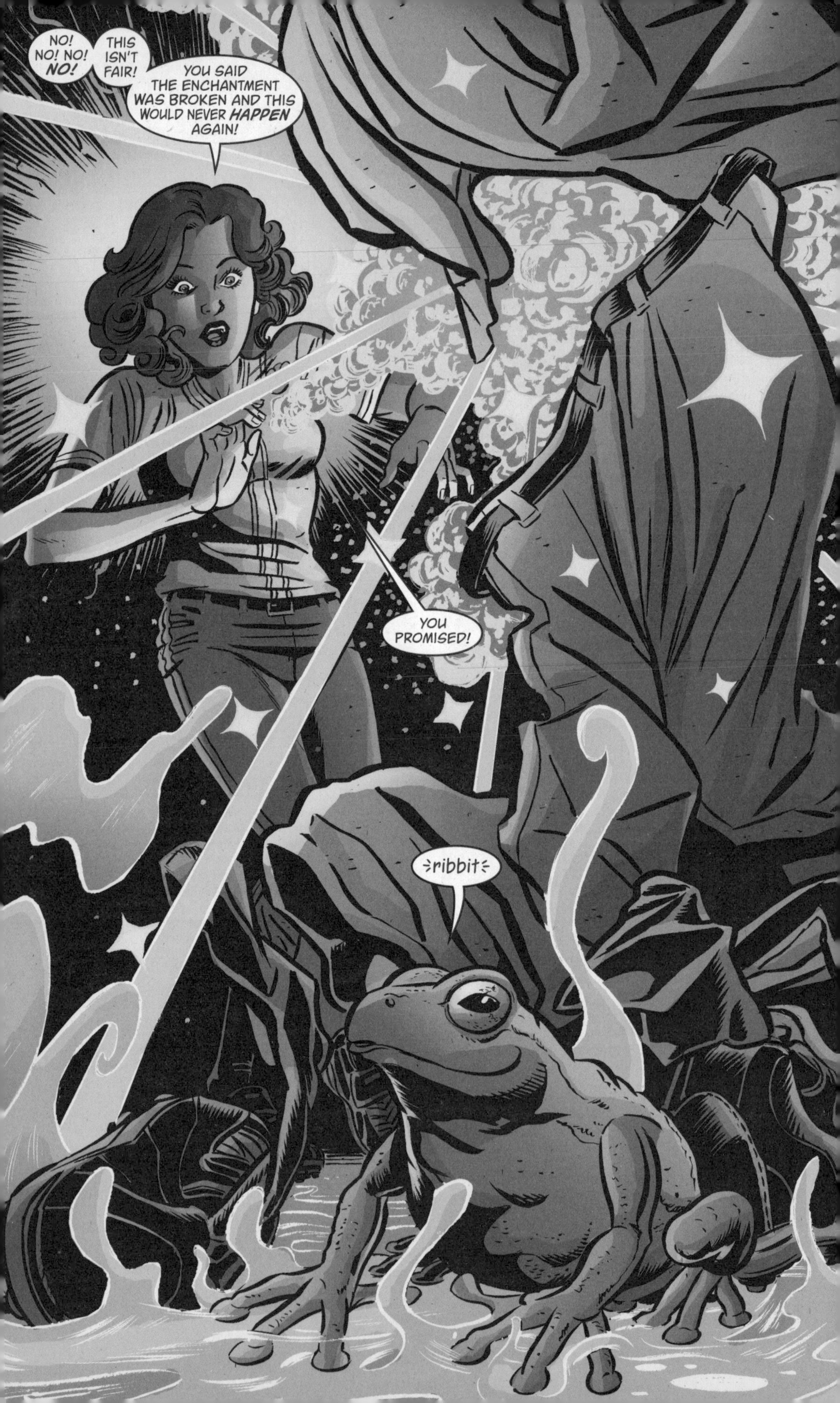
NO! NO! NO! NO!
THIS ISN'T FAIR!
YOU SAID THE ENCHANTMENT WAS BROKEN AND THIS WOULD NEVER HAPPEN AGAIN!
YOU PROMISED!
ribbit

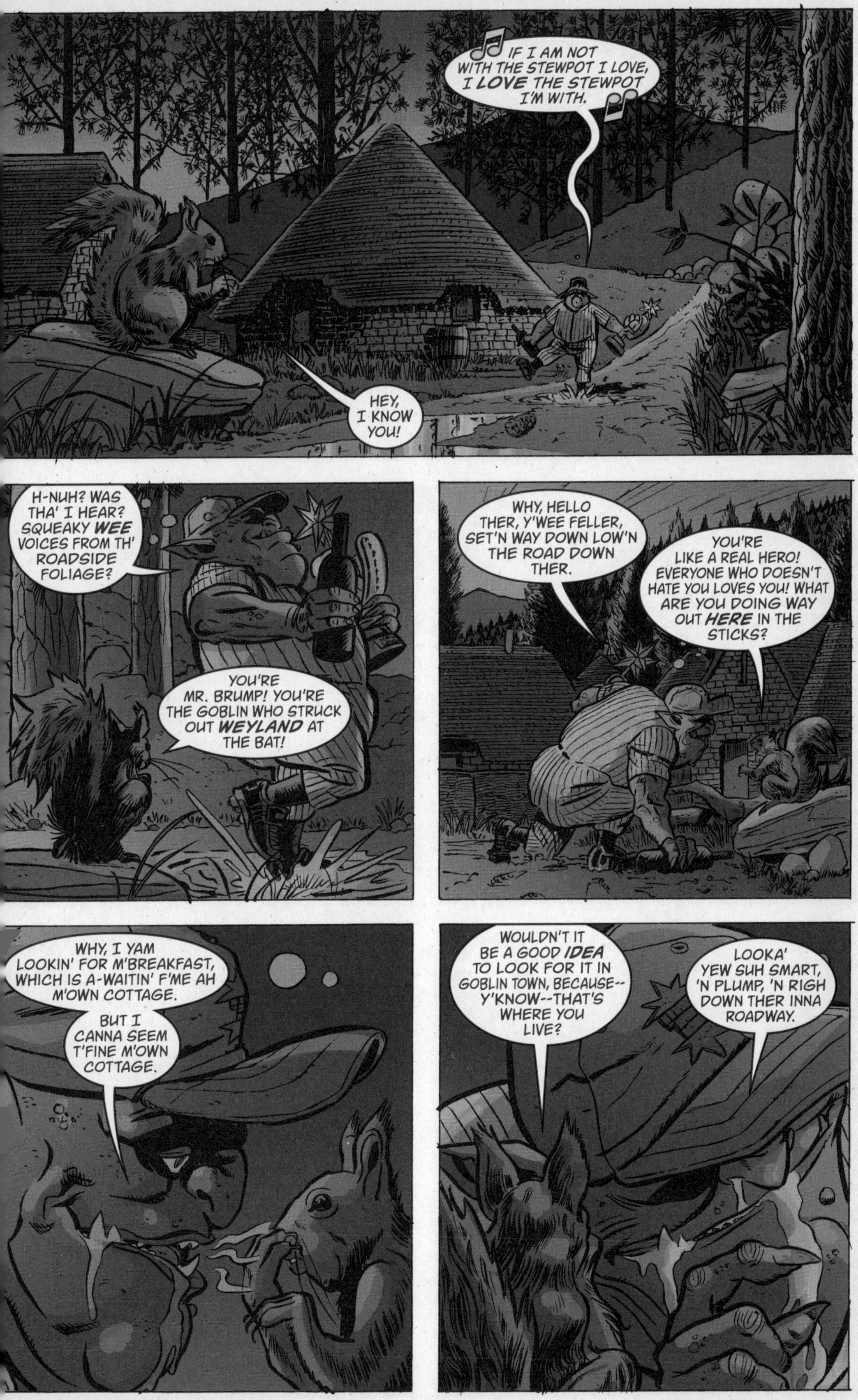
IF I AM NOT WITH THE STEWPOT I LOVE, I LOVE THE STEWPOT I'M WITH.
HEY, I KNOW YOU!
H-NUH? WAS THA' I HEAR? SQUEAKY WEE VOICES FROM TH' ROADSIDE FOLIAGE?
YOU'RE MR. BRUMP! YOU'RE THE GOBLIN WHO STRUCK OUT WEYLAND AT THE BAT!
WHY, HELLO THER, Y'WEE FELLER, SET'N WAY DOWN LOW'N THE ROAD DOWN THER.
YOU'RE LIKE A REAL HERO! EVERYONE WHO DOESN'T HATE YOU LOVES YOU! WHAT ARE YOU DOING WAY OUT HERE IN THE STICKS?
WHY, I YAM LOOKIN' FOR M'BREAKFAST, WHICH IS A-WAITIN' F'ME AH M'OWN COTTAGE.
BUT I CANNA SEEM T'FINE M'OWN COTTAGE.
WOULDN'T IT BE A GOOD IDEA TO LOOK FOR IT IN GOBLIN TOWN, BECAUSE-- Y'KNOW--THAT'S WHERE YOU LIVE?
LOOKA' YEW SUH SMART, 'N PLUMP, 'N RIGH DOWN THER INNA ROADWAY.

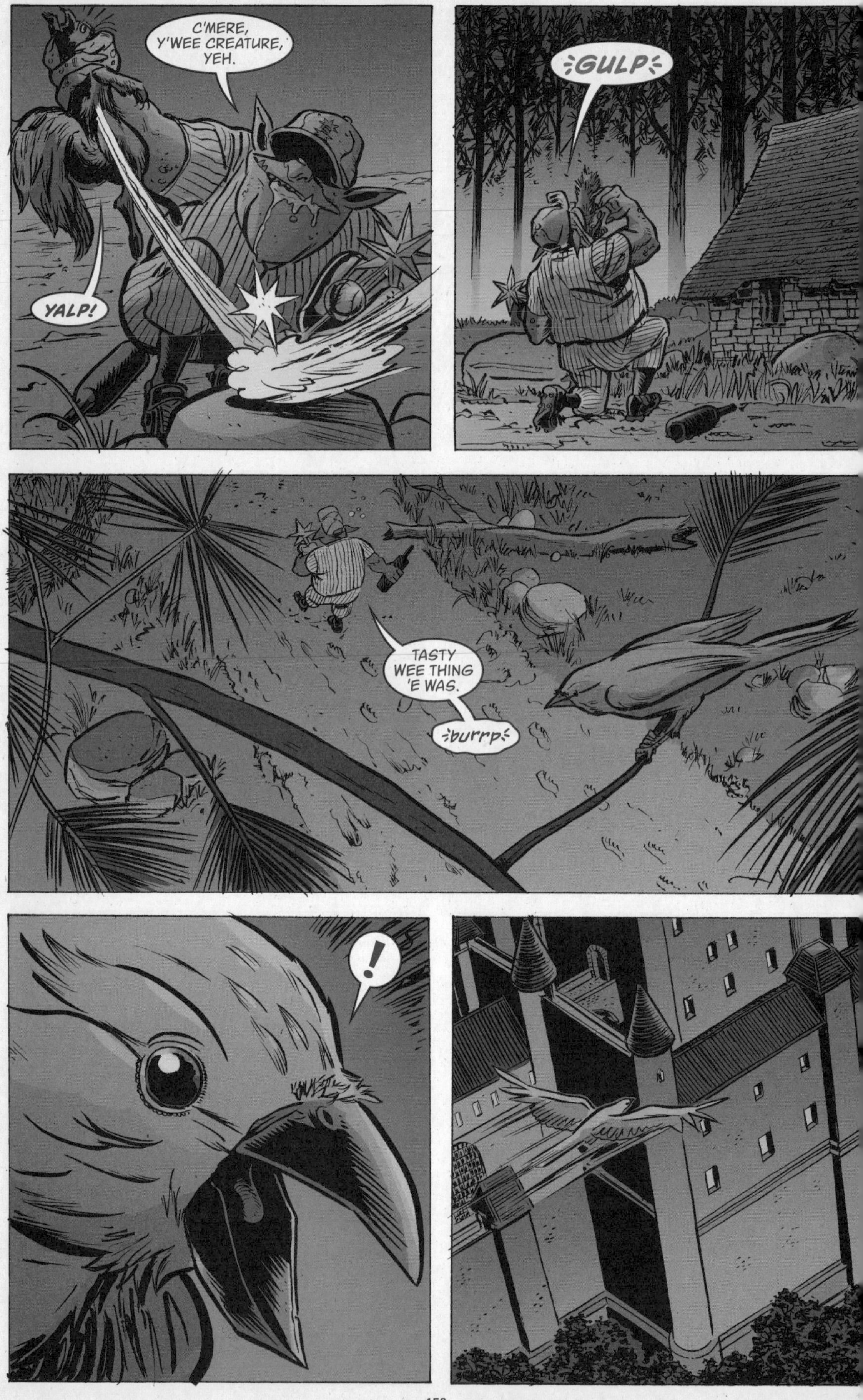
C'MERE, Y'WEE CREATURE, YEH.
YALP!
GULP
TASTY WEE THING 'E WAS.
burrp
!

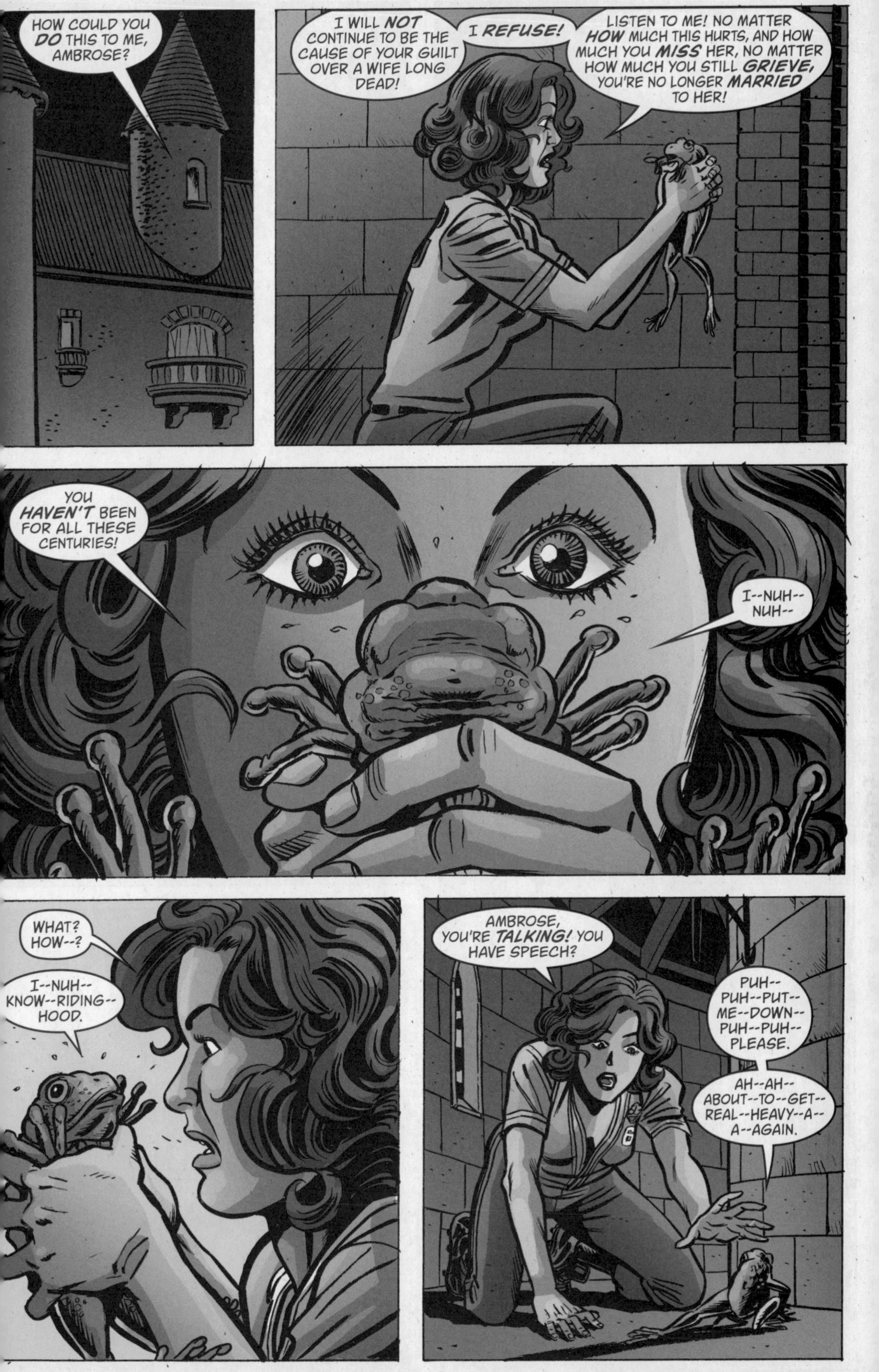
HOW COULD YOU DO THIS TO ME, AMBROSE?
I WILL NOT CONTINUE TO BE THE CAUSE OF YOUR GUILT OVER A WIFE LONG DEAD!
I REFUSE!
LISTEN TO ME! NO MATTER HOW MUCH THIS HURTS, AND HOW MUCH YOU MISS HER, NO MATTER HOW MUCH YOU STILL GRIEVE, YOU'RE NO LONGER MARRIED TO HER!
YOU HAVEN'T BEEN FOR ALL THESE CENTURIES!
I--NUH--NUH--
WHAT? HOW--?
I--NUH--KNOW--RIDING--HOOD.
AMBROSE, YOU'RE TALKING! YOU HAVE SPEECH?
PUH--PUH--PUT--ME--DOWN--PUH--PUH--PLEASE.
AH--AH--ABOUT--TO--GET--REAL--HEAVY--A--A--AGAIN.

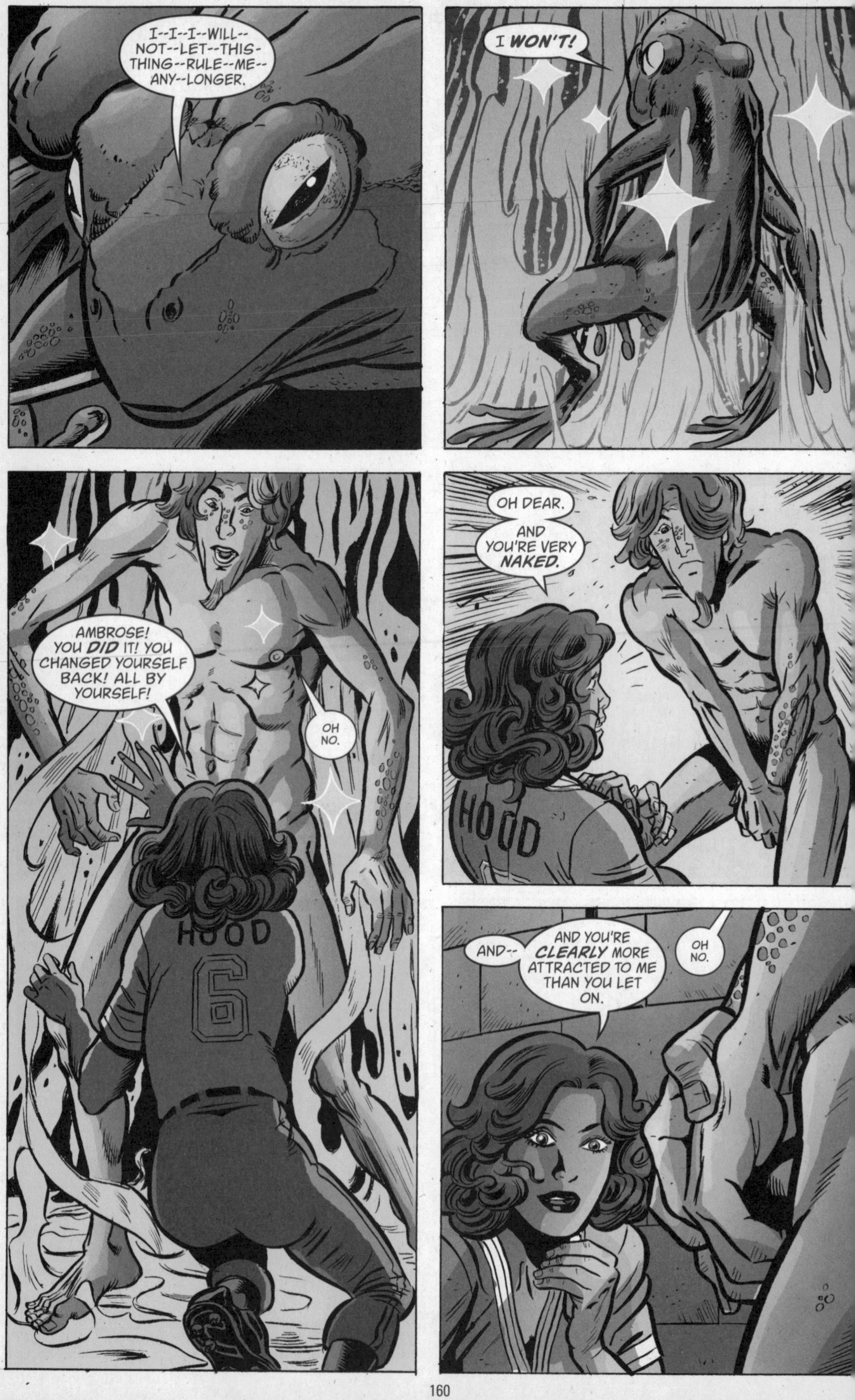
I--I--I--WILL--NOT--LET--THIS-THING--RULE--ME--ANY--LONGER.
I WON'T!
AMBROSE! YOU DID IT! YOU CHANGED YOURSELF BACK! ALL BY YOURSELF!
OH NO.
OH DEAR.
AND YOU'RE VERY NAKED.
HOOD
HOOD 6
AND--
AND YOU'RE CLEARLY MORE ATTRACTED TO ME THAN YOU LET ON.
OH NO.

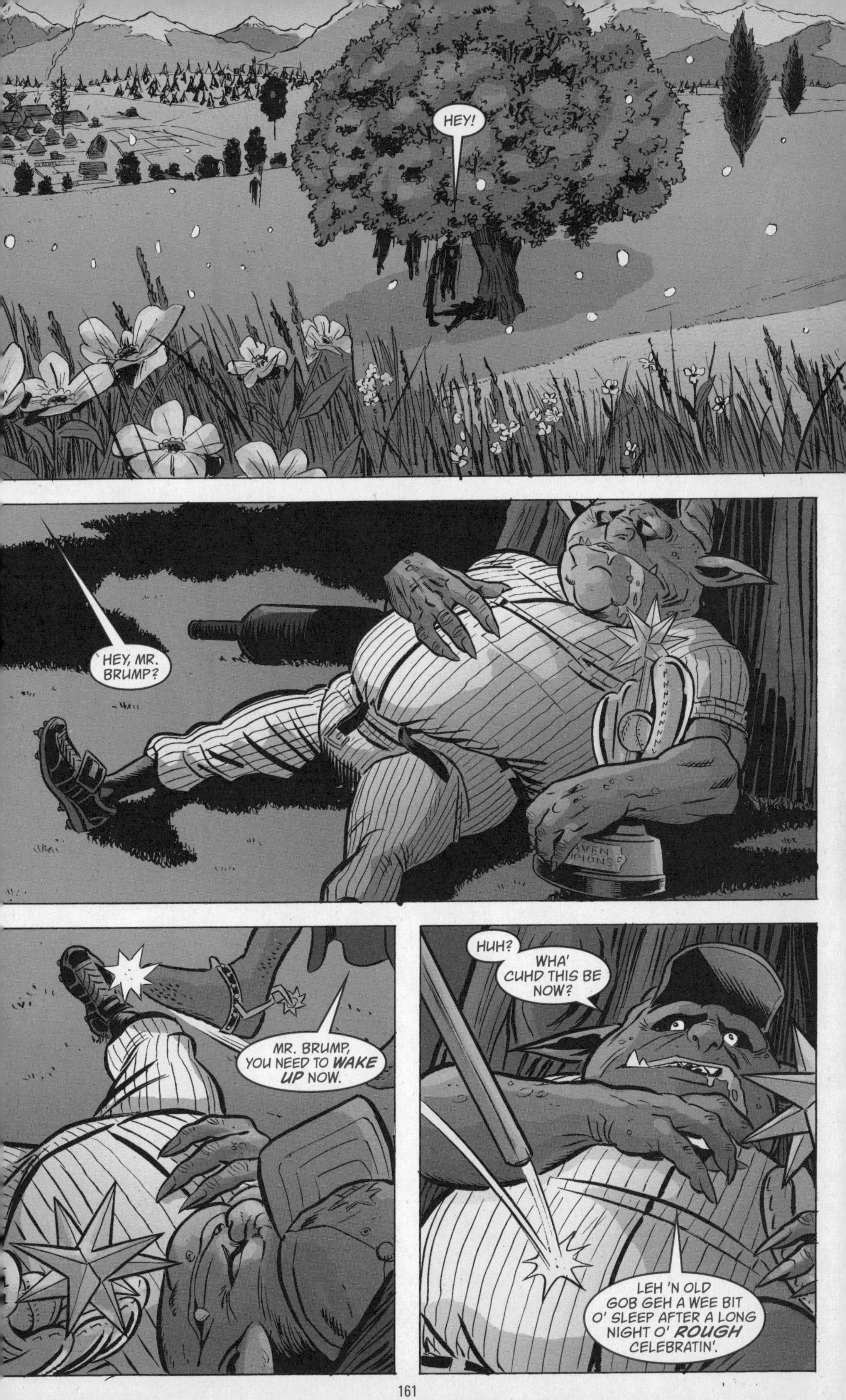
HEY!
HEY, MR. BRUMP?
MR. BRUMP, YOU NEED TO WAKE UP NOW.
HUH?
WHA' CUHD THIS BE NOW?
LEH 'N OLD GOB GEH A WEE BIT O' SLEEP AFTER A LONG NIGHT O' ROUGH CELEBRATIN'.

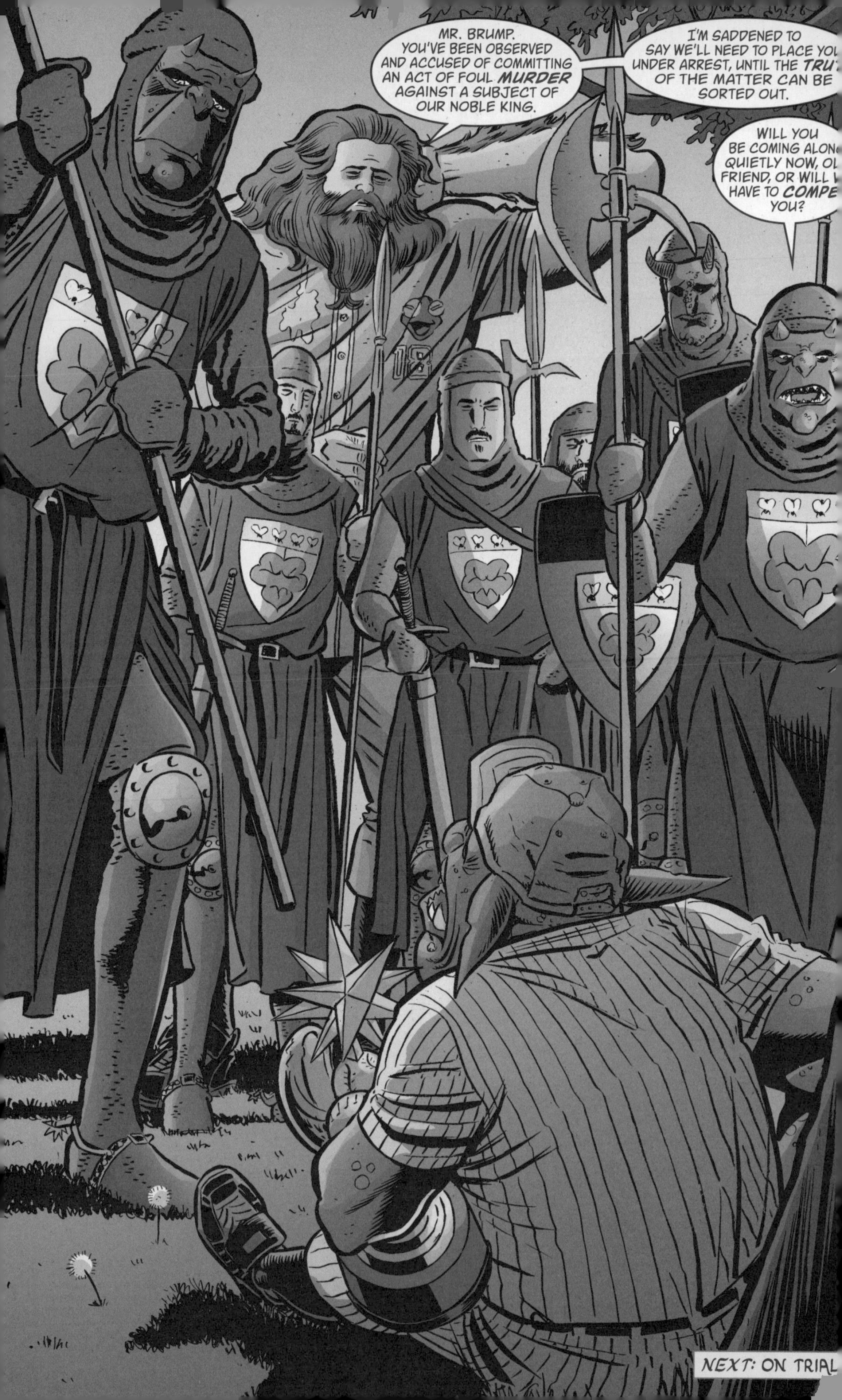
MR. BRUMP. YOU'VE BEEN OBSERVED AND ACCUSED OF COMMITTING AN ACT OF FOUL MURDER AGAINST A SUBJECT OF OUR NOBLE KING.
I'M SADDENED TO SAY WE'LL NEED TO PLACE YO UNDER ARREST, UNTIL THE TRU OF THE MATTER CAN BE SORTED OUT.
WILL YOU BE COMING ALON QUIETLY NOW, OL FRIEND, OR WILL HAVE TO COMPE YOU?
NEXT: ON TRIAL

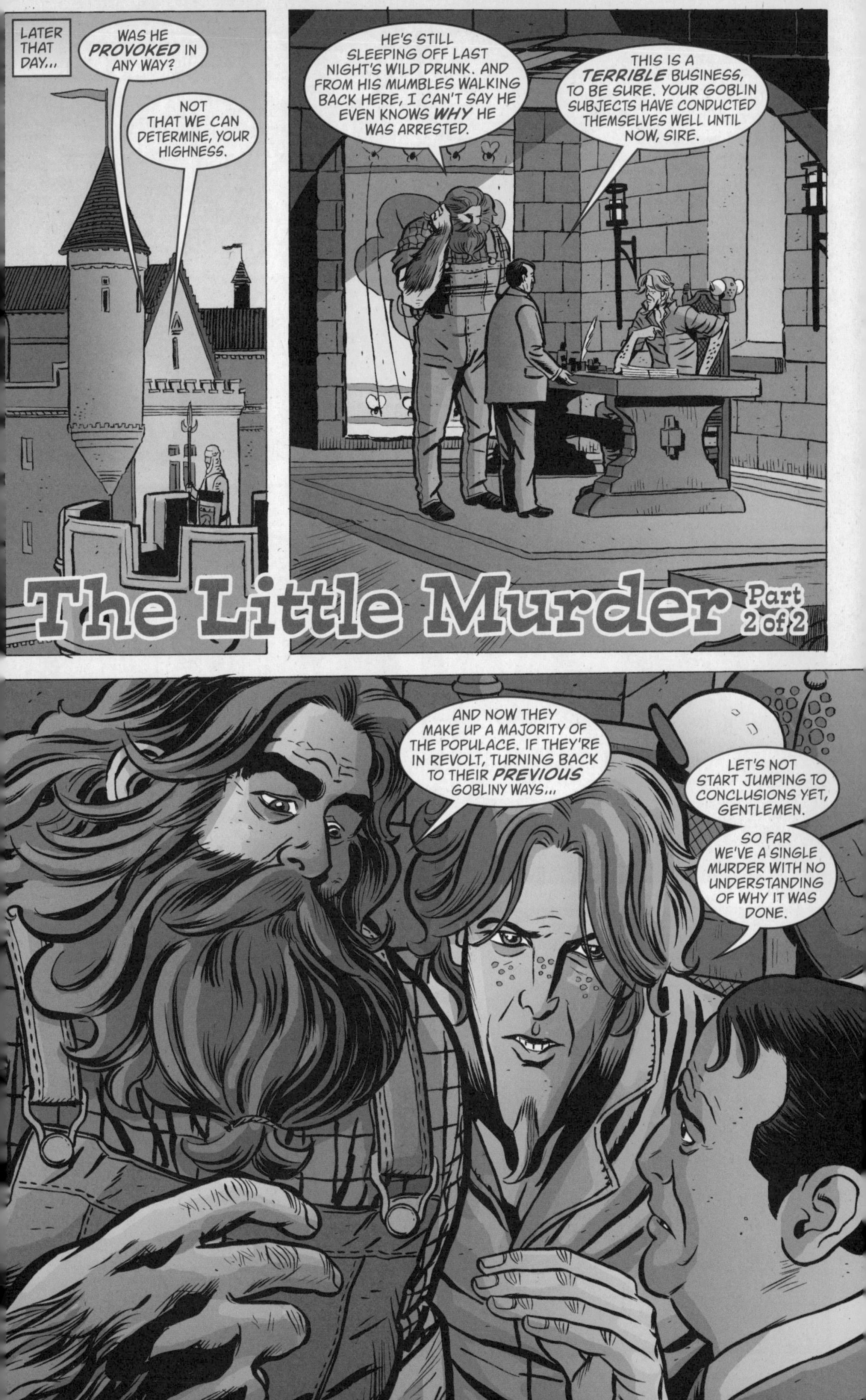
LATER THAT DAY...
WAS HE PROVOKED IN ANY WAY?
NOT THAT WE CAN DETERMINE, YOUR HIGHNESS.
HE'S STILL SLEEPING OFF LAST NIGHT'S WILD DRUNK. AND FROM HIS MUMBLES WALKING BACK HERE, I CAN'T SAY HE EVEN KNOWS WHY HE WAS ARRESTED.
THIS IS A TERRIBLE BUSINESS, TO BE SURE. YOUR GOBLIN SUBJECTS HAVE CONDUCTED THEMSELVES WELL UNTIL NOW, SIRE.
The Little Murder Part 2 of 2
AND NOW THEY MAKE UP A MAJORITY OF THE POPULACE. IF THEY'RE IN REVOLT, TURNING BACK TO THEIR PREVIOUS GOBLINY WAYS...
LET'S NOT START JUMPING TO CONCLUSIONS YET, GENTLEMEN.
SO FAR WE'VE A SINGLE MURDER WITH NO UNDERSTANDING OF WHY IT WAS DONE.

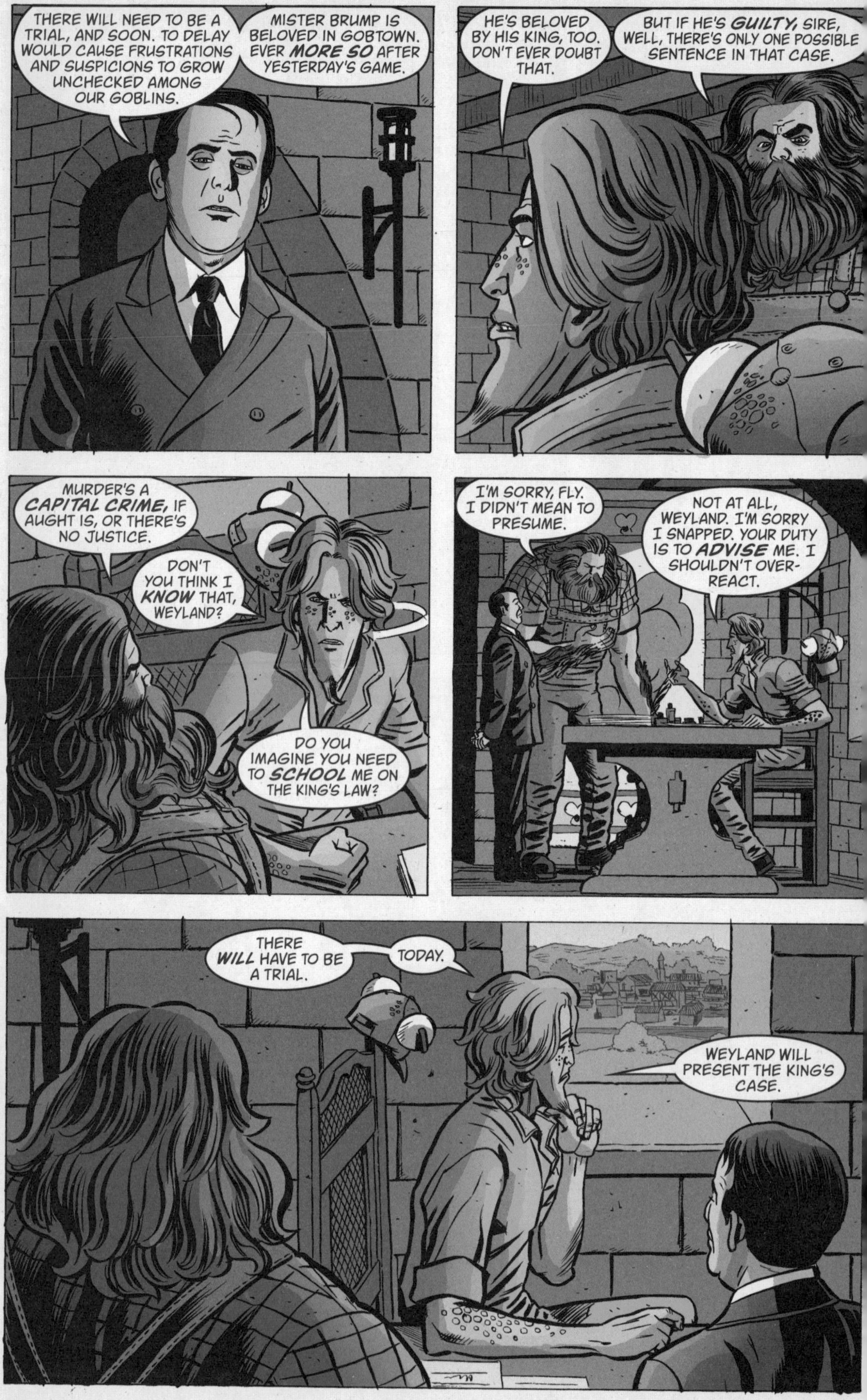
THERE WILL NEED TO BE A TRIAL, AND SOON. TO DELAY WOULD CAUSE FRUSTRATIONS AND SUSPICIONS TO GROW UNCHECKED AMONG OUR GOBLINS.
MISTER BRUMP IS BELOVED IN GOBTOWN. EVER MORE SO AFTER YESTERDAY'S GAME.
HE'S BELOVED BY HIS KING, TOO. DON'T EVER DOUBT THAT.
BUT IF HE'S GUILTY, SIRE, WELL, THERE'S ONLY ONE POSSIBLE SENTENCE IN THAT CASE.
MURDER'S A CAPITAL CRIME, IF AUGHT IS, OR THERE'S NO JUSTICE.
DON'T YOU THINK I KNOW THAT, WEYLAND?
DO YOU IMAGINE YOU NEED TO SCHOOL ME ON THE KING'S LAW?
I'M SORRY, FLY. I DIDN'T MEAN TO PRESUME.
NOT AT ALL, WEYLAND. I'M SORRY I SNAPPED. YOUR DUTY IS TO ADVISE ME. I SHOULDN'T OVER-REACT.
THERE WILL HAVE TO BE A TRIAL.
TODAY.
WEYLAND WILL PRESENT THE KING'S CASE.

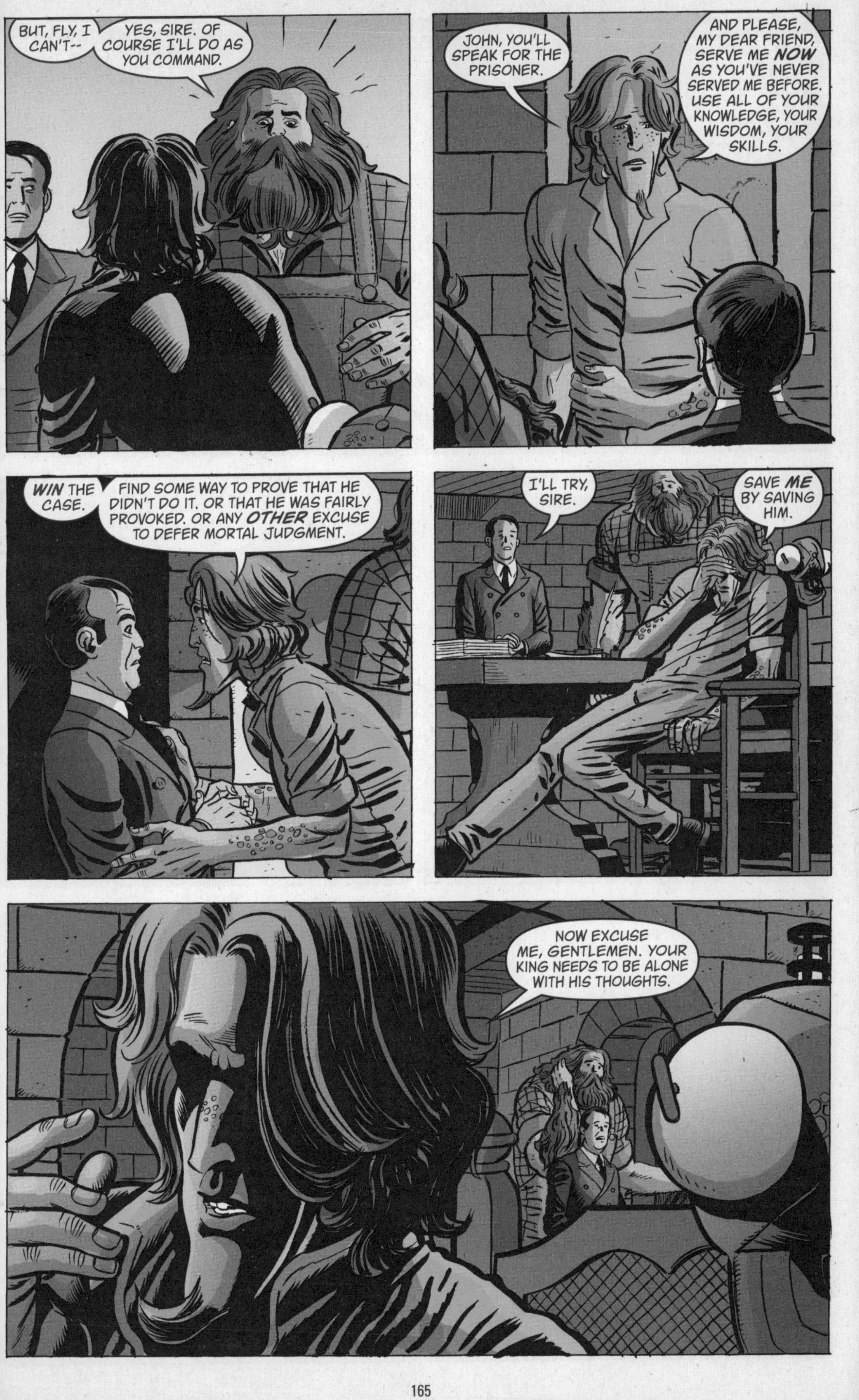

BUT, FLY, I CAN'T--
YES, SIRE. OF COURSE I'LL DO AS YOU COMMAND.
JOHN, YOU'LL SPEAK FOR THE PRISONER.
AND PLEASE, MY DEAR FRIEND, SERVE ME NOW AS YOU'VE NEVER SERVED ME BEFORE. USE ALL OF YOUR KNOWLEDGE, YOUR WISDOM, YOUR SKILLS.
WIN THE CASE.
FIND SOME WAY TO PROVE THAT HE DIDN'T DO IT. OR THAT HE WAS FAIRLY PROVOKED. OR ANY OTHER EXCUSE TO DEFER MORTAL JUDGMENT.
I'LL TRY, SIRE.
SAVE ME BY SAVING HIM.
NOW EXCUSE ME, GENTLEMEN. YOUR KING NEEDS TO BE ALONE WITH HIS THOUGHTS.

HOW MUCH OF THAT DID YOU HEAR?

ALL OF IT. WHAT ARE YOU GOING TO *DO*, AMBROSE?

WHAT *CAN* I DO?

DESPITE MY CHILDISH HOPES OTHERWISE, WE'RE GOING TO FIND OUT THAT MISTER BRUMP IS GUILTY. THEN I'VE NO CHOICE. I'LL HAVE TO *COMMAND* HIS EXECUTION.

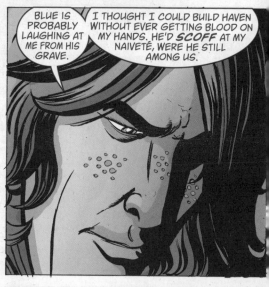

BLUE IS PROBABLY LAUGHING AT ME FROM HIS GRAVE.

I THOUGHT I COULD BUILD HAVEN WITHOUT EVER GETTING BLOOD ON MY HANDS. HE'D *SCOFF* AT MY NAIVETÉ, WERE HE STILL AMONG US.

THERE'S ONE THING YOU CAN DO. GO *AWAY*. GO OUT ON ONE OF YOUR EXPLORATIONS AND DON'T COME BACK FOR SOME TIME.

LET US HOLD THE TRIAL IN YOUR ABSENCE. NO GREAT KING CAN BE EXPECTED TO ALWAYS BE ON HAND, EVERY DAY OF EVERY YEAR. YOU NEEDN'T TROUBLE YOURSELF WITH--

WITH DOING MY SACRED *DUTY*?

NO, RIDE. I LOVE YOU FOR TRYING, BUT I CAN'T SHIRK THIS RESPONSIBILITY BY SHIFTING IT TO OTHERS. THIS IS ON *ME*. NO ONE ELSE.

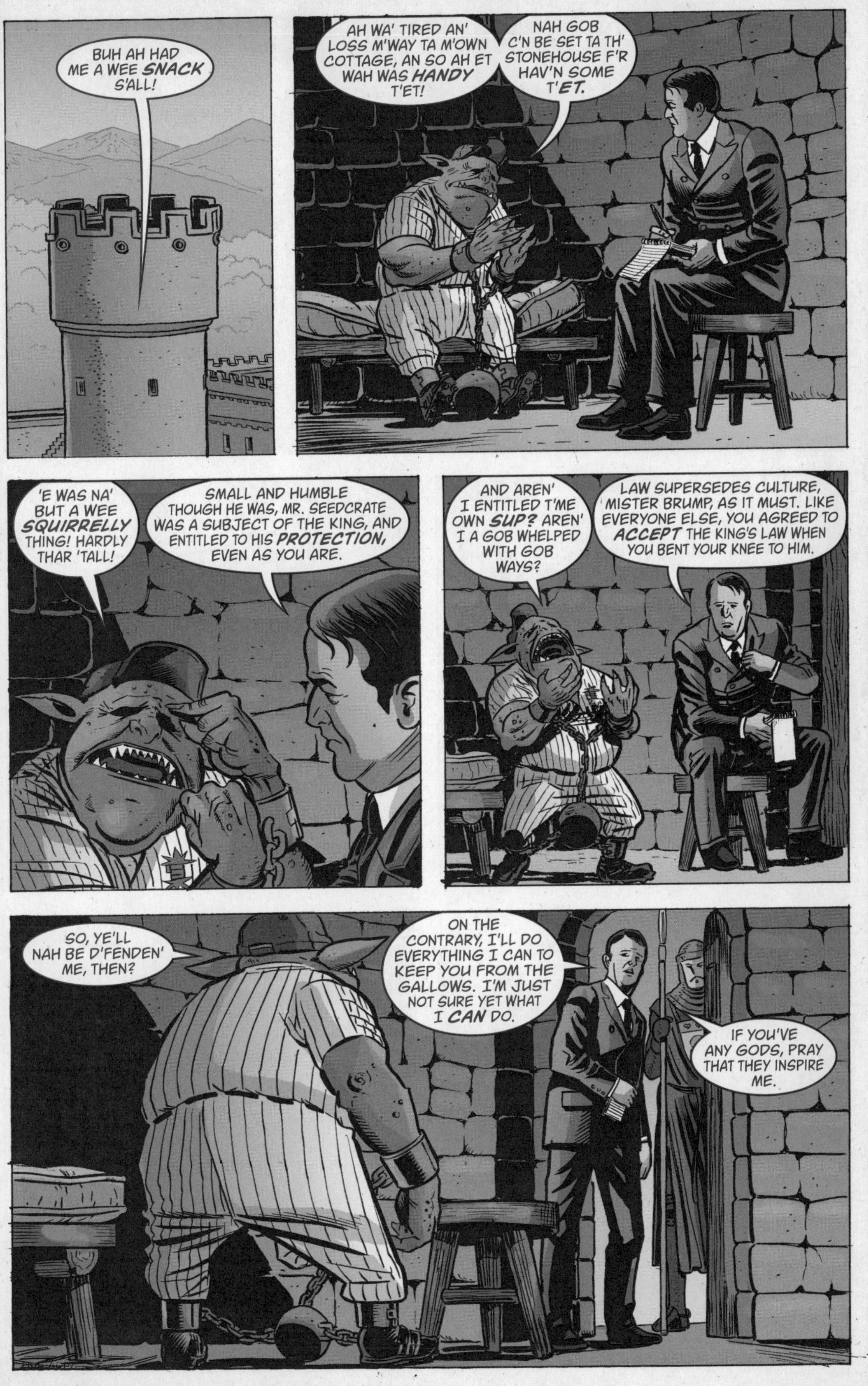
BUH AH HAD ME A WEE SNACK S'ALL!
AH WA' TIRED AN' LOSS M'WAY TA M'OWN COTTAGE, AN SO AH ET WAH WAS HANDY T'ET!
NAH GOB C'N BE SET TA TH' STONEHOUSE F'R HAV'N SOME T'ET.
'E WAS NA' BUT A WEE SQUIRRELLY THING! HARDLY THAR 'TALL!
SMALL AND HUMBLE THOUGH HE WAS, MR. SEEDCRATE WAS A SUBJECT OF THE KING, AND ENTITLED TO HIS PROTECTION, EVEN AS YOU ARE.
AND AREN' I ENTITLED T'ME OWN SUP? AREN' I A GOB WHELPED WITH GOB WAYS?
LAW SUPERSEDES CULTURE, MISTER BRUMP, AS IT MUST. LIKE EVERYONE ELSE, YOU AGREED TO ACCEPT THE KING'S LAW WHEN YOU BENT YOUR KNEE TO HIM.
SO, YE'LL NAH BE D'FENDEN' ME, THEN?
ON THE CONTRARY, I'LL DO EVERYTHING I CAN TO KEEP YOU FROM THE GALLOWS. I'M JUST NOT SURE YET WHAT I CAN DO.
IF YOU'VE ANY GODS, PRAY THAT THEY INSPIRE ME.

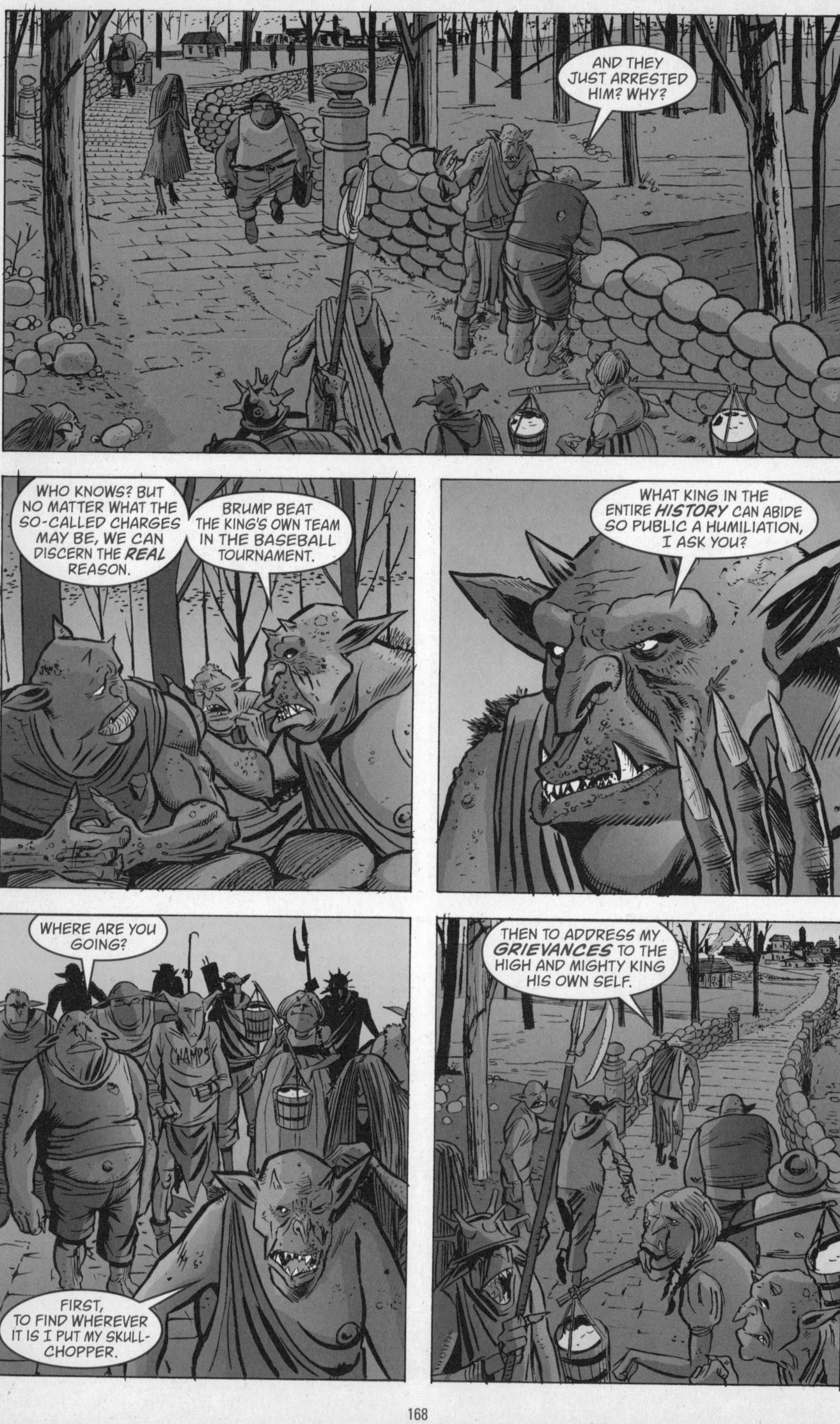

AND THEY JUST ARRESTED HIM? WHY?
WHO KNOWS? BUT NO MATTER WHAT THE SO-CALLED CHARGES MAY BE, WE CAN DISCERN THE REAL REASON.
BRUMP BEAT THE KING'S OWN TEAM IN THE BASEBALL TOURNAMENT.
WHAT KING IN THE ENTIRE HISTORY CAN ABIDE SO PUBLIC A HUMILIATION, I ASK YOU?
WHERE ARE YOU GOING?
CHAMPS
FIRST, TO FIND WHEREVER IT IS I PUT MY SKULL-CHOPPER.
THEN TO ADDRESS MY GRIEVANCES TO THE HIGH AND MIGHTY KING HIS OWN SELF.

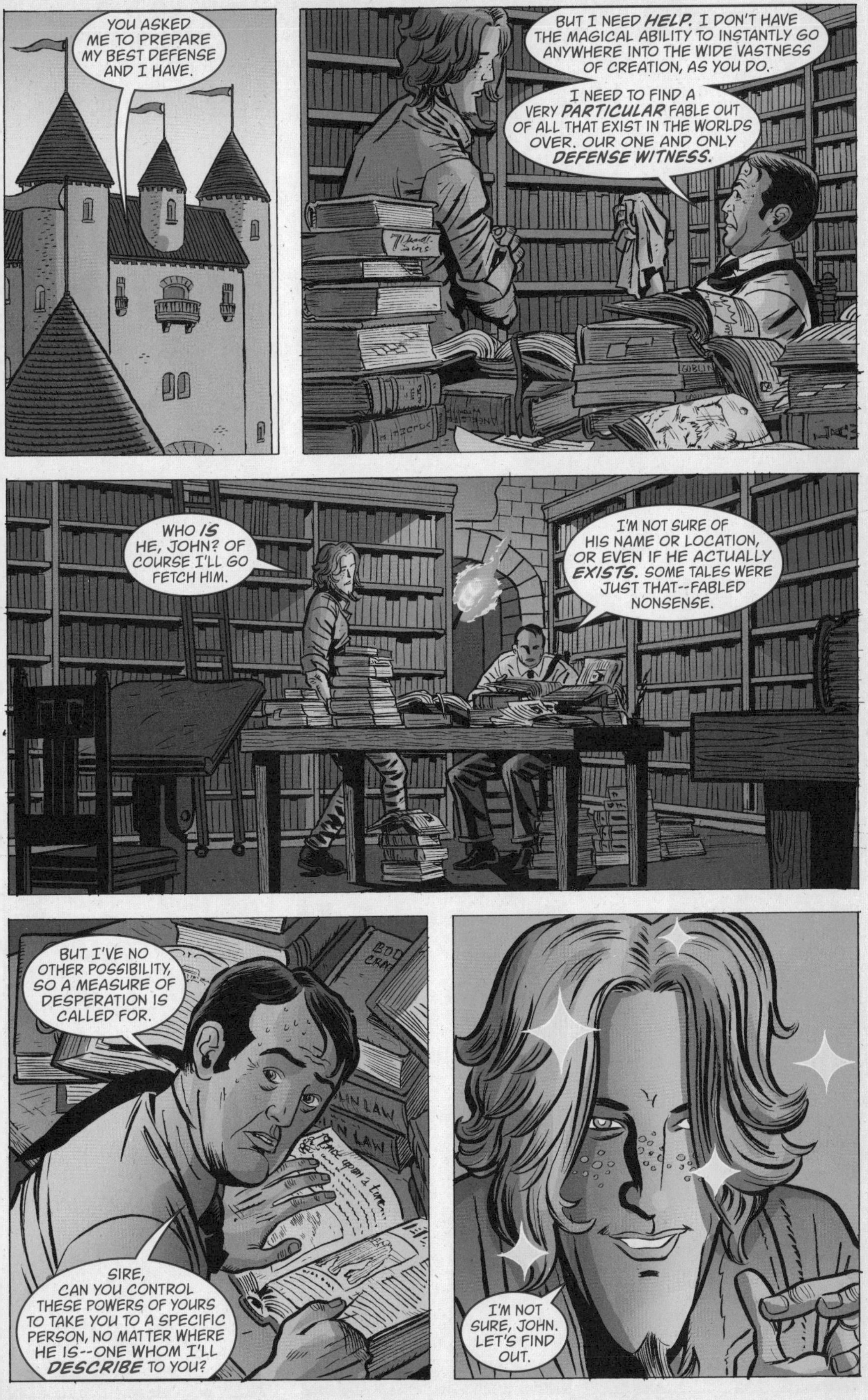

YOU ASKED ME TO PREPARE MY BEST DEFENSE AND I HAVE.
BUT I NEED HELP. I DON'T HAVE THE MAGICAL ABILITY TO INSTANTLY GO ANYWHERE INTO THE WIDE VASTNESS OF CREATION, AS YOU DO.
I NEED TO FIND A VERY PARTICULAR FABLE OUT OF ALL THAT EXIST IN THE WORLDS OVER. OUR ONE AND ONLY DEFENSE WITNESS.
GOBLIN
WHO IS HE, JOHN? OF COURSE I'LL GO FETCH HIM.
I'M NOT SURE OF HIS NAME OR LOCATION, OR EVEN IF HE ACTUALLY EXISTS. SOME TALES WERE JUST THAT--FABLED NONSENSE.
BUT I'VE NO OTHER POSSIBILITY, SO A MEASURE OF DESPERATION IS CALLED FOR.
JOHN LAW
SIRE, CAN YOU CONTROL THESE POWERS OF YOURS TO TAKE YOU TO A SPECIFIC PERSON, NO MATTER WHERE HE IS--ONE WHOM I'LL DESCRIBE TO YOU?
I'M NOT SURE, JOHN. LET'S FIND OUT.

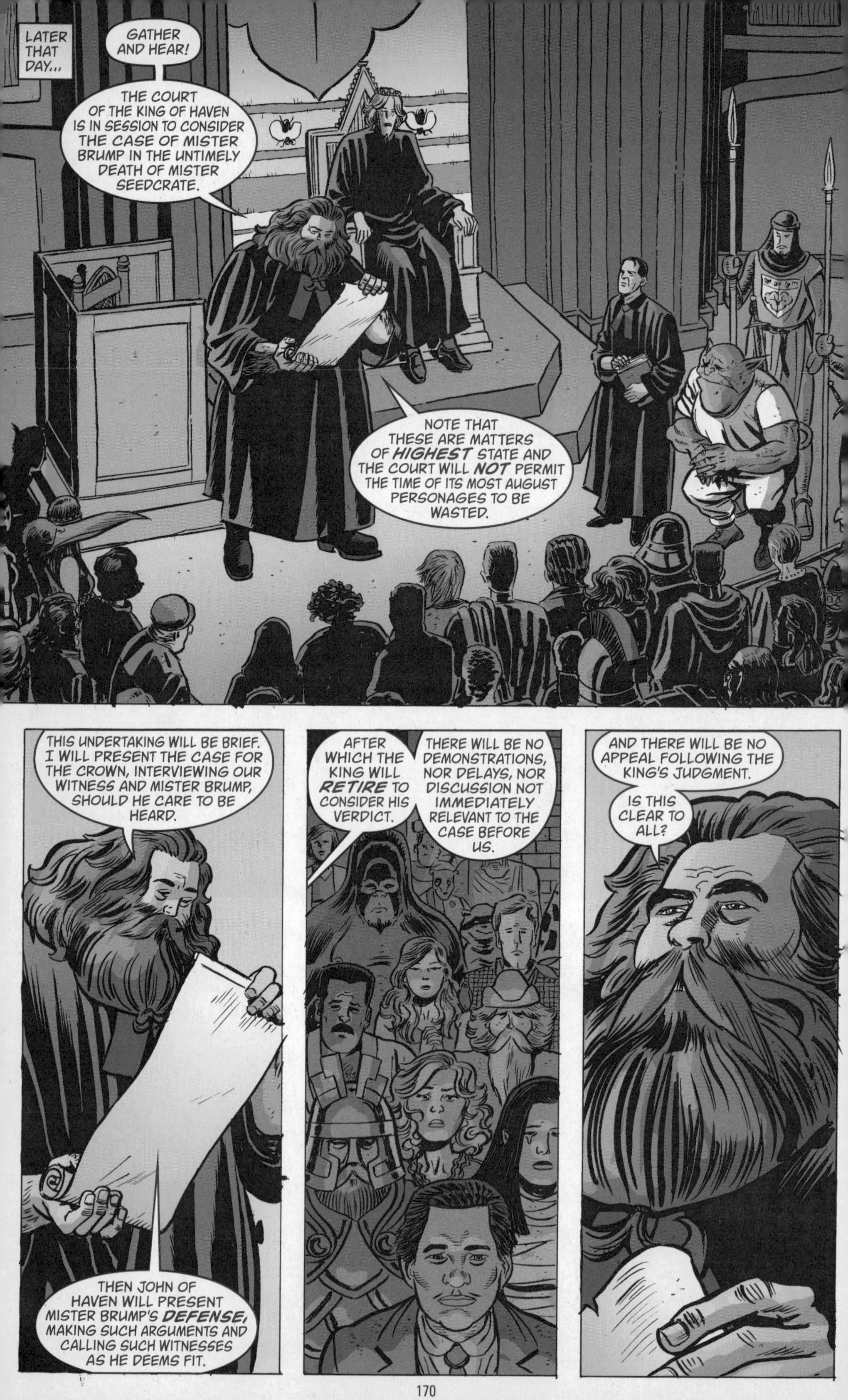
LATER THAT DAY...
GATHER AND HEAR!
THE COURT OF THE KING OF HAVEN IS IN SESSION TO CONSIDER THE CASE OF MISTER BRUMP IN THE UNTIMELY DEATH OF MISTER SEEDCRATE.
NOTE THAT THESE ARE MATTERS OF HIGHEST STATE AND THE COURT WILL NOT PERMIT THE TIME OF ITS MOST AUGUST PERSONAGES TO BE WASTED.
THIS UNDERTAKING WILL BE BRIEF. I WILL PRESENT THE CASE FOR THE CROWN, INTERVIEWING OUR WITNESS AND MISTER BRUMP, SHOULD HE CARE TO BE HEARD.
THEN JOHN OF HAVEN WILL PRESENT MISTER BRUMP'S DEFENSE, MAKING SUCH ARGUMENTS AND CALLING SUCH WITNESSES AS HE DEEMS FIT.
AFTER WHICH THE KING WILL RETIRE TO CONSIDER HIS VERDICT.
THERE WILL BE NO DEMONSTRATIONS, NOR DELAYS, NOR DISCUSSION NOT IMMEDIATELY RELEVANT TO THE CASE BEFORE US.
AND THERE WILL BE NO APPEAL FOLLOWING THE KING'S JUDGMENT.
IS THIS CLEAR TO ALL?

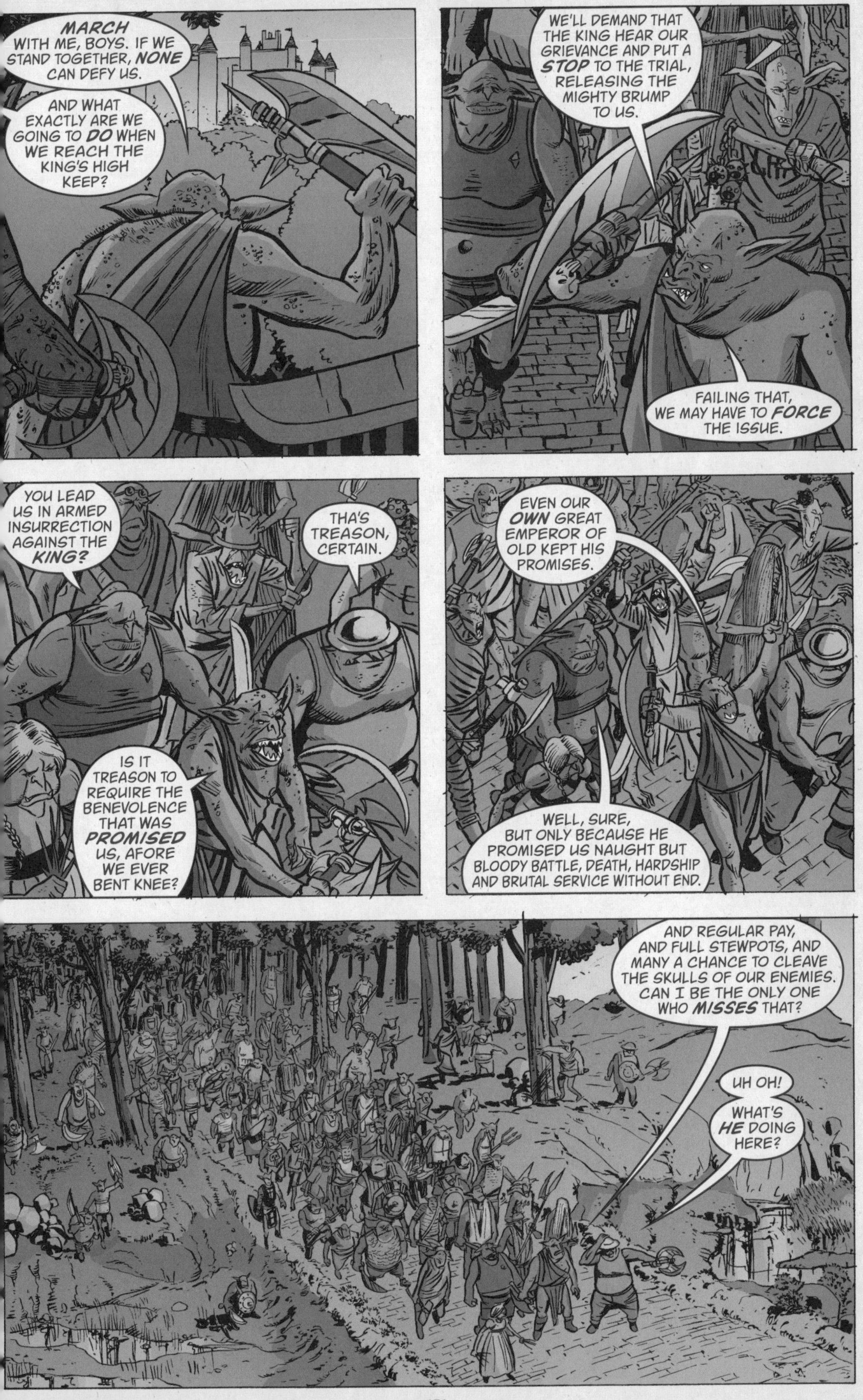
MARCH WITH ME, BOYS. IF WE STAND TOGETHER, NONE CAN DEFY US.
AND WHAT EXACTLY ARE WE GOING TO DO WHEN WE REACH THE KING'S HIGH KEEP?
WE'LL DEMAND THAT THE KING HEAR OUR GRIEVANCE AND PUT A STOP TO THE TRIAL, RELEASING THE MIGHTY BRUMP TO US.
FAILING THAT, WE MAY HAVE TO FORCE THE ISSUE.
YOU LEAD US IN ARMED INSURRECTION AGAINST THE KING?
THA'S TREASON, CERTAIN.
IS IT TREASON TO REQUIRE THE BENEVOLENCE THAT WAS PROMISED US, AFORE WE EVER BENT KNEE?
EVEN OUR OWN GREAT EMPEROR OF OLD KEPT HIS PROMISES.
WELL, SURE, BUT ONLY BECAUSE HE PROMISED US NAUGHT BUT BLOODY BATTLE, DEATH, HARDSHIP AND BRUTAL SERVICE WITHOUT END.
AND REGULAR PAY, AND FULL STEWPOTS, AND MANY A CHANCE TO CLEAVE THE SKULLS OF OUR ENEMIES. CAN I BE THE ONLY ONE WHO MISSES THAT?
UH OH!
WHAT'S HE DOING HERE?

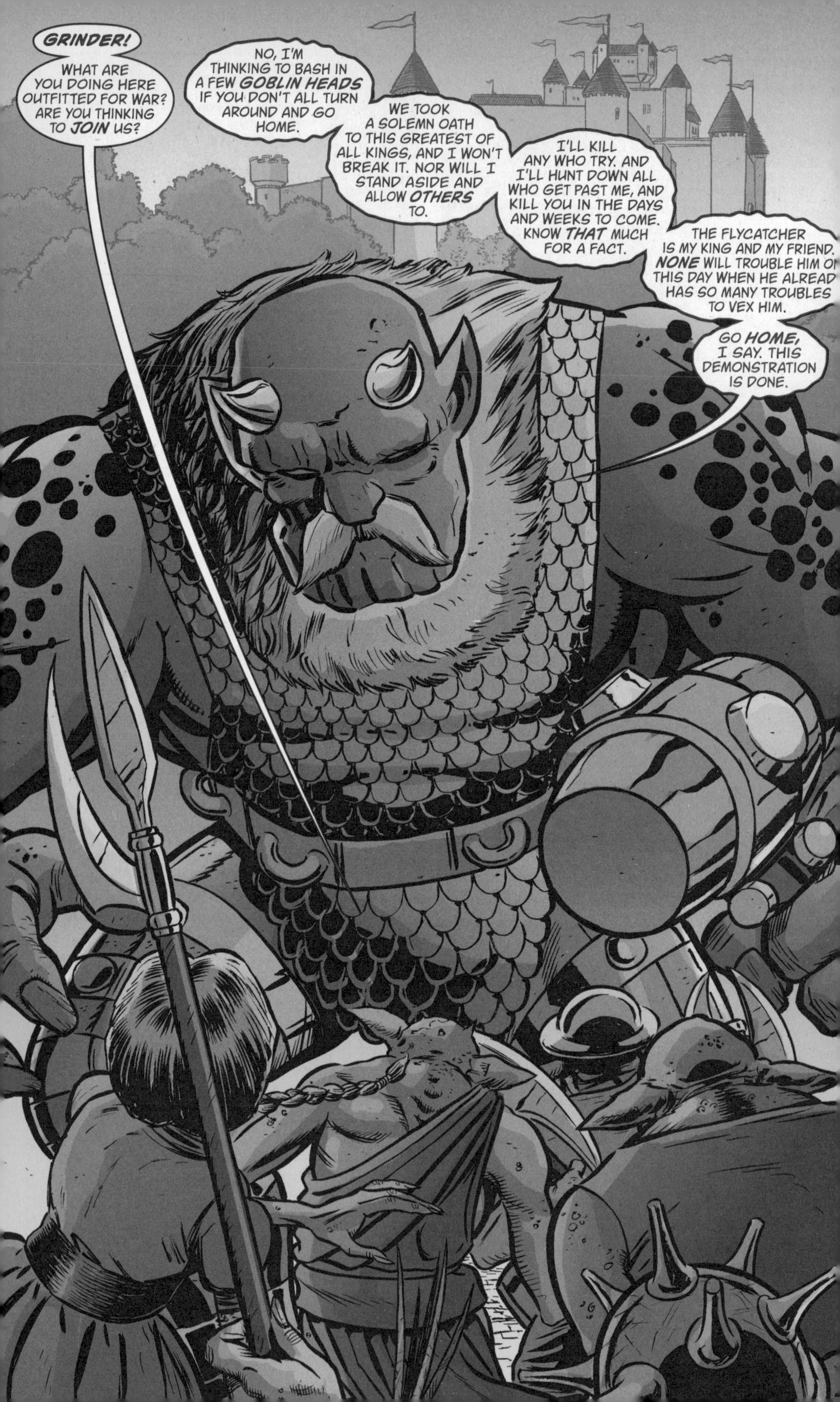
GRINDER!
WHAT ARE YOU DOING HERE OUTFITTED FOR WAR? ARE YOU THINKING TO JOIN US?
NO, I'M THINKING TO BASH IN A FEW GOBLIN HEADS IF YOU DON'T ALL TURN AROUND AND GO HOME.
WE TOOK A SOLEMN OATH TO THIS GREATEST OF ALL KINGS, AND I WON'T BREAK IT. NOR WILL I STAND ASIDE AND ALLOW OTHERS TO.
I'LL KILL ANY WHO TRY. AND I'LL HUNT DOWN ALL WHO GET PAST ME, AND KILL YOU IN THE DAYS AND WEEKS TO COME. KNOW THAT MUCH FOR A FACT.
THE FLYCATCHER IS MY KING AND MY FRIEND. NONE WILL TROUBLE HIM O THIS DAY WHEN HE ALREAD HAS SO MANY TROUBLES TO VEX HIM.
GO HOME, I SAY. THIS DEMONSTRATION IS DONE.

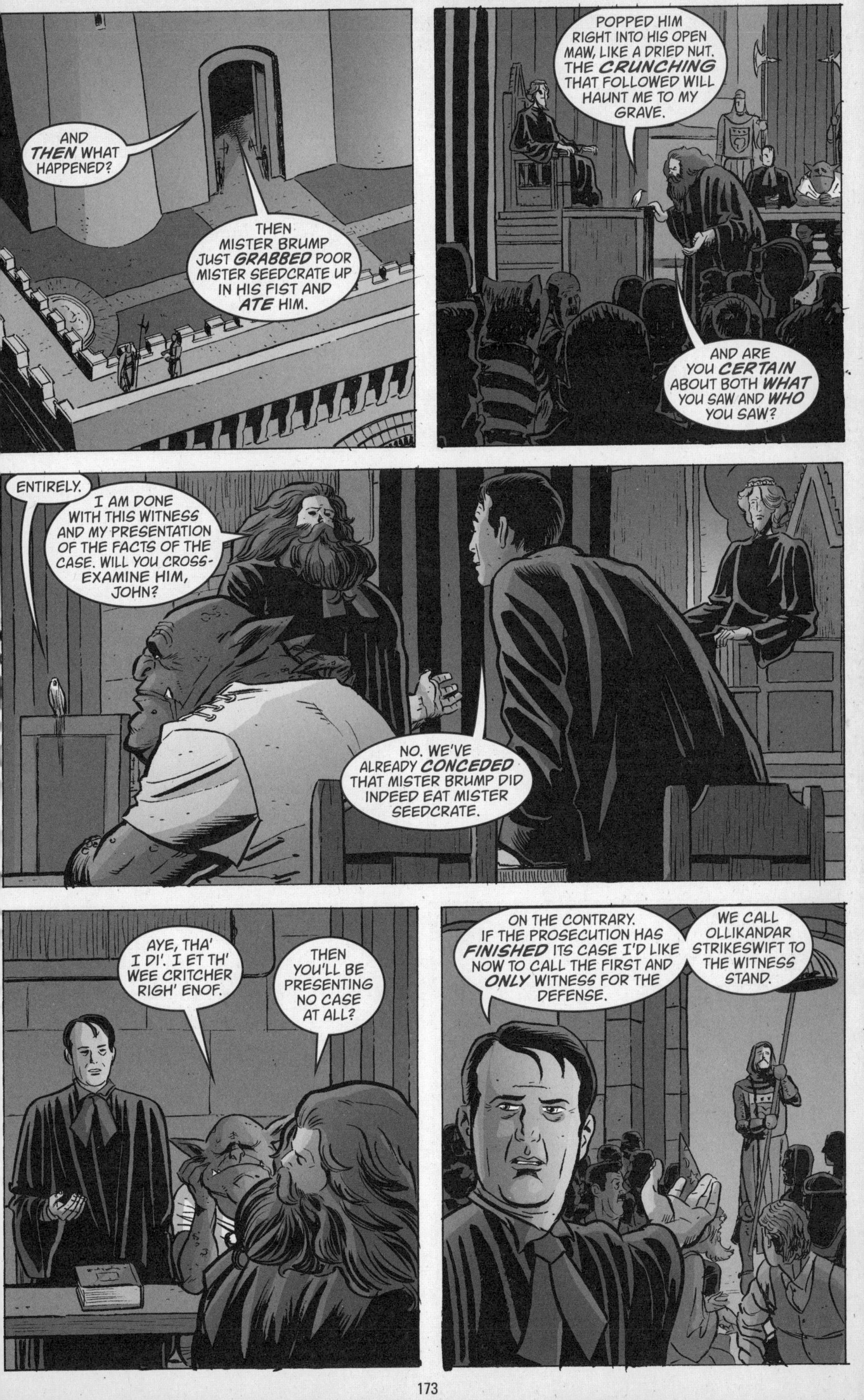
AND THEN WHAT HAPPENED?
THEN MISTER BRUMP JUST GRABBED POOR MISTER SEEDCRATE UP IN HIS FIST AND ATE HIM.
POPPED HIM RIGHT INTO HIS OPEN MAW, LIKE A DRIED NUT. THE CRUNCHING THAT FOLLOWED WILL HAUNT ME TO MY GRAVE.
AND ARE YOU CERTAIN ABOUT BOTH WHAT YOU SAW AND WHO YOU SAW?
ENTIRELY.
I AM DONE WITH THIS WITNESS AND MY PRESENTATION OF THE FACTS OF THE CASE. WILL YOU CROSS-EXAMINE HIM, JOHN?
NO. WE'VE ALREADY CONCEDED THAT MISTER BRUMP DID INDEED EAT MISTER SEEDCRATE.
AYE, THA' I DI'. I ET TH' WEE CRITCHER RIGH' ENOF.
THEN YOU'LL BE PRESENTING NO CASE AT ALL?
ON THE CONTRARY. IF THE PROSECUTION HAS FINISHED ITS CASE I'D LIKE NOW TO CALL THE FIRST AND ONLY WITNESS FOR THE DEFENSE.
WE CALL OLLIKANDAR STRIKESWIFT TO THE WITNESS STAND.

ARE YOU OLLIKANDAR, BROTHER TO GALLIFAR STRIKESWIFT?

YES, I AM. I *TOLD* YOU AS MUCH, DIDN'T I?

AND WHERE IS YOUR BROTHER NOW?

DEAD.

AND HOW DID YOUR BROTHER DIE?

HE *DROWNDED* AT THE BOTTOM OF THE GREAT WIGGLY RIVER.

AND HOW DID THAT HAPPEN?

WELL, WE ALL NEEDED TO CROSS THE RIVER, DIDN'T WE? YES, WE DID.

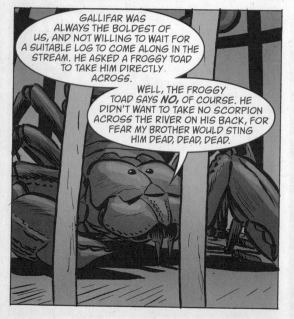

GALLIFAR WAS ALWAYS THE BOLDEST OF US, AND NOT WILLING TO WAIT FOR A SUITABLE LOG TO COME ALONG IN THE STREAM. HE ASKED A FROGGY TOAD TO TAKE HIM DIRECTLY ACROSS.

WELL, THE FROGGY TOAD SAYS *NO*, OF COURSE. HE DIDN'T WANT TO TAKE NO SCORPION ACROSS THE RIVER ON HIS BACK, FOR FEAR MY BROTHER WOULD STING HIM DEAD, DEAD, DEAD.

BUT MY BROTHER TELLS HIM, "WHY WOULD I *STING* YOU, BECAUSE THEN I'D SURELY *DROWN?*" WELL, THE FROGGY TOAD CONSIDERS THIS AND AGREES TO TAKE HIM ACROSS.

SO MY BROTHER JUMPS ON THE FROGGY TOAD'S BACK AND THEY START ACROSS THE RIVER. WE WERE *ALL* IMPRESSED WITH GALLIFAR ON THAT DAY, LET ME TELL YOU.

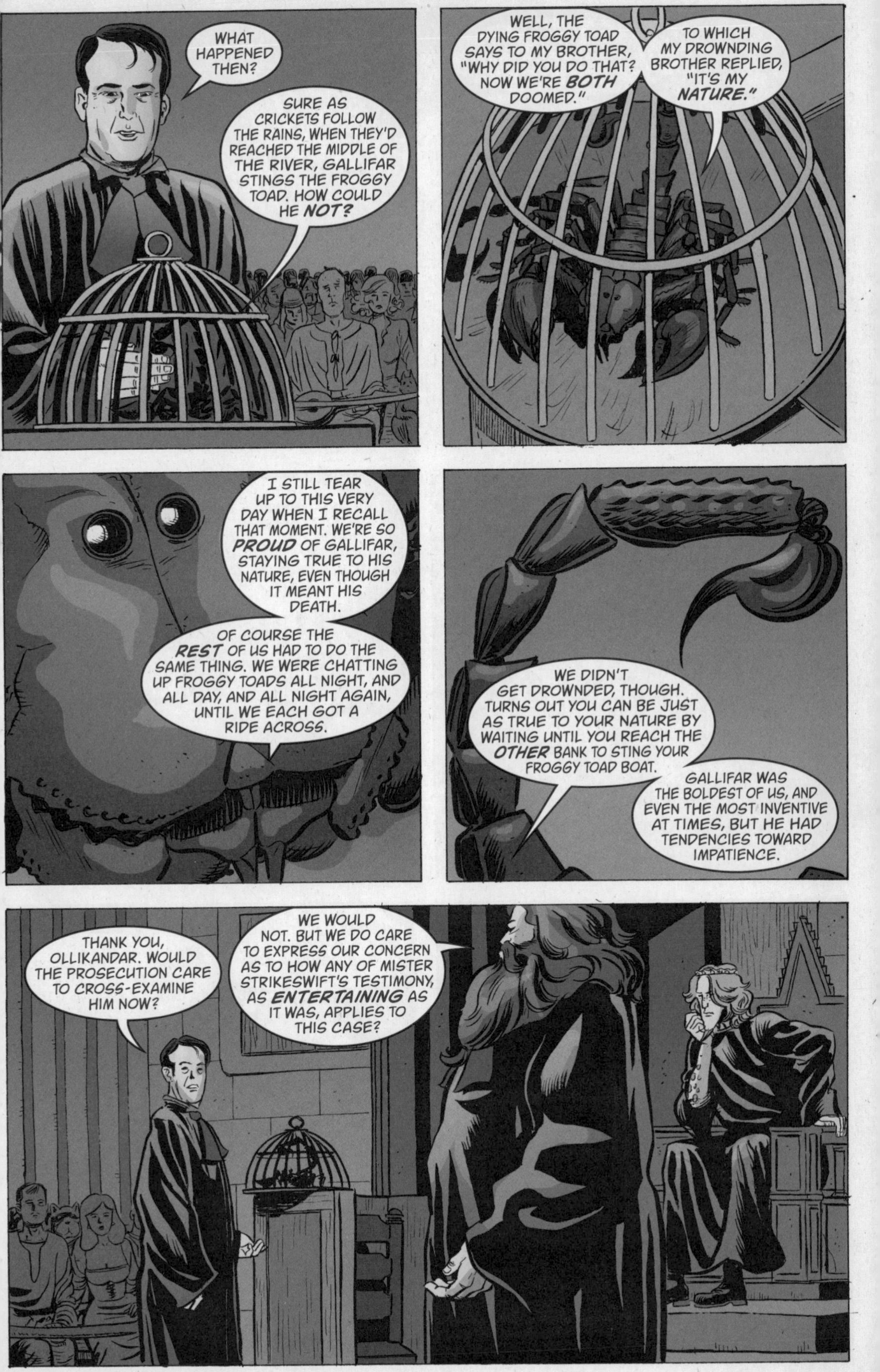
WHAT HAPPENED THEN?
SURE AS CRICKETS FOLLOW THE RAINS, WHEN THEY'D REACHED THE MIDDLE OF THE RIVER, GALLIFAR STINGS THE FROGGY TOAD. HOW COULD HE NOT?
WELL, THE DYING FROGGY TOAD SAYS TO MY BROTHER, "WHY DID YOU DO THAT? NOW WE'RE BOTH DOOMED."
TO WHICH MY DROWNDING BROTHER REPLIED, "IT'S MY NATURE."
I STILL TEAR UP TO THIS VERY DAY WHEN I RECALL THAT MOMENT. WE'RE SO PROUD OF GALLIFAR, STAYING TRUE TO HIS NATURE, EVEN THOUGH IT MEANT HIS DEATH.
OF COURSE THE REST OF US HAD TO DO THE SAME THING. WE WERE CHATTING UP FROGGY TOADS ALL NIGHT, AND ALL DAY, AND ALL NIGHT AGAIN, UNTIL WE EACH GOT A RIDE ACROSS.
WE DIDN'T GET DROWNDED, THOUGH. TURNS OUT YOU CAN BE JUST AS TRUE TO YOUR NATURE BY WAITING UNTIL YOU REACH THE OTHER BANK TO STING YOUR FROGGY TOAD BOAT.
GALLIFAR WAS THE BOLDEST OF US, AND EVEN THE MOST INVENTIVE AT TIMES, BUT HE HAD TENDENCIES TOWARD IMPATIENCE.
THANK YOU, OLLIKANDAR. WOULD THE PROSECUTION CARE TO CROSS-EXAMINE HIM NOW?
WE WOULD NOT. BUT WE DO CARE TO EXPRESS OUR CONCERN AS TO HOW ANY OF MISTER STRIKESWIFT'S TESTIMONY, AS ENTERTAINING AS IT WAS, APPLIES TO THIS CASE?

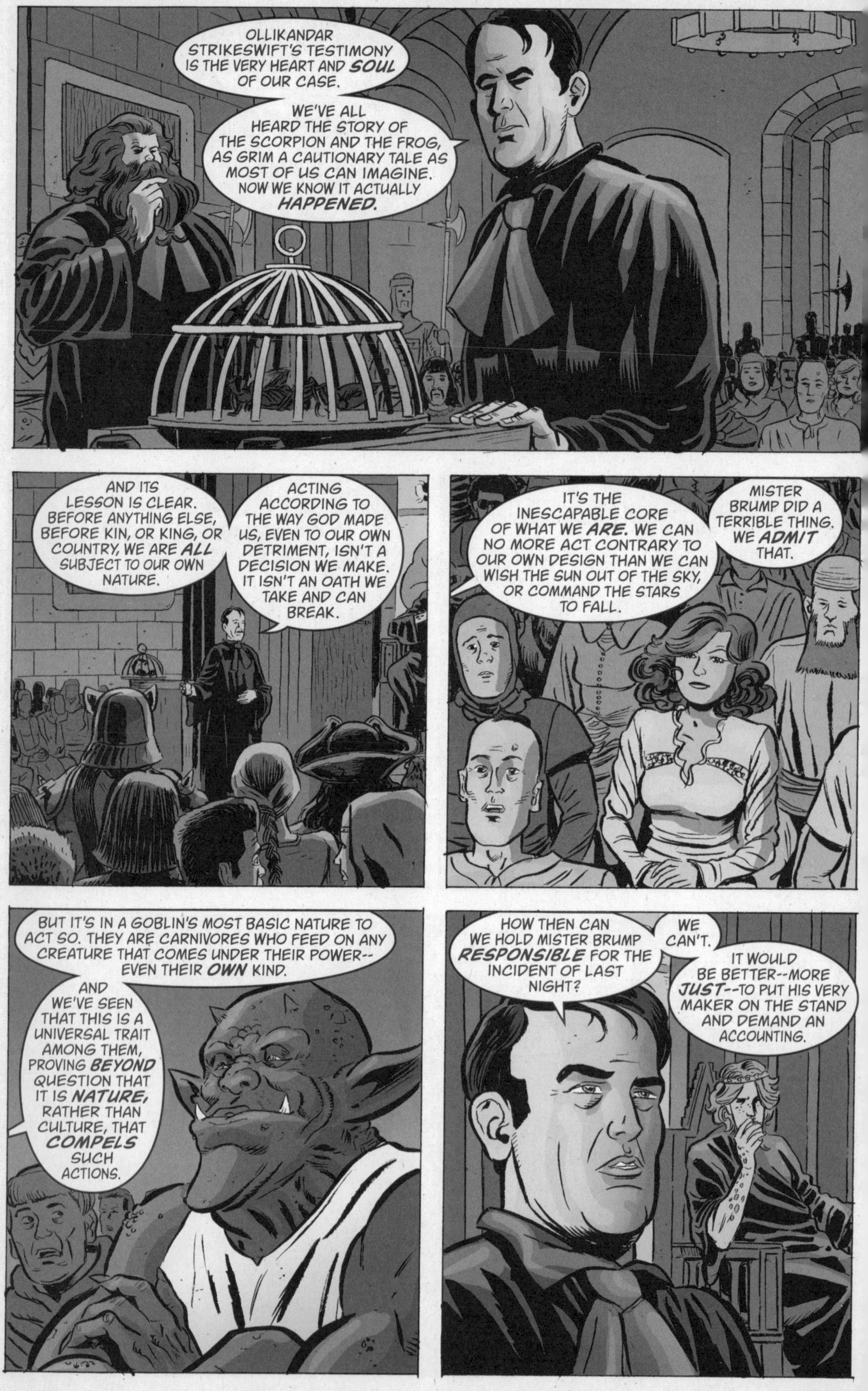
OLLIKANDAR STRIKESWIFT'S TESTIMONY IS THE VERY HEART AND SOUL OF OUR CASE.
WE'VE ALL HEARD THE STORY OF THE SCORPION AND THE FROG, AS GRIM A CAUTIONARY TALE AS MOST OF US CAN IMAGINE. NOW WE KNOW IT ACTUALLY HAPPENED.
AND ITS LESSON IS CLEAR. BEFORE ANYTHING ELSE, BEFORE KIN, OR KING, OR COUNTRY, WE ARE ALL SUBJECT TO OUR OWN NATURE.
ACTING ACCORDING TO THE WAY GOD MADE US, EVEN TO OUR OWN DETRIMENT, ISN'T A DECISION WE MAKE. IT ISN'T AN OATH WE TAKE AND CAN BREAK.
IT'S THE INESCAPABLE CORE OF WHAT WE ARE. WE CAN NO MORE ACT CONTRARY TO OUR OWN DESIGN THAN WE CAN WISH THE SUN OUT OF THE SKY, OR COMMAND THE STARS TO FALL.
MISTER BRUMP DID A TERRIBLE THING. WE ADMIT THAT.
BUT IT'S IN A GOBLIN'S MOST BASIC NATURE TO ACT SO. THEY ARE CARNIVORES WHO FEED ON ANY CREATURE THAT COMES UNDER THEIR POWER-- EVEN THEIR OWN KIND.
AND WE'VE SEEN THAT THIS IS A UNIVERSAL TRAIT AMONG THEM, PROVING BEYOND QUESTION THAT IT IS NATURE, RATHER THAN CULTURE, THAT COMPELS SUCH ACTIONS.
HOW THEN CAN WE HOLD MISTER BRUMP RESPONSIBLE FOR THE INCIDENT OF LAST NIGHT?
WE CAN'T.
IT WOULD BE BETTER--MORE JUST--TO PUT HIS VERY MAKER ON THE STAND AND DEMAND AN ACCOUNTING.

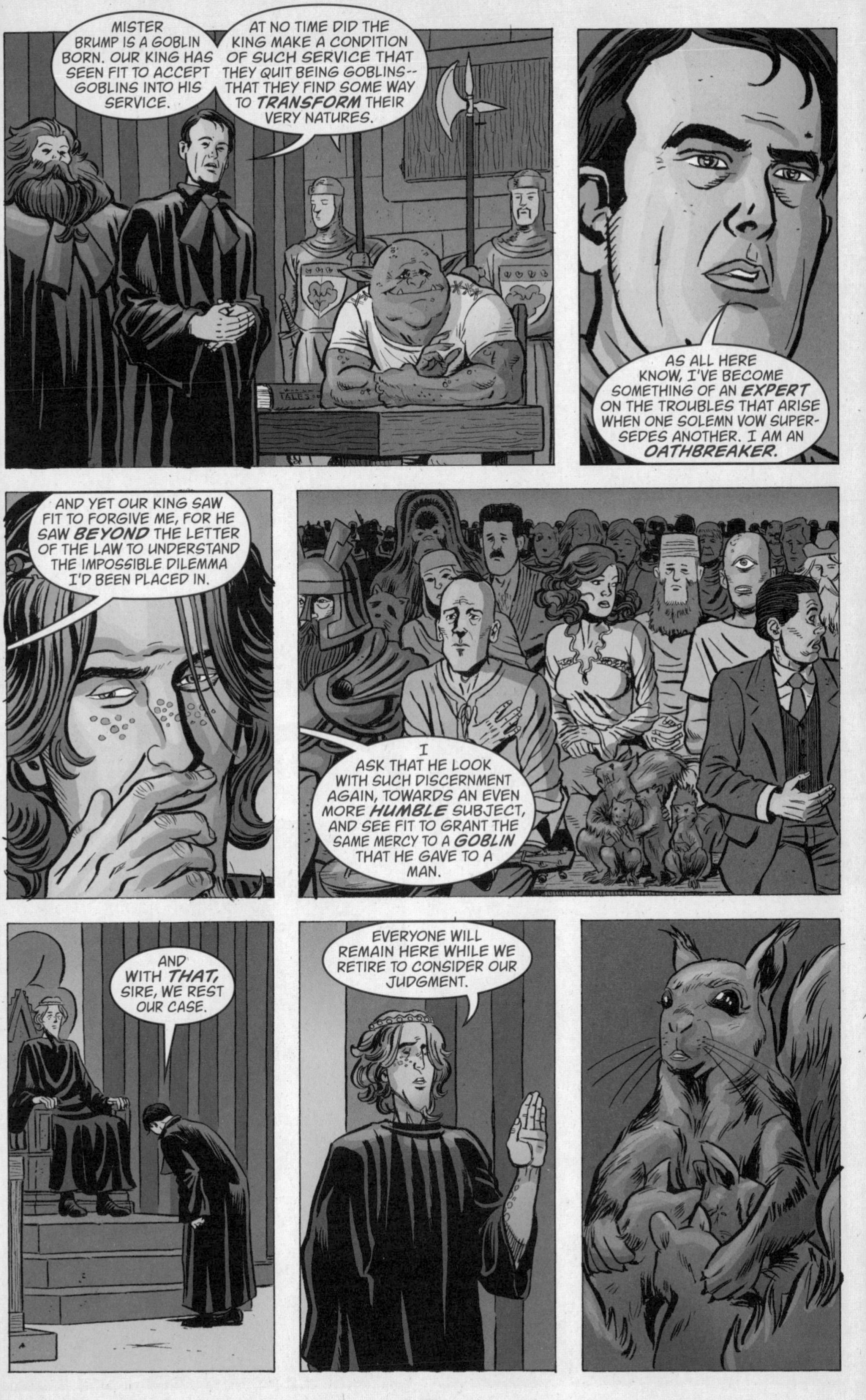
MISTER BRUMP IS A GOBLIN BORN. OUR KING HAS SEEN FIT TO ACCEPT GOBLINS INTO HIS SERVICE.
AT NO TIME DID THE KING MAKE A CONDITION OF SUCH SERVICE THAT THEY QUIT BEING GOBLINS-- THAT THEY FIND SOME WAY TO TRANSFORM THEIR VERY NATURES.
AS ALL HERE KNOW, I'VE BECOME SOMETHING OF AN EXPERT ON THE TROUBLES THAT ARISE WHEN ONE SOLEMN VOW SUPERSEDES ANOTHER. I AM AN OATHBREAKER.
AND YET OUR KING SAW FIT TO FORGIVE ME, FOR HE SAW BEYOND THE LETTER OF THE LAW TO UNDERSTAND THE IMPOSSIBLE DILEMMA I'D BEEN PLACED IN.
I ASK THAT HE LOOK WITH SUCH DISCERNMENT AGAIN, TOWARDS AN EVEN MORE HUMBLE SUBJECT, AND SEE FIT TO GRANT THE SAME MERCY TO A GOBLIN THAT HE GAVE TO A MAN.
AND WITH THAT, SIRE, WE REST OUR CASE.
EVERYONE WILL REMAIN HERE WHILE WE RETIRE TO CONSIDER OUR JUDGMENT.

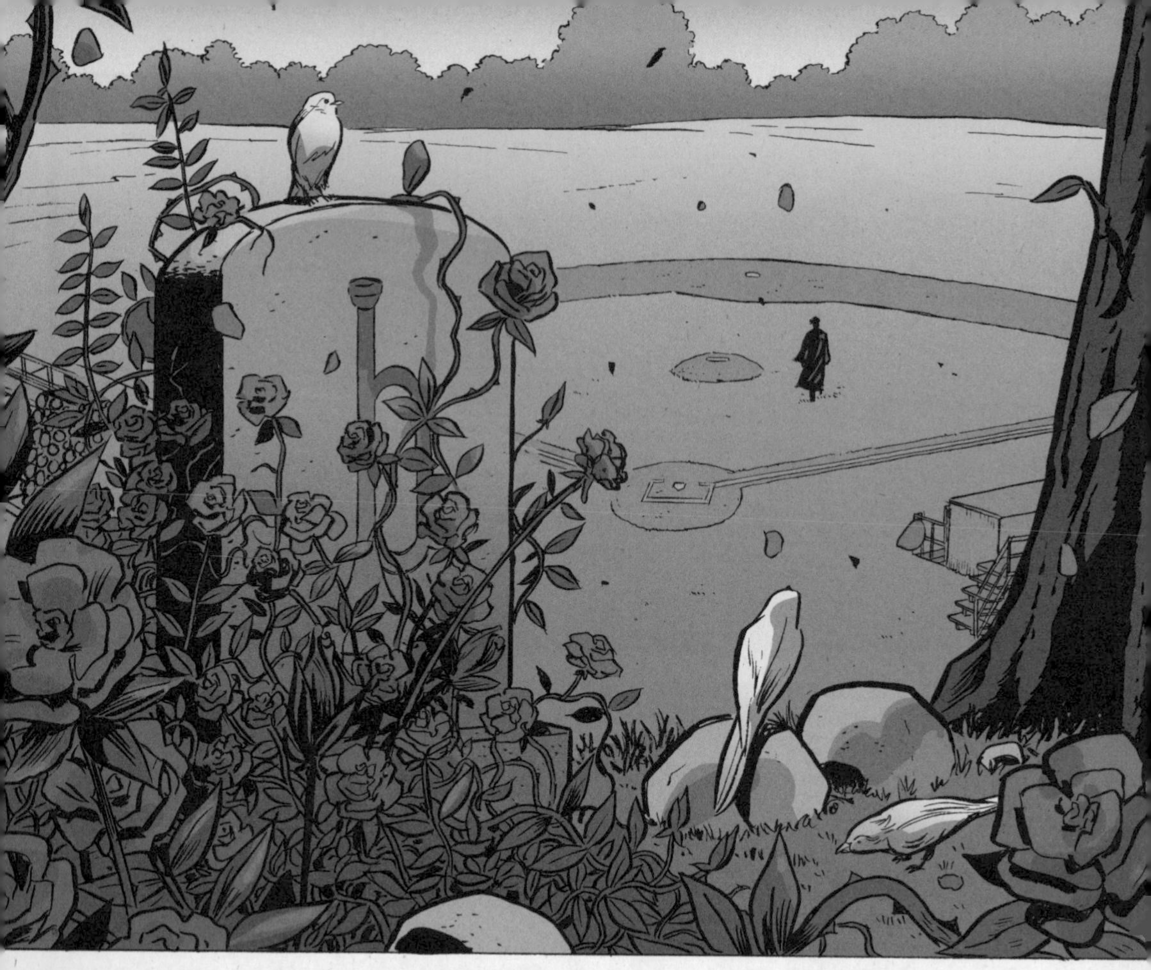

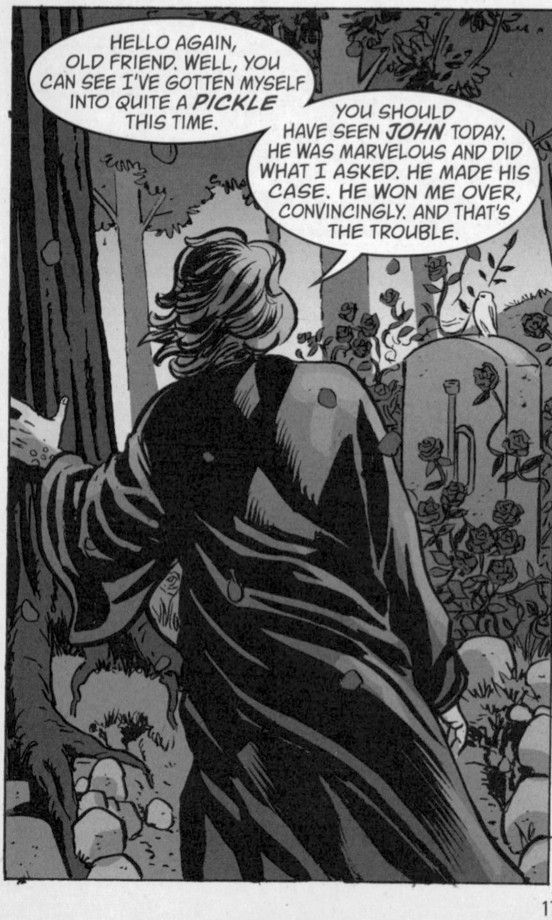
HELLO AGAIN, OLD FRIEND. WELL, YOU CAN SEE I'VE GOTTEN MYSELF INTO QUITE A PICKLE THIS TIME.
YOU SHOULD HAVE SEEN JOHN TODAY. HE WAS MARVELOUS AND DID WHAT I ASKED. HE MADE HIS CASE. HE WON ME OVER, CONVINCINGLY. AND THAT'S THE TROUBLE.

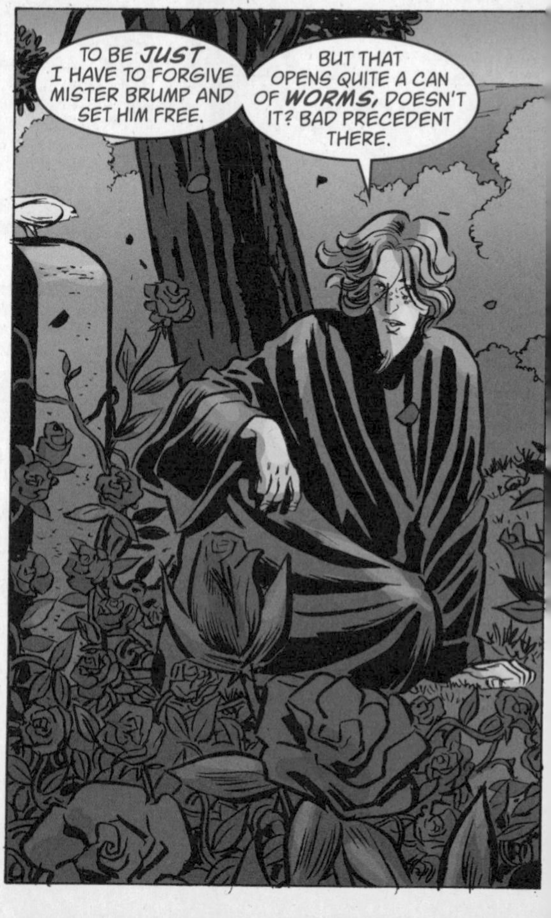
TO BE JUST I HAVE TO FORGIVE MISTER BRUMP AND SET HIM FREE.
BUT THAT OPENS QUITE A CAN OF WORMS, DOESN'T IT? BAD PRECEDENT THERE.

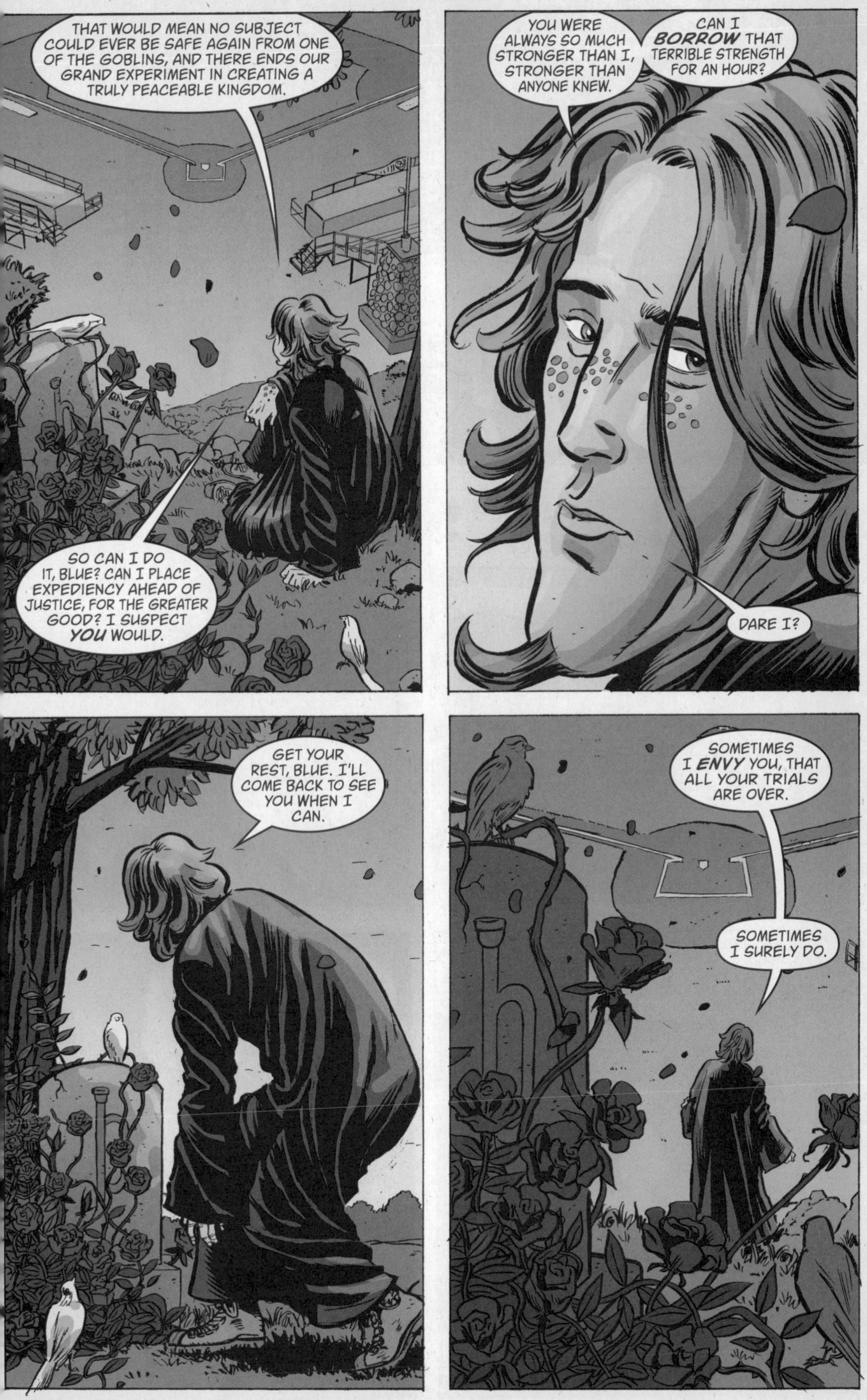
THAT WOULD MEAN NO SUBJECT COULD EVER BE SAFE AGAIN FROM ONE OF THE GOBLINS, AND THERE ENDS OUR GRAND EXPERIMENT IN CREATING A TRULY PEACEABLE KINGDOM.
SO CAN I DO IT, BLUE? CAN I PLACE EXPEDIENCY AHEAD OF JUSTICE, FOR THE GREATER GOOD? I SUSPECT YOU WOULD.
YOU WERE ALWAYS SO MUCH STRONGER THAN I, STRONGER THAN ANYONE KNEW.
CAN I BORROW THAT TERRIBLE STRENGTH FOR AN HOUR?
DARE I?
GET YOUR REST, BLUE. I'LL COME BACK TO SEE YOU WHEN I CAN.
SOMETIMES I ENVY YOU, THAT ALL YOUR TRIALS ARE OVER.
SOMETIMES I SURELY DO.

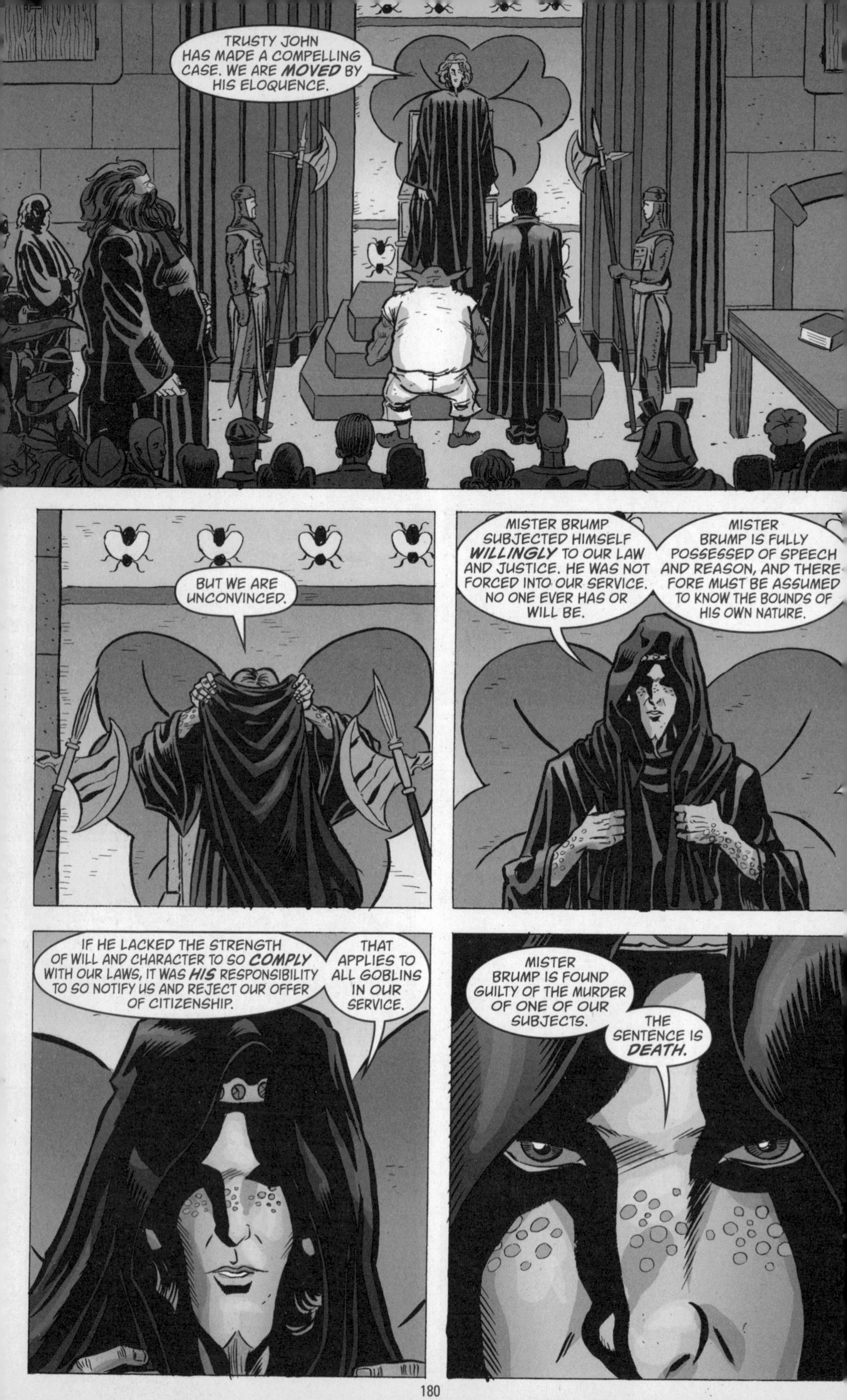
TRUSTY JOHN HAS MADE A COMPELLING CASE. WE ARE *MOVED* BY HIS ELOQUENCE.
BUT WE ARE UNCONVINCED.
MISTER BRUMP SUBJECTED HIMSELF ***WILLINGLY*** TO OUR LAW AND JUSTICE. HE WAS NOT FORCED INTO OUR SERVICE. NO ONE EVER HAS OR WILL BE.
MISTER BRUMP IS FULLY POSSESSED OF SPEECH AND REASON, AND THERE FORE MUST BE ASSUMED TO KNOW THE BOUNDS OF HIS OWN NATURE.
IF HE LACKED THE STRENGTH OF WILL AND CHARACTER TO SO *COMPLY* WITH OUR LAWS, IT WAS *HIS* RESPONSIBILITY TO SO NOTIFY US AND REJECT OUR OFFER OF CITIZENSHIP.
THAT APPLIES TO ALL GOBLINS IN OUR SERVICE.
MISTER BRUMP IS FOUND GUILTY OF THE MURDER OF ONE OF OUR SUBJECTS.
THE SENTENCE IS *DEATH.*

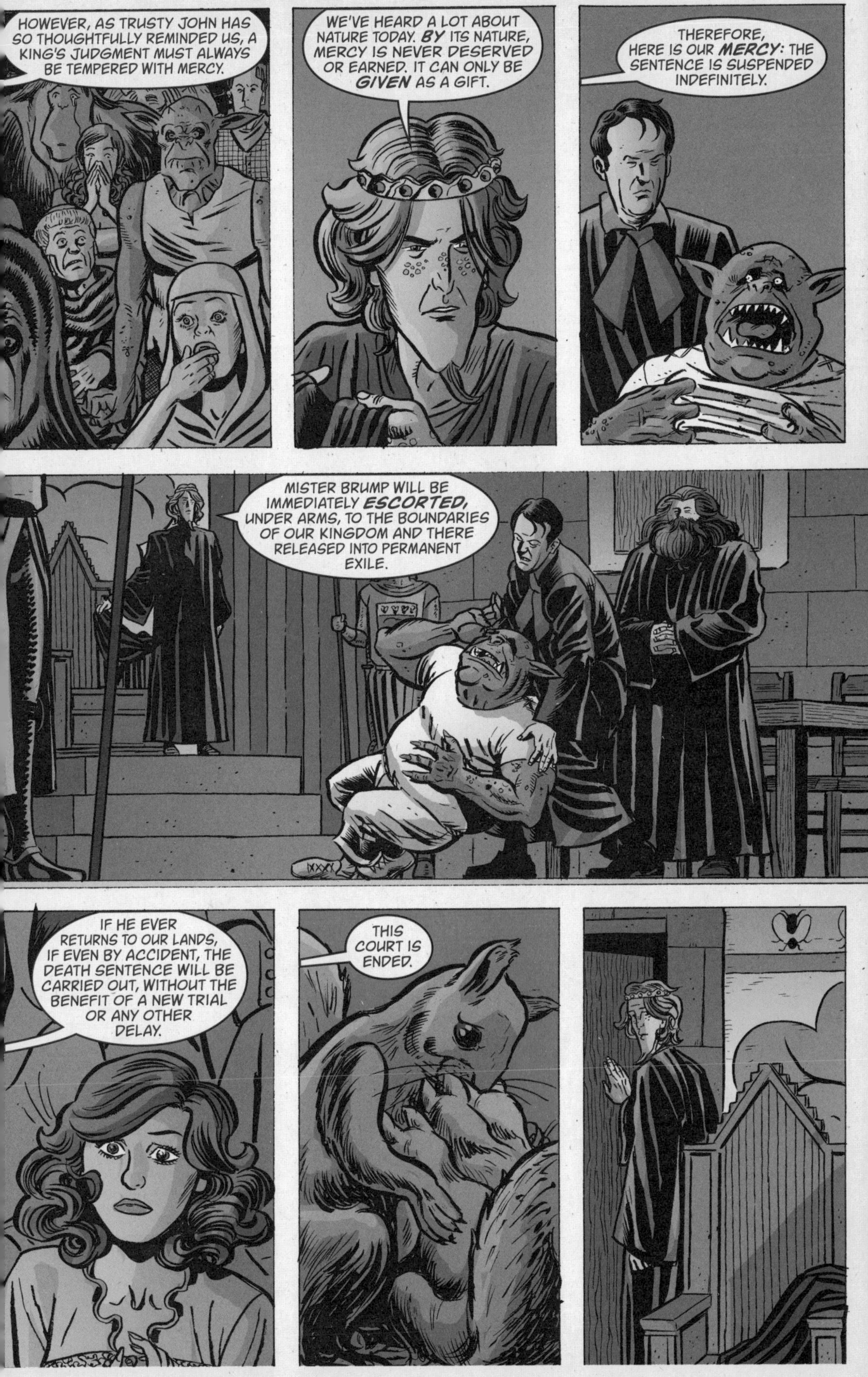
HOWEVER, AS TRUSTY JOHN HAS SO THOUGHTFULLY REMINDED US, A KING'S JUDGMENT MUST ALWAYS BE TEMPERED WITH MERCY.
WE'VE HEARD A LOT ABOUT NATURE TODAY. BY ITS NATURE, MERCY IS NEVER DESERVED OR EARNED. IT CAN ONLY BE GIVEN AS A GIFT.
THEREFORE, HERE IS OUR MERCY: THE SENTENCE IS SUSPENDED INDEFINITELY.
MISTER BRUMP WILL BE IMMEDIATELY ESCORTED, UNDER ARMS, TO THE BOUNDARIES OF OUR KINGDOM AND THERE RELEASED INTO PERMANENT EXILE.
IF HE EVER RETURNS TO OUR LANDS, IF EVEN BY ACCIDENT, THE DEATH SENTENCE WILL BE CARRIED OUT, WITHOUT THE BENEFIT OF A NEW TRIAL OR ANY OTHER DELAY.
THIS COURT IS ENDED.

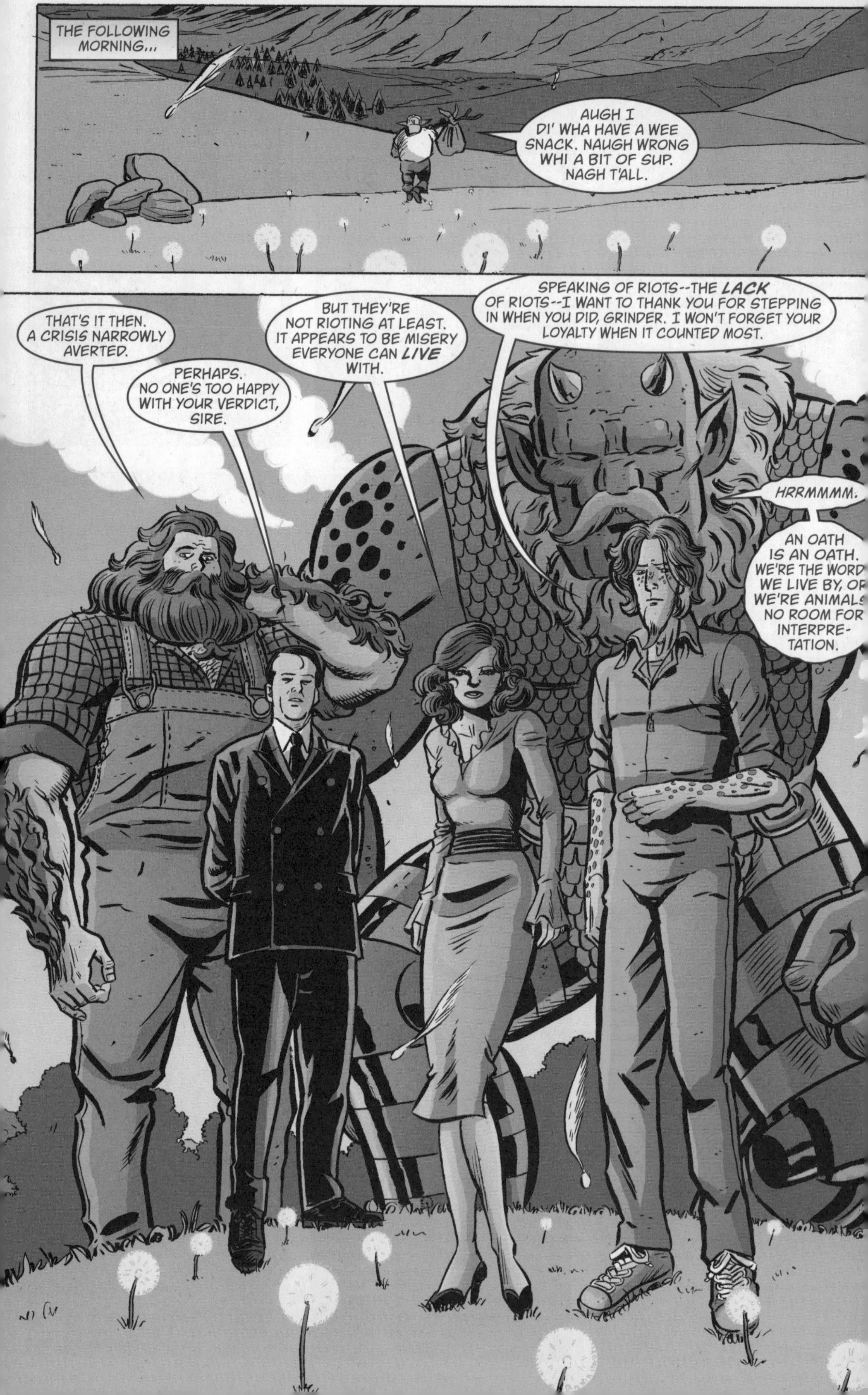
THE FOLLOWING MORNING...
AUGH I DI' WHA HAVE A WEE SNACK. NAUGH WRONG WHI A BIT OF SUP. NAGH T'ALL.
THAT'S IT THEN. A CRISIS NARROWLY AVERTED.
PERHAPS. NO ONE'S TOO HAPPY WITH YOUR VERDICT, SIRE.
BUT THEY'RE NOT RIOTING AT LEAST. IT APPEARS TO BE MISERY EVERYONE CAN *LIVE* WITH.
SPEAKING OF RIOTS--THE *LACK* OF RIOTS--I WANT TO THANK YOU FOR STEPPING IN WHEN YOU DID, GRINDER. I WON'T FORGET YOUR LOYALTY WHEN IT COUNTED MOST.
HRRMMMM.
AN OATH IS AN OATH. WE'RE THE WORD WE LIVE BY, OR WE'RE ANIMALS NO ROOM FOR INTERPRE-TATION.

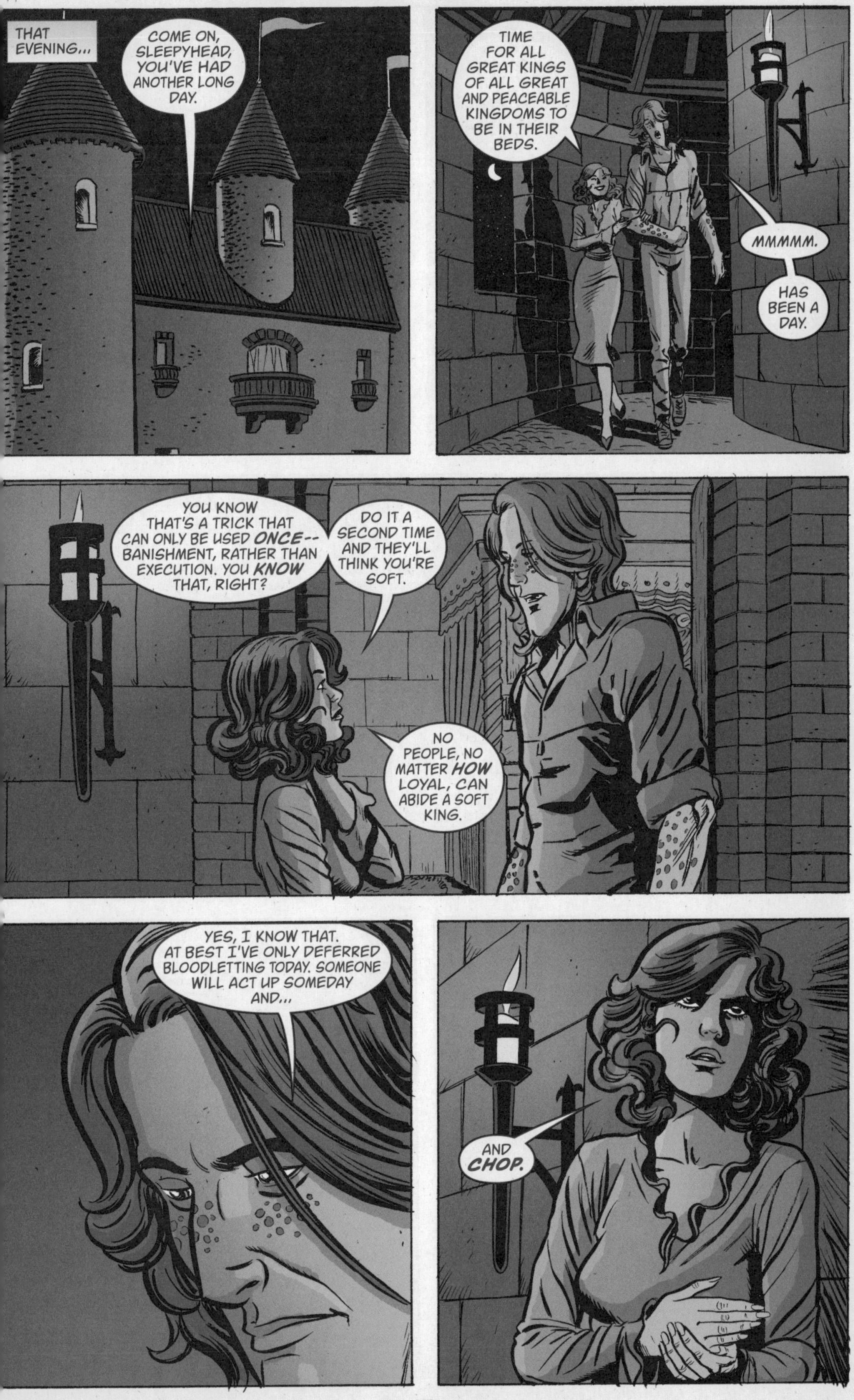

THAT EVENING...
COME ON, SLEEPYHEAD, YOU'VE HAD ANOTHER LONG DAY.
TIME FOR ALL GREAT KINGS OF ALL GREAT AND PEACEABLE KINGDOMS TO BE IN THEIR BEDS.
MMMMM.
HAS BEEN A DAY.
YOU KNOW THAT'S A TRICK THAT CAN ONLY BE USED ONCE-- BANISHMENT, RATHER THAN EXECUTION. YOU KNOW THAT, RIGHT?
DO IT A SECOND TIME AND THEY'LL THINK YOU'RE SOFT.
NO PEOPLE, NO MATTER HOW LOYAL, CAN ABIDE A SOFT KING.
YES, I KNOW THAT. AT BEST I'VE ONLY DEFERRED BLOODLETTING TODAY. SOMEONE WILL ACT UP SOMEDAY AND...
AND CHOP.

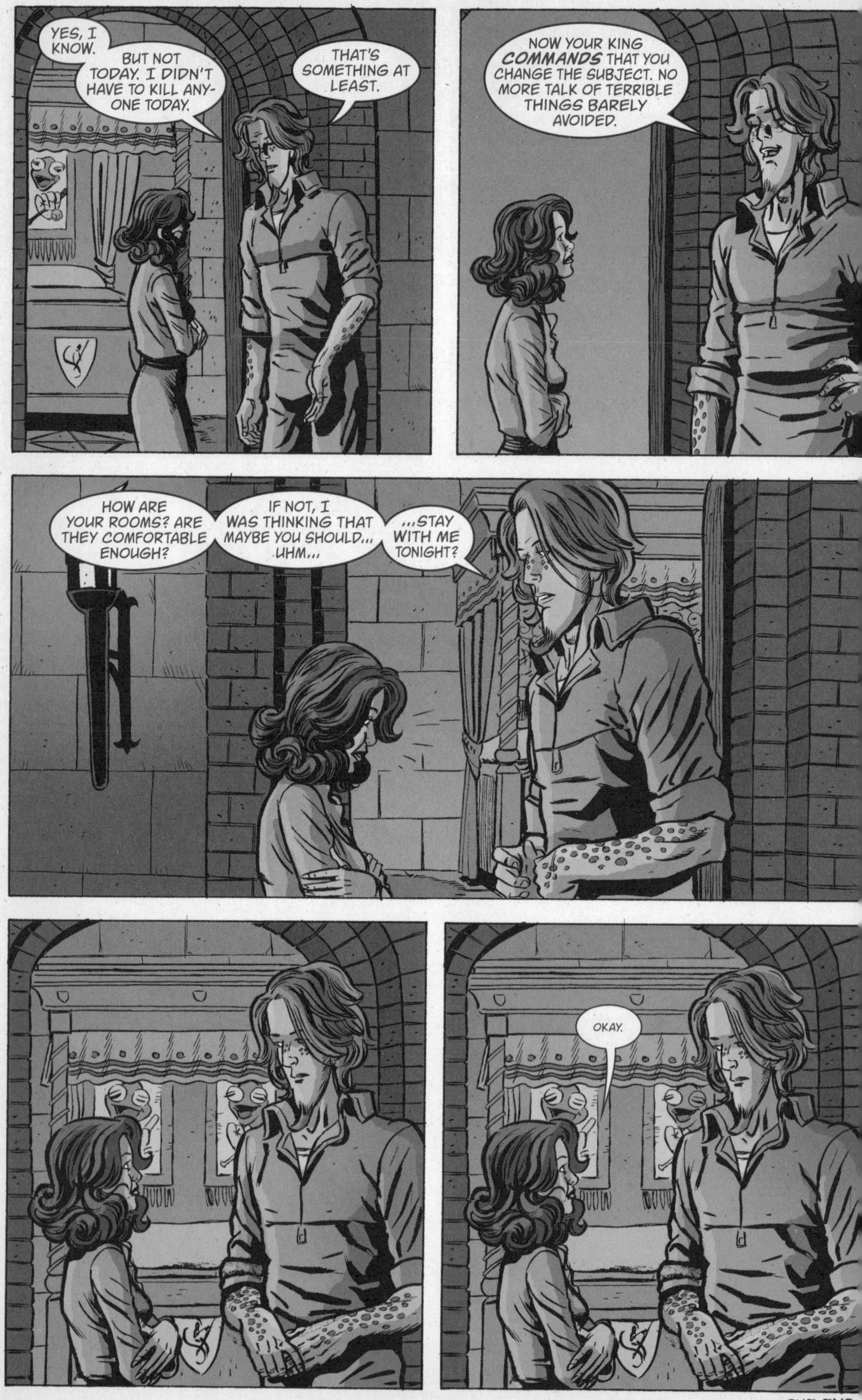
YES, I KNOW.
BUT NOT TODAY. I DIDN'T HAVE TO KILL ANY-ONE TODAY.
THAT'S SOMETHING AT LEAST.
NOW YOUR KING COMMANDS THAT YOU CHANGE THE SUBJECT. NO MORE TALK OF TERRIBLE THINGS BARELY AVOIDED.
HOW ARE YOUR ROOMS? ARE THEY COMFORTABLE ENOUGH?
IF NOT, I WAS THINKING THAT MAYBE YOU SHOULD... UHM...
...STAY WITH ME TONIGHT?
OKAY.

THE END

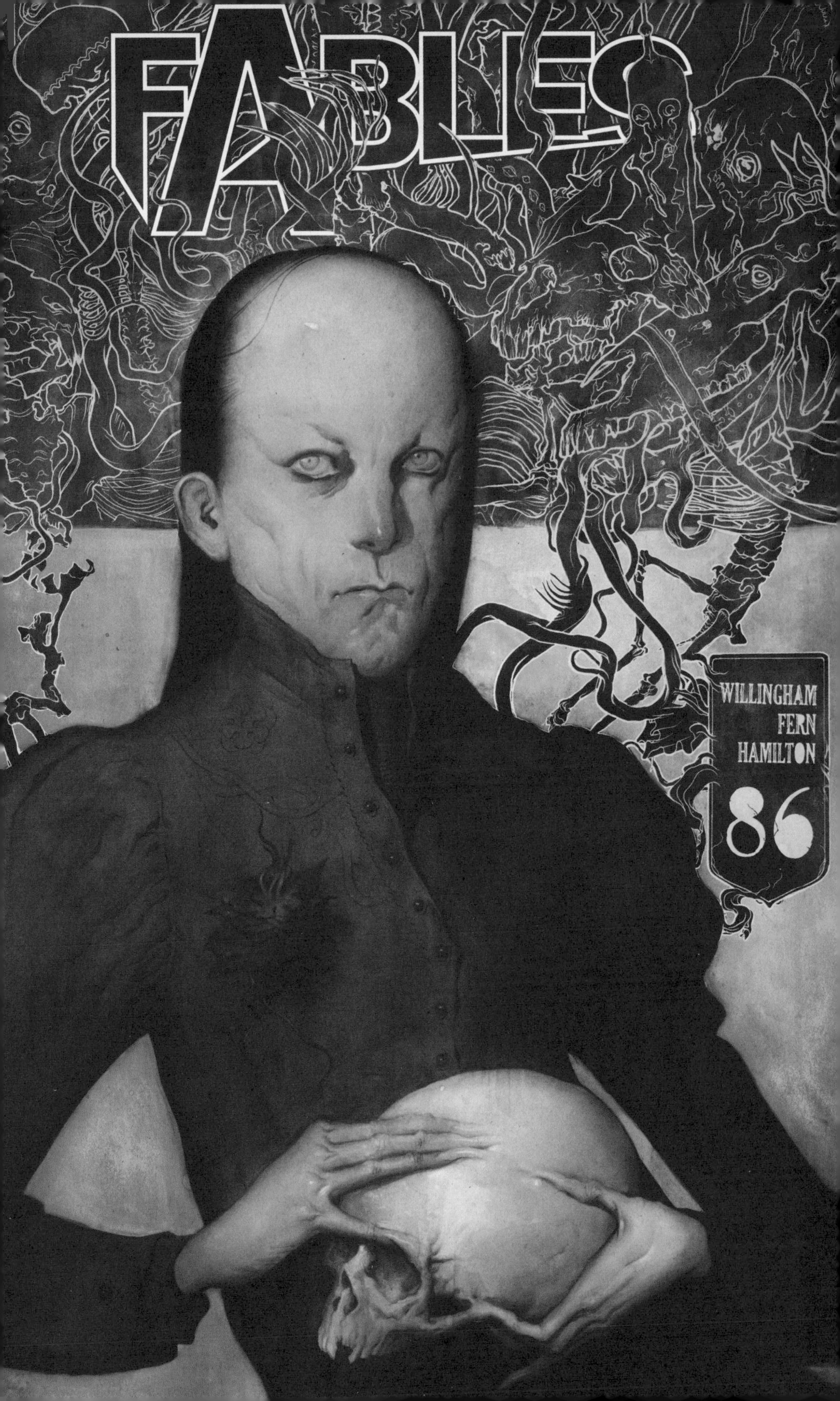
FABLES
WILLINGHAM
FERN
HAMILTON
86

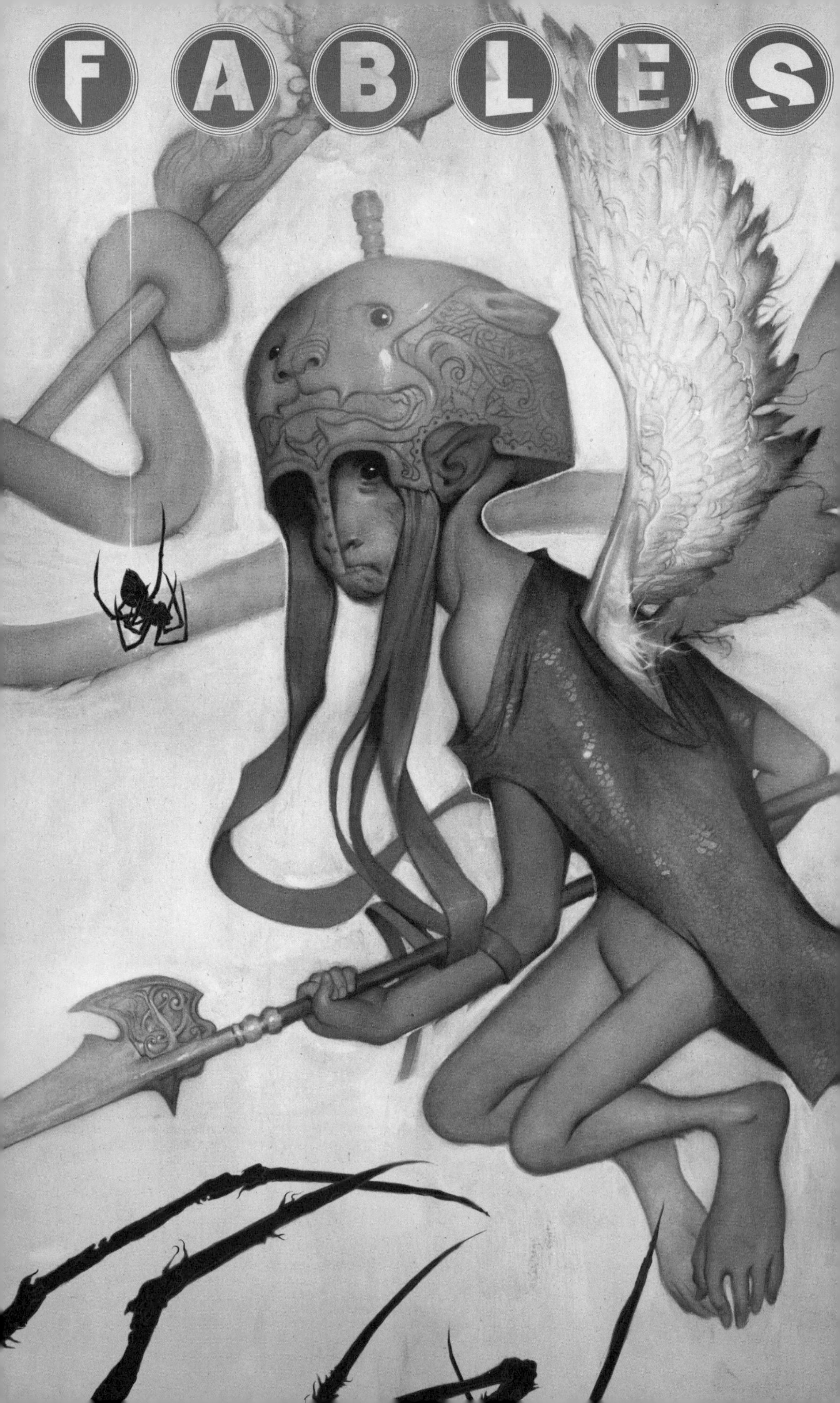
FABLES

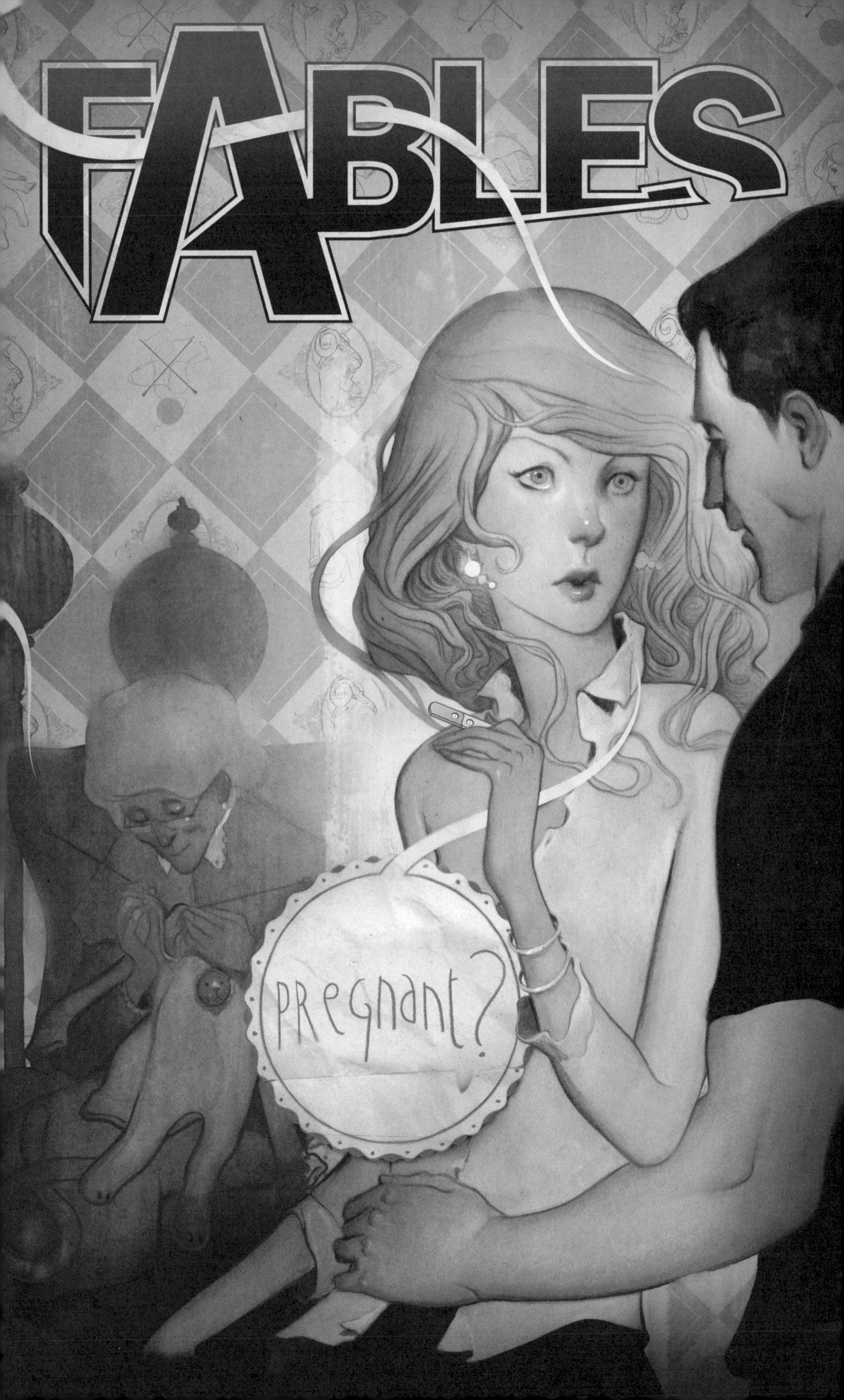
FABLES
pregnant?

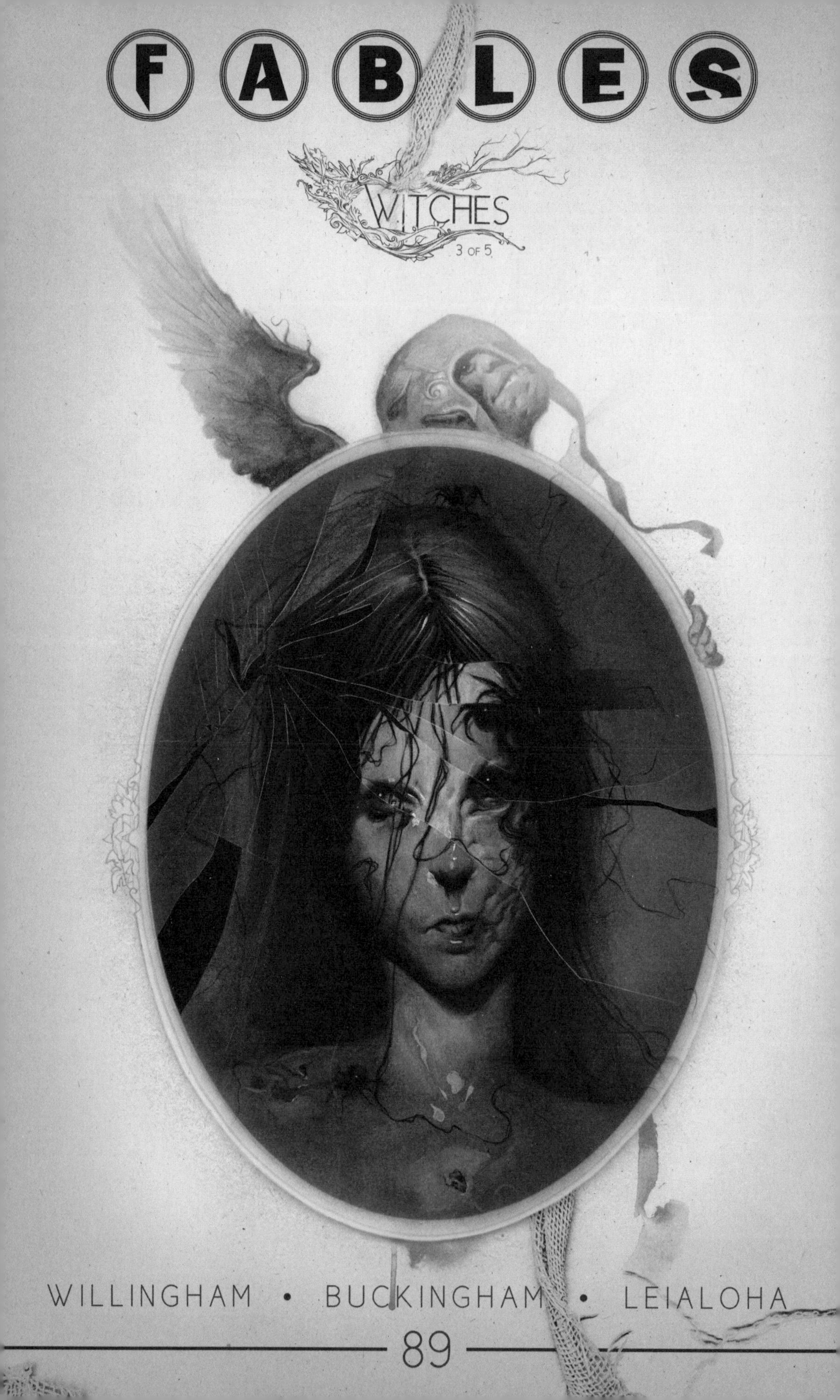
FABLES
WITCHES
3 OF 5
WILLINGHAM • BUCKINGHAM • LEIALOHA
89

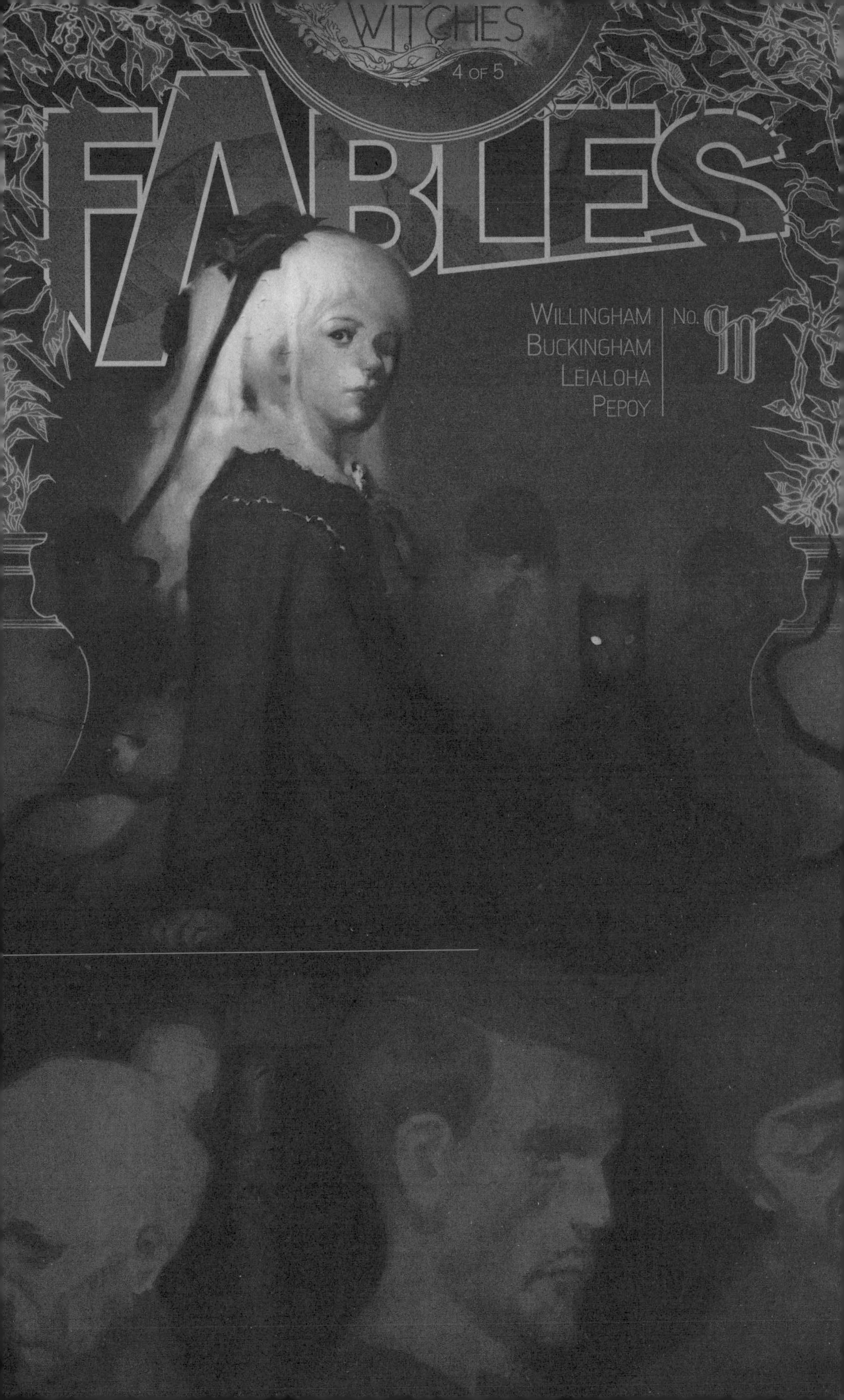
WITCHES
4 OF 5
FABLES
WILLINGHAM
BUCKINGHAM
LEIALOHA
PEPOY
No. 90

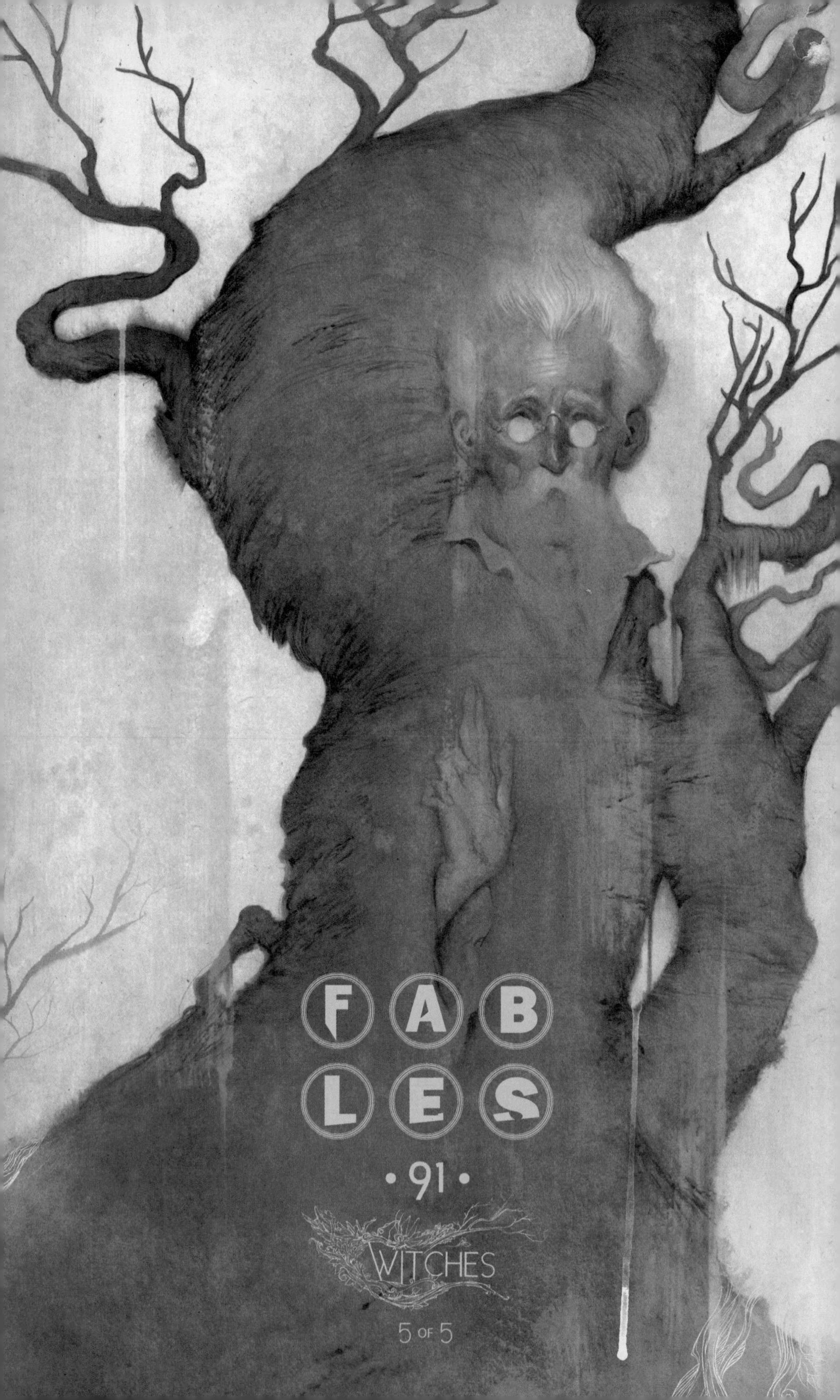
FABLES
91
WITCHES
5 of 5

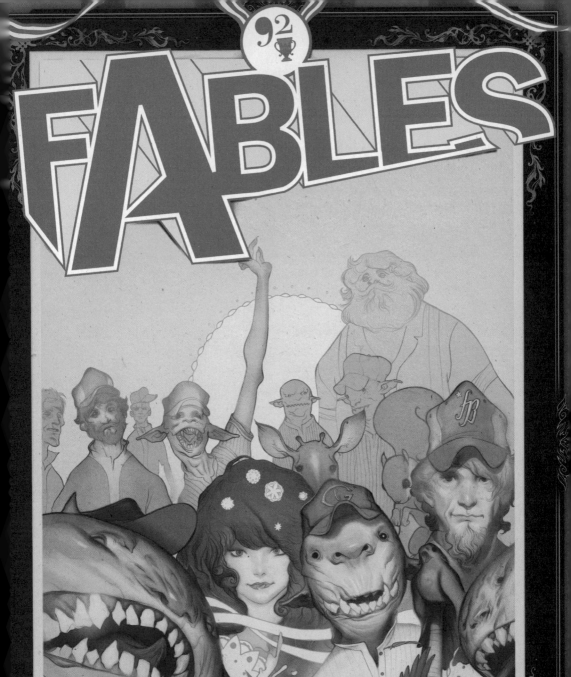

92

FABLES

Gobtown Crushers
·PENNANT WINNERS·

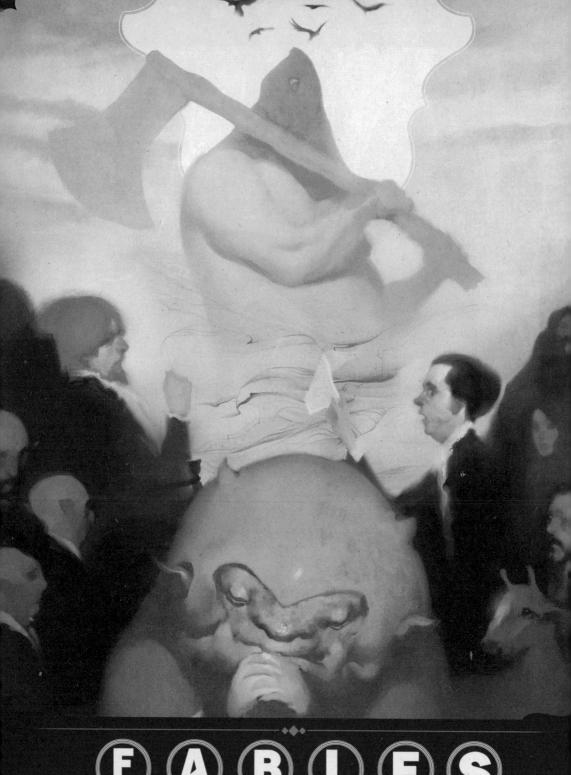

F A B L E S

· WILLINGHAM ·

· LAPHAM ·